Nonprofit Organizations and Civil Society in the United States

LeRoux and Feeney's *Nonprofit Organizations and Civil Society in the United States* makes a departure from existing nonprofit texts on the market: rather than focus on management, it focuses on nonprofit organizations and their contributions to the social, political, and economic dimensions of society. The book also covers the nexus between nonprofits and civil society. This text offers a theory-oriented undergraduate introduction to the nonprofit field and an examination of the multifaceted roles these organizations play in American society.

Kelly LeRoux is an Associate Professor in the Department of Public Administration at the University of Illinois at Chicago, where she teaches courses in nonprofit management. Before beginning an academic career, she worked for 11 years as an administrator for a nonprofit behavioral health and housing organization, and has served on numerous nonprofit boards. Her research has been published in more than a dozen public and nonprofit management journals and has been sponsored by the National Endowment for the Arts, Center on Philanthropy at Indiana University, Kresge Foundation, the Institute for Policy and Civic Engagement, the Institute for Research on Race and Public Policy, and the Great Cities Institute.

Mary K. Feeney is an Associate Professor at the School of Public Affairs at Arizona State University and is the Lincoln Professor of Ethics in Public Affairs. She also serves as the Associate Director for the Center for Science Technology and Environmental Policy Studies at ASU. Her research focuses on public and nonprofit management and science and technology policy. Feeney has published over 30 peer-reviewed articles in public management, science and technology policy, and higher education research and co-authored the book *Red Tape Research: A Prism for Public Administration Theory* with Barry Bozeman.

Nonprofit Organizations and Civil Society in the United States

Kelly LeRoux and
Mary K. Feeney

Routledge
Taylor & Francis Group

NEW YORK AND LONDON

First published 2015
by Routledge
711 Third Avenue, New York, NY 10017

and by Routledge
Park Square, Milton Park, Abingdon, Oxon, OX14 4RN

Routledge is an imprint of the Taylor & Francis Group, an informa business

© 2015 Taylor & Francis

The right of Kelly LeRoux and Mary K. Feeney to be identified as authors of this work has been asserted by them in accordance with sections 77 and 78 of the Copyright, Designs and Patents Act 1988.

Library of Congress Cataloging in Publication Data
LeRoux, Kelly.
 Nonprofit organizations and civil society in the United States/
Kelly LeRoux, Mary K. Feeney. — 1 Edition.
 pages cm
 Includes bibliographical references and index.
 1. Nonprofit organizations—United States—History. 2. Nonprofit organizations—Social aspects. I. Feeney, Mary K. II. Title.
 HD2769.2.U6L47 2015
 338.7—dc23
 2014017568

ISBN: 978-0-415-66144-7 (hbk)
ISBN: 978-0-415-66145-4 (pbk)
ISBN: 978-0-203-07343-8 (ebk)

Typeset in Adobe Caslon & Copperplate Gothic
by Florence Production Ltd, Stoodleigh, Devon, UK

To my parents
Ann P. and Larry S. LeRoux
who shaped my experience with civil society long
before I heard the term
To Mary Ellen Feeney, Barry Bozeman, and Eric W. Welch
—for always encouraging me to be me

Brief Contents

DETAILED CONTENTS

An overview of the size, scope, boundaries, and defining characteristics of the nonprofit sector. Introduces cross-cutting economic, social, and political themes that affect and shape the nonprofit sector.

Highlights historical and legal foundations of the nonprofit sector, describing charity, philanthropy, religious, social, political, and economic roots of the nonprofit sector.

Describes theories of why nonprofit organizations exist and explains their critical social, economic, and legal role in the US.

Describes the roles of nonprofit organizations in community-building, noting the importance of civil society, laws, norms, and customs that shape the sector. Outlines the relationships between civil society, nonprofits, and social capital.

Explores the traditional and emerging dimensions of community services and volunteering in the US, discussing the importance of volunteer labor for nonprofit organizations and the various factors that motivate individuals to volunteer their time and energy to the nonprofit sector.

6 PHILANTHROPY, FOUNDATIONS, AND GIVING   169

Examines the role of philanthropy and giving in civil society and the nonprofit sector. Outlines different types of foundations and their role in shaping civil society and social change and discusses trends in individual giving and motivations for giving.

Provides an overview of nonprofits in the American political landscape, noting the role of nonprofits in policy-making, including lobbying, advocacy, and mobilization activities.

Defines and examines major social movements in the US and the role of
nonprofits in those movements. Describes more contemporary social
movements and the role of nonprofits in those movements.

Outlines the role of nonprofits as a major provider of jobs for the
American workforce, and also examines the efforts of various types of
nonprofit organizations in promoting local economic development.

Examines contemporary issues facing the nonprofit sector and civil society in the US including changing population demographics, shifts in income inequality and suburban poverty, and challenges to tax-exempt status for nonprofit organizations.

PREFACE

Motivation for This Book

As social scientists and instructors with a particular interest in the role of nonprofits in society and their relationship to government, we have often found ourselves without the perfect textbook for teaching undergraduates about nonprofit organizations. Many of our "go-to" nonprofit textbooks focus on management or are intended for a professional audience—written for practitioners who are often assumed to have a good deal of experience working in the nonprofit sector, or are in the process of learning nonprofit management skills in the classroom and through internships. [1] Yet, these texts are not ideal for interdisciplinary courses at the undergraduate level. Our book, *Nonprofit Organizations and Civil Society in the United States,* makes a departure from existing nonprofit texts on the market, in that it does not focus on management, but rather offers a more general approach to understanding nonprofit organizations and their contributions to the social, political, and economic dimensions of society; it also covers the nexus between nonprofits and civil society. Our text fills a unique niche, offering a theoretically oriented undergraduate introduction to the nonprofit field and an examination of the multifaceted roles these organizations play in American society.

Students in a variety of fields have interest in the nonprofit sector—interests ranging from employment, volunteer opportunities, political activism, or the desire to better understand the role of nonprofits in business, government, and society. Today, many undergraduates are considering careers in public service (in government, nonprofits, and with for-profit firms), but few have the opportunity to gain a broad understanding of the nonprofit sector and its place in American civil society. Nonprofit courses aimed at undergraduates are emerging at universities throughout the United States, and are embedded in a variety of disciplines including public administration and public affairs, business, economics, philosophy, public policy, political science, sociology, and social work. Our book targets this emerging audience.

The primary focus of this book is nonprofit organizations in the United States. While we discuss international nonprofit organizations and often describe US-based nonprofits in comparison to non-US nonprofits, it is important to note that nonprofit and civil society organizations are partly an outcome of the political, social, and economic environment in which they operate. This is especially true in the US, where nonprofit organizations have special legal, financial, and social status in society. We hope that the comparative international segments of the book will provide an avenue for additional discussion in the classroom. And, of course, faculty looking to take a more international focus in the classroom can use this as a springboard for that type of discussion.

The primary audience for this book is not disciplinary; our goal is for this book to speak across a variety of disciplines. To that end, we have kept the presentation of material interdisciplinary, broad, and comprehensive. We touch upon basic aspects of government and political science, basic economic theory and terminology, and general sociological theories. Students will become familiar with these various disciplinary lenses and how they relate to nonprofits, but do not require expertise in any one discipline in order to effectively consume the material presented in this book. Our expectation is that instructors focused on a particular discipline can use this book as a base text which can be supplemented with readings, lectures, and case studies that are particular to the discipline (e.g. business, economics, public health, criminology, etc.) or area of interest (e.g. healthcare, education policy, welfare policy, etc.).

Graduate Courses

While the primary audience is undergraduate, we believe this book provides a useful starting point for graduate instruction. This textbook can serve as a companion text on nonprofit organizations. For example, instructors of *public management* courses will find this book to be a useful guide for understanding how nonprofit organizations are similar and dissimilar to public organizations, the relationships between nonprofit organizations and public organizations, and the ways in which the nonprofit sector is increasingly delivering public services via government contracts and grants. It could easily be paired, for instance, with Hal G. Rainey's (2009) *Understanding and Managing Public Organizations* (Jossey-Bass).

For those teaching in graduate programs in *social work*, this book will provide a nice perspective on the economic and political aspects of nonprofit organizations. Moreover, it offers detailed descriptions of the organizational structure of many nonprofits and their relationships to government, groups, and communities. This book helps to describe the environment and organizations where many MSW graduates will work. For those teaching about nonprofits from a *communications* perspective, this book could be paired with Patterson and Radtke's *Strategic Communications for Nonprofit Organizations* (2nd), offering a well-rounded approach to understanding the complex nature of nonprofit organizations and their relationship to civil society.

For instructors working in *business* schools, this book can serve as a companion to texts such as *Good to Great and the Social Sectors* (Collins, 2011), *Business Model Generation* (Osterwalder and Pignuer, 2013), and *Philanthro-Capitalism* (Bishop and Green, 2008), offering a complementary focus on the role of public service and mission-driven organizations. We also highlight the ways in which nonprofit organizations can operate within, or next to, corporate structures or as philanthropic arms to larger for-profit activities. This book can be easily paired with more advanced, graduate texts on social entrepreneurship and corporate philanthropy. In short, the book is introductory in nature, easily comprehended, and relies on contemporary examples and debates, making it useful for grounding students' understanding of nonprofits, as supplemental readings can be used to teach the topic from a wide variety of disciplinary perspectives.

What to Expect from This Book

This book is divided into four sections. Section I includes three chapters (1, 2, and 3) that provide an introduction to the nonprofit sector and civil society. Section II includes three chapters (4, 5, and 6) which detail nonprofits in American social life, in particular a focus on community-building, volunteering, philanthropy, and giving. Section III (Chapters 7, 8, and 9) centers on the political and economic aspects of the nonprofit sector. Section IV concludes with a chapter (10) that focuses on the current and future challenges and opportunities for the nonprofit sector.

Instructors and students will note that each chapter opens with an **Opening Story** or application of the key concepts from the chapter. These modern stories are intended to draw students in and prepare them for the material that follows. In some cases, these opening stories are "ripped from the headlines" with the hopes of stimulating interest in the chapter content and also serving as easy-to-understand platforms for further discussion. Instructors are encouraged to use these examples, and others, to integrate the materials in the chapter into a discussion of current events or issues that are particularly relevant to students.

Chapter Learning Objectives are outlined at the start of each chapter. At the close of each chapter we have provided a list of **Key Terms**. These key terms are bolded within the text of the chapter. We also provide discussion questions at the close of each chapter. The **Discussion Questions** can be used for in-class discussion or as study questions for students. We also provide a variety of **Website Links** for additional student research or classroom use. Instructors may wish to incorporate these websites into their lecture presentations or ask students to visit them to learn more about particular organizations and programs. In some chapters, we provide recommended readings, video clips, and additional materials that can be used to supplement the chapter content and provide points of discussion for lectures and seminars.

Finally, many of the chapters include small **Boxes** that highlight short case examples or challenges and controversies that pertain to chapter content. These materials are intended to be provocative. In many cases they present a slanted view of an issue or challenge students to think about alternative approaches to the issues at hand. The cases, examples, and illustrations used throughout the books do not necessarily represent the views of the authors or the publishers, but instead are presented to stimulate thoughtful discussion and critical thinking. We hope that these examples can be used as a springboard for lively discussion and debate in the classroom, whether it is a large group discussion moderated by the instructor or in small groups.

What to Expect from Specific Chapters

Section I: Introduction to the Nonprofit Sector & Civil Society

Chapter 1 presents a detailed discussion of what is meant by the term "nonprofit sector," and a variety of other terms (e.g. third sector, independent sector, etc.) used to describe the sector. We note how the nonprofit sector is similar to, and different from, public and for-profit sectors and discuss the ways in which the context of the nonprofit sector is changing along with the economic, technological, and social changes in society. This first chapter outlines the size, scope, and boundaries of the US nonprofit sector, highlighting examples of nonprofits that represent the diversity of the sector. We also define civil society and note the ways in which the nonprofit sector contributes to, and is shaped by, civil society. In the first chapter, we also begin to introduce cross-cutting themes that appear throughout the book including: the role of technology in civil society and transforming nonprofit and voluntary action; collaboration, partnerships, and inter-sector linkages and influences; and the increasingly blurred boundaries of the sector including the emergence of new hybridized forms of social purpose organizations.

Chapter 2 examines the origins of our contemporary nonprofit sector in the United States. The chapter highlights the historical and legal foundations of the nonprofit sector, noting how these features result in a distinct American nonprofit sector. The chapter is divided into five parts. First, we outline the values that underlie the nonprofit sector, including the impulses for charity and philanthropy that are grounded in Judeo-Christian beliefs and teachings, and many world religions, American values of individualism and pluralism, and attitudes toward welfare, capitalism, entrepreneurship, and how these values have shaped a preference for personal responsibility, a limited welfare state, and preferences for private solutions/responses to problems whenever feasible.

Second, we discuss the roots of nonprofits in American social life. We offer a brief history of associations that have emerged and how nonprofit culture has been shaped by the social structure and history of the US. Third, we outline the roots of nonprofit organizations in American political life, noting the ways in which American political values, preferences, and history have shaped the nonprofit sector and vice versa. Fourth, we discuss the nonprofit sector and its relationship to the economy, noting its role in job creation and revenue. We detail the legal structure of nonprofits in the US, noting the meaning and purpose of tax exemption. This chapter concludes with a discussion of the overlap between the public, nonprofit, and for-profit sectors and the context in which nonprofits operate, enabling students to gain a better understanding of the ways in which the US nonprofit sector contributes to the American economy and some of the challenges facing the sector.

Chapter 3, Theories of the Nonprofit Sector, outlines theoretical explanations for why nonprofits exist, and why nonprofits often represent preferred providers in markets where for-profits also provide goods and services. For the sake of simplicity, the discussion of nonprofit theories is divided into economic and non-economic explanations. Economic explanations for why nonprofits form include market failures, government failures, and interdependence theory. The chapter also examines limitations of economic theories and considers some alternative theoretical perspectives including the theory of the commons, pluralism, and collective action perspectives on nonprofit organizations and civil society groups. Although brief, this chapter introduces important concepts that serve as a frame of reference for material and examples introduced in later chapters.

Section II: The Nonprofit Sector in Civil Society

Chapter 4, Nonprofits and Community-Building, borrows from Anheier's (2005)[2] definition to describe civil society as the macro-level institutional structure of laws, norms, customs that create the social structure for nonprofit organizations and associations. This chapter explores how nonprofit and civil society organizations contribute to the social fabric of America. We build on the previously discussed definitions of "nonprofit" and civil society and introduce the concept of social capital. We then examine how civil society and social capital relate to one another and the nonprofit sector. Specifically, we discuss traditional voluntary associations and local civic groups, political parties, neighborhood associations, trade and labor unions, sports clubs, churches, PTAs, twelve-step and other self-help programs, and community-based organizations. We include a discussion of the "dark" side of social capital. We also discuss the ways in which the Internet and social media have supplemented, complemented, and, in some cases, replaced many traditional forms of face-to-face associating.

Chapter 5 explores the traditional and emerging dimensions of volunteering in the US. This chapter, titled Community Service and

Voluntary Action, begins by describing the prevalence of volunteering in the US and the patterns of volunteering by gender, age, race, and ethnicity. We discuss why volunteering is important to the nonprofit sector and consider the various motivations for volunteering. We note the differences between formal and informal volunteering, compulsory volunteering, intermediary organizations that promote or support volunteering, and newer forms of volunteering including virtual volunteering, micro-volunteering, and various new technologies that are shaping volunteer experiences.

Chapter 6 examines the role of philanthropy and giving in US civil society. The chapter focuses on the changing nature of philanthropy, foundations, and giving. We begin by defining philanthropy and offering a quick introduction to the history of philanthropy in the US. The chapter opens with a description of the Giving Pledge, the giving commitments of billionaires. Following the description of philanthropy we include a profile of Andrew Carnegie. We note the distinction between philanthropy and charity and discuss the values that support philanthropy and charitable giving. We then provide an overview of the modern foundation sector, noting different types of foundations (grant-making, operating, community, and corporate) and the ways in which foundations redistribute resources, stimulate innovation, and foster social change, to manifest the personal values of their creators. Following the discussion of philanthropy, we move on to consider giving patterns in the US. We discuss individual giving, including who gives and who receives. We note annual giving trends, including which organizations benefit most from private giving and interesting facts on giving tendencies among the very wealthy and low-income individuals. We also note key motivations for giving, including altruistic, coercive, and egoist motives. Finally, we discuss how technology is transforming giving with new forms of giving such as mobile donations, and personal fundraising pages created via social media and other examples.

Section III: Political, Social, & Economic Aspects of the Nonprofit Sector

Chapter 7, The Influence of Nonprofit Organizations on the Political Environment, provides an overview of the various roles that nonprofits play in the American political landscape, with particular attention to their roles in policy-making and elections. The chapter introduces concepts such as pluralism, collective action, and representation and then discusses the role that nonprofits play in our democracy. We discuss nonprofits as interest groups and their activities including lobbying, advocacy, and grassroots mobilization. We then note the critical distinctions between 501(c)(3) and 501(c)(4) nonprofits with regard to lobbying, advocacy, and mobilization activities. We note important transparency issues that have emerged in response to the political activities of nonprofit organizations. We highlight the role of nonprofits in elections, voter registration, and get-out-the-vote campaigns.

Chapter 8, titled Nonprofit and Voluntary Activism: Social Movements and Protest Politics, defines and examines some of the major social movements of the 20th century, in particular the civil rights and the role of nonprofits in that movement. We then shift to discuss more contemporary social change organizations and movements including the Gay Rights Movement and the Economic Justice Movement. We discuss the logic and theories that aim to explain social and protest movements that work to effect political and social change. We also touch on some important, modern international social movements including the Arab Spring, the Saffron Revolution in Myanmar (Burma), the Twitter Revolution in Iran, and the Women's Rights Movement in India.

Chapter 9, Economic Contributions of Nonprofit Organizations, turns to a discussion of the role that nonprofit organizations play in the US economy, both as a major employer of American workers, and also the roles played in local economic development by job training and community development organizations throughout the US. The chapter begins by identifying major industries within the nonprofit sector that serve as sources of jobs for the American workforce, and considers some of the factors that have contributed to nonprofit employment growth in recent years. The chapter then takes an in-depth look at some of the ways that job training and community development organizations promote local economic development, helping to repair local economies from the bottom up in many of America's poorest communities. Chapter 9 concludes with a discussion of nonprofits focused on business attraction, development, and promotion, organizations, and considers how these organizations help to fulfill local economic development goals.

Section IV: Nonprofit Sector Challenges & Opportunities
Chapter 10, The Future of Nonprofits and Civil Society, examines some contemporary and emerging trends that will affect the nonprofit sector in

the next decade and beyond. These trends create both significant challenges and opportunities for nonprofits and civil society. The trends discussed in this chapter include changing population demographics and what they mean not only for nonprofit service delivery but also for diversity in the nonprofit workforce and nonprofit governance; fiscal stress and uncertainty in government spending and the turbulence it creates for nonprofits; increased demands for transparency and accountability; increased market competition and pressures for performance; blending and blurring of sector distinctions; and the rise of technology and social media.

Notes

1   Outstanding textbooks for these audiences include Helmut Anheier's (2005) *Nonprofit Organizations: Theory, Management, Policy*; J. Steven Ott and Lisa Dicke's (2011) *Understanding Nonprofit Organizations: Governance, Leadership, and Management*; Peter Frumpkin's (2002) *On Being Nonprofit*; Robert Herman & Associates' (2004) *Jossey Bass Handbook of Nonprofit Leadership and Management*. Additionally, Gary Grobman's many editions of *The Nonprofit Handbook* are wonderful textbooks for graduate courses in nonprofit management and public affairs.
2   Anheier, Helmut K. 2005. *Organizations: Theory, Management, Policy*. New York, NY: Routledge Press.

ACKNOWLEDGMENTS

This book would not have been possible without the initial inspiration of Kate Pravera. Kate is the Academic Director for the School of Continuing Studies and has dedicated countless hours to developing the curriculum for nonprofit studies at the University of Illinois at Chicago (UIC). She has worked with graduate students, undergraduate students, and practitioners to share her enthusiasm for the nonprofit sector and public service. Kate played a critical role in identifying the need for this textbook, pitching the idea to Routledge, and encouraging us to develop it. We are thankful for her encouragement and contributions in the early stages of this project.

We are also thankful for the support and enthusiasm of the many UIC students who served as test subjects as we piloted early drafts of the book's chapters. In particular, we would like to thank the students enrolled in Dr. LeRoux's PA 230 class in Fall 2013. We appreciate your patience in reading unedited versions of the chapters and your thoughtful feedback about the content, exercises, and presentation of the material. We would also like to thank Cecilia Tobias for supplying the Reddit example in Chapter 10.

We also owe thanks to the many reviewers who took the time to carefully read, comment upon, and critique each chapter of the draft manuscript:

Al Lyons	Indiana University-Purdue University Indianapolis
Bruce Sievers	Stanford University
David Campbell	Binghamton University
Ken Menkhaus	Davidson College
Rebecca Nannery	Indiana University
Katie Korkosz	University of Central Florida
Victoria Johnson	University of Michigan
Jennifer Shea	San Francisco State University
Robert Rycroft	University of Mary Washington
Charles Epp	University of Kansas
Carl Milofsky	Bucknell University
Heath A. Brown	Seton Hall University
Laurance Geri	Evergreen State University
Donald Ritzenheim	Eastern Michigan University

Along with our students' input, we took the reviewers' feedback seriously and incorporated many valuable suggestions. All of the feedback we received along the way helped to improve the book and enhance the quality of the final product.

Finally, we owe a huge debt of gratitude to Julie Langer, a fantastic PhD student in the UIC Department of Public Administration, who provided unending support and cheer while reading draft chapters, developing tables, sorting through data, and responding to our many requests. Not only did Julie perform all the typical organizational tasks of a graduate assistant, we were fortunate to also have such a bright mind to bounce ideas off, share examples, and offer critiques. We are certain Julie is on her way to becoming an excellent scholar, and we know that her future colleagues and students will be equally lucky to work with her.

SECTION I

INTRODUCTION TO THE NONPROFIT SECTOR & CIVIL SOCIETY

1
DEFINING THE NONPROFIT SECTOR AND CIVIL SOCIETY

CHAPTER LEARNING OBJECTIVES

By the end of this chapter, students will be able to:

1. Identify various terms used to describe the nonprofit sector

2. Define civil society and its relationship to the nonprofit sector

3. Describe the major subsectors, or groups of organizations, that make up the US nonprofit sector

4. Describe general patterns of growth within the US nonprofit sector

5. Identify the key characteristics that make nonprofit organizations different from public and for-profit organizations

6. Identify characteristics that nonprofit organizations share in common with public and for-profit organizations

---

Introduction

Whether it involves chaperoning a child's field trip to the zoo, attending weekly church service, participating in a workplace blood drive, or attending class at a private college or university, Americans interact with the nonprofit and civil society sector in numerous ways in the course of their daily routines, often without realizing it. With nearly 1.6 million registered non-profits in the US today,[4] these institutions are playing increasingly important roles not only in American society and culture, but throughout the world. In addition to these registered, or formal, organizations there are tens of thousands of unregistered groups, clubs, churches, associations, coalitions, and initiatives, some of which operate on a strictly voluntary basis, without any paid staff. These unregistered organizations exist alongside, and sometimes in partnership with the registered organizations. Together, these registered and unregistered organizations constitute the nonprofit and civil society sector. The organizations and activities of this sector shape the social, political, and economic dimensions of American life in vital ways. While we will soon examine the definition of nonprofit organizations and civil society in detail, it will be noted here that the terms are often used interchangeably. However, **civil society** carries a somewhat broader meaning, referring to organizations and action initiated by citizens, outside of government and the market, along with the laws, norms, and customs that enable citizen-driven organizations and action.

In helping to create the social fabric of American life, nonprofit and civil society organizations provide spaces for people with common interests to associate, network, and volunteer. Sometimes nonprofit and civil organizations enable people with similar values to come together to share experiences, for example a community church or a cultural group like the Polish American Association. In other cases, nonprofits aim to solve a social problem or provide support to a group of people, for example Children of Lesbians and Gays Everywhere (COLAGE). In other cases, nonprofit organizations are distinguished by their service to communities, for example the Children's Hospital of Denver, or the Central Austin Neighborhood Association serving one of Chicago's very low-income neighborhoods. Other nonprofit organizations play an integral part in politics and policy-making at all levels of government by raising public awareness of salient issues, lobbying for legislation or public funding for important causes, and mobilizing citizens to vote, contact their elected officials, and participate in protests. For example, consider the Rock the Vote movement which works to increase voter participation among youth, or the National Organization for Rare Disorders, which lobbies to raise awareness and get government funding allocated to researching rare illnesses.

INVESTING IN A CURE FOR MALARIA: WHO SHOULD PAY FOR IT?

According to a recent article, "Bill Gates has declared capitalism 'flawed' because it channels more resources to curing minor ailments such as male baldness than to addressing the diseases that destroy millions of lives every year".[1] Why do we spend more in the United States on research to cure androgenetic alopecia, or male pattern baldness, than to eradicate malaria, a preventable and curable disease?

The answers, though not necessarily reassuring, are clear. The US spends more on research for male pattern baldness because (1) in the US male pattern baldness is more prevalent than malaria, (2) male pattern baldness is more common among people with financial means than is malaria, (3) there is a market for the treatment of male pattern baldness (e.g. there are people who want the medication/treatment and will pay for it), and finally (4) malaria is not generally considered an American problem—it mostly affects people outside of the US.

"What?!" you cry. "But I live in the US and I care about people dying from malaria. I want scientists to develop a vaccine for malaria. I think we should prevent malaria, and when it occurs, I want those who are sick with malaria to be treated."

That may be what you want. That may be what many of us want. But are you willing to pay for it? Are all Americans willing to pay for it? Should a portion of every American's taxes pay to invest in research for a malaria vaccine and support the treatment of malaria victims in Africa and Pakistan?

Alternatively, maybe the government shouldn't pay for this. So, let's turn to the private, for-profit sector. Maybe there is a pharmaceutical company that is willing to invest millions of its own profits to develop a malaria vaccine and treatment. But, once they have developed those drugs, who will buy them? Not Americans, as they don't suffer from malaria. Can the pharmaceutical company rely on those with malaria in Afghanistan, Pakistan, and parts of Africa and South America to buy these drugs—and to buy enough to make back the costs of the research and development (R&D) and turn a profit? Or should pharmaceutical companies invest in research to cure male pattern baldness and then sell that cure to Americans who are willing and able to pay for it? (Note: 35 million men in the US are affected by male pattern baldness.)[2]

Do you see the problem here? It is a **market failure** and a **government failure**. Market failure refers to the fact that there is not a private market for malaria R&D in poorer nations—there is not enough demand for investment and consumers lack the ability to pay for the treatment. It is a government failure because malaria is a public health problem, something that requires government investment because it is expensive and affects all of society. But, it also affects parts of the world where many governments

continued

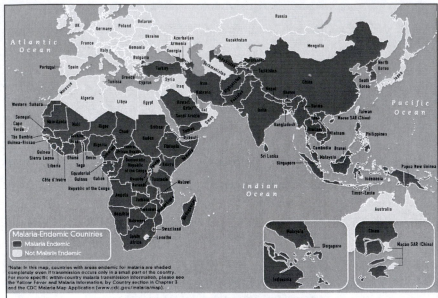

Eastern and Western Hemisphere Maps of Malaria Endemic Countries, 2011

lack the resources and capacity to invest in the science and market distribution required to eradicate the disease. Those governments that can afford to eradicate the disease (e.g. the US, UK, France, etc.) have already eradicated it at home, but lack the political will to tax their own people to fight the disease worldwide.

continued

Who will invest in developing a malaria vaccine and provide widespread treatment? The Bill and Melinda Gates Foundation has taken on the charge. Focusing on global health problems since their trip to Africa in 1993, Bill and Melinda Gates have stepped in where governments and private markets have failed. The Gates Foundation has funded more than $258 million in grants in anti-malaria work, the Millennium Scholar program for minority students pursuing advanced degrees in science, funded Sound Families to address homelessness in the Puget Sound area in Washington state, and launched an HIV/AIDS prevention program in India.[3] This is just one example of the important role that nonprofit organizations play in society, filling in where governments and private for-profit organizations fail to meet a need.

Nonprofit and civil society organizations of all types play a vital and growing role in the economy, employing more than 9% of the American workforce, and accounting for roughly 5.5% of **Gross Domestic Product (GDP)** in 2010.[5] Gross Domestic Product can be defined as the total monetary value of goods and services produced by a particular industry. Figure 1.1 highlights the nonprofit sector's growth from 1950 through 2010, showing both nonprofits' contributions to GDP and wages nonprofits have paid to US workers.[6] As illustrated in Figure 1.1, nonprofits' economic contributions began to rise beginning around 1970, and began to rise sharply beginning around 1980. As compared to 1950 when nonprofits' contributions to GDP hovered around 5 billion, in 1970 it had reached nearly 33 billion and by 1980 had soared to 97 billion. As the figure also suggests, the trend has continued to tick upward, with nonprofits contributing more than $804 billion in GDP in 2010. Similar trends can also be seen when examining the number of dollars that nonprofit organizations paid out to US workers. In 1950, wages paid out to US nonprofit workers neared 4 billion. However, by 1980 those numbers reached an impressive 71.6 billion and, by 2010, almost 577 billion. Taken together, these trends highlight the sector's tremendous growth over the time span of 60 years in the United States.

In the United States and abroad, nonprofit and civil society organizations emerge, grow, and succeed for a variety of social, political, and economic reasons. The role of the nonprofit and civil society sector in each of these dimensions of American life is the focus of this book. In the chapters that

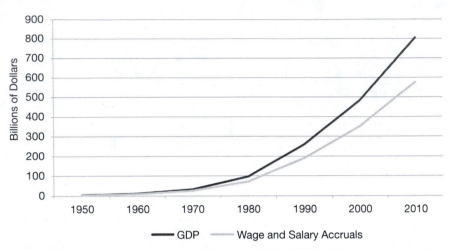

FIGURE 1.1 Economic Roles of the Nonprofit Sector (1950–2010).

Note: Data provided were adapted from *The Nonprofit Almanac 2012*. The originating data source, The Bureau of Economic Analysis at the Department of Commerce, measures the nonprofit sector by looking at organizations that fall into the following categories: religious and welfare, medical care, education and research, recreation and personal business. Those nonprofit organizations serving businesses such as credit unions and chambers of commerce are not accounted for in the data provided in Figure 1.1.

follow, we will examine the ways that nonprofit and civil society organizations contribute to the social, political, and economic dimensions of American culture, and in turn how American citizens shape the nonprofit sector and help to foster and create civil society. Throughout this discussion, we propose a dynamic view of the nonprofit and civil society sector; although the sector has a rich history that is grounded in distinct values and traditions, it is constantly evolving and changing, taking on roles typically handled by governments, and it has also moved into profit-making activities causing some nonprofits to mimic for-profit businesses. Technology, globalization, economic shifts, cross-sector partnerships, immigration, and the changing demographics of America are just a few of the key factors contributing to the on-going flux and transformation of the sector, and represent some themes we will visit throughout the book.

Before delving into these roles, however, it is important for the sake of common understanding that we define and describe the organizations that make up the US nonprofit sector, and examine more closely the meaning of civil society. In this chapter, we will consider some of the various labels used to describe the nonprofit sector, with special attention given to the term civil society, and will explore how the two concepts fit together. Next we will look at the size and scope of the nonprofit and civil society sector in the US. We will then discuss the boundaries of the nonprofit sector, discussing some of the attributes that make organizations within the nonprofit sector distinct, as well as consider some ways that nonprofit roles and characteristics blend with those of for-profit and public organizations.

Terms Used to Describe the Nonprofit Sector

Experts on nonprofit and civil society organizations have found it difficult to agree upon any one term for the sector, and thus a variety of labels are used to refer to it such as voluntary sector, civil society sector and so on. One reason there is no single "best term" for the sector stems from the immense diversity of organizations and activities contained within it. For example, American Jewish University, The Mayo Clinic, Planned Parenthood, The Bill & Melinda Gates Foundation, The Sierra Club, the American Bar Association, and the Catholic Worker Movement might describe themselves as educational organizations, healthcare providers, advocacy groups, philanthropies, voluntary organizations, environmental activists, professional associations, or religious organizations, but all fall under the general categorization of nonprofit organizations. Organizational diversity is one reason that makes the perfect terminology elusive. Another reason is that the sector has "fuzzy boundaries." We will examine both of these issues in greater detail later in this chapter.

In addition to the mission-impossible task of counting all the un-registered groups and organizations, the boundaries of the nonprofit and voluntary sector are made fuzzy by the growth of partnerships between nonprofits and government and for-profit organizations.[7] Nonprofit organizations are working as consultants and contractors to government agencies, delivering public services such as mental healthcare, distributing and monitoring welfare benefits, and running after-school programs. They are also affiliated with for-profit organizations, often as a philanthropic branch of a for-profit company, such as the Target Foundation or Google.org, which "develops technologies to help address global challenges and supports innovative partners through grants, investments and in-kind resources."[8] As some nonprofit organizations take on the delivery of public services, like government organizations, or strive to maximize revenue, like for-profit organizations, it can become difficult to see what exactly defines the nonprofit and civil society sector. Is the nonprofit sector simply comprised of organizations that are not traditionally government organizations and not clearly for-profit private corporations? Some have argued that the term "nonprofit" is itself problematic because it does not tell us what the sector *is*, but rather what it *is not*.[9]

A variety of labels are used to refer to the nonprofit and civil society sector. Some of these terms, outlined in Table 1.1, include the **third sector, independent sector, voluntary sector, charitable sector, social sector**, and **philanthropic sector**.

Each of these terms is useful for describing a particular aspect of the sector but, in doing so, conceals other characteristics. For example, the term "independent sector" implies that nonprofit organizations are autonomous actors that stand apart from government and for-profit organizations. While this label is accurate for describing some types of nonprofit and voluntary groups such as lobbying organizations that are privately funded, this term is not accurate for describing all nonprofits, as some rely heavily or even fully on government for the funding they need to operate, as is the case for many health and human service organizations. Similarly the term "third sector" suggests that organizations of the nonprofit sector are mutually exclusive from the "first" sector of the economy which is comprised of privately owned, for-profit businesses, and the "second" sector which is made up of government or public organizations. Yet, in reality, many nonprofit organizations are heavily engaged in partnerships with for-profit and government organizations, or have profit-making programs or subsidiary organizations under the same corporate umbrella, making the "third" sector label not entirely accurate for organizations in this category.

The term "voluntary sector" would also be inappropriate as a general label for the sector, as many organizations are highly professionalized and carry out their operations entirely through paid staff. While some nonprofit organizations are run entirely through donated labor, or through a mix of paid staff and volunteers, many are not. The label "philanthropic sector" is limiting in a similar way. The term derives from the word "philanthropy" which means altruistic concern for human kind, often expressed through giving of time or financial resources. But some nonprofits do not rely at all on private giving to conduct their operations. Thus, while some nonprofits are philanthropic, many organizations in the sector are not.

TABLE 1.1 Common Labels for the Nonprofit Sector

Label	Description	Strengths	Weakness
Nonprofit Sector	Nonprofit organizations are those that are not constructed for the primary purpose of making and distributing profits to shareholders.	Addresses the broader issue of organizational profit and accurately notes that many organizations are not primarily driven by profits.	Many nonprofit organizations make profits but are restricted in what they can do with those profits. Some argue that government organizations are not driven by profit.
Third Sector	Nonprofit organizations collectively comprise a sector different from the for-profit or governmental sectors.	A catchall phrase for all organizations that are not clearly private for-profit firms or government organizations.	Does not tell us what distinguishes this sector from the other two sectors (private and public).
Independent Sector	Nonprofit organizations are autonomous actors that stand apart from government and for-profit organizations.	Suggests that nonprofit organizations work independently from government and for-profit, private entities.	Implies the other two sectors are "dependent." Does not accurately represent financial dependence of nonprofit organizations in other sectors.
Voluntary Sector	Nonprofit organizations comprised of self-selecting individuals that come together voluntarily to work towards an organization's mission.	Highlights a primary feature that can distinguish nonprofit organizations from government and private for-profit organizations	Limits sector only to organizations that are run by volunteers. Not all nonprofits are run by volunteers; many have full-time staff members.
Charitable Sector	Nonprofit organizations that provide charitable services directly to intended beneficiaries.	Captures the essence of the sector as typically promoted by ordinary knowledge or by daily experiences, media influence, etc.	Limits sector to only charitable organizations. Many nonprofit organizations do not operate as charities (see all IRS 501(c) designations).
Philanthropic Sector	A sector where work is defined by altruistic concern for human kind, often expressed through giving of time or financial resources.	Highlights unique emotions driving the work of many nonprofit organizations. This term captures the nature of the sector most often promoted publicly.	Limits sector to only philanthropic organizations. For-profit organizations can engage in philanthropy. Not all nonprofits are driven by altruism and like emotions.
Social Sector	A sector where a concern for society takes center stage and work is geared towards improving social conditions.	Focuses positively on the sector's primary social purpose, rather than on what it is not (i.e. nonprofit, non-governmental).	Expansive term that can include not only formal social organizations but also informal collectives working for social purposes.
Non-Governmental Sector	Organizations that are nonprofit and serve a public mission, but are not governmental	This term aims to separate private, nonprofit organizations from government organizations also serving a public mission	Private organizations, whether for-profit or nonprofit, might be considered non-governmental. Some nonprofit organizations might rely on governmental funding.

Similarly, the term "charitable sector" is an appropriate label for the large number of benevolent organizations that exist for the collective good of society; it is far less appropriate in describing other types of nonprofit organizations that primarily provide benefits to their own members such as professional associations and labor unions.

Still, many of these alternative terms are used to describe or define the nonprofit and civil society sector. The use of each of these terms might be better understood if we consider the social, political, and economic complexity of US society and the ways in which we think about organizations and sectors. In the US, many nonprofit organizations describe their origins as a response to social need, and in some cases a social need to which the government or the private for-profit sector has not provided a level of service to meet the demand. When the government fails to provide a service and there is not a sufficient market for private, for-profit organizations to provide a particular service, nonprofit organizations might emerge to fill that gap. For example, consider the provision of services to the poor and hungry. Churches and other religious organizations might provide this service as an expression of their faith, or because the government is failing to fulfill all of the needs of the poor. Similarly, while there is a private market for the production of fine art and literature, there might not be a way for the general public to experience art and literature. An individual might personally own a painting by Picasso, but how do we ensure that the public can see an original Picasso, or have access to books and learning? In communities where the government could not afford to build art museums and libraries, wealthy philanthropists created libraries or donated personal art collections for public benefit. In this case, we might describe these organizations as philanthropic, as compared to the charitable organizations that give food and shelter to the poor. In both of these cases, we see private actors (organizations or individuals) providing a good or service that the private, for-profit sector and the government have failed to provide. In some ways, the nonprofit sector can be seen as filling in the gaps between government services and the private market for goods and services, giving rise to the term "third sector."

Civil Society

The term "civil society sector" has become more commonly used in American discourse and is often used interchangeably with the term "nonprofit sector." What is meant by the term civil society? Are civil society and the nonprofit sector the same thing or can we draw distinctions between them? And, if they are distinct, what is the relationship between the two?

It is important to note that there is substantial ambiguity surrounding the notion of civil society. According to the *Journal of Civil Society*, "civil society is a contested concept. There is little agreement on its precise meaning, though much overlap exists among core conceptual components." Most definitions converge in their agreement that civil society involves citizen action and organizations outside of the market and the state that advance common interests. Many definitions are limited to a set of organizations that comprise civil society. For example, the *World Alliance for Citizen Participation* defines civil society as "networks and organisations, trade unions, faith-based networks, professional associations, NGO capacity development organisations, philanthropic foundations, and other funding bodies."[10] Civil Society International, a nonprofit capacity-building organization, offers a similar definition, referring to civil society as a collection of "'intermediary institutions' such as professional associations, religious groups, labor unions, and citizen advocacy organizations that give voice to various sectors of society and enrich public participation in democracies."[11]

Other definitions account for a broader view of civil society that includes not only organizations, but also laws (free speech) and norms (regard for others) that make society a better place to live. For example, Helmut Anheier defines civil society as "the macro-level institutional structure of laws, norms, and customs that give rise to the organizations and associations that citizens create (outside of government and the market)."[12]

In the chapters that follow, we operate from a view of civil society that is consistent with Anheier's broader definition. Figure 1.2 depicts the three key components of civil society: institutions, ideas and action, and organizations. Institutions are the laws, norms, and values of society. Ideas and action are the common interests, associations, and citizen initiatives that often mobilize individuals and groups. Organizations are the formal and informal structures that enable action. These three components are inter-related, as civil society is the larger context within which formally registered nonprofit organizations as well as informal

FIGURE 1.2 Components of Civil Society.

groups, clubs, and citizen initiatives operate. Registered nonprofit organizations play a key role in shaping and creating civil society, but the notion of civil society is not limited to these formal organizations. Moreover, civil society encompasses the values, norms, customs, and legal infrastructure that allow for the expression of group interests and actions.

As this discussion suggests, each term used to describe the nonprofit sector is incomplete as it highlights a particular dimension, feature, or value of the sector, but in doing so conceals other realities about it. In the following sections, we describe the nonprofit sector and outline some of the ways that there are overlapping components between the nonprofit sector and private and public sectors.

Size and Scope of the US Nonprofit Sector

Tax–Exempt Status

The size and scope of the nonprofit sector are relatively easy to draw boundaries around if we limit it to the conventional understanding of the sector as consisting of all organizations designated as tax-exempt entities by the federal Internal Revenue Service (IRS). The IRS is the federal organization best known for processing income tax returns. However, this is also the agency that has primary oversight of nonprofit organizations at the federal level. The IRS determines whether or not to grant **tax-exempt status** to organizations that apply for it. The vast majority of applicants that apply for this status receive approval, absolving the organization from paying taxes. However, as we mentioned earlier, the true size and scope of the nonprofit and civil society sector is much larger than the number of formally registered tax-exempt entities. While the precise number of these organizations and thus exact size of the sector can never fully be known, the National Center for Charitable Statistics estimates that roughly 2.3 million voluntary organizations operate in the US, nearly 1.6 million of which are registered as tax-exempt entities with the US Internal Revenue Service.[13] Organizations that are formed for certain purposes (which we shall soon examine) may apply to the IRS to seek status as a tax-exempt corporation, and must also register with the state in which the organization plans to do business.

Tax exemption is a financial privilege granted by the federal government which allows certain organizations permanent exemption from payment of corporate income taxes at the federal level, and in the majority of states exemption from payment of all state and local taxes including property, sales, franchise and use taxes; tax-exempt organizations are also eligible for reduced postal rates.[14] The US government allows tax exemption status to nonprofit organizations so that they can dedicate more of their earnings to improving the quality of life in our society. Tax exemption is considered a subsidy to encourage pro-social behavior and is generally justified by the "quid pro quo" logic.[15,16] **Quid pro quo logic** suggests that nonprofits should receive tax subsidies because they provide benefits to neighborhoods, communities, cities, states, and our society in general. Many of the important nonprofit organizations in our communities enjoy tax-exempt status, including colleges, nonprofits, charter schools, religious organizations, fraternal groups, and community programs. The challenges and benefits of nonprofit tax exemption are discussed in more detail in Chapter 2. For now, it is simply important to know that nonprofit organizations are often identified by their tax-exempt status and registration with the IRS.

National Taxonomy of Exempt Entities Classification

The **National Taxonomy of Exempt Entities (NTEE)** codes offer a useful way to categorize nonprofit organizations according to their mission or purpose. The NTEE system was created during the 1980s and is a classification scheme used today by the IRS and the National Center for Charitable Statistics, the national clearinghouse for compiling data on the US nonprofit sector. The NTEE classification system categorizes all nonprofit organizations into 26 major groups under 10 broad subsectors of arts and culture, education, environment and animal welfare, health, human services, international and foreign affairs, public and social benefit, religious organizations, mutual/membership benefit, and unknown/unclassified. While a full listing of more than 400 codes can be found through the National Center for Charitable Statistics, http://nccs.urban.org/classification/NTEE.cfm, we will briefly examine eight of the broad subsectors that form the skeleton of the NTEE system and look at some examples of organizations that make up these groups.

Arts, Culture, and Humanities

A wide variety of organizations make up the arts subsector including museums, performing arts centers, symphony orchestras, opera and ballet companies, history and science museums, theaters, historical societies, film and video production groups, television and radio productions, arts education programs, arts advocacy organizations, and all other arts-related organizations. Examples of nonprofit organizations in this subsector include the J. Paul Getty museum in Los Angeles, National Public Radio, Dog and Pony Theatre Company in Chicago, Detroit Symphony Orchestra, Arts Alliance Illinois, and the San Francisco Arts Education Project.

Education

A large nonprofit educational subsector exists alongside, and as a supplement to, the public sector educational system. The nonprofit education subsector consists of private elementary and secondary schools (including religious and parochial schools), charter schools, two- and four-year private colleges and universities, preschools, organizations that lobby for education, scholarship funds and student financial aid organizations, sororities and fraternities, alumni associations, and parent teacher associations. Examples of some organizations within the nonprofit education subsector include the Asians and Pacific Islander American Scholarship Fund, Harvard University, the Center for Education Reform, Russell Byers Charter School in Philadelphia, and the Ohio State University Alumni Association.

Environment and Animal Welfare

Organizations within the environmental and animal welfare subsector include pollution abatement and control groups, water, wetlands, energy and forest conservation groups, gardening clubs, fisheries, wildlife sanctuaries, zoos and aquariums, groups concerned with the protection of endangered species, and animal protection and welfare advocacy groups. Many organizations within this sector are national in scope, having state or local chapters/groups, while others are limited to a local focus. Examples of organizations found within this subsector include the Chicago Botanic Gardens, the Dallas Arboretum, Trout Unlimited, San Diego Zoological Society, the Nature Conservancy, People for the Ethical Treatment of Animals (PETA), and the Humane Society.

Health

The healthcare sector in the US consists of a mix of nonprofit, for-profit, and public organizations. Types of nonprofit organizations found in this subsector include general and specialty hospitals, community mental health centers, family planning centers, substance abuse prevention and treatment programs, blood, organ, and tissue banks, psychiatric hospitals and residential treatment centers, professional associations representing physicians and other health professionals with medical specialties, and research institutes and advocacy groups organized around specific diseases and disorders. Examples of organizations represented in the nonprofit healthcare subsector include Mayo Clinic, Susan G. Komen, National Alliance for the Mentally Ill, St. Jude's Children's Hospital, Planned Parenthood, American Cancer Society, Alzheimer's Association, AIDS Research Alliance, Autism Society of America, and the American Medical Association.

Human Services

The human services subsector represents what is perhaps the most visible face of the nonprofit sector. Organizations within this subsector provide a range of services at the community level, many of which are targeted to help the needy and members of specific populations. Types of organization within this subsector include domestic violence programs, food pantries, homeless shelters, senior centers, ethnic and immigrant service centers, emergency assistance programs, child and family service programs, disability service centers, legal assistance, and job training programs. Examples of well-known organizations within this subsector include the Salvation Army, American Red Cross, YMCA/YWCA, Habitat for Humanity, and thousands of locally formed service providers.

International and Foreign Affairs

Organizations that make up the international and foreign affairs subsector have missions that are designed to foster international understanding, promote agriculture and economic development overseas, provide international relief, promote international peace and security, human rights, conduct research on foreign policy and globalization issues, international economic and trade policy, or international migration or refugee issues. The nonprofit organizations found within this subsector that are engaged in these issues may directly provide services, perform research related to these issues, or lobby for these causes. Examples of organizations within this subsector include Sister Cities International, Kiva Microfunds, Heifer Project International, Oxfam-America, Amnesty International, Human Rights Watch, and the Center for New American Security.

Public and Societal Benefit

The public and social benefit category of nonprofit organizations is one of the most diverse. Within this subsector are nonprofit community and economic development organizations, rights organizations representing the interests of specific populations, as well as philanthropic and grant-making organizations. The community and economic development group itself is highly diverse, containing neighborhood and block clubs, community action agencies, community development organizations whose purpose is to expand the benefits of local economic growth to the poor, as well as organizations that serve or represent other constituencies including both aspiring and already successful business entrepreneurs, commercial, industrial, and residential developers, convention and visitors bureaus, hotel and restaurant associations, and real estate associations, among others. Examples of organizations in this group include Community Action

Agencies, Chambers of Commerce, the American Hotel and Lodging Association, and the National Association of Real Estate Brokers.

Also included within this subsector are civil rights groups that exist to protect and promote the interests of specific populations, such as racial minorities, women, persons with disabilities, and senior citizens. Examples of these organizations include the American Association of Retired Persons (AARP), the National Organization for Women (NOW), the NAACP, and the National Gay and Lesbian Task Force. The public and social benefit subsector also encompasses philanthropy, volunteerism, and grant-making organizations. This set of organizations includes private, corporate, and community foundations, named trusts, programs that promote voluntarism, and federated giving organizations. Well-known examples of organizations in this category include the Rockefeller Brothers Fund, Cleveland Community Foundation, Junior Leagues, Hewlett Packard Foundation, United Way, and the Jewish Federation.

Religious Institutions

The religious subsector includes not only churches and places of worship for a variety of Christian denominations and other faith practices in the US such as Judaism, Islam, and Buddhism, but also includes religious television, radio, and print publications, interfaith coalitions, missionary and outreach programs, and human service programs operated through the church. It is difficult to estimate the size of this subsector because churches are automatically considered tax-exempt and are thus not required to apply for tax-exempt status from the IRS, nor are they required to submit annual filing of financial reports, so while they are considered part of the nonprofit sector, they are not included in the records of tax-exempt organizations available to the public. That said, some churches voluntarily choose to seek recognition of tax-exempt status from the IRS in an effort to enhance their legitimacy and transparency in the eyes of their members and the public. Churches that operate social service or missionary programs must obtain recognition of tax-exempt status in order to engage in fundraising and solicitation of charitable donations for these programs. In addition to churches of all types, some examples of organizations included in this subsector include Christian Broadcasting Network, Interfaith Alliance Foundation, and Jewish Community Centers.

Figure 1.3 highlights the growth and decline of the number of nonprofit organizations in these eight broad subsectors over time. As indicated by the figure, education, human services, and religious organizations were the largest nonprofit subsectors in the US from 1995 through 2013. In 2010, there were more than 400,000 organizations in health and human services. There have been around 170,000 education organizations during this time period and the number of religious organizations has continued to increase, from 100,00 in 1995 to more than 250,000 in 2013. In 2013, education organizations made up approximately 16% of the sector, and religious organizations comprised about 21%. The largest subsector in 2013 according to the total number of organizations was human services, which accounted for nearly 30% of the total organizations. Though most nonprofit subsectors saw a slight decline in the total number of registered organizations in 2010 and 2011, overall the total number of registered nonprofits in the US increased by approximately 40% from 1995 to 2013.

If we consider the total revenue brought in by each subsector, we can see the trends vary slightly from the previous analysis of the subsectors by total number of organizations. Figure 1.4 shows the distribution of the eight broad subsectors by total revenue reported from 1995 through 2013.

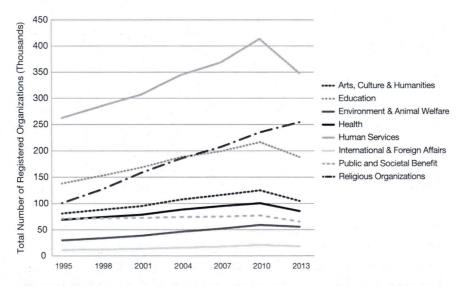

FIGURE 1.3 Registered Nonprofit Organization Growth & Decline, by Subsector (1995–2013).

Note: All data were derived from the National Center for Charitable Statistics database. Only those organizations registered with the IRS are accounted for in this visual model.

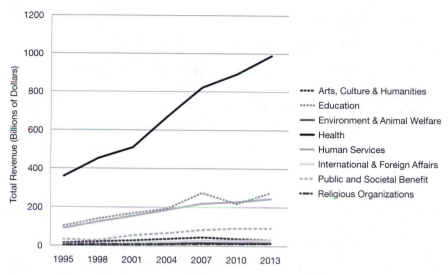

FIGURE 1.4 Nonprofit Revenue Growth & Decline, by Subsector (1995–2013).

Source: National Center for Charitable Statistics—http://nccs.urban.org/

According to the figure, we can see that the three largest subsectors according to total revenue are health, education, and human services, a fact we shall examine more closely in Chapter 9. In 2013, health organizations contributed 53% of the total revenue of the sector, while the next two largest contributions came from education and human services, which contributed 15% and 13%, respectively. Though each subsector saw peaks and valleys over the 18-year period in terms of revenue growth and decline, overall the revenue generated by these eight nonprofit subsectors increased by approximately 38% from 1995 through 2013.

This overview of tax-exempt organizational categories and the subsectors helps to highlight the wide variety of organizations that make up the nonprofit and civil society sector. The vast diversity of the sector and its tendency to elude a simple and clear terminology raises the question of whether we can make any generalizations about the sector at all. What are the common features of organizations that comprise the US nonprofit and civil society sector? In the next section, we examine a set of characteristics that define this sector, and make the organizations within it distinct. We also examine some ways that nonprofit organizations are similar to, and distinct from, for-profit organizations and public organizations.

The Blurring Boundaries of the Nonprofit Sector

Distinguishing Characteristics of the Nonprofit Sector

Despite the diversity of organizations and activities that are represented within it, the nonprofit sector can be regarded as a distinct sector based on the following attributes: being mission-directed, community-governed, and reliance on charitable donations and voluntary resources. There are of course exceptions to these attributes and sometimes nonprofit organizations share characteristics of private, for-profit organizations, and public organizations.

Mission-Directed

Nonprofit organizations share in common the fact that they are formed in order to fulfill some particular mission, cause, or social purpose. Nonprofit organizations are "mission-directed" in the sense that the mission generally serves as the orienting point of reference, or anchor, for organizational activities and decision-making. Historically, nonprofit organizations have been described as "mission-driven rather than profit-driven,"[17] yet this implies a false dichotomy because nonprofit organizations must also make money if they are to have the capacity to fulfill their missions. The "mission-directed" attribute makes nonprofit organizations distinct from for-profit organizations, some of which may value social responsibility but have a primary objective of generating profits. Of course, one might argue that certainly private, for-profit organizations have missions too; for example, Google's mission to "Do no evil." But what makes nonprofit organizations different is that the mission is meant to be more important than the pursuit of profits. Whereas, the financial bottom line is often the most important determinant of whether a for-profit organization survives or not.

Additionally, we know that many government organizations are public serving and are mission-driven, putting the public-serving mission ahead of making profits. However, some types of nonprofits, while still mission-directed, exist to provide specific benefits to those who choose to become a member of the organization, which typically requires the payment of dues or premiums on some sort of regular schedule. As compared with public and social benefit nonprofits which provide **collective benefits** for all of society, mutual membership benefit organizations provide **selective**

benefits, which are limited to members only. So, while government and nonprofit organizations might both put mission ahead of profits, many types of nonprofit organizations do have the ability to exclude individuals or refuse services, whereas public organizations generally must serve everyone who is eligible for services.

Voluntary Governance

The second distinguishing characteristic of nonprofit organization is that they are governed by boards of directors, whose members carry out their duties as volunteers. Board members may hold a variety of titles in their professional and personal lives, but regardless of whether the board member is the CEO of a corporation, a real estate developer, nurse, lawyer, ex-offender, professor, elected official, or stay-at-home parent, he or she carries out the role of nonprofit board member without compensation. Generally, persons volunteer to serve as board members because of a personal experience related to the organization's mission or a deep commitment to the cause the organization represents. In many instances, board members are asked, or volunteer themselves, to serve because they have some particular skill, expertise, or perspective that can provide a valuable contribution to the organization. The boards of directors, composed of volunteers, are a key characteristic of voluntary governance.

Boards of nonprofit organizations are often made up of members of the community in which the organization is physically located, and some organizations, such as the Bickerdike Redevelopment Corporation in Chicago's Humboldt Park neighborhood, require the board to be comprised of community members. Other types of nonprofit organizations place a premium on securing board representation from members of the population for whom the organization exists. This practice is common among nonprofit organizations providing mental health and substance abuse treatment, such as Wyandot Center for Community Behavioral Healthcare in Kansas City which requires that at least one client of the organization serves as a member on the board of directors. As a result of these practices, nonprofit boards tend to be much more diverse and demographically representative of their stakeholders than other kinds of organizations.

Voluntary governance, governance from a set of volunteer board members, means that nonprofit organizations are fundamentally different from for-profit organizations, which are governed by boards of stockholders who own shares of the company. The voluntary governance feature also makes nonprofit organizations distinct from public organizations, which are governed by a mix of elected officials and political appointees. While the feature of voluntary governance offers many benefits such as increased diversity and community representation, it can be a double-edged sword as volunteers may not have adequate time to devote to their board roles, or may lack the expertise and technical knowledge needed to provide effective oversight and financial accountability of the organization.

Reliance on Voluntary Resources

One of the most important distinguishing features of the nonprofit sector is its reliance on voluntary resources. Specifically, many nonprofits generate revenues from donations and philanthropic giving, and rely on the donation of time, expertise, and other non-financial resources. While not every single nonprofit organizations relies on private donations, most receive at least a small portion of their income from individual contributions and/or institutional philanthropy (foundations, funding intermediaries, etc.). We shall examine private giving to nonprofit organizations more closely in Chapter 6. For now, we will simply emphasize that this tendency to receive income from voluntary, private donations and philanthropic giving is a feature of the nonprofit sector that makes it distinct from private for-profit organizations as well as government organizations.

Voluntary contributions of time are another characteristic distinguishing nonprofits from for-profit and government organizations. Although not every nonprofit organization relies on voluntary labor to carry out its mission, all nonprofits rely on volunteers to serve on the board of directors, and thus volunteers represent a critical resource for the sector. In Chapter 5, we will examine in detail the issue of volunteering and community service, and the use of voluntary labor by the nonprofit sector.

Reliance on Diverse Sources of Income

While not every nonprofit organization has a highly diverse revenue portfolio, roughly 90% of nonprofit organizations rely on multiple sources of funding.[18] As shown in Figure 1.5, reporting public charities in 2010 were funded through numerous sources.[19] Specifically, in 2010, public charities reported receiving the majority of their revenue from private fees for goods and services, which can range from tuition payments and hospital patient revenues to ticket sales. The second largest source of nonprofit income in 2010, as highlighted by Figure 1.5, was from fees received from government sources such as Medicare, Medicaid, and government contracts. Together, government grants and contracts comprise about 32% of nonprofit revenue. The reliance on diverse sources of income and on voluntary resources is a key feature that distinguishes organizations in the nonprofit sector from different types of organizations in other sectors. For example, for-profit firms rely primarily on profits generated through consumer payments for goods and services for their income, while public organizations rely primarily on taxes for their operating revenues, which citizens pay on a compulsory rather than a voluntary basis.

Nonprofit organizations rely on a diverse mix of resources for their success. Some of these resources include voluntary contributions from

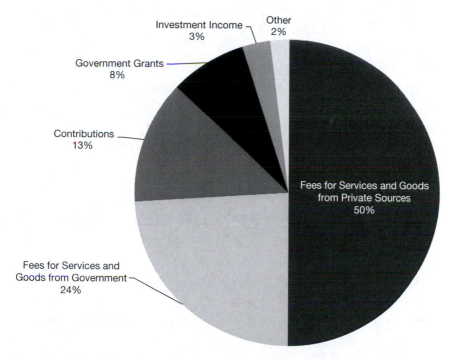

FIGURE 1.5 Primary Revenue Sources of Reporting Public Charities, 2010.

Note: The data in Figure 1.5 were drawn from a 2012 report by the Urban Institute. See http://www.urban.org/UploadedPDF/412674-The-Nonprofit-Sector-in-Brief.pdf

individual donors, government contracts and grants, corporate contributions, earned income such as fees, commercial activity, interest and investment income, and other nonprofit organizations including foundations, funding intermediaries, and churches. Consider National Public Radio (NPR), for example, which relies on a mixture of federal funding, listener contributions, and the sale of airtime to private organizations and individuals to support its operations. While NPR, like some government and private organizations, relies on a mix of public and private funding, it also relies on charitable donations, which is not a characteristic that is typical of organizations in the government and for-profit sectors. Of course, there are some cases where private, for-profit organizations operate with government contracts and grants: for example, defense contractors. But in these cases, government funding is used to provide some service to the government, while still providing a benefit or profit to the organization's owners or shareholders. In comparison, nonprofits relying on government grants and contracts are often delivering public services on behalf of the government and not returning a profit to the organization.

Figure 1.6 provides an example of revenue diversity in four different nonprofit organizations at the national and local level including: National Public Radio, the Salvation Army World Office, The Cara Program, and World Business Chicago.[20] Figure 1.6 highlights the percentage of revenue relied upon by each of these four organizations. Take a moment to look up and read about each of the four organizations listed in Figure 1.6. Can you hypothesize as to why these organizations would rely on such different revenue streams given their mission, client base, and scope of services?

Nonprofit Similarities with For-Profit and Public Organizations

While nonprofit organizations are distinct from government and for-profit organizations in the ways described above, they share numerous features in common with for-profit and government organizations. Nonprofit organizations share many of the social and public-serving missions of government organizations, seeking to provide goods and services to the general public or those in our society who might need extra support. In other ways, nonprofit organizations can operate like for-profit organizations, as individuals can choose who belongs to the organization, limit membership to their groups, provide services to a specific set of people,

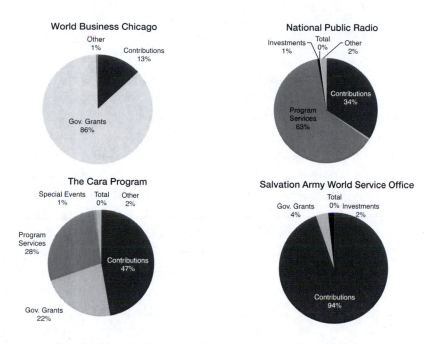

FIGURE 1.6 Revenue Diversity, Examples of National & Local Nonprofits, 2010.

Note: Revenue streams investigated for each organization were taken from Guidestar's reported financial figures for the fiscal year 2010, on the IRS 990. Revenue streams included contributions, government grants, investments, program services, special events, sales, and other. Those streams not included on the pie chart for each organization indicate a zero was reported.

or redefine their mission, budgets, and revenue-generating activities based on their leadership and preferences, without input from the general public, tax payers, or elected political officials.

The similarities between the public, for-profit, and nonprofit sectors can be especially apparent when nonprofits are joined in financial partnerships with government or for-profit organizations, as they tend to absorb characteristics of their funding partners. For example, when a small, faith-based homeless shelter operated mostly by volunteers decides to partner with the local city government through a contract to provide services to the poor, the government might require that the shelter "scale up" their operations to serve more people, become more professionalized in their service delivery, institute new policies, hire staff with professional degrees, and adhere to government regulations. Because the homeless shelter is accepting public funds, it must also now accept the requirements that come with public funding. Because city resources are intended to be distributed to all needy residents, the faith-based group can no longer limit its services to church members or people of the same faith. Instead, it must expand its services to the general public. Similarly, the government funding might require public reporting of spending activities, compelling the shelter to hire a professional accountant to track financial activities and complete reports to the government. Thus, while the homeless shelter may benefit from a more reliable source of funding it must also now take on some of the activities and characteristics we would normally attribute to a government organization. Additionally, while accepting government funding allows the shelter to expand their mission to serve more people, it will likely come with trade-offs including loss of control over some aspects of decision-making, and increased levels of accountability and reporting.

Similarly, nonprofit organizations that rely mostly on service fees for their income may behave like for-profit firms by placing a premium on customer service and satisfaction, in an attempt to maximize market share. Consider nursing homes, for example, which rely primarily on payments from Medicare and Medicaid for each patient residing in their facility. In an effort to become the most attractive and desirable facility in town (and thus attract the most "customers"), nursing homes may replace their outdated televisions with flat-screen HDTVs, offer premium TV and movie selections, menu options, extensive recreation and activity options, and modern furnishings.

Even in the absence of government-funding partnerships, however, nonprofit organizations share some fundamental characteristics in common with public organizations, and in other ways they share a likeness to for-profit firms. Below, we will examine some of these similarities, as well as highlight some similarities across organizational forms. Table 1.2 summarizes the attributes that define the nonprofit sector as unique and distinct, as well as the attributes of nonprofit organizations that are shared in common with for-profit and public organizations.

Similarities with Public Organizations

As we mentioned earlier, nonprofit organizations must make money in order to have the capacity to fulfill their missions. This is also true for public organizations. However, nonprofit and public organizations are fundamentally different from for-profit organizations in the sense that they are legally prohibited from distributing profits to employees or board

TABLE 1.2 Primary Attributes of the Nonprofit Sector

Attribute	Description	Example—The Cara Program
Mission-Directed	Organization has an orienting reference point for activity and decision-making.	*Mission*: "The Cara Program prepares and inspires motivated individuals to break the cycle of homelessness, transform their lives, strengthen our communities, and forge paths to real and lasting success."
Community-Governed	Organization is reliant to some degree on charitable giving and voluntary labor.	The Cara Program cites generous community support, local employers, volunteers, funders, and its Board of Directors as critical components for continued organizational success.
Non-Distribution Constraint	Like public organizations, nonprofits cannot distribute profits to employees or board members.	The Cara Program is an IRS-registered 501(c)(3) organization. As such, they are legally prohibited from distributing profits to employees or shareholders and all donations go directly to their Annual General Operating Fund, and are tax deductible.
Provision of Public Goods	Like public organizations, nonprofits provide goods and services similar to the government that private organizations are unable or unwilling to provide.	Much like the Department of Family and Support Services and the Illinois Department of Commerce and Economic Opportunity, The Cara Program primarily provides workforce development services to high barrier populations in the communities they serve.
Transparency/ Accountability	Like public organizations, many nonprofits strive for high levels of transparency and public accountability.	To ensure donors and the public have updated information The Cara Program publishes performance updates, annual reports, and its IRS 990 form online.
Innovative and Entrepreneurial	Like for-profit organizations, nonprofit organizations can engage freely in innovative and entrepreneurial activities.	The Cara Program launched its own Social Enterprise in 2005 called CleanSlate. This multi-million dollar enterprise provides transitional jobs to at-risk individuals in the Chicagoland area.

members. Thus while they need enough money to survive and to buffer themselves from emergencies, they lack an incentive to generate profits to a large extent. This characteristic of nonprofit and public organizations is known as the "non-distribution constraint" and shall be examined more closely in Chapter 3.

Nonprofit and public organizations are similar in that they both provide public goods that for-profit organizations cannot or will not provide because is it either inappropriate or unprofitable. While we will examine this issue more closely in Chapter 3, a brief example using environmental protections helps to illustrate this point. Public organizations provide for environmental protection through a variety of efforts including regulations and monitoring of private industry, and public education. Nonprofit organizations supplement this work through environmental research, public education, and putting pressure on policy-makers to pass laws that protect the environment. Similarly, the public sector through the National Park Service, US Forest Service, and other public lands programs sets aside land for preservation and conversation in the United States. The Nature Conservancy, a private, nonprofit organization, has taken on this mission as well, pooling private funds and donations to buy land that can be conserved for a public good. These cases exemplify the ways in which public and nonprofit organizations might seek the same provision of public goods and services for society. Yet it is also the case that not *all* nonprofit organizations provide public goods, as some exist to provide selective benefits exclusively to a set of members as we mentioned earlier.

In some ways, nonprofit and public organizations are alike in their level of transparency and accountability to the public. Most registered nonprofit organizations must disclose their financial statements, lists of board members, salaries of the five highest paid employees, and basic organizational information each year, which is made publicly available via Guidestar as well as the National Center for Charitable Statistics business master files. The availability of information from public organizations via websites varies, depending on the level of government and the type of organization, but most citizen queries particularly with regard to local and state government issues can be readily answered by visiting these organizations' websites. The Freedom of Information Act (FOIA) enables citizens to request information from public organizations when not readily available, and also applies to nonprofit programs that are funded by government. Just as much of the operations, financial details, and personnel information of for-profit organizations is proprietary—meaning the public does not have a legitimate claim to it nor does the organization have a responsibility to disclose it—private nonprofit organizations can also treat this information as proprietary. Thus, the source of funding for nonprofit organizations and their reliance on government organizations can often help to explain how similar or dissimilar they are to public organizations.

Similarities with For-Profit Organizations

Innovation and entrepreneurship are two characteristics generally associated with the business world. Yet nonprofit organizations are similar to for-profit organizations in this regard, and have become increasingly so over time.[21] As the number of nonprofit organizations has increased and traditional sources of revenue (such as government funding) have not kept pace with this growth, nonprofit organizations have adopted new tactics to become more competitive. Many nonprofits are improving the quality of their services to attract and retain clients, members, and customers, publicizing performance outcomes, marketing their services, expanding into new markets, and developing profit-making ventures. These profit-making ventures of nonprofit organizations, often called "social enterprises," are growing in number, and represent a larger trend toward a market-based orientation within the nonprofit sector. Social enterprises and hybrid organizational models such as the low-profit, limited-liability corporation (L3C), which we shall discuss further in Chapter 10, serve as examples of the way that traditional boundaries between for-profit and nonprofit forms are blurring. While these newer organizational models hold the promise of greater efficiency and more effective solutions to some of our most pressing problems in society, they raise new questions and challenges for the nonprofit sector.

Table 1.3 illustrates the ways in which the three sectors—public, for-profit, and nonprofit—overlap with one another and remain distinct from one another. We see that the distinguishing features of nonprofit organizations are relying on volunteers and donations, and being community governed. We also see that, like public organizations, nonprofits sometimes provide public goods, are mission-driven, and seek to serve the public interest above profit-making. When nonprofit organizations rely heavily

TABLE 1.3 Distinct and Shared Characteristics in Nonprofit, For-Profit & Public Sectors

	For-Profit Sector	Nonprofit Sector	Public Sector
Profit Distribution	Yes	No	No
Public Service Mission	No	Sometimes	Yes
Reliance on Voluntary Labor & Donations	No	Yes	No
Ability to Tax for Resources	No	No	Yes
Provision of Public Goods	No	Sometimes	Yes
Community-Governed	No	Yes	No
Innovate Freely in Response to Market	Yes	Yes	No

on public funding, they become subject to public sector standards of accountability to the general population of citizens, but public organizations remain distinct from nonprofit organizations in that they are owned and operated by the government and can levy taxes to obtain resources. Table 1.3 also shows us how nonprofit organizations are similar to for-profit organizations in their entrepreneurship and innovation, enabling them to respond to market pressures. While Table 1.3 is a useful guide for understanding the general similarities and distinctions between the three sectors, it is important to note that there are organizations that sit at the borders of these sectors or in the overlapping zones, and as the sectors become more intertwined and financially interdependent in their efforts to address social problems, we will find increasing complications in defining them as separate sectors.

Similarities between Nonprofit, For-Profit, and Public Sectors

As our discussion has demonstrated, the nonprofit, for-profit, and public sectors each have distinctive qualities. But organizations are organizations, and they share some features in common regardless of their type. Organizations within all three sectors depend on resources for their survival. Moreover, they all need to manage and remain responsive to multiple stakeholders, including citizen/customers, suppliers, employees, and board members/governing bodies. Another unifying feature of nonprofit, public, and for-profit organizations is the growing reliance on technology to conduct day-to-day business and to engage stakeholders. Reliance on technology has evolved from simple Internet websites for displaying information and conducting transactions, to ongoing two-way and multi-party communication through social media. These new, emerging technologies enable new possibilities for engaging and sustaining the attention of stakeholders. This reliance on technology presents both new challenges and opportunities for organizations, and we will explore many of the ways that technology is transforming the nonprofit and civil society sector throughout the chapters that follow.

CHALLENGES AND CONTROVERSIES

The Role of Sector in Adoptions in America

Adoptions are a relatively common practice in the United States. In 2008 there were 136,000 reported adoptions, up from 128,000 in 2000.[22] It is estimated that the number of adopted children in the US is around 2 million.[23]

Many of us have a friend or family member who was adopted or who is planning to adopt a child. Parents seeking to adopt children face a number of important decisions. Should they adopt domestically or internationally? Should they adopt a child from an orphanage, through an agency, or from an individual mother? Adoptions are regulated by states, so the rules vary from state to state across the country. People seeking to adopt a child must learn the rules in their state and then decide how they will approach the process. Will they use a government agency or a private agency? And if they use a private agency, will they choose a for-profit or a nonprofit organization? What kind of services and rules should adopting parents expect based on the type of organization they choose? If they adopt overseas, will a nonprofit organization be more trustworthy than a for-profit organization? What do these organizations do with all of the processing fees—do those funds go to navigating the bureaucratic rules in the other country, to supporting the birth mother, or to supporting other children in the system? Are some of the organizations more transparent than others? Are there reports or tax forms that parents can read to get a sense of how the adoption agency is run? Should they choose an agency based on reputation and stereotypes of government, for-profit, and nonprofit adoption agencies? Who should they trust with their money and the important process of ensuring that they can adopt a child safely into their home? These are all important questions that adopting parents will need to consider.

There are two types of adoption agencies in the US: public and private.

Public adoption agencies are operated by the county or state in which they are located and are supported by tax dollars. The main function of public agencies is to find homes

continued

for children for whom the government state has assumed responsibility. Often the types of adoptions facilitated by public agencies are for waiting children or special-needs children, often currently residing in the foster care system. Usually, adopting through a public agency is at a lower cost than through private organizations since the state subsidizes the legal and processing fees. Some public agencies will have sliding scale fees based on the income of the adoptive parents and some states will offer tax deductions based on the type of adoptions that the state is hoping to encourage. Many times adoptions through public agencies are closed (no contact between the birth parent and adoptive parents) because the adopted child is the full responsibility of the state. When seeking to understand the process for adoption, associated costs, and practices for placing children, the records for public adoption agencies are open to the public and can be requested by adopting parents through a Freedom of Information Act request.

Private adoption agencies are privately-operated businesses that are licensed to conduct adoptions by the state where they operate. Some private adoption agencies are nonprofit, some are for-profit, some are religious, and others are not. Like other businesses, private adoption agencies charge fees for their services and must make enough profit to maintain their business. While some private adoption agencies operate as for-profit businesses, in some cases the state requires that all adoption agencies be nonprofit, since there is some fear of adoption agencies turning over a profit and appearing to be "selling" children. Nonprofit adoption agencies often receive financial assistance from religious institutions or larger charities like the United Way. The financial records of private adoption agencies are typically not open to public scrutiny, so the adopting parents might not be able to learn as much about the organization and the process as they would like. Of course, private adoption agencies can choose to be as transparent as they would like.

The similarity among all adoption agencies is that, regardless of sector, they must be licensed by the state. Beyond that, private and public adoption agencies can vary dramatically in when and how they manage adoptions. Fees for adoptions will range based on the type of agency, the type of service offered, and the tax and fee structure of the state. Whether the adoption is open or closed will also vary by agency type, as will the criteria for being an adoptive parent (e.g. some agencies require adoptive parents to be married, others will not conduct adoptions for same sex couples or couples who are over the age of 40).

Some people worry about relying on private organizations to place children in adoptive homes. In 2010, an Atlanta Journal Constitution (AJC) investigation in Georgia reported that there can be lucrative rewards in the adoption business. Georgia law requires that all private adoption agencies operate as nonprofit organizations, but the law does

continued

not preclude large executive salaries and high overhead expenses that do not directly benefit the children the agencies seek to serve. In their review of federal tax returns, the AJC reported that many executives in these nonprofits were making 1/4 to 1/3 of the agency's budget and that administrative costs exceeded expenses on direct services for children.

According to Pablo Eisenberg, a researcher at the Center for Public and Nonprofit Leadership at Georgetown University, "a lack of industry standards and government rules enable people running such agencies to spend freely for their own benefit."[24] Others note a lack of transparency in the industry. For example, Faithbridge Foster Care Inc. generally avoids public scrutiny, so much so that Faithbridge tax documents state that it "does not make its governing documents, conflict of interest policy and financial statements available to the public."[25]

The AJC investigation concluded that the state offers weak oversight of the 336 private agencies that arrange adoptions and foster care in Georgia.[26] The AJC reported that more than 1,500 inspections and investigations uncovered that regulators regularly overlooked violations of adoption rules including the failure to check parents' criminal records and not document safe environments in adoptive homes. In some cases, private agencies failed to show payments to birth mothers that were intended to cover medical or living expenses and in one case an agency director received a direct deposit into a personal bank account from an adoptive parent. The AJC noted that the lack of oversight is demonstrated by the fact that in the previous two years the state had only imposed three penalties, two fines and one license revocation.[27]

The variation in adoption processing, costs, and rules from public agencies to private agencies and between private for-profit and private not-for-profit agencies raise important questions about sector differences and our expectations of these organizations when managing a complex issue such as adoption and the placement of children in to safe homes. In this example we see the ways in which public agencies can differ from private, but also the ways in which nonprofit organizations might not be operating with the best interests of clients in mind—and in fact might be making a great profit for CEOs and other staff members. Drawing on what you know about the different sectors with regard to accountability, regulatory power, bureaucracy, transparency, mission, values, and profit, consider the following questions:

DISCUSSION QUESTIONS

1. If you were interested in adopting a child, would you want to work with a public agency or a private adoption agency? Why?

continued

2. If you were to choose a private agency, would you prefer a for-profit or nonprofit agency? Why?

3. Would you make your decision based on the cost of the adoption, the type of adoption, the speed with which the adoption could be completed, or the sector of the adoption agency?

4. What kind of research would you want to do before choosing an adoption agency?

KEY TERMS

- Charitable sector
- Civil society
- Collective benefit
- Gross Domestic Product (GDP)
- Government failure
- Independent sector
- Market failure
- National Taxonomy of Exempt Entities (NTEE)
- Philanthropic sector
- Quid pro quo logic
- Selective benefit
- Social sector
- Tax-exempt status
- Third sector
- Voluntary governance
- Voluntary sector

DISCUSSION QUESTIONS

1. Why have experts found it difficult to arrive at a single, universally accepted term to describe the sector? How would you describe the US nonprofit sector in one or two sentences?

2. What is the relationship between the nonprofit sector and civil society?

3. What are some of the defining characteristics of the nonprofit sector? What makes it distinct from the public and for-profit sectors?

4. What are some of the features that nonprofits share in common with for-profit and public (government) organizations?

ACTIVITY

Consider the following 10 organizations and develop a table or chart to determine if they are best categorized as being in the nonprofit, public, or for-profit sector. Be sure to note issues that might indicate that the organization sits across two sectors or along the boundaries of the sectors.

1. US Department of Transportation
2. American Diabetes Association
3. City of Los Angeles
4. Boy Scouts of America
5. Carnegie Foundation
6. PricewaterhouseCoopers LLP
7. National Organization of Women
8. Sierra Club
9. Heritage Foundation
10. National Public Radio
11. Google Inc.

When comparing these organizations be sure to consider the following important characteristics:

a. Is the organization accountable to the general public or private membership?
b. Is it tax exempt?
c. Are the financial records publicly available?
d. How is the leader chosen?
e. Is there a board of directors?
f. What is the mission? Is it associated with a public purpose?
g. Does the organization make a profit?
h. Who determines how the organization spends its earnings?
i. Who are the clients or patrons of the organization? Who does the organization serve?

Websites

National Center for Charitable Statistics: http://nccs.urban.org/classification/NTEE.cfm

Additional Reading

Frumkin, Peter. 2005. *On Being Nonprofit: A Conceptual and Policy Primer*. Harvard University Press.

Salamon, Lester. 2002. *The State of Nonprofit America*. Brookings Institution Press and the Aspen Institute.

Notes

1   Chu, Ben. 2013. Bill Gates: Why do we care more about baldness than malaria? Saturday, 16 March 2013. Accessed April 2, 2013 at http://www.independent.co. uk/news/world/americas/bill-gates-why-do-we-care-more-about-baldness-than-malaria-8536988.html

2   Chu (2013).

3   Gates Foundation website. Accessed May 23, 2013 at http://www.gatesfoundation. org/Who-We-Are/General-Information/History

4   Roeger, Katie L., Blackwood, Amy S., and Pettijohn, Sarah L. 2012. *The Nonprofit Almanac 2012*. Washington, DC: Urban Institute Press. Accessed August 23, 2013 at http://nccsdataweb.urban.org/NCCS/extracts/nonprofitalmanacflyerpdf.pdf. Data reported in the Almanac are from 2010.

5   Roeger et al. (2012).

6   According to Roeger et al. (2012), "The Bureau of Economic Analysis at the Department of Commerce measures the size of the US economy. It divides the economy into four sectors: government, business, households, and nonprofit institutions serving households (NPISH). The BEA definition of nonprofits organizations varies from the IRS definition. The BEA's NPISH definition does not include all tax-exempt organizations. It excludes organizations that serve businesses, such as chambers of commerce, and nonprofits such as credit unions and university presses that are also counted as serving business because they sell goods and services in the same ways as for-profit businesses. Nonprofits that fall under the NPISH definition include those that provide services in one of the following five categories: religious and welfare (social services, grant-making foundations, political organizations, museums, and libraries), medical care, education and research, recreation (cultural, sports, and civic and fraternal organizations), and personal business (labor unions, legal aid, and professional associations). In 2010, NPISHs contributed $804.8 billion to the gross domestic product (GDP)" (p. 9).

7   Salamon, L. M. 1995. *Partners in Public Service: Government-Nonprofit Relations in the Modern Welfare State*. Baltimore: Johns Hopkins University Press.

8   Accessed May 18, 2013 at http://www.google.org/about.html

9   Lohmann, Roger. 1989. And Lettuce is Non-animal: Toward a Positive Economics of Voluntary Action. *Nonprofit and Voluntary Sector Quarterly*, 18(4): 367–383.

10 Civicus: The World Alliance for Citizen Participation. Accessed November 8, 2012 at http://www.civicus.org/about-us-125

11 http://www.civilsoc.org/ Accessed November 8, 2012.

12   Anheier, Helmut K. 2005. *Organizations: Theory, Management, Policy*. New York, NY: Routledge Press.

13   Roeger et al. (2012).

14   Ott, J. Steven. 2001. *The Nature of the Nonprofit Sector*. Boulder, Colorado: Westview Press.

15   Kenyon, Daphne A. and Adam Langley. 2010. Payments in Lieu of Taxes: Balancing Municipal and Nonprofit Interests. *Policy Focus Report of the Lincoln Institute of Land Policy*, Cambridge, MA.

16   Brody, Evelyn. 2007. The States' Growing Use of a Quid-Pro-Quo Rationale For The Charity Property Tax Exemption. *The Exempt Organization Review*, 56(3): 269–288.

17   Hammer, Michael and Steven A. Stanton. 1995. *The Reengineering Revolution*. New York, NY: Harper Collins.

18   Fischer, Robert L., Amanda Wilsker, and Dennis R. Young. 2011. Exploring the Revenue Mix of Nonprofit Organizations: Does It Relate to Publicness? *Nonprofit and Voluntary Sector Quarterly*, 40: 662–681.

19   Roeger, K. L. Blackwood, A., and Pettijohn, S.L. 2012. The Nonprofit Sector in Brief: Public Charities, Giving and Volunteering, 2012.

20   Guidestar Financial Records. 2010. Revenue streams for individual organizations from Guidestart Financial Figures for Fiscal Year 2010 on the IRS 990. Accessed Dec 15, 2012 at http://www.guidestar.org/Home.aspx.

21   Weisbrod, Burton. 1998. *To Profit or Not to Profit: The Commercial Transformation of the Nonprofit Sector*. Cambridge University Press.

22   Child Welfare Information Gateway. 2011. How many children were adopted in 2007 and 2008? Washington, DC: U.S. Department of Health and Human Services, Children's Bureau. Accessed November 26, 2013 at https://www.childwelfare. gov/pubs/adopted0708.pdf#Page=26&view=Fit

23   Adopted Children and Stepchildren. 2000. Issued October 2003. U.S. Department of Commerce Economics and Statistics Administration, U.S. Census Bureau. Accessed November 26, 2013 at https://www.census.gov/prod/2003pubs/censr-6.pdf

24   Judd, Alan. 2010b. Nonprofit adoption agencies often profit someone other than children, families: AJC investigation: Big portions of agency budgets go to top executives. The Atlanta Journal-Constitution. Updated: 11:07 a.m. Monday, April 26, 2010 | Posted: 4:53 a.m. Monday, April 26, 2010. Accessed November 26 2013 at http://www.ajc.com/news/news/local/nonprofit-adoption-agencies-often-profit-someone-o/nQfWR/

25   Judd (2010b).

26   Judd, Alan. 2010a. Adoption agencies break rules, escape punishment: AJC investigation: Weak oversight on private adoption agencies. The Atlanta Journal-Constitution. Updated: 7:27 p.m. Sunday, April 25, 2010 | Posted: 8:26 a.m. Sunday, April 25, 2010. Accessed November 26 2013 at http://www.ajc.com/news/news/local/adoption-agencies-break-rules-escape-punishment/nQfTt/

27   Judd (2010a).

2

HISTORICAL AND LEGAL FOUNDATIONS OF THE NONPROFIT SECTOR

CHAPTER LEARNING OBJECTIVES

By the end of this chapter, students will be able to:

1. Recognize the cross-cultural values and human impulses that have shaped the development of the nonprofit and civil society sector across the globe

2. Identify distinct values that have shaped the development of the US nonprofit sector and civil society

3. Explain the roots of nonprofit organizations in American social, political, and economic spheres of society

4. Identify key features of the legal framework that governs nonprofit organizations

5. Describe the basic rationale for allowing nonprofits to be exempt from taxes

6. Discuss some of the controversies related to the tax privileges enjoyed by nonprofits

---

Introduction

Long before there was a formally established nonprofit sector in the United States, individuals formed associations to pursue common interests, organized efforts to support or oppose laws and government actions, and

WHO WILL SPEAK FOR THE POWERLESS?

You are a senior in high school, preparing for graduation with two of your friends, Julia and Thomas. The three of you have known each other since grade school. You went to the same church and attended the same schools. You are the valedictorian at your high school graduation and Julia is the salutatorian. Thomas is a state all-star in baseball. Now, here you are, preparing for graduation and the world ahead of you. Thomas has enrolled at a nearby community college where he has a full-ride scholarship to play baseball. You and Julia have both been accepted to Texas A&M where you plan to major pre-med and Julia will pursue a pre-law track. But the night before graduation, Julia informs you that she will not be attending college. She cannot afford the tuition and does not qualify for federal or state financial aid—she is not a legal resident of the United States.

You begin brainstorming solutions to Julia's problem. Maybe she can return to Colombia and apply to law school there? A great idea, but all of Julia's family is living in the United States. And, moreover, she does not speak Spanish very well. Life in Colombia would be pretty difficult for Julia. Thomas suggests that he marry Julia, so that she can become a US citizen. The problem is, a spousal sponsor for citizenship would require Julia to return to Colombia and there is no telling how long it might take to process the application—maybe two years? Maybe more? And, anyway, Thomas and Julia are not in love and have no real interest in being married. Moreover, what would Thomas' girlfriend think of this plan?

Julia has lived in the US for over 18 years. She worked in high school as a lifeguard and worked during the school year at the local library shelving books. Each year she paid social security, Medicare, and other taxes. Her family and friends raised money for her to go to college and she qualified for a private academic scholarship. She is one of the smartest students you know and has been a good friend to you and many others in your class. She has the potential to be a top-notch lawyer and would most likely contribute greatly to our society. But, there is this issue of her legal status— how can you convince the US government and future employers that she deserves to be here?

Julia's problem is not hers alone. Thousands of young people in the United States face similar challenges. How will they fund a college education? Once they complete a college education, how will they get good jobs, or jobs for which they are qualified? Even if Julia can fund her time at law school, what law firm will hire her after graduation? While the federal government has a system for processing immigrants, it does not have the capacity (or political will) to solve this problem for young people

continued

raised in the US. Will the private sector provide solutions? Companies might like to hire qualified workers, like Julia, but they take a substantial risk hiring undocumented people. Julia would like to contact her congressional representative, but fears that if people know she is undocumented she might get deported. Who will fight for the rights of young people like Julia? Who can speak for those who live in fear of speaking up for themselves?

Nonprofit and civil society organizations are ideally suited to work on behalf of those who lack full political rights in the US. These organizations can lobby government and political actors to develop policies and pass legislation to protect people like Julia and offer financial support to undocumented students, ensuring that a good education does not go to waste. Civil society organizations can help to bridge the gap between the government and private organizations that would like to hire people like Julia. Civil society organizations and associations are often formed to connect resources from people like Thomas, who care about this issue, with those who have the ability to provide solutions.

When the political system and government regulations create barriers for individuals who lack political power, the vote, or rights in the system, nonprofit and civil society organizations can be an important vehicle for mobilizing resources and voicing the concerns of the voiceless. In this case, those who are empowered with citizenship, or a vote, can work on behalf of the disempowered. Nonprofit and civil society organizations can fill the gap between what people need (or deserve) and what our society is currently providing. And as we shall see in this chapter, these organizations have played an instrumental role throughout US history in helping immigrants become more politically empowered and economically better off, and they continue to play an important role today in helping people like Julia.

took it upon themselves and their communities to provide care for the poor and disabled. Even prior to the appearance of the first statutory reference to nonprofit organizations in 1894,[1] the spirit of the nonprofit sector was alive and well in America. In fact, the values, impulses, and activities associated with nonprofit organizations and civil society predate the founding of the American republic and have roots that can be traced far earlier, not only in the US but in many other cultures.[2]

This chapter examines the origins of the contemporary nonprofit sector in the US, as well as the distinct values and legal infrastructure that have helped to grow and sustain it. First, we consider some of the fundamental values underlying nonprofit and civil society activities across countries and cultures, as well as the values that are more distinctly American. Next, we examine the roots of nonprofit organizations in social, political, and economic life in the United States by focusing on some key points in history in which civil society groups and associations helped to shape our society. Lastly, we look at some of the details of the US tax code that enable nonprofit sector organizations to operate, including provisions that encourage private citizens to give resources (time and money) to support these organizations. This chapter just scratches the surface when it comes to historical perspectives on the nonprofit sector and civil society. For true philosophers and history buffs, a list of additional readings is provided at the end of the chapter.

Values of the Nonprofit Sector and Civil Society

As we learned in Chapter 1, charity and philanthropy are two key terms associated with the nonprofit sector, and indeed represent important values that have helped shape civil society and the nonprofit sector throughout history. Charity is defined as "generosity and helpfulness especially toward the needy or suffering, or aid given to those in need,"[3] while philanthropy is similarly defined as "goodwill toward fellow members of the human race; especially active effort to promote human welfare" or "an act or gift done or made for humanitarian purposes."[4] Impulses for charity and philanthropy are deeply grounded in the beliefs and teachings in major world religions, which impart a sense of obligation among followers to care for the poor and needy. Given the origins of charity and philanthropy in religious teachings, these values are not unique to the US nonprofit sector, but rather they are fundamental principles underlying the nonprofit sector in other countries and cultures. Despite vast differences in beliefs, traditions, and rituals of religions across the globe, charity and philanthropy represent a common thread among all of them. The Second Harvest Food Bank of Orange County offers some statements from religious texts that help to illustrate this point:[5]

Christianity (the Bible):
"For the poor shall never cease out of the land: therefore I command thee, saying, Thou shalt open thine hand wide unto thy brother, to thy poor, and to thy needy, in thy land."—Deut. 15:11.

"Defend the poor and fatherless: Do justice to the afflicted and needy."—Ps. 82:3.

"But when thou makest a feast, call the poor, the maimed, the lame, the blind: And thou shall be blessed; for they cannot recompense thee: For thou shalt be recompensed at the resurrection of the just."—Luke 14:13–14.

Judaisim (the Tanakh, cannon of the Hebrew Bible):
"Learn to do good. Devote yourselves to justice; aid the wronged. Uphold the rights of the orphan; defend the cause of the widow." —Isaiah 1:17.

"He upheld the rights of the poor and needy—then all was well." —Jeremiah 22:16.

"When you reap the harvest of your land, you shall not reap all the way to the edges of your field, or gather the gleanings of your harvest. You shall not pick your vineyard bare, or gather the fallen fruit of your vineyard; you shall leave them for the poor and the stranger."—Leviticus 19:9–10.

Islam (the Quran): 6
"Give generously for the cause of God and do not with your own hands cast yourselves into destruction. Be charitable; God loves the charitable."—The Cow 2:195

"God loves those who do good."—The Table 5:13

"To be charitable in public is good, but to give alms to the poor in private is better and will atone for some of your sins. God has knowledge of all of your actions."—The Cow 2:271

Religious teachings calling for charity and philanthropy serve as the foundation of a great deal of activity that occurs within the US nonprofit sector. Well-known organizations such as the Salvation Army, Habitat for Humanity, and Catholic Charities are just a few examples of the many nonprofit organizations in the US that were founded on religious principles and have maintained their faith basis. On the other hand, there are also many secular nonprofits, and some organizations that originated with a faith base have evolved into more secular organizations such as the Young

The Older YMCA Logo and the Newer Y Logo

Men's Christian Association (YMCA). This organization re-branded itself in 2010 with a new name, "The Y", to reflect the organization's mission shift away from spiritual development toward a mission of inclusiveness, promoting healthy lifestyles and building strong communities.

While charity and philanthropy are fundamental tenets of the nonprofit sector throughout the world, other values associated with the US nonprofit sector are particular to America. For example, *liberty* and *diversity* are two key values not only expressed but formalized in the US Constitution. In fact, many of the values detailed in the US Constitution, from freedom of religion and speech to pluralism, play a pivotal role in defining the boundaries and the reach of the US nonprofit sector. Unlike many other countries in Europe, Latin America, and the Middle East, the United States does not have a national religion. The US Constitution mandates the separation of church and state, and the First Amendment guarantees American citizens the freedom to practice any religion they choose, including the freedom to not practice a religion at all. This legal freedom has paved the way for tremendous diversity of religious expression in the US and served as the basis for the development of thousands of nonprofit churches, religious congregations, houses of worship, and informal religious and spiritual groups in the US.

The First Amendment guarantees freedom of speech, which includes the press and the right of citizens to assemble. Since the US won its independence from Great Britain through the Revolutionary War in 1783, Americans have maintained a preference for limited government and a system of checks and balances, including citizen voice, to prevent government tyranny. Americans enjoy the freedom to express their discontent and disagreement with political leaders through organized protests, petitions, lobbying campaigns. In countries governed by authoritarian regimes and those that do not put a high value on personal liberties, citizens may be persecuted for these acts. The liberties guaranteed in the US Constitution set the basis for the establishment of nonprofit organizations and a civil society that aims to protect these rights, including organizations designed to coordinate protests, develop lobbying campaigns, and dedicated to personal liberties (e.g. American Civil Liberties Union) and protecting other constitutional rights: for example, the National Rifle Association (NRA), which lobbies to protect citizens' rights to keep and bear arms as outlined in the Second Amendment.

Other constitutional provisions extend voting rights and civil rights and guarantee citizens' freedom from discrimination on the basis of age, sex, race, or religion. The freedoms of expression outlined in the First Amendment combined with the racial, ethnic, and religious diversity of the US population have resulted in the creation of numerous, diverse, and often competing groups in our society. The characteristic of our society that allows for individuals to freely associate and for multiple groups to co-exist without any single one of them being the center of power is called **pluralism**. Pluralism is defined as "a state of society in which members of diverse ethnic, racial, religious, or social groups maintain and develop their traditional culture or special interest within the confines of a common civilization."[7] Pluralism is a key component of US society that helps to explain the establishment and success of nonprofit organizations and civil society. For example, the relatively peaceful co-existence of numerous religions in the US such as Catholicism, Protestantism, Judaism, Islam, along with Eastern religions such as Buddhism, are reflective of a pluralist society.

At the same time that diversity and pluralism have helped to shape the US nonprofit and civil society sector, the American value of individualism[8] has also played a key role in our civil society. **Individualism** stems from a belief that citizens should not rely on the state to provide for their basic needs, but rather should "pull themselves up by their bootstraps" and take personal responsibility for achieving and maintaining economic self-sufficiency for themselves and their immediate families. Americans tend to hold motivation, hard work, and entrepreneurship in high esteem, and have a general preference for a limited **welfare state**—a government where the state plays a key role in protecting and promoting economic and social well-being of citizens through equality of opportunity, distribution of wealth, and public programs that provide for a good life. Individualism has thus been a key value in shaping the social service system in America.

Values of individualism, self-government, and liberty are deeply embedded in American political culture,[9] and have fostered a general preference among Americans for limited government. Given this preference, over time the privatization of public goods and services has become more common. By contracting out for things like healthcare and human services, governments are able to continue investing in services the public needs while limiting the growth of the government workforce. This is a subject we shall examine further in Chapter 3.

The Roots of Nonprofits in American Social Life

Long before a nonprofit sector was formally recognized in the US, citizens formed neighborhood groups, associations, and congregations through which to socialize, worship, share common interests, and they engaged in voluntary efforts to meet social needs of the less fortunate in their communities. These kinds of groups, even prior to their formalization into nonprofit organizations, have played a critical role in building the social fabric of America. Neighborhood groups, associations, congregations, and service organizations contribute to social life in America by creating spaces and places for inter-personal interaction. This interaction promotes social capital, or connections among individuals.[10] Social capital can be viewed as the glue that holds communities together; it is developed through social networks and the personal bonds that arise from networking. Although the Internet has radically altered the way we define communities and networking over the past decade, what remains constant is the fact that association and interaction builds social capital and strengthens human bonds, and several types of nonprofit organizations, like their early predecessors, create the space both physically and virtually for this interaction to occur.

Americans have been creating voluntary associations since before the republic was formed. By the 19th century, so prolific in number were associations that while traveling in the US in 1981 the French philosopher Alexis de Tocqueville observed the tendency of Americans to form associations for a seemingly endless number of causes. Moreover, de Tocqueville characterized this tendency as unique to America, arguing that other nations would rely on the government to fulfill many of the purposes for which Americans form associations. As de Tocqueville stated in his famous text *Democracy in America*,

> Americans of all ages, all stations of life, and all types of disposition are forever forming associations. Americans combine to give fêtes, found seminaries, build churches, distribute books, and send missionaries to the antipodes. Hospitals, prisons, and schools take shape in that way. Finally, if they want to proclaim a truth or propagate some feeling by the encouragement of a great example, they form an association. In every case, at the head of any new undertaking, where in France you would find the government or in England some territorial magnate, in the United States you are sure to find an association. I have come across several types of association in America of which, I confess, I had not previously the slightest conception, and I have often admired the extreme skill they show in proposing a common object for the exertions of very many and in inducing them voluntarily to pursue it.[11]

As de Toqueville suggests, some of the early associations formed in America carried out critical functions such as healthcare or education, while others served as outlets for socialization and making civic contributions to the local community. Before the Internet made it possible to keep up with the daily events of friends, family, neighbors, and co-workers through Facebook and Twitter, or to find casual get-togethers with people who share your interests through meetup.com, Americans joined local clubs and community groups to socialize and contribute to civil society. Just a few prominent examples of the thousands of these groups include Parent Teacher Associations (PTA), the League of Women Voters, the Knights of Columbus, Rotary, Veterans of Foreign Wars (VFW), and youth organizations such as Boy Scouts of America, Campfire Girls, and Boys' and Girls' Clubs.

Parent Teacher Associations (PTAs) and Organizations (PTOs) are some of the most visible and active remnants of the association era. Founded in 1897 as the *National Congress of Mothers* by Alice McLellan Birney and Phoebe Apperson Hearst, the PTA's purpose is to work toward the health, safety, and educational success of all children and the promotion of family engagement in schools. The founders started the organization when women did not have the right to vote and social activism was not popular. However, they believed mothers would support their mission and they were right. Early in 1897, they started a nationwide campaign and on February 17, 1897, more than 2,000 people—mostly mothers, but also fathers, teachers, laborers, and legislators—attended the first convocation of the National Congress of Mothers in Washington, DC. Twenty years later, 37 chartered state congresses existed.[12] Today, there are more than 20,000 local PTA groups in the US and the PTA functions as the largest child advocacy organization in the nation.[13] Local PTA groups thus not only benefit the children they represent, but also serve as a convening space for parents, particularly mothers of young children, to associate and build bonds with other parents in their neighborhood or community, while performing a volunteer service.

Other types of organizations engage in little advocacy, existing mainly to provide community service, some of them secular in nature, others faith-based. For example, Rotary Club is an international service organization founded by Paul Harris in 1905 in Chicago. Rotary's stated purpose is "to bring together business and professional leaders in order to provide humanitarian services, encourage high ethical standards in all vocations, and help build goodwill and peace in the world" and Rotary's primary motto is "service above self." Local chapters of Rotary engage in a variety of service projects at the community level and abroad. There are currently 34,282 Rotary clubs and over 1.2 million members worldwide.[14] By contrast to this secular organization, the Knights of Columbus was formed as a faith-based club whose religious principles still serve as primary points of guidance for the organization today. The Knights was founded by Father Michael J. McGivney in 1882 in honor of Christopher Columbus. Originally serving as a mutual benefit society to low-income, immigrant Catholics, it developed into a fraternal service organization dedicated to providing charitable services and promoting Catholic education. Charity is the foremost principle of the Knights, as evidenced by the more than $158 million given directly to charity by the organization in 2011 and the performance of over 70 million hours of volunteer service. The Knights have more than 1.8 million members in 15,000 councils, most of whom are US citizens, but councils also exist in roughly seven other nations.[15]

While all of these organizations still exist in local communities today, many have lost membership over time[16] and have had to work to reinvent themselves for the new fast-paced, digital culture in which we now live. All of these organizations are part of a **federation**, meaning that a national or "parent" organization is created to dictate the mission, values, and rules of the organization, giving the organization its "brand," while local chapters of these organizations formed throughout the country, led by volunteers who then recruit local community members to also volunteer to get involved in the work of the chapter.

In addition to these types of clubs and groups, churches and congregations have played an important role in building the social fabric of America. The US has a long and rich history of participation in organized religion dating back to the emigration of large numbers of Puritans from Great Britain to New England from 1620–1640,[17] and the Quaker settlements that emerged in the Northeast territory in the 1680s. Religious diversity has proliferated throughout the centuries, and today more Americans belong to religious congregations than to any other kind of voluntary association.[18] The more than 300,000 congregations in America today, including synagogues, mosques, and temples, make a robust contribution to American social life. And they are automatically considered nonprofit organizations without having to obtain tax-exempt status from the federal government. Despite the fact that participation in organized religion has declined in recent years, places of worship remain vital community institutions, offering citizens of shared belief systems opportunities to con-gregate, interact, volunteer, share their problems, and perform good works for one another.

Human service organizations also play a critical role in American social life. Human service organizations embody the values of charity and philanthropy, and create opportunities for citizens to give of their time and financial resources to help improve the plight of the less fortunate. Prior to the 1930s, social welfare needs were largely met through purely voluntary efforts by local community members. Before there was a formal-ized system of government aid in place to help the poor, a strong sense of responsibility to one's neighbor guided an informal and largely voluntary system of care for the sick, disabled, elderly, widowed, and orphaned.

Early philanthropists such as Andrew Carnegie, whose 1889 dictate "The Gospel of Wealth"[19] called on the rich to use their wealth to improve society, encouraged other men of wealth such as John D. Rockefeller and John D. MacArthur to embrace philanthropy. These early pioneers, and others such as Edsel Ford and Ewing Marion Kaufman, helped to shape the concept of modern philanthropy and giving. The work of the early philanthropists of the 19th and 20th century served as the template for modern foundations which today invest heavily in **social programs** both throughout the US and abroad.

Perhaps the most well-known pioneer of social welfare was Jane Addams; the best model of early social service programming was the settlement house. Jane Addams led the American settlement house movement, founding Hull House, the first settlement house in the nation in 1889 in Chicago's west-side neighborhood largely inhabited by low-income, Italian immigrants. The settlement house movement was a reform-oriented social movement and had, at its center, the goal of integrated living among the social classes. Its main objective was the establishment of "settlement houses" in poor urban areas, in which educated, volunteer middle-class "settlement workers" would live together with poor residents, sharing knowledge and culture with their low-income neighbors. Hull House, and the hundreds of settlement houses modeled after it, provided services such as job linkages, daycare, education, and healthcare to low-income citizens living in the houses and in surrounding neighborhoods.

By 1913, there were 413 settlement houses in 32 states. Thus, settlement houses might be regarded as the earliest version of a formal system of

Jane Addams' Hull House Museum, at University of Illinois, Chicago

social service provision in the US. Long after the settlement house movement lost traction, Jane Addams remained an inspiration to charitable-minded community leaders working toward social justice. She inspired many to continue her work and form new social service organizations. She is widely regarded as the founder of the Social Work profession. Many modern-day human service organizations operating in the US carry out their work according to the principles of equity and social justice endorsed by Addams.

The Roots of Nonprofits in American Politics

In the same way that Americans formed associations to support their needs for socialization and basic welfare provision, they have created organizations to engage in the political system, lobbying for the passage of new laws, protesting current legislation, and advocating for political change. Many of the early associations that sought to have an impact on federal policy were organized on a federated structure and relied on approaches that are strikingly similar to today's lobbying and political change organizations. The American Anti-Slavery Society (AASS), for example, was founded in 1833 by William Lloyd Garrison and Arthur Tappan with the mission to abolish slavery in the United States. The national organization worked to build a broad base of support by developing state and local chapters. By 1838, the society had 1,350 local chapters and approximately 250,000 members. The AASS engaged in public education and worked to keep members informed of legislative actions pertaining to abolition through a weekly newspaper.[20]

The National Society Daughters of the Revolution (DAR) was founded in 1890 to promote patriotism, preserve American history, and secure better education for children. Although the organization describes itself as a non-political volunteer women's service organization, it takes on a mission of advancing patriotism and honoring the memory of ancestors who fought to make the US free and independent. The organization promotes three objectives:

> Historical—to perpetuate the memory and spirit of the men and women who achieved American Independence; Educational—to carry out the injunction of Washington in his farewell address to the American people, "to promote, as an object of primary importance, institutions for the general diffusion of knowledge, thus developing an enlightened public opinion{.}"; and Patriotic—to cherish, maintain, and extend the institutions of American freedom, to foster true patriotism and love of country, and to aid in securing for mankind all the blessings of liberty.[21]

Thus, US civil society includes organizations that seek to promote and protect US political values, some of which remain non-political organizations, like DAR.

Other historical examples of civil society action include those that have sought to bring about policy change. For example, the American temperance movement was concerned with limiting and banning alcohol and gave rise to more than twenty voluntary groups that worked toward this goal during the late 18th and early 19th centuries. Organizations such as the Anti-Saloon League, Daughters of Temperance, and the Catholic Total Abstinence Union of America are just a few of the voluntary groups that worked to affect public policies related to the sale and consumption of alcohol.[22] The largest and most influential among these groups was the

American Temperance Society, which was formed in Boston in 1826 by a Presbyterian minister named Lyman Beecher.[23] At the turn of the 19th century, Beecher and other reform-minded activists who condemned drinking as immoral attributed many social problems to the consumption of alcohol. The American Temperance Society initially worked to promote voluntary abstinence, recruiting members to sign a pledge to abstain from drinking alcohol. Within three years of its founding, the Society had spread across the country in the form of local chapters, and within ten years it had 8,000 local groups and had registered over 1.5 million members through its pledge program. After it had achieved a large following, the Society shifted its efforts toward mandatory prohibition and began advocating for laws banning alcohol throughout the states.[24]

Civil society has also played a key role in political reforms such as passing equal rights legislation. For example, voluntary groups were critical in the battle for women's voting rights—partly because they offered a mechanism for women to become engaged in a political system of which they were being excluded. Women's **suffrage**, or right to vote, in the US was achieved largely through the efforts of two organizations, the National Woman Suffrage Association, founded in New York City in 1869 by Susan B. Anthony and Elizabeth Cady Stanton, and the American Women's Suffrage Association founded the same year by Lucy Stone. The two organizations joined forces and merged in 1890 to become the National American Women's Suffrage Association (NAWSA).[25] The efforts of these organizations throughout the late 19th and early 20th century culminated in the passage of the Nineteenth Amendment to the US Constitution in 1920, which states: "The right of citizens of the United States to vote shall not be denied or abridged by the United States or by any State on account of sex." These organizations were critical in bringing together women, funds, and men who supported women's suffrage to fundamentally change the male-dominated political structure. The ability to organize and mobilize through civil society offers an alternative political avenue for many disenfranchised groups in the United States. We can easily draw parallels to the civil rights movements of the 1960s and onward, to the immigration rights movements today. When the politically disenfranchised seek a voice in the political system, civil society and nonprofit organizations provide the ideal vehicles for that voice.

Good Government

Many other voluntary groups formed during the **Progressive Era** (1980s–1920s) in order to pursue reforms related to political corruption, child welfare, and industrial safety and economic security for laborers. The Progressive Era saw the rise of many "good government" and "political watchdog" groups that are still in existence today and widely known for their nonpartisan approaches. For example, the International City/County Management Association (ICMA) was founded in 1914 for the purpose of disseminating principles and practices of professional local government management throughout the US and helped to bring about a paradigm shift among municipal and county governments that had previously functioned on a system of patronage, bribery, and corruption. Another good government group formed during this era was the League of Women Voters (LWV), founded in 1920 with a mission of providing education to help citizens become informed voters. Today, the LWV remains one of the most visible and reputable nonpartisan organizations, working to register voters and produce candidate voting records and nonpartisan voter information guides specific to the cities and states in which their chapters are located.

Labor Unions

Demands for increased production during the industrial revolution led to dangerous working conditions, long working hours, and general exploitation of workers, which brought about a distinct type of nonprofit organization during the Progressive Era that has left an enduring mark upon the political landscape: labor unions. The American Federation of Labor founded by Samuel Gompers in 1886, as well as the United Mine Workers founded in 1890, are just two prominent examples of the hundreds of nonprofit labor organizations that formed during this period with the purpose of uniting workers to collectively bargain over wages, benefits, and working conditions. Through their collective efforts, labor unions were effective in building a broad-based movement across the US that elevated public consciousness about the plight of workers and resulted in landmark legislative reforms including the National Labor Relations Act of 1935 which guaranteed the rights of private sector employees to collectively bargain, and the Fair Labor Standards Act of 1939 which brought a host of improvements including the establishment of a federal minimum wage, requirements for paying overtime, and established prohibitions on the employment of minors. While the power of labor unions, as well as public opinion of them, has waned somewhat in recent years, they remain a considerable force in American politics. Not only are labor unions at the forefront of policy debates pertaining to labor and employment at both the federal and state levels, but they are also instrumental in the mass mobilization of voters during national election years, typically encouraging their members to vote for Democratic candidates.[26]

Civil Rights

The battle for racial equality during the Civil Rights era saw the creation of numerous minority rights and identity-based organizations, some of which are still in operation today, although many have broadened their missions. While the strategies and tactics of these groups varied, they were all part of a larger national movement that shared a common goal of achieving full equality under the law for African Americans, and furthering the social, economic, and, especially, political empowerment of this group. Perhaps the most well-known nonprofit organization associated with this era—and the monumental policy changes that emerged from it—is the Southern Christian Leadership Conference. Co-founded by Dr. Martin Luther King in 1957, the SCLC emphasized nonviolent protest, and relied on civil disobedience and mobilizing mass participation in boycotts and marches as means of exerting influence in the marketplace, and raising public awareness over the economic and social injustices suffered by African Americans at the hands of both government and private businesses.[27] The tactics of the SCLC differed from those of another key group associated with the movement, the National Association for the Advancement of Colored People. Founded in 1961,[28] the NAACP took an approach that was distinctly more oriented toward challenging violations of the law and relied on lawsuits, legislative lobbying, and professional education campaigns in their attempts to influence federal policy.[29]

The efforts of the SCLC and NAACP, combined with that of dozens of other nonprofit groups such as the Congress of Racial Equality and Student Nonviolent Coordinating Council, ultimately led to the passage of the Civil Rights Act of 1964 which brought sweeping reforms in racial equality, including desegregation of public schools, ended inequalities in voter registration requirements, and outlawed discrimination based on *"race, color, religion or national origin"* in all public places. Several critical policy changes occurred subsequent to the enactment of the Civil Rights Act, including the passage of the Voting Rights Act of 1965, which outlawed discriminatory voting practices, and the creation of the Equal Employment Opportunity Commission in 1965, a federal administrative law enforcement agency whose purpose is to arbitrate in complaints of discrimination workplace practices.

The monumental public policy changes to emerge from the Civil Rights Movement (catalyzed in large part by nonprofit groups) were important in their own right but were significant also in that they paved the way for several subsequent rights movements including the Feminist Movement of the late 1960s and 70s, the Disability Rights Movement of the 1980s and 90s, and the Lesbian, Gay, Bisexual, Transgender, and Queer (LGBTQ) Rights Movement of the last decade and present day. Nonprofit organizations playing a critical role in the forefront of advocating for women's issues today are the same organizations founded in the 1960s and 70s. Key examples of these groups include the National Organization for Women (NOW), co-founded by Betty Friedan in 1966 to advocate for gender equality and the advancement of women,[30] and the National Abortion and Reproductive Rights Action League (now NARAL Pro-Choice America), established in 1969 to advocate for women's health and reproductive rights.[31] These organizations not only serve as the preeminent voices of today in women's policy issues, but were influential in the passage of historic legislation that benefitted women's interests, including the Equal Employment Opportunity Act of 1972 and the Equal Opportunity in Science and Engineering Act of 1980, which specifically targeted women as an underrepresented group in medicine, science, and engineering.

Legislative victories for persons with disabilities were another outcome of the efforts of nonprofit rights organizations in the late 20th century. Nonprofit disability rights groups such as the National Alliance for the Mentally Ill (founded 1979) and United Cerebral Palsy (founded 1949) were among the many groups influential in expanding civil rights to persons with disabilities through passage of key federal policies. These policies include the Americans with Disabilities Act of 1990 which prohibited discrimination on the basis of disability against qualified individuals in hiring and promotion decisions by employers, and mandated accessibility and accommodations for persons with disabilities in all public and commercial places,[32] as well as the Individuals with Disabilities Education Act of 2004, which extended the right to a "free and appropriate" education to children with disabilities.[33]

Nonprofit organizations are also playing a key role in another type of civil rights battle, one that has gained momentum during the 21st century: the quest for full equality under the law for LGBTQ persons. While national organizations such as Gay, Lesbian, Straight Education Network (GLSEN), Human Rights Campaign, Triangle Foundation, and the National Gay and Lesbian Task Force have been working to represent the needs and interests of members of the LGBTQ community for many decades, it is only recently that these organizations have witnessed major progress in legislative changes that benefit the LGBTQ community. These older gay rights groups, along with newer ones such as Freedom to Marry, have collectively played a key role in shaping public opinion and creating the climate that led the US Supreme Court in 2013 to strike down the main part of the federal Defense of Marriage Act (DOMA). The Defense of Marriage Act granted states the authority to refuse to recognize same-sex marriages granted under the laws of other states, which had the effect of barring same-sex married couples from being recognized as "spouses" for purposes of federal laws, or receiving federal marriage benefits.[34] Just days before, the Supreme Court overturned California's Proposition 8, which banned same-sex marriage in that state.

The Gay Rights Movement has benefited from changes in public opinion that seem to have shifted in support of gay marriage rights. In 2013, a series of Gallup polls showed that, for the first time in history, a majority of Americans supported same-sex marriage, a trend which is partially driven by generational change as younger voters overwhelmingly endorse gay rights including same-sex marriage.[35] Nonprofit gay rights groups have played a role in shaping opinion with regard to the inequities of excluding gays from the same legal benefits extended to other married couples. These groups have been influential in advocating for other major policy changes that benefit the gay community. In December 2010, President Barack Obama persuaded Congress to enact a legislative repeal of the military's "Don't Ask, Don't Tell" policy which prohibited gays and lesbians from serving openly in the armed forces. The repeal of the law legally prohibits discrimination and harassment on the basis of sexual orientation and affirms the contributions to military service made by gay men and women. Finally, gay rights organizations have been instrumental in helping to elect candidates that represent the needs and interests of the LGBTQ community. Nationwide, an increased number of openly gay politicians have been elected to public office including city councils, state legislative bodies,[36] and in November 2012, Tammy Baldwin (WI) made history by becoming the first openly gay person elected to the US Senate.

While the Gay Rights Movement has been bolstered by these shifts in public opinion, recent legislative victories, and greater political representation by gay and lesbian politicians, there remains a great deal of work for gay rights organizations to do before LGBTQ citizens have the same protections and benefits as the rest of the population. As of 2013, fifteen US states plus the District of Columbia have legalized gay marriage. Thus it will not happen overnight, but gay rights advocacy groups such as Freedom to Marry appear on track to eventually achieve their goal of seeing legalized gay marriage in all fifty states.

The Roots of Nonprofits in America's Economy

In addition to playing a foundational role in the sociological and political make-up of the modern United States, nonprofit organizations play important roles in the US economy. The contributions of nonprofit organizations to the American economy can be assessed in several ways including the nonprofit sector's share of US Gross Domestic Product (GDP), and the share of the US workforce employed by nonprofit organizations. While the number of formal nonprofit organizations is vast, the total count of organizations is not an accurate reflection of their contribution to the economy, since most nonprofits are small and operate on little or no money. As we learned in Chapter 1, nonprofits' share of contribution to US GDP has grown dramatically over the past few decades. The change in nonprofits' share of GDP over time is an indication that the nonprofit sector is a sizable and growing share of the US economy.[37] Moreover, we learned in the last chapter that nonprofit organizations played a relatively minor role in the American economy up until the 1960s. In fact, it is estimated that more than 70% of the nonprofits organizations that exist today were established since the mid-1960s.[38] The US nonprofit sector witnessed small growth in the 1930s and a substantial growth in their contribution to the US economy from the 1960s onward.

While the nonprofit sector provided some paid jobs prior to the 1930s, nonprofit organizations at the turn of the 20th century relied mostly on private contributions, and extensively on voluntary labor. The 1930s marked a time when the federal government expanded its reach into local service provision and the scope of its roles on a dramatic scale, which in turn led to growth in the number and size of nonprofit organizations also providing public services. President Franklin Delano Roosevelt's **New Deal** was a series of economic programs established between 1933 and 1936 to provide relief, recovery, and reform during the Great Depression. The New Deal was a broad domestic policy agenda that made extensive public investments in expanding infrastructure, workforce development, and social welfare programs including Social Security and Aid to Dependent Children. Complementing the growth of government social service provision, nonprofit human service organizations were in transition during this era, beginning to move from small, voluntary efforts to more formalized organizations that gradually employed more paid staff. As a result of government's new commitments to the people, some types of nonprofits were able to benefit from the increased government funding during this era, while others expanded through private funding as it became clear which needs of the public government could not meet.

The events of the 1960s also served to put the nonprofit sector on course to play the significant role that it does in the American economy today. President Lyndon B. Johnson declared a **"War on Poverty,"** infusing an unprecedented level of government funding into local communities throughout the US, especially in poor and blighted urban areas. The term War on Poverty refers to the policies that resulted from President Johnson's 1964 State of the Union address when he pushed congress to pass legislation that would lower the national poverty rate, which at the time was around 19%. Johnson argued that expanding government's role in education and healthcare could help to reduce poverty, leading him to push Congress to pass the Economic Opportunity Act and establish the Office of Economic Opportunity (OEO) to target federal funds at reducing poverty.

Stimulated by available government money, many new nonprofits formed during this time, including anti-poverty Community Action Agencies (CAAs) and Headstart programs that still operate today. The funding appropriated from the federal government for these services was largely used to contract with community-based nonprofits to deliver these services, allowing nonprofits to scale up their operations and swell their ranks of paid employees. A new federal cabinet, the US Department of Housing and Urban Development (HUD), was created in 1965 as part of the war on poverty strategy, and this organization today remains the primary source of funds for addressing homelessness and low-income housing needs, the vast majority of which are contracted out to community-based nonprofit organizations.

Part of President Lyndon B. Johnson's vision for a **Great Society**, a set of domestic programs aimed at reducing poverty and racial injustice, also included health insurance for the elderly, poor, and disabled, leading to the creation of Medicare and Medicaid in 1965. Unlike some War on Poverty programs that were short-lived (such as Model Cities), Medicare and Medicaid were created as **entitlement programs,** meaning that government established eligibility criteria for these programs and is then obligated from that point on to provide these services for all citizens who meet the criteria. These dedicated funding streams provided the catalyst for thousands of new nonprofit hospitals, healthcare clinics, family planning centers, community mental health centers, nursing homes, assisted living facilities, hospice programs, and home-based service providers that now employ more than half (57%) of today's nonprofit workforce.[39]

The War on Poverty led to the genesis of another type of nonprofit organization that plays a key role in the economic sphere of society— Community-Based Development Organizations (CBDOs), also known as Community Development Corporations (CDCs). Community-based development organizations primarily exist in lower-income communities, both urban and rural, and work to help residents of a specific community or neighborhood to achieve economic progress through a variety of services, including job training and workforce development, education, advocacy, community organizing, affordable housing and real estate development, and fostering small, locally-owned businesses and microenterprises. Many of the more than 3,800 CBDOs in existence today were conceived through federal funding in the 1960s or began as Community Action Agencies.[40] These organizations exist alongside nonprofit Chambers of Commerce, convention and visitors' bureaus, and other economic planning and business recruitment organizations, to create the nonprofit economic development subsector.

The 1960s was a watershed decade for the US nonprofit sector. The unprecedented government spending for social welfare and legal commitments made to the elderly, poor, and disabled for government-paid healthcare during this decade carved out an important role for nonprofit organizations in the economy. As we saw in the last chapter, nonprofit organizations, and especially those in the health sector, have steadily grown in number since the 1960s. Today healthcare, education, and social services collectively account for the majority of nonprofit jobs (84%).[41]

At the same time as nonprofit employment was growing, the 1980s brought increased regulation and oversight of the sector, along with a growing public skepticism about government spending for social services. President Reagan pursued a policy of retrenchment for social welfare spending during the 1980s that had a marked impact on the nonprofit sector. Operating from a conservative ideology and "small government" policy agenda, the Reagan administration cut federal support to nonprofit organizations (not including Medicare and Medicaid) by approximately 25% in real dollar terms in the early 1980s and this did not return to its 1980 level until the late 1990s.[42] The nonprofit sector continued to thrive under the improved economic times of the 1990s and President Clinton's welfare reform policy, the Personal Responsibility and Work Opportunity Reconciliation Act of 1996 (PRWORA), which re-directed federal income assistance for low-income, women and children into new streams of federal money for job training, workforce development, and child care, the majority of which was contracted out to nonprofit organizations.

Despite the Great Recession of 2009 and the diversion of federal resources toward Homeland Security and wars abroad during President George W. Bush's (2000–2008) and President Barack Obama's administrations (2008 onwards), the nonprofit sector has maintained its place in the US economy. As seen in Figure 2.1, which shows the percentage of GDP that is comprised by nonprofit labor (volunteer and paid), the number of nonprofit organizations grew steadily from 2000 through 2010. Even with the slight decline in the total number of organizations from 2010 to 2012,[43] overall since 2000 the number of nonprofits has increased by approximately 23%. In addition, nonprofit employment grew every year between 2000 and 2010, while the for-profit sector lost jobs in most of these years.[44] This continued growth of nonprofit employment during the

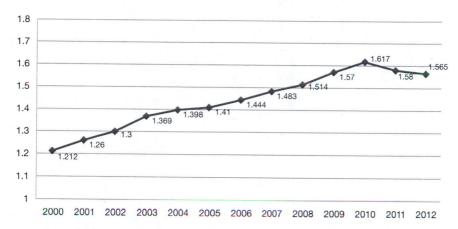

FIGURE 2.1 Number of Nonprofit Organizations, 2000–2012 (Millions).

Source: National Center for Charitable Statistics—by organization type including public charities, foundations, and all other nonprofit organizations.

harshest economic times the US has seen in almost a century suggests that, indeed, today's nonprofit sector is a vital force in the US economy. Moreover, the accomplishments of the community development sector (CBDOs and CDCs) in revitalizing high-poverty urban neighborhoods and rural communities[45] are another indicator of the important role nonprofit organizations play in the economic sphere of society.

The Legal Framework for Nonprofit Organizations

The provisions of the US Constitution provide not only an important historical backdrop to the activities of modern-day civil society, but remain the fundamental legal basis for the wide-ranging organizations and activities that make up civil society today, whether these activities involve practicing religion of one's own choosing, protesting the federal government's policy of phone surveillance, or joining associations that work to defend the second amendment (the right to bear arms). Beginning in the 20th century however, the US tax code emerged an equally important component to the legal framework for nonprofit organizations.

As we mentioned briefly in Chapter 1, the tax code—the rules of which are written and enforced by the federal Internal Revenue Service (IRS)[46]— provides the primary legal framework for nonprofit organizations in the US and serves as the basis by which we can draw boundaries around the sector. Organizations that are part of the formal nonprofit sector are those

TABLE 2.1 Internal Revenue Service Codes for Tax-Exempt Organizations

Section of Code	Description of Categories	Tax-deductible Contributions Allowable	Example
501(c)(1)	Corporations Organized under Act of Congress (including Federal Credit Unions)	Yes, if made for exclusively public purposes	ACE Community Credit Union
501(c)(2)	Title-Holding Corporation for Exempt Organization	No[2]	Sanctuary Park Realty Holding Company
501(c)(3)	Public Charities and Private Foundations	Yes, generally	YMCA Ford Foundation
501(c)(4)	Civic Leagues and Social Welfare Organizations	No, generally[2,3]	National Rifle Association (NRA) American Association of Retired Persons (AARP)
501(c)(5)	Labor, Agricultural, and Horticultural Organizations	No[2]	American Federation of Teachers AFL-CIO, IBEW
501(c)(6)	Business Leagues, Chambers of Commerce, Real Estate Boards, etc.	No[2]	National Football League (NFL) American Medical Association (AMA)
501(c)(7)	Social and Recreational Clubs	No[2]	Los Angeles Country Club Chi Omega Fraternity
501(c)(8)	Fraternal Beneficiary Societies and Associations	Yes, for certain Sec. 501(c)(3) purposes	Knights of Columbus
501(c)(9)	Voluntary Employees Beneficiary Associations	No[2]	Wal-Mart Stores Inc. Associates Health & Welfare Trust
501(c)(10)	Domestic Fraternal Societies and Associations	Yes, for certain Sec. 501(c)(3) purposes	Free Masons Shriner's International
501(c)(11)	Teacher's Retirement Fund Associations	No[2]	Boston Public School Teachers Retirement Fund
501(c)(12)	Benevolent Life Insurance Associations, Mutual Ditch or Irrigation Companies, Mutual or Cooperative Telephone Companies, etc.	No[2]	Paul Bunyon Rural Telephone Cooperative Great Lakes Energy Cooperative
501(c)(13)	Cemetery Companies	Yes, generally	Mount Elliott Cemetery
501(c)(14)	State Chartered Credit Unions, Mutual Reserve Funds	No[2]	Consolidated Credit Unions of Virginia

Code	Description	Deductible	Examples
501(c)(15)	Mutual Insurance Companies or Associations	No[2]	Farm & Home Life Insurance Company First National Life Insurance Company of America
501(c)(16)	Cooperative Organizations to Finance Crop Operations	No[2]	National Livestock Credit Corporation
501(c)(17)	Supplemental Unemployment Benefit Trusts	No[2]	Goodyear Tire Company Superfund
501(c)(18)	Employee-Funded Pension Trust (created before June 25, 1959)	No[2]	Interlocal Pension Fund of the Inter-Brotherhood of Teamsters
501(c)(19)	Post or Organization of Past or Present Members of the Armed Forces	No, generally[7]	American Legion Military Order of the Purple Heart
501(c)(21)	Black Lung Benefit Trusts	No[4]	North American Coal Corporation Black Lung Benefit Trust
501(c)(22)	Withdrawal Liability Payment Fund	No[5]	No organizations currently registered with the IRS
501(c)(23)	Veterans Organizations (created before 1880)	No, generally[7]	Navy Mutual Aid Association
501(c)(25)	Title-Holding Corporations or Trusts with Multiple Parents	No	225 West Wacker Street Acquisition Corporation
501(c)(26)	State-Sponsored Organization Providing Health Coverage for High-Risk Individuals	No	North Carolina Health Insurance Risk Pool
501(c)(27)[11]	State-Sponsored Workers' Compensation Reinsurance Organization	No	Missouri Employers Mutual Insurance Company
501(c)(28)[12]	National Railroad Retirement Investment Trust	No	No organizations currently registered with the IRS

Note: Re-printed and adapted from Guidestar: http://www.guidestar.org/rxg/help/irs-subsection-codes.aspx 1. For exceptions to the filing requirement see chapter 2 of Publication 557 and the general instructions for Form 990. 2. An organization exempt under a subsection of Code sec. 501 other than 501(c)(3) may establish a charitable fund, contributions to which are deductible. Such a fund must itself meet the requirements of section 501(c)(3) and the related notice requirements of section 508(a). 3. Contributions to volunteer fire companies and similar organizations are deductible, but only if made for exclusively public purposes. 4. Deductible as a business expense to the extent allowed by Code section 192. 5. Deductible as a business expense to the extent allowed by Code section 194A. 6. Application is by letter to the address shown on Form 8718. A copy of the organizing document should be attached and the letter should be signed by an officer. 7. Contributions to these organizations are deductible only if 90% or more of the organization's members are war veterans. 8. For limits on the use of Form 990-EZ, see chapter 2 of Publication 557 and the general instructions for Form 990-EZ (or Form 990). 9. Although the organization files a partnership return, all distributions are deemed dividends. The members are not entitled to *pass-through* treatment of the organization's income or expenses. 10. Form 1120-POL is required only if the organization has taxable income as defined in IRC 527(c). 11. The 501(c)(27) organizations (State-Sponsored Workers' Compensation Reinsurance Organizations) do not appear on GuideStar because they are not included on the I.R.S. Business Master File (BMF). 12. There is only one 501(c)(28) organization (the National Railroad Retirement Investment Trust), which was created by an act of Congress. It is not included on the BMF and therefore does not appear on GuideStar.

that have applied for and have been granted tax-exempt status by the IRS. Tax exemption is both a legal status and financial privilege granted by the federal government which allows certain organizations permanent exemption from payment of corporate income taxes at the federal level, and, in the majority of states, exemption from payment of all state and local taxes including property, sales, franchise and use taxes; tax-exempt organizations are also eligible for reduced postal rates.[47]

The "quid pro quo" logic helps to illustrate the underlying rationale of a federal policy that allows for such an extensive system of tax-exempt organizations. The quid pro quo logic suggests that tax exemption is an appropriate subsidy because the government, or public at-large, benefits from the existence of organizations that receive the subsidy.[48] Therefore, favorable tax treatment is granted under the assumption that the organization will provide public benefit and will "operate to improve the quality of life in a community."[49] In other words, the quid pro quo logic implies that nonprofits are deserving of tax subsidies because these organizations provide benefits to society, including the fact that they reduce the service burdens of government (however, this logic does not apply to all types of nonprofit organizations, which is a source of controversy that we will examine shortly).

Because they provide benefits for neighborhoods, communities, cities, states, and our society in general, nonprofit organizations are absolved of paying taxes so that they can dedicate more of their resources to providing goods and services to the public. While federal, state, and local governments thus "lose out" on billions of dollars each year in tax revenue, the public and social benefit that nonprofits provide are considered a worthwhile investment by American citizens and policy-makers. The IRS recognizes 28 categories of tax-exempt organizations. Table 2.1 provides a list of these categories, along with examples of organizations that fit these categories.

As Table 2.1 demonstrates, a wide variety of organizations and activities fall under the umbrella of the tax exemption. However, it is important to note that some of these categories are extremely small, with only a handful of organizations or none at all at present, while others have tens of thousands. Indeed, the majority of tax-exempt organizations in the US fall under the 501(c)(3) code. Just over one million of all tax-exempt organizations are 501(c)(3)—the majority of which are public charities and a smaller portion of which are private foundations. Organizations within the 501(c)(3) category make up just over two thirds of the entire formal nonprofit sector.[50] In order for an entity to obtain 501(c)(3) status, the IRS requires that it must be organized to fulfill one or more of the following specific purposes: religious, educational, charitable, scientific, literary, testing for public safety, fostering national or international amateur sports competition, or prevention of cruelty to children or animals. While 501(c)(3) organizations make up the largest group of registered non-profits, there are a wide variety of public charity types in this group. Figure 2.2 shows the distribution of the types of 501(c)(3) public charities registered as of July 2013 in the United States. The figure shows the breakdown of registered nonprofits according to major NTEE categories. For example, human service organizations include those whose missions range from agriculture and nutrition and housing to youth development and sporting. Some of the largest human service organizations in the US include the American National Red Cross and Habitat for Humanity

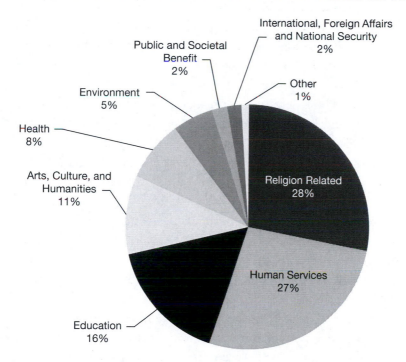

FIGURE 2.2 Distribution of Types of 501(c)(3) Public Charities Registered in the US, 2013.

Source: National Center for Charitable Statistics—registered nonprofit organizations by type.

International. Public benefit organizations, on the other hand, include those organizations whose primary function centers on advocacy, community improvement, philanthropy, and volunteerism. Power players in this arena of organizing include organizations such as the American Civil Liberties Union Foundation, Local Initiatives Support Corporation (LISC), and the George Kaiser Family Foundation.

Organizations with the 501(c)(3) public charity designation differ in an important way from those in the other categories of tax exemption. In addition to their freedom from paying taxes, nonprofit organizations within this category enjoy an additional financial benefit in that they can issue donors a tax receipt, which creates an incentive for private giving to these organizations. The federal tax code encourages individuals and corporations to contribute cash and other items of value to nonprofits with the 501(c)(3) designation by allowing them to deduct the value of their donation from their federal income taxes, and in most cases from their state income taxes as well. This creates an incentive for Americans to give to nonprofit organizations, something that is typically not done in other countries—which can be one explanation for why the nonprofit sector is so large in the US as compared to other nations (see Figure 2.3). As Figure 2.3 shows, the nonprofit sector makes up 5.5% of the gross domestic product (GDP) in the United States as compared to 2.8% in Brazil, 1.9% in Norway, and 0.8% in Thailand. Those percentages rise a bit more when voluntary labor is taken into account. In the case of Norway and New Zealand, volunteer labor increases the sector's contribution to the GDP by almost 3%.

Numbering slightly more than 110,000 "social welfare" organizations, the 501(c)(4)s make up a much smaller but sizable share of the nonprofit sector. These organizations exist primarily to lobby for and against various causes, and to shape public opinion through issue education. The Sierra Club and the American Association of Retired Persons (AARP) are example organizations that fall within this category. The remaining 400,000 plus organizations are spread among the other (c)(3) codes, and cover organizations as diverse as labor unions, fraternal societies, insurance and mutual aid funds, sports and recreational clubs, and cemeteries.

Given that the government forgoes billions of dollars in tax revenue every year as a result of granting tax exemptions to nonprofit organizations, these financial privileges have come under greater scrutiny in recent years, particularly where certain types of nonprofit organizations are concerned.

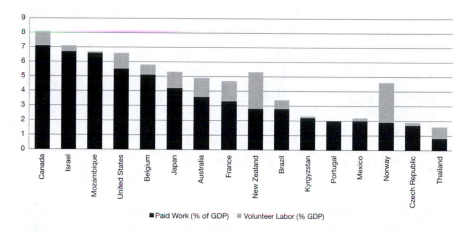

FIGURE 2.3 Percent of Nonprofit Contributions to GDP: United States and Other Nations.

Note: Reprinted and adapted from UN Nonprofit Handbook (March 2013). Accessed at http://ccss.jhu.edu/wp-content/uploads/downloads/2013/04/JHU_Global-Civil-Society-Volunteering_Final_3.3013.pdf

A number of controversies exist related to the current tax treatment of nonprofits. One such controversy stems from the increasing trend of cash-strapped local governments across the country either directly assessing property taxes, or finding more subtle ways to tax nonprofit organizations for the municipal services they rely on to operate. While we will examine this issue in greater depth in Chapter 10, Box 2.1 offers an illustration of how this controversy has played out in the City of Chicago.

Another source of contention in the current system of tax exemption arises from competition between for-profit businesses and nonprofit organizations that provide the same services. As we mentioned in Chapter 1, there are a number of industries in which both nonprofits and for-profits exist to provide services, including hospitals, nursing homes, day care centers, private colleges and universities, and many others. As we also discussed in Chapter 1, nonprofit and for-profit organizations share a number of features in common including the need to generate revenue in order to survive. The controversy between the nonprofit and for-profit organizations in the same field stems from the numerous tax advantages that nonprofit organizations have, which is argued by some[51] to create an uneven playing field as nonprofits may have an unfair advantage in competing for customers. This is a complex issue, as competition and conflict do not emerge in every scenario (in fact partnerships and collaboration between

BOX 2.1 THE CHALLENGE OF TAX EXEMPTION

Federal, state, and local governments "lose out" on billions of dollars each year in tax revenue. Despite the public benefits from the social services and goods that nonprofits provide, many nonprofits occupy large tracts of valuable land where not only are they exempt from property taxes, but they often receive free or reduced city services such as water or emergency services. Some communities have sought to alter this relationship between local governments and nonprofit organizations, removing some of the privileges that have historically come with tax exemption in the United States.

In 2013, the City of Chicago proposed a plan for raising revenues among nonprofit organizations in the city. Mayor Rahm Emanuel and the City Council argued that although nonprofits provide important services to the community, they are also a significant burden on the city and, in a time of economic recession, the city could no longer afford to provide major hospitals, religious organizations, and educational institutions with a free ride. In 2012, the City of Chicago announced that nonprofit organizations would no longer get free water from the City of Chicago. Many nonprofits protested this proposal, arguing that they could not afford the water rates and that paying for water would divert important funds away from services for the poor, children, etc. The city argued that, in this time of economic recession, it could not afford to subsidize these nonprofits, and moreover, because nonprofits get free water, they are wasteful in their use of water. The city noted that installing water meters at nonprofit organizations would require them to be responsible and accountable for their water usage and waste.

After much negotiation between the mayor, city council members, and nonprofit agencies, in April 2013 Mayor Emanuel proposed a four-tier structure for water rates, where nonprofits with fewer assets would continue to enjoy free water, while those with higher valued assets would pay a percentage of their water bill. Specifically, nonprofits with overall assets under $1 million would not pay for water; those valued between $1 and $10 million would get a 60% exemption; those valued $10–$250 million would get a 25% exemption; and those valued at more than $250 million would receive no exemption. The proposal still included an exemption of 20% for public museums and a Disproportionate Share Hospitals' water exemption would remain in place, with a minimum exemption of 25%.

Should communities provide free water to nonprofit organizations that provide services to their communities? Should large hospitals be responsible for paying a larger percentage of their water bills than smaller organizations (a progressive tax of sorts)? What is fair in this situation?

nonprofits and for-profits are increasingly common). However, the possibility exists for this conflict to arise anytime there are nonprofit and for-profit businesses providing the same or highly similar services in a community. Box 2.2 provides a brief illustration.

BOX 2.2 AN UNEVEN PLAYING FIELD?

Social enterprises, or profit-making ventures run by nonprofit organizations, are another controversial issue related to the special tax treatment that nonprofits receive under the current tax code. Given that nonprofit organizations do not have to pay income, property, or sales taxes, some have questioned whether this creates an uneven playing field for small business owners that provide similar goods and services in the community.

Consider the following example: founded in 2004, the Boston-area nonprofit *More than Words* (MTW) is a youth-run, used bookstore and café with the mission to *"empower youth who are in foster care, court-involved, homeless, or out of school, to take charge of their lives by taking charge of a business."*[52] The charitable purposes of the organization include youth development, employment, job training, and education. In 2011, MTW had annual revenues of roughly $1.2 million with assets exceeding $600k.[53] Providing job training and educational opportunities to disadvantaged youth is a noble and worthy cause, however it does raise questions of equity for the handful of local, indie-owned, used bookstores in Boston, such as *Rodney's Books*. As neighboring small businesses must compete with MTW in the regional market of used book-buyers, some might question whether MTW has an unfair advantage not only because they are exempt from taxes, but also because they can offer potential customers a tax write-off in exchange for donated books (and of course monetary donations). The locally-owned, for-profit booksellers may be at a financial disadvantage as they must pay potential customers for used books (through either cash or store credit). Additionally, while the profits made from MTW's book and café sales must be reinvested in the organization to further its mission of teaching business skills to disadvantaged youth, its preferential tax treatment also allows the organization to devote more of its resources to the marketing and visibility of the organization.

Are these tax advantages fair to the small businesses in the community that provide comparable goods and services? Is it appropriate for nonprofits to receive these kinds of subsidies when small business owners in the same industry are struggling financially? Or does it depend on the size of the local market, and its "carrying capacity" for the particular good or service the nonprofit is providing? For example, a city the size of Boston may be able to bear a larger number of used bookstores before any one business feels the impact of competition.

In addition to enjoying a special tax status to help nonprofit organizations operate, the US tax code also creates incentives for individuals to donate to nonprofit organizations. When Americans file their tax returns each year, they are able to deduct charitable donations from their income, a tax rule known as the **charitable deduction**. This rule creates incentives for wage earners to donate to nonprofit organizations. But this individual tax incentive creates yet another controversy related to the tax code vis-à-vis nonprofit organizations—the current rules pertaining to charitable deductions provide the greatest financial benefits to individuals who are already reasonably well-off in the socioeconomic spectrum. In order to receive tax deductions from charitable contributions, taxpayers must itemize their returns. Taxpayers in higher tax brackets are much more likely to itemize than those in lower brackets. For example, only 16.2% of taxpayers in the lowest 10% bracket itemize. In comparison, if we look at the lower 33% of taxpayers, 70.9% itemize, while 89.4% of taxpayers in the 35% bracket itemize. This means that those who earn more money are more likely to itemize their taxes and claim deductions for donations to nonprofit organizations.[54]

BOX 2.3 CHANGING THE CHARITABLE DEDUCTION RULES?

In January 2013, President Obama introduced several proposals to amend the charitable deduction as part of a larger package of reforms aimed at "closing tax loopholes" that benefit the wealthiest citizens (those with household incomes over $250,000). Some of these proposals have included reducing the value of itemized deductions that are taken by wealthiest taxpayers to 28%, down from 39.6%, and limiting the total deductions a person can take to 2% of adjusted gross income.[55] The Obama administration has been unsuccessful in achieving any major changes in the tax code, due not only to a lack of bipartisan support in Congress, but also because the nonprofit community has pushed back against the President to oppose any reforms to the current rules governing charitable deductions. Advocacy groups such as the Charitable Giving Coalition have fought against the changes, arguing that the changes would discourage charitable giving and reduce private donations to the nonprofit sector by as much as $9 billion annually[56] (although there is some evidence suggesting that tax benefits play a relatively minor role in individuals' reasons for giving[57]—a topic we'll look at more closely in Chapter 6). While the issue of tax reform is still very much an on-going debate in Washington DC, it remains to be seen whether or not there will be any major policy changes to the tax code that would affect nonprofit organizations.

In essence, the charitable deduction could be considered another tax cut for the wealthy. Further adding to this controversy is that a large share of tax-deductible contributions in America is given to elite institutions of higher education, arts and cultural organizations, private K-12 schools, and other nonprofit institutions associated with affluence. While we shall examine this issue and general patterns of giving in much greater detail in Chapter 6, it is worth noting here that reforming the charitable deduction remains a hotly contested issue. Box 2.3 examines some of the proposals the federal government has considered with regard to reforming the charitable deduction.

Summary

This chapter highlights the origins of nonprofit and civil society organizations in the social, political, and economic spheres of American life. Nonprofit organizations fulfill an important social role in the US, functioning as associations for organizing based on religious and personal preferences, uniting to combat social injustices, and filling in when the public and for-profit sectors fail to fulfill citizen needs. Throughout history and into the modern day, nonprofit and civil society organizations have been important players in the American political arena, representing the interests of various groups and fighting for favorable policies on their behalf. Nonprofit organizations have a shorter history of economic contributions, but this role has been growing steadily over the past 50 years and the nonprofit sector today represents a major source of jobs in the US, particularly in health, human services, and education.

Along with cross-cultural values of charity and philanthropy, American values of individualism and pluralism have played a major role in the growth, development, and definition of the US nonprofit sector. The diversity that exists within American society helps to explain the size and complexity of the nonprofit sector. The provisions of the US Constitution provide not only an important historical backdrop to the activities of modern-day civil society, but remain the fundamental legal basis for the wide-ranging organizations and activities that make up the nonprofit and civil society sector today. Beginning in the 20th century, the US tax code became an equally important component of the legal framework for nonprofit organizations. The US tax code creates special opportunities to establish and operate nonprofit organizations, and offers incentives for

Americans to donate money to these organizations. Despite a number of contemporary challenges and controversies surrounding the tax code as it relates to nonprofits, a majority of citizens and law-makers alike remain inclined toward favorable tax treatment of nonprofit organizations. Underlying this favorable disposition is an assumption that nonprofits provide public or social benefit and improve the quality of American life in some fashion.

KEY TERMS

- Charitable deduction
- Entitlement programs
- Federation
- Great Society
- Individualism
- New Deal
- Pluralism
- Progressive Era
- Suffrage
- War on Poverty
- Welfare state

DISCUSSION QUESTIONS

1. What are some of the modern-day equivalents of Jane Addams' Hull House in your city or community? In what ways do these organizations aid immigrant groups? In your view, have the newer organizations been more successful in helping immigrants assimilate, find gainful employment, and become politically engaged? How do the newer immigrant service organizations of today differ from early settlement houses?

2. Thinking back to the opening story of this chapter, what advice would you give to Julia and her friends?

3. Does the charitable deduction represent just another tax loophole for the wealthy? Or does it offer more broad-based benefits? Do you think the charitable deduction needs to be reformed? If so, what changes to the current rules might yield the greatest benefit to society?

4. What issues in contemporary American society warrant the most attention and action from nonprofits? Why does this issue, or issues, demand action from the nonprofit sector, and to what extent is the nonprofit sector already addressing this issue? What role can you, as an individual, play in improving this issue that you identified as important to society?

ACTIVITY

Working within small groups of four to five people, identify a nonprofit organization most of the group is familiar with (either a national nonprofit or one that is well-known in your city/community) that has worked to create social change. Examine whether the organization has primarily contributed to the social, political, or economic dimension of society (or whether its contributions have overlapped these dimensions). What are some of the values that influenced the decision and work of the person (people) who founded this organization? If it is an organization that has been around for many years, what values might guide its current leaders? Are the values and impulses that influence Americans who are drawn to charity/philanthropy different today than they were one hundred years ago? Fifty years ago? Ten years ago? How have modern influences changed our values and attitudes toward charity and philanthropy?

Additional Reading

Arnburger, Paul, Melissa Ludlum, Margaret Riley, and Mark Stanton. 2008. *A History of the Tax-Exempt Sector: An SOI Perspective.* The Internal Revenue Service: Statistics of Income Bulletin. Winter 2008.

Hammack, David C. 1998. *Making the Nonprofit Sector in the United States: A Reader.* Bloomington, IN: Indiana University Press.

Robbins, Kevin C. 2011. The Nonprofit Sector in Historical Perspective: Traditions of Philanthropy in the West, in J. Steven Ott and Lisa Dicke (eds), *The Nature of the Nonprofit Sector*, 2nd ed. Boulder, CO: Westview Press. 2012.

Simon, John G. 1987. The tax treatment of nonprofit organizations: A review of federal and state policies, in Walter W. Powell and Richard Steinberg (eds), *The Nonprofit Sector: A Research Handbook,* 2nd ed. Yale University Press. 2006.

Notes

1 Arnburger, Paul, Melissa Ludlum, Margaret Riley, and Mark Stanton. 2008. *A History of the Tax-Exempt Sector: An SOI Perspective.* The Internal Revenue Service: Statistics of Income Bulletin. Winter 2008. Accessed May 30, 2013 at http://www.irs.gov/pub/irs-soi/tehistory.pdf

2 For discussion of charitable and philanthropic in ancient times, see Kevin C. Robbins' reading in Ott, J. Steven and Lisa A. Dicke. 2011. *The Nature of the Nonprofit Sector.* Boulder, CO: Westview Press.

3 http://www.merriam-webster.com/dictionary/charity. Accessed June 21, 2013.

4 http://www.merriam-webster.com/dictionary/philanthropy. Accessed June 21, 2013.

5 http://feedoc.org/AgencyAccess/ReligiousViews.aspx. Accessed June 21, 2013.

6 According to Second Harvest of Orange County, the Quran "was given to humankind via Muhammad in the Arabic language so that its message would not be distorted or

misunderstood. When any presentation of the Koran is made in any other language, the reader/listener is cautioned to refer to the original Arabic test for the complete and accurate wording and meaning. The Penguin Classics Edition from which the following are quoted includes the full text in Arabic." Accessed June 21, 2013 at http://feedoc.org/AgencyAccess/ReligiousViews/Koran.aspx.

7   http://www.merriam-webster.com/dictionary/pluralism. Accessed June 22, 2013.

8   Ott and Dicke (2011) have also identified pluralism and individualism as two key values associated with the nonprofit sector in America (p. 51).

9   Patterson, Thomas E. 2002. *We the People: A Concise Introduction to American Politics*, 4th ed. New York, NY: McGraw-Hill.

10   Putnam, Robert D. 2000. *Bowling Alone. The Collapse and Revival of American Community*. New York, NY: Simon & Schuster.

11   De Tocqueville, Alexis. 1838. *Democracy in America*. New York: George Dearborn and Co.

12   http://www.pta.org/ Accessed September 6, 2013.

13   https://www.pta.org/about/content.cfm?ItemNumber=946&navItemNumber=551. Accessed September 6, 2013.

14   https://www.rotary.org/en/about-rotary. Accessed September 6, 2013.

15   http://www.kofc.org/un/en/about/aboutus.html. Accessed September 6, 2013.

16   Putnam (2000).

17   http://www.greatmigration.org/new_englands_great_migration.html. Accessed October 5, 2013.

18   Chaves, Mark. 2004. *Congregations in America*. Cambridge, MA: Harvard University Press.

19   Carnegie, A. (1903). *The Gospel of Wealth*. Eigaku-Shimpo-Sha.

20   http://www.wwhp.org/Resources/Slavery/aass.html. Accessed October 5, 2013.

21   http://www.dar.org/natsociety/history.cfm. Accessed October 5, 2013.

22   http://www.njwomenshistory.org/Period_3/daughters.htm; Blocker, Jack S. (1989). *American Temperance Movements: Cycles of Reform*. Boston: Twayne Publishers; http://www2.potsdam.edu/hansondj/Controversies/The-American-Temperance-Society.html#. Accessed October 5, 2013.

23   Blocker, J. S., D. M. Fahey, and I. R. Tyrrell (eds). 2003. *Alcohol and Temperance in Modern History: An International Encyclopedia* (Vol. 1). ABC-CLIO.

24   Blocker et al. (2003).

25   http://www.archives.gov/education/lessons/woman-suffrage/awsa-memorial.html. Accessed October 5, 2013.

26   Endorsement of political candidates is illegal for most nonprofit organizations. Labor unions, and other nonprofit organizations of specific types, are permitted to engage in partisan activity, a topic that will be explored in greater detail in Chapter 7.

27   http://sclcnational.org/our-history/. Accessed October 5, 2013.

28   The NAACP's website suggests that the organization was founded in 1909, and is the "nation's oldest and largest civil rights organization." However, the IRS identifies the organization's ruling year as 1961.

29   http://www.naacp.org/pages/naacp-history. Accessed June 13, 2013.

30   http://www.now.org/history/the_founding.html. Accessed June 13, 2013.

31 http://www.prochoiceamerica.org/assets/files/about-naral-history.pdf. Accessed June 13, 2013.

32 http://www.eeoc.gov/eeoc/history/35th/1990s/ada.html. Accessed June 13, 2013.

33 http://idea.ed.gov/ Accessed June 13, 2013.

34 http://www.gpo.gov/fdsys/pkg/BILLS-104hr3396enr/pdf/BILLS-104hr3396enr.pdf. Accessed June 13, 2013.

35 Silver, Nate. 2013. How Opinion on Gay Marriage is Changing and What it Means. March 26, 2013. Accessed June 13, 2013 at http://fivethirtyeight.blogs.nytimes.com/2013/03/26/how-opinion-on-same-sex-marriage-is-changing-and-what-it-means/?_r=0

36 Haider-Markel, Donald. 2010. *Gay and Lesbian Candidates, Elections, and Policy Representation.* Washington, DC: Georgetown University Press.

37 Salamon, Sokolowski, and Geller. 2012. *Holding the Fort: Nonprofit Employment in a Decade of Turmoil.* The Johns Hopkins Nonprofit Economic Data Project. Employment Bulletin #39. Johns Hopkins Center for Civil Society Studies. January 2012.

38 Drucker, Peter. 1994. *The Age of Social Transformation.* Glencoe, IL: The Free Press.

39 Salamon et al. (2012).

40 Swanstrom, Todd and Julia Koschinsky. 2000. Rethinking the Partnership Model of Government-Nonprofit Relations: The Case of Community Development. Chapter 4 in Richard C. Hula, and Cynthia Jackson-Elmoore (eds), *Nonprofits in Urban America.* Westport, CT: Quorum Books.

41 According to Salamon et al. (2012), healthcare accounts for 57% of all nonprofit jobs, education accounts for 15%, and social services account for 12%.

42 Salamon, Lester A. 2002. *The State of Nonprofit America.* Washington, DC: Brookings Institution Press.

43 Some of the reduction in the number of nonprofits after 2010 can be explained by the revocations that happened as a result of the 2008 reforms to the IRS 990 forms, triggering the first revocations in 2011.

44 Salamon et al. (2012).

45 Wright, Nathaniel S. Revitalizing Community Development Corporations: Do CDCs Matter? Working Paper, RGK Center on Philanthropy at University of Texas-Austin. Accessed September 6, 2013 at http://www.rgkcenter.org/sites/default/files/file/research/Wright2010.pdf

46 Agency bureaucrats write the rules in conjunction with members of Congress who ultimately approve these rules.

47 Ott and Dicke (2011).

48 Kenyon, Daphne A. and Adam Langley. 2010. Payments in Lieu of Taxes: Balancing Municipal and Nonprofit Interests. Policy Focus Report of the *Lincoln Institute of Land Policy,* Cambridge, MA; and Brody, Evelyn. 2007. The States' Growing Use of a Quid-Pro-Quo Rationale For The Charity Property Tax Exemption. *The Exempt Organization Review,* 56(3): 269–288. For a detailed discussion of cases in which the quid pro quo logic was used by state governments to justify tax exemption, see Brody 2007.

49 Hoyt, Christopher. 2001. Tax-Exempt Organizations, in Steven J. Ott (ed.), *The Nature of the Nonprofit Sector.* Boulder, CO: Westview Press, p. 148.

50 According to the NCCS there are 1,006,670 public charities and 120,617 foundations designated as 501(c)(3) organizations. Accessed November 9, 2012 at http://nccs.urban.org/

51 Grobman, Gary. 2011. *The Nonprofit Handbook*, 6th ed., Chapter 25, Nonprofits and Small Business Competition. Harrisburg, PA: Whitehat Communications.

52 http://www.guidestar.org/organizations/04–2784985/more-than-words.aspx. Accessed May 30, 2013.

53 http://www.guidestar.org/organizations/04–2784985/more-than-words.aspx. Accessed May 30, 2013.

54 Baneman, Daniel and Benjamin Harris. 2011. *Who Itemizes Deductions?* The Urban Institute. Accessed June 7, 2013 at http://www.urban.org/publications/1001486.html

55 Donovan, Doug. March 15, 2013. Senate Democrats Call for Limits on Charitable Deductions, *Chronicle of Philanthropy*. Accessed June 7, 2013 at http://philanthropy.com/article/Senate-Democrats-Call-for/137953/

56 Donovan, Doug, April 8, 2013. Obama to Renew Call to Limit Charitable Dedection, *Chronicle of Philanthropy*. Accessed June 7, 2013 at http://philanthropy.com/article/Obama-to-Renew-Call-to-Limit/138425/

57 Mount, Joan. 1996. Why Donors Give. *Nonprofit Management and Leadership*, 7: 3–14.

3
THEORIES OF THE
NONPROFIT SECTOR

CHAPTER LEARNING OBJECTIVES

By the end of this chapter, students will be able to:

1. Describe several theories that explain the existence of the nonprofit sector
2. Explain key economic theories of the nonprofit sector
3. Explain several non-economic theories of the nonprofit sector
4. Apply one or more theories to explain the reasons why a specific nonprofit organization exists in your community

---

Introduction

Why do we have a nonprofit sector? Do we really need one? Why do nonprofits exist in industries where government and for-profit organizations also provide services? These are the types of questions that nonprofit theories seek to explain and that we explore in this chapter. As we discovered in Chapter 2, the formal nonprofit sector began to grow to its current large scale about 50 years ago, therefore theories about the nonprofit sector are relatively new. Nonprofit theories are not "fixed" but, like other

Students from Tulane University volunteer with Habitat for Humanity

Many of you have probably heard of Habitat for Humanity. In fact, some of you might have volunteered with Habitat for Humanity. Have you ever wondered why it exists? Specifically, why does this organization build and repair houses all over the world, and then sell those houses through no-profit, no-interest mortgage loans or unconventional financing methods?[1] Habitat for Humanity is "a nonprofit, ecumenical Christian ministry that builds with people in need regardless of race or religion" which welcomes "volunteers and supporters from all backgrounds."[2]

There are thousands of home-building companies in the world. Governments often provide housing to the poor, in the form of free public housing, subsidized rents, or vouchers to rent properties. So why does Habitat for Humanity build homes? Maybe because home-building companies are selling the homes they build for large profits, making them unaffordable for lower income families. While there is a profitable market for those with good, stable incomes and a history of good credit, there remains a need for affordable homes and financing assistance for lower-income families who may face challenges in saving money for a down payment, and affording the added costs of mortgage interest that drive up monthly home payment costs. And in some cases, governments are not able to provide enough housing for low-income families. In other cases, the housing that the government provides is temporary or has restrictions that can make it difficult for families to move toward successful home ownership.

continued

A Habitat for Humanity project sponsored by Bank of America and Roanoke College

Habitat for Humanity exists to help families and individuals overcome these and other barriers to home ownership. There is need, or demand, for affordable, simple homes. In fact, according to Habitat's website, worldwide around 827.6 million people live in slums and in the US 48.5 million people are living in poverty. At the same time, there is a supply of able-bodied volunteers who are eager to give their time and money to others. Instead of turning a profit and building homes that are expensive and have high labor and supply costs, Habitat for Humanity relies on donations of time, supplies, and labor. By using donated building supplies and volunteer labor, Habitat for Humanity can build homes at a low cost, enabling Habitat to sell those homes at a lower cost. Additionally, Habitat foregoes the profits from the homes they build because their mission is to help people in need, rather than to make money. Habitat does its work because housing provides stability for families and children; a sense of dignity and pride; health, safety, and security; and increased educational and employment opportunities.

As you can see, some of the explanations for the existence of Habitat for Humanity are economic (the supply of volunteers, donated goods and funds, and the demand for housing), others are political (governments cannot provide enough housing), and still others are social (permanent housing provides stability for families, children, and communities, and helps families escape the cycle of poverty, all of which are good for society in general). These are useful explanations for understanding Habitat for Humanity, but would these same characteristics explain why other types of nonprofits exist?

theories, are open to interpretation and revision as society continues to evolve and change. As we acquire new knowledge and understanding of how nonprofits fit within the larger context of organizations and institutions of American society, so too our theories can evolve.

Theories of the nonprofit sector can be grouped into economic and non-economic theories. As we discover in this chapter, nonprofit theories can help to explain why certain types of nonprofits exist and can serve as guides for decisions about nonprofit formation. The following discussion of theories suggests that these decisions largely come down to a need, demand, or intense preference for some service or good (tangible or intangible) that is not currently fulfilled by either government or the for-profit sector.

What Is a Theory?

When social scientists use the word "theory" it has a very specific meaning, and it is probably different from the meaning of theory when we hear it used in everyday life. A social science theory is quite different from having a theory, or an idea or suspicion, about why two friends are fighting or why people choose to use Twitter instead of Facebook. A social science theory is a testable framework about social phenomena, or social occurrences or relationships. Social science theories are tested repeatedly with empirical data, experiments, and analysis. When a theory is tested over and over again using valid and reliable research methods, social scientists are able to develop a better understanding of social relationships and phenomena —and ultimately the world around us.

A social science theory can be used to explain and predict behavior of individuals, groups, or organizations in particular contexts. When we find consistent relationships by testing hypotheses, we can gain support for a theory and confidence that the theory is an accurate representation of social experiences. Theories help us to know what to predict and expect in particular situations. A theory of nonprofits might aim to understand the social, economic, and political conditions that predict the formation of nonprofit organizations or civil society groups. Other theories might explain the conditions under which particular nonprofit organizations will be successful at achieving their missions. For our purposes, non-profit theories are important because they help to explain why nonprofit organizations exist, what gaps they fill in civil society, and what explains nonprofit success and failure. Additionally, nonprofit theories help us to move away from a single example of a nonprofit organization succeeding or failing to generalize about the larger nonprofit community. By studying data from many cases we can develop information that is more accurate and more useful for understanding how to advance our collective and individual interests.

In sum, if we know why nonprofits exist and the important role they play in civil society, this can better shape the ways in which we work in the nonprofit sector, our obligations as public service professionals, volunteers, citizens, and the decisions we make to help achieve the nonprofit's mission. Below we discuss some of the important theories about the existence and success of nonprofit organizations in civil society. First, we discuss economic theories and then non-economic theories.

Economic Theories

Economic theories have provided the predominant set of modern explanations for the existence of nonprofit organizations in the US.[3] Economic theories are primarily concerned with the role of nonprofits as producers of goods and services desired or needed by various segments of the public, and the role of individuals as consumers of the goods and services that nonprofits offer. Economic theories of the nonprofit sector emphasize the inherent limitations of private markets and government, and highlight the emergence of nonprofit organizations as a response to addressing those limitations.[4] Three theoretical frameworks arising from economic principles that help us to better understand the existence of the nonprofit sector include market failures, government failure, and government-nonprofit partnership theory.

Market Failure Perspectives

Private, for-profit businesses produce the vast majority of goods and services within the US. The prominence of the for-profit business sector in the US stems from a long-standing belief in the virtues of free market capitalism. This norm of holding the business sector in high regard and maintaining a preference for limited government (and sometimes a distrust of government) uses values that are deeply embedded in American culture. Americans often idealize the private for-profit, or "first sector", because private businesses are believed to operate with the greatest efficiency and effectiveness, as a result of being disciplined by market forces. Indeed, the competitive nature of the for-profit marketplace creates pressures for private firms to keep prices low and maintain high quality goods and services.

However, private, for-profit markets sometimes fail to achieve the ideals of efficiency and effectiveness, which can lead to problems of undersupply of the good or service and negative consequences for the consumer. When the private, for-profit market is not able to efficiently provide a good or service we call this a market failure. Several types of "market failures" can occur, creating a need for government intervention in the form of overseeing private production through regulation, or creating certain incentives for private firms to adjust their behavior, both of which could correct the market failure. In other instances government can prevent or correct market failures by directly producing the goods or services through government agencies. Or, as we will soon learn through some examples, sometimes the nonprofit sector provides goods and services in response to market failures. We discuss three common types of market failures —failures to supply collective goods, information asymmetries, and externalities—which lead to governments and sometimes nonprofit organizations (formal or informal) stepping in to correct the problems associated with a for-profit organization providing the good or service.

Failure to Supply Collective Goods

Collective goods are those that benefit all of society or all members of a particular group, and where it would be difficult to impossible to exclude individuals from enjoying the benefit of the good (e.g. law and order, peace, clean air). Private markets frequently fail to provide a good or service demanded by some segment of the population because the economic incentives to provide the good are not strong enough. Because private, for-profit firms are in the business of making money, it does not make sense for them to provide certain goods and services that would be freely available to everyone. For example, most business entrepreneurs would not be interested in providing fire protection services in local communities because it would not be profitable to do so. Fires occur relatively infrequently, and yet a cadre of trained and willing fire fighters must be ready to answer the call on those rare occasions fires occur. For-profit companies are not in the business of fire protection because even if they charged a fee for fighting fires at local residences or commercial settings, fires occur so infrequently that it would be difficult for the business to make a profit; indeed money would be lost as they would have to pay firefighters to be on duty around the clock even when they were not responding to a fire, possibly for weeks or months. Thus, in many cases, especially in larger communities, government fulfills the need for fire protection by collecting taxes and providing one or more municipal or county fire stations. However, some local communities cannot generate enough money through taxes for government to provide this essential service, so the informal nonprofit sector fills the gap when a community leader organizes an all-volunteer fire protection force, a tendency that is particularly common in rural parts of the US. In short, private businesses are not likely to invest in situations of high risk and low profit margins, but if society needs the good or service, government will often step in to produce the good or subsidize its production. Additionally, voluntary action (informal nonprofit organization) may fulfill the public need, if neither the for-profit sector nor government sector acts to address the need or problem.

Information Asymmetries

Information asymmetry refers to different amounts or quality of information between two parties who are engaged in a transaction. This occurs when a seller and a buyer have different types of information about the product, the price of the product, or supply and demand in the marketplace. Asymmetrical information creates a market failure problem when the *seller* of a good or service has more information than the *buyer* about the quality of the product, or when the buyer has more information about the marketplace for reselling the product (e.g. consider buying a car, where the seller knows more about the car's history, features, and problems).

Information asymmetries, or information imbalances, are problematic if the firm or producer uses their information advantage to deceive consumers and exploit profits. For example, the tobacco industry discovered that cigarettes cause cancer. Fearing that this information would cause a decline in sales, tobacco companies did not reveal this information to the public and continued to sell cigarettes that were detrimental to the health of consumers. It was not until the federal government mandated (forced) the companies to report the dangers that they began to provide this information to consumers. In this example, the government corrected the information asymmetry by requiring cigarette manufacturers to post disclosure labels on each package warning potential buyers of the risks associated with consuming tobacco.

In similar ways, nonprofits can help to correct information asymmetries related to goods and service in the marketplace. In some cases, information asymmetries are the result of a lack of transparency or trust between buyers and sellers. One of the ways that buyers and sellers (consumers and producers) interact is through contracts. Contracts or more formal agreements help to specify requirements, expectations, and commitments in order to reduce information asymmetry. Contract failure occurs when there are problems with the agreement or transaction. Contract failure is a theory of nonprofits developed specifically upon the problems associated with information asymmetries.[5] Many times, nonprofit organizations can deliver goods or services to reduce information asymmetry and increase trust in transactions. When buyers lack information about the quality of a good or service, or do not trust the producer of a good or service, a nonprofit organization might be ideal for reducing information asymmetry and increasing trust and communication between the two actors in a transaction. Because nonprofits are not primarily driven by profits, consumers usually trust them more than for-profit firms. Nonprofits are often considered especially preferable producers of goods and services for which consumers might not be able to adequately judge the quality and make adjustments based on their level of satisfaction with the service. Below we discuss a few examples of nonprofit organizations helping to reduce information asymmetries in the marketplace.

Suppose, for example, that you are a parent of an infant and shopping for the best day care center, and you have a choice of either a for-profit or a nonprofit day care center. As a parent, you want to enroll your child in the day care with the highest ratio of caregivers to infants. You visit both centers and are told that the ratio of caregivers to infants is 1 to 3. You also note that the cost of the day cares is about the same. Should you send your child to the for-profit day care or the nonprofit day care? You might decide that daycares working to make money will do more to provide excellent services to children and parents. On the other hand, you might worry that in order to make a profit, the for-profit organization is paying below market wages to the caregivers, which may result in poor care for your child. Or maybe the for-profit organization is cutting costs by purchasing cheaply made toys and low-quality, higher-toxicity cleaning products. Upon further investigation, you might find that the for-profit center provides a 1 to 3 caregiver to child ratio only during peak times of the day. Since the bottom-line goal of the center is to maximize profits, they have fewer total staff on duty and, for part of the day, the caregiver-to-infant ratio is more like 1 to 5. The nonprofit day care center, on the other hand, has a mission of nurturing infants to help them achieve their maximum development so they maintain the caregiver-to-infant ratio of 1 to 3 throughout the day. Thus, you might decide that though the costs are the same, the nonprofit organization, with a mission of nurturing infants before making profits, is more aligned with your values. In this example, there are clear information asymmetry problems arising from the for-profit provision of childcare. Since nonprofits lack the profit incentive and serve as a proxy for trust for consumers, nonprofit provision can help to correct the information asymmetry problem in the market for childcare.

Nursing home services provide a similar illustration. Private, for-profit nursing homes have been shown to use twice as many sedatives as non-profit nursing facilities,[6] allowing them to capitalize on profits by saving on personnel costs. Since nonprofits are prohibited from distributing their surplus revenue to staff or board members they lack the incentive to maximize profits and instead operate with the goal of achieving their mission. Nonprofit organizations are more likely to be transparent in their operations and reveal the true costs of providing care, whereas for-profit nursing homes and day care centers may cut corners to maximize profits, but fail to fully represent these cost-cutting measures to the consumer.

Externalities

Externalities, also known as "spillover effects," are unintended conse-quences that are borne by a third party who is neither the buyer nor the seller in a market exchange. Externalities can be positive or negative. Positive externalities occur when a third party does not have to pay for a benefit. For example, your neighbors may invest in a beautifully landscaped yard that not only increases the value of their homes, but also increases the desirability of your neighborhood in the housing market. Negative externalities occur when a third party is harmed or made worse off in some way and is not compensated for it. For example, people may breathe in pollutants generated by a nearby manufacturing plant without even realizing they are being harmed. Government typically uses regulations and fines to eliminate or minimize negative externalities such as pollution. For example, government ensures that third parties are not harmed by pollution through enacting clean air standards and monitoring firms to make sure they do not exceed allowable emission levels.

Although government often intervenes in private, for-profit markets in order to reduce negative externalities, nonprofits can help to correct this source of market failure as well. Let's consider the ways in which nonprofit organizations might mediate negative externalities. Fishing is an important industry in the world. One of the negative externalities of fishing activities is that when one fishing company harvests in the ocean, it depletes the stock of available fish for other companies. Additionally, it diminishes the presence of particular types of fish which might result in detrimental changes to other species or alter the oceanic ecosystem altogether. The market for harvesting fish and selling them to consumers does not account for this additional "cost" to other fishing companies, other fish, the ocean, or society. A nonprofit organization, concerned with the existence of a particular fish or the oceanic ecosystem in general, might raise public awareness of these negative externalities or directly lobby for new laws and stricter regulations to combat the negative externality. Thus, while there is no private market for buying and selling these types of services, mediating fish depletion and environmental damage, there are individuals and groups who are motivated to create organizations to address these issues. Society at large benefits from these efforts, even though only a small percentage "pay" for this mobilization and advocacy through their contributions and membership dues.

Nonprofits can also help to generate positive externalities. For example, many people unknowingly enjoy the benefits of their friends, neighbors, and co-workers having received flu vaccines. Individuals, even when they do not receive the vaccine themselves, are less likely to catch the flu when surrounded by people who have been immunized. The immunization of others reduces the chances of exposure for every person in their environment. Nonprofit health clinics often offer these and other disease-prevention services for free or at reduced cost to those with an inability to pay. We might also think of the many examples of neighborhood organizations that invest in revitalizing or beautifying our communities. The Mile of Murals Project[7] in Chicago is one example of a community-based neighborhood organization that creates positive externalities for neighborhood residents, passersby, and train riders. The project is a collaboration of public, private, and nonprofit organizations such as the Glenwood Avenue Arts District, the Rogers Park Business Alliance, community and youth groups, individual artists, and the Chicago Transit Authority and Streets and Sanitation Departments to create murals along the train line as a means to vitalize the neighborhood, improve the quality of life for residents, support artists, and attract visitors.[8] By investing in local artists, this community-based organization creates positive benefits for members of the public, even for those who did not pay for or otherwise contribute to the production of these murals.

Government Failure Theory

The government failure theory provides another explanation for the existence of nonprofit organizations and voluntary action. When provision of goods and services by for-profit firms would lead to the kinds of market failure problems described above, government often intervenes as an alternate producer of the goods and services. However, government is often only equipped to provide goods and services for which the majority of the public is willing to support with their tax dollars. Weisbrod argues that government goods and services are generally responsive to the average citizen or "median voter." Developed by Weisbrod (1975),[9] the government failure theory suggests that there are inherent limitations to the types and levels of goods and services governments can provide because the public is unable and unwilling to fully provide for every need presented by the population.

For example, the federal government directly provides military, defense, and security services, because a majority of Americans agree these services are necessary and desirable. Americans consent to have their tax dollars used for this purpose. Similarly, most Americans are willing to help fund the Social Security program through their taxes, because even though it only benefits certain segments of the population (the elderly and disabled), the median voter expects to benefit from it at some point in their life. By contrast, the median voter might be less willing to pay a tax that would be used to protect and restore coldwater trout and salmon habitats in wild areas across the US. Although the government makes some effort in this area through various conservation laws, it does not do nearly enough from the perspective of American fly fisherman who, fishing only for sport, have a vested interest in seeing the wild trout and salmon populations thrive. Since those affected by this issue represent a fairly narrow segment of the population, a nonprofit such as Trout Unlimited forms to fill this gap. In this example, people who care intensely about this issue, people who would have been willing to support such a service with their taxes, can voluntarily contribute their money, time, and resources time to this cause, rather than the government requiring all Americans to pay for this service.

Consider another example. It is unlikely that the average citizen would be inclined to pay a special tax to support persons with cystic fibrosis, a serious disorder but one that affects a very narrow segment of the population. There are roughly 30,000 persons in the US affected by cystic fibrosis who have needs for medical treatment, social support, and the hope for an eventual cure through research. The unmet needs of these 30,000 people have given rise to a nonprofit organization, the Cystic Fibrosis Foundation, which exists solely to fulfill the needs of this interest.

In sum, the government failure theory suggests that nonprofit organizations emerge to fill gaps in the market created by failures of government provision. Government cannot provide for every need that exists within US society. Government failures occur because the public is generally unwilling to support, with their tax dollars, goods and services that only benefit narrow segments of the population. Government generally supplies only those services that are responsive to the needs and preferences of median voter.

Government–Nonprofit Partnership Theory

The **government-nonprofit partnership theory**, also known as the "interdependence theory," suggests that much of the nonprofit sector exists because extensive government funding has been made available for the creation and maintenance of certain types of nonprofits. As we learned in the last chapter, much of the growth in the nonprofit sector over the past 50 years has been catalyzed by the creation of entitlement programs such as Medicare and Medicaid as well as new investments in anti-poverty, housing, and community development programs. According to Young (2000), since the 1980s, the US government has been taking a more fiscally conservative role in providing public services, increasingly relying on the nonprofit sector to deliver these goods and services.

Proposed by Salamon (1995),[10] the interdependence theory assumes that both government and nonprofits have inherent weaknesses, but by creating a partnership in which government provides limited funding for certain goods and services needed by the public but which the for-profit market will not or should not fulfill, these goods and service can be produced and delivered in a more creative, flexible, and efficient manner by nonprofit organizations. In essence, government-nonprofit partnerships can take advantage of the strengths of the two sectors: the authority and funding of government organizations and the flexibility and autonomy of nonprofit organizations.

According to Salamon, nonprofit organizations were limited by several weaknesses, often described as problems of "voluntary failure." Voluntary failure includes insufficiency, paternalism, particularism, and amateurism (Salamon, 1995). Insufficiency refers to the instability of nonprofit financial resources, as private giving ebbs and flows. Paternalism describes the historical tradition of nonprofits being governed by white, wealthy, civic elites who typically have made decisions for the organizations without soliciting client input. Particularistic tendencies stem from the fact that nonprofits are often formed to serve a particular racial, ethnic, religious, or demographic group. Amateurism refers to the historical reliance of non-profits on voluntary labor, which can limit nonprofits' capacity, professionalism, and expertise. Partnerships with government can help to alleviate these weaknesses, or voluntary failure.

Partnering with governments can alleviate or supplement some of these weaknesses of nonprofits. Government funding can offset the uncertainty of private giving, providing a stable revenue base for nonprofits and thus reducing the problem of insufficiency. Similarly, government funding can reduce the problem of paternalism (overreliance on governance by white, civic elites) by increasing the likelihood that nonprofit boards will be more representative of the persons served, requiring mechanisms for client participation, and, in some cases, setting a public-serving agenda of governance that goes beyond the preferences of elites. While private, nonprofit organizations may limit their services based on ethnic, religious, gender, or other preferences, government funding requires nonprofits to distribute public services on an equitable basis, without regard for ethnic, religious, or other status. Thus government funding and its requirements can help to eliminate nonprofit particularism. Finally, partnering with governments can reduce the amateurism in nonprofits since government funding can help nonprofits to support more long-term hiring of professional staff and investment in their training. For their part, nonprofits benefit from this partnership primarily from government-based financial resources, which allow nonprofits to expand the scope and scale of their operations and extend their missions to serve more people.

The increase in government-nonprofit partnerships is not only a result of nonprofits seeking government funding to adjust for their own weaknesses, but governments are seeking partnerships with nonprofits to adjust for their own weaknesses. Governments are also seeking government-nonprofit partnerships because of the trend toward government outsourcing that has been prevalent in the US since the early 1980s. Big government is an unpopular idea among Americans, who prefer a government that can "do more with less," be efficient, rely on private sector providers when possible, and reduce the number of people working for government. Government outsourcing of functions to nonprofits is viewed as a "win-win" situation for both parties and society. Government benefits from this partnership by expanding the programs and services needed by some segments of the public, but does so without increasing the size of the government workforce. Government also benefits by capturing the creative potential for programming that exists within the nonprofit sector and contracting to providers who are often embedded in the communities that they serve.

Nonprofits often develop programs and service models that are more effective in treating a problem than the programs or services offered by government bureaucracies which are often slow to move and rule-bound. In sum, nonprofits are often a more efficient provider of services because they are disciplined by market forces in ways that government is not. Outsourcing government services to nonprofits also enables the use of volunteers, which is not only "value-added" labor but creates social capital within communities. Finally, government-nonprofit partnerships enable nonprofits to pair government funding with private donations and volunteer labor, thus bringing additional resources to bear on social problems. In sum, the government-nonprofit partnership theory suggests that nonprofits exist in large part because government cannot supply all the goods and services necessary for a thriving, healthy civil society, but can invest in and provide funding for many of them. Nonprofits serve as vehicles for indirectly

TABLE 3.1 Theories Explaining the Nonprofit Sector

Theory	Features	How Nonprofits Address the Problem	Examples
Market failure	Occurs when for-profit businesses have little or no economic incentive to provide a good or service.	Nonprofits create goods or services on the basis of their mission and values, not profits.	Volunteer fire departments Free health clinics
	Information asymmetries: the seller of a good or service has more information than the buyer, and may not disclose information that the buyer needs.	Buyers (consumers) are more comfortable with a nonprofit provider of goods or services because of a higher trust level.	Nursing homes
	Externalities: unintended consequences that fall upon a third party who is neither the buyer nor seller in a market exchange. Can be positive or negative.	Government reduces negative externalities through regulation. Nonprofits reduce negative externalities through education, advocacy, organizing, and direct action.	Environmental organizations
Government failure theory	When the government steps in due to market failures, but can only provide goods and services which the majority of the public (i.e. the median voter) is willing to support.	Nonprofits merge to fill gaps in the market created by failures of government provision.	Museums Arts organizations
Government–nonprofit partnership (inter-dependence theory)	Government cannot supply all goods and services directly, but can invest in and provide limited funding for many of them.	Nonprofits serve as vehicles for indirectly carrying out the policy and program objectives of government, often in a more creative and flexible manner.	Affordable housing development organizations

carrying out government policy and program objectives, in an innovative and flexible manner.

Table 3.1 provides a summary of theories explaining why we have non-profits, including market failure, government failure, and government-nonprofit partnership theory. The table notes the general features of these theories, how nonprofits address particular problems, and lists examples of the types of nonprofits that exemplify the theory.

Criticisms of Economic Theories

Economic theories of nonprofit organizations, while historically providing the main theoretical lens through which to understand nonprofits, have become the subject of criticism in recent years. Economic models emphasize the roles of producers and consumers in a market transaction or exchange, yet some goods and services produced by nonprofits cannot be purchased in a market transaction, and in other instances the producer and consumer roles cannot be neatly separated or are intangible. For example, in Alcoholics Anonymous, and similar self-help groups, participants serve as both producers and consumers of the benefits created by group. Similarly, Habitat for Humanity beneficiaries are not only the consumers of the good (a new home) but also the producers of the good (hours contributed in "sweat equity" helping to build or rehab the home). Another criticism of economic theories is that they cannot explain why some types of goods and services are found within multiple sectors.[11] For example, hospitals and many other types of healthcare facilities can be found within all three sectors: nonprofit, for-profit, and government. Similarly, there are thriving public, nonprofit, and for-profit colleges and universities in the US. Clearly there is a private market for hospitals and colleges—there is demand and there is supply. So why are governments and nonprofits also in the business of running hospitals and colleges? Are they filling in where the market fails? Are they providing collective goods?

Roger Lohmann (1989)[12] launched the first major critique of economic theories explaining the creation of nonprofit organizations. Lohmann argued that economic theories misclassify all nonprofits as enterprises, arguing that a large portion of voluntary organization and activity does not function like an enterprise. For example, consider churches, synagogues, mosques, and other religious establishments—they are voluntary in nature and do not operate as enterprises. Moreover, Lohmann objects to economic models because they portray nonprofits as having no independent basis of their own for forming, but rather emerging into the market place only to fill gaps left by other sectors—emerging in response to a failure of private, for-profit organizations or government failure. Certainly, we can think of examples of nonprofit organizations that arise because a group of individuals comes together for some shared purpose, not simply in response to market forces.

Economic theories provide a limited perspective because they fail to account for the fact that many nonprofits arise out of the ideas and initiative of committed individuals or small groups of citizens. Finally, Lohmann denounces economic theories because they "tell us more about what a nonprofit is not than what a voluntary action is" (p. 367).[13] In response to these criticisms, Lohmann proposed a new theory, the theory of the commons, which offers a more affirmative perspective of the nonprofit sector and will be examined more closely in the next section.

Non-Economic Theories

Several other theories help to explain the existence of the nonprofit sector. Unlike economic theories, which share a common set of assumptions about demand, supply, and exchange of goods and services, non-economic theories of the nonprofit sector tend to be multi-disciplinary, drawing from diverse perspectives within sociology, political science, and other disciplines. Several key non-economic theories will be explored in the next section, including the theory of the commons, mediating theory, pluralism, and collective action.[14] A summary of these theories, their features, and some examples is provided in Table 3.2.

Theory of the Commons

The **theory of the commons** was proposed by Lohmann (1992)[15] as a direct response to the perceived inadequacies of economic theories in explaining voluntary action. It is an affirmative theory, describing what the non-profit sector is and does, rather than what it is not. The theory of the commons suggests that nonprofits, whether legally incorporated or not, "are formed with *deliberate intent* to fulfill artistic, scientific, social, athletic, or religious purposes within a community space, or 'commons'" (p. 46).

The theory of the commons is premised upon eight key assumptions of **social action**: affluence, authenticity, continuity, rationality, near-universality, autonomy, intrinsic valuation, and ordinary language. Social action means that the commons do not exist in name only; action is purposeful and participants attach subjective meaning to it. The condition of affluence suggests that participants in the commons must have their basic needs met in order to contribute to, and advance the purposes of, the commons. Authenticity dictates that people who comprise a commons are who they say they are, that their motives are pure, and that they are there for the stated or common purpose and not for personal gain or some other ulterior motive. Continuity is another defining feature meaning that commons are characterized and sustained over time by distinct traditions, rituals, symbols, ceremonies, and the like. Rationality describes the logic and reasoning exercised by participants in adhering to the goals of the commons, making decisions, and solving daily problems that arise within the course of action.

Near-universality means that commons exist in all human cultures, in the form of "self-defining collectives of people who voluntarily associate and act jointly outside of markets and households and independent of the state" (Lohmann, 1992, p. 169). Autonomy assumes that participants have the ability to act independently, to display individual and group self-control, and they are there of their own free will and un-coerced decision. Intrinsic valuation is the assumption that the values of the commons arise from within and it is these values that motivate action rather than the individual conforming to some externally imposed expectations of action or behavior. Finally, commons rely on ordinary language, meaning that terms used to describe their forms and functions must be comprehensible to the average person.

As noted by the key assumptions, the commons are sustained by rules, routines, and generally accepted norms of behavior, along with assets of monetary and non-monetary resources, such as knowledge and commitment. According to Lohmann, the collective benefits or "goods" produced by and within commons are often intangible and cannot be quantified. Moreover, these collective benefits are not necessarily monetary or key to the markets outlined in economic theories. Playing on the economic theorists' notion of nonprofits as productive enterprises or "factories," Lohmann coined the term **"benefactories"** which he views as a more accurate way to describe nonprofit and voluntary organizations since the "goods" manufactured by nonprofit and voluntary organization are often intangible, but nonetheless important, benefits. Nonprofit and voluntary benefactories can either benefit organizational members (intrinsic) or benefit non-members (extrinsic), or both.

Mediating Theory

Berger and Neuhaus (1977)[16] propose the theory of nonprofits as **mediating structures**. Berger and Neuhaus (1977) argue that voluntary organizations exist as mediating structures that bridge the private lives of individuals with shared experiences of public life. Proponents of mediating theory suggest that citizens have become alienated from government and the large institutions of public life. As a remedy to this alienation, smaller, more personal institutions emerge to help to restore community by serving as intermediaries between individuals in their private lives and public life. Examples of nonprofits that function as mediating structures include churches, neighborhood groups, voluntary associations, and social service organizations.

Berger and Neuhaus note that mediating organizations both formal and informal, aim to serve those who are disempowered by the current social, economic, and political system and structure. They suggest that nonprofits serving as mediating structures exist to empower people, particularly the poor who have not been well served by traditional institutions of government in their view. They assert that "the paradigm of mediating structures aims at empowering poor people to do the things the more affluent can already do; it aims to spread the power around a bit more" (Berger and Neuhaus, 1977, p. 8). Mediating theory holds that ad hoc and random meetings of individuals are not sufficient to effectively connect the private lives of individuals to the larger public sphere. Instead, Berger and Neuhaus insist that in order for mediation to occur "it cannot be sporadic and occasional; it must be institutionalized in structures" (1977, p. 4) as in the types of nonprofits they identify. Thus, mediating theory argues that many nonprofit organizations emerge and formalize to mediate the relationships between disempowered individuals and the social, political, and economic world in which they exist—a mediation between individuals and civil society.

Pluralism and Collective Action Theories

While the theories we discussed earlier view nonprofits as forming in response to economic markets, pluralist theories see nonprofits as forming in response to governments. Specifically, **pluralist theory** views nonprofits as forming in order to foster a healthy democracy and to counteract government tyranny. Pluralist theory suggests that when governments alone make decisions about public resources, we run the risk of falling victims to government tyranny. Pluralists argue that multiple, competing groups contribute to a more robust democracy and ensure a fairer and more just distribution of public resources. Pluralists view nonprofits as competing interest groups vying for political influence, public resources, and greater expression of their values in the public arena. When there is adequate representation of various group interests in the political decision-making arena, groups can expect to get their way on some issues, some of the time, but not on all issues, all of the time. Pluralism dictates that nonprofits will form to ensure that multiple viewpoints can be represented and to ensure that government tyranny does not result. Box 3.1 provides an illustration of pluralist theory in action in Yellowstone National Park.

Collective action theory suggests that nonprofits arise based on group demand for organized action. Nonprofits emerge as organizational vehicles

---

BOX 3.1 PLURALIST THEORY IN ACTION—WOLF REINTRODUCTION IN YELLOWSTONE NATIONAL PARK

Wolves were reintroduced to Yellowstone National Park in 1995 after nearly 30 years of dispute and compromise to determine the best method for creating, implementing, and enforcing policies about their presence in the national park system. Wolf reintroduction was first discussed in the US Congress in 1966 when biologists suggested reintroducing wolves to deal with the critically high populations of elk and coyotes in Yellowstone, which had resulted in ecological damages. Biologists argued that wolves were important natural predators that could help to maintain healthy populations of elk and other wildlife in the Park. Ranchers who owned land near Yellowstone disputed the proposal arguing that wolves would kill important livestock in the area. Environmentalists wanted wolves to be declared endangered species and given special protection both inside and outside of the Park's borders. Other environmental groups argued that wolves were already in the Park and did not need reintroduction efforts

continued

but better protection. The government conducted a number of studies to determine the feasibility of reintroducing wolves to the Park. The states that house Yellowstone National Park, Montana, Idaho, and Wyoming, responding to their constituents, were against the reintroduction of wolves since they threatened the livelihood of local ranchers.

In 1974, a wolf recovery team was appointed by the federal government and in 1982 released the first official recovery plan for public comment. By 1985, surveys indicated that 74% of visitors to the Park thought wolves would improve the park, and 60% favored reintroducing wolves to the Park. In 1994, while the government worked to develop an environmental impact assessment and full plan for wolf recovery in the area, two lawsuits were filed by nonprofit organizations. The first by the Wyoming Farm Bureau and the second by the Idaho Conservation League and the Audubon Society. While both of these lawsuits were dismissed, they raised important concerns among a variety of communities—the first concerned with protecting ranching interests, the second concerned with protecting an endangered species that they argued was already living in the Park. The debate about wolf reintroduction and the protection efforts for wolves continued for nearly three decades, with multiple interests arguing for and against the plans proposed by the federal government, the National Park Service, and the US Fish and Wildlife Service. The dialogue between all of these actors, governmental, private, and nonprofit, represents the ways in which pluralist dialogue can bring multiple actors to the table and push policy away from the narrow interests of the government toward a negotiated plan where everyone gets something, but no one gets everything.

As of today, wolves are present in Yellowstone. They receive some environmental protections, but there are also robust plans for compensating ranchers who lose livestock to wolves. Tourism related to wolf observation is thriving (e.g. wolf-viewing outfitting). Vegetation such as aspen and willow trees that had been overgrazed by elk are now recovering and coyote populations are increasingly under control.

The Idaho, Montana, and Wyoming, state governments opposed the reintroduction of wolves into the Park. Ranchers and hunters also opposed the reintroduction efforts. But many environmentalist groups, tourism organizations, and wildlife groups supported the reintroduction. The federal government supported the reintroduction plan. In this case, had the states had their way, there would be no wolves in Yellowstone, though the public and many other actors supported the reintroduction. Here is an example of a pluralist solution to the problem of state control, where a variety of actors, federal, state, private, and nonprofit, came together to negotiate a solution, where the Park thrives, the public gets to observe wolves in their wild habitat, ranchers are compensated for their losses to wolves, and a pluralistic solution provides the most positive outcomes to the largest number of involved stakeholders.

for accomplishing what one person cannot do alone. Collective action theory portrays nonprofits as organizations arising to express group interests—members of a group share something in common such as values, beliefs, preferences, or goals. By uniting around these shared values, beliefs, preferences, or goals, individuals can form voluntary groups joining together to raise money and awareness related to their cause, and lobby for new programs or laws, or oppose changes to laws that conflict with the group's preferences. Some examples of modern-day collective action groups abound. Anytime a major event occurs and people organize to protest, mobilize, or act, we see collective action groups. For example, consider when Hurricane Sandy struck the coast of New York City and New Jersey in 2013. Immediately following the storm, groups organized to provide information to residents, organize donations, and distribute resources. As another example, consider the movement against bullying in American schools. After increased violence against teens, assaults, physical bullying, and increased incidents of cyber bullying, organizations such as the Bully Police USA,[17] an all-volunteer organization, began advocating for anti-bullying legislation. As a result of those efforts, in 1999 Georgia passed the first anti-bullying legislation and, as of 2013, 49 states have such legislation (all but Montana).

Collective action organizations rely on a strong base of like-minded persons to support their work. But because of this reliance on supporters who strongly support the goals of the group, collective action groups can suffer from the problem of "free riders". Free-ridership occurs when benefits generated by the organization are non-excludable, meaning that others (non-members, or the public in general) will receive the benefits of the organization's efforts even if they did not directly contribute to it. For example, when Bully Police USA advocates for anti-bullying legislation, although a small group of individuals may have financially supported that effort and volunteered their time and efforts, all residents of the state will benefit from the resulting legislation. In another example, relatively few people outside of those affected by a drunk driving accident would choose to give money to Mothers Against Drunk Driving (MADD). Yet the social benefits produced by this group (stricter drunk driving laws and greater enforcement) cannot be confined to only those who pay to support the cause; everyone in society benefits from having fewer drunk drivers on the road. Due of the potential for free ridership, collective action organizations

TABLE 3.2 Why Do We Need a Nonprofit Sector? Non-Economic Theories

Theory	Features	Role of Nonprofits	Types
Theory of the commons	Developed as a response to economic theories of nonprofits; views such theories as inadequate.	Nonprofits are formed with deliberate intent and are engaged in purposeful social action.	Most nonprofits
	Describes what the nonprofit, voluntary sector is and does, rather than what it is not.	Nonprofits do not exist primarily as a response to negative forces or gaps created in other sectors.	
Mediating theory	Recognizes an unprecedented dichotomy between public life and private life today.	Nonprofits serve as mediating structures, providing a remedy to alienation in society.	National Public Radio
	Views citizens as alienated from the megastructures of public life.	Four categories: churches, neighborhood groups, voluntary associations, and social service organizations.	Greater New Orleans Disaster Recovery Partnership
			Settlement Music School of Philadelphia
Pluralist theory	Nonprofits form to foster a healthy democracy and counteract tyranny.	Competition among nonprofits creates a pluralism of interest groups vying for political influence and public resources.	National Rifle Association (NRA)
	Recognizes the need for multiple competing groups to help ensure a fair and just distribution of public resources.		Mothers against Gun Violence
			Pro Gun Coalition to Stop Gun Violence
Collective action theory	Nonprofits arise based on group demand for organized action.	Nonprofits emerge as organizational vehicles for what one person cannot do alone: raise money and awareness, lobby for new programs, or change existing laws.	Occupy Wall Street
	Group members share common values, beliefs or goals.		Greenpeace
			National Pro–Life Alliance

can only survive by maintaining a core group of committed individuals who are willing to pay to support the cause with their time and money.

Table 3.2 summarizes the non-economic theories for explaining the presence of the nonprofit sector in the US. Specifically, Table 3.2 outlines the theory of the commons, mediating theory, pluralist theory, and collective action theory, noting their primary features, the ways in which each theory views the role of nonprofits, and some examples of the types of nonprofits that are described by the theory.

Summary

As this chapter has demonstrated, theories of the nonprofit sector are diverse and arise from a wide variety of disciplinary perspectives, including economics, sociology, and political science. This chapter conveys that no single theory can adequately explain the existence of the nonprofit sector. Certain theories may be better suited to describing specific types or classes of nonprofits. Moreover, it is sometimes the case that the existence of any given nonprofit organization may be logically explained by multiple theories. For example, economic theories may best explain the existence of nonprofits that produce and deliver tangible services that can be bought and sold in the marketplace (such as healthcare organizations), while pluralist theory and collective action theory may best explain nonprofit lobbying and advocacy groups.

Moreover, economic theories of the nonprofit sector suggest several different ways of understanding the relationship between government and private, not-for-profit organizations. In particular, different strands of theory support the alternative views that nonprofits (a) operate independently as supplements to government, (b) work as complements to government in a partnership relationship, or (c) are engaged in an adversarial relationship of mutual accountability with government.[18] In sum, theories of the nonprofit sector are relatively new and remain open to interpretation and revision as the field continues to change and evolve. It is likely that new theories related to the nonprofit sector will be developed in the future as the sector continues to expand in both size and scope and takes on new roles and functions in society.

KEY TERMS

- Benefactories
- Collective action theory
- Collective goods
- Externalities

- Government-nonprofit partnership theory
- Information asymmetries
- Mediating structures

- Pluralist theory
- Social action
- Theory of the commons

DISCUSSION QUESTIONS

1. Identify a nonprofit organization that is currently in the news. It must be large enough to have a website and Facebook page. (Many smaller organizations do not.)

   a Based on information found on the organization's website and Facebook page, write down all the reasons that the organization says communicates about why it exists. Look for explanations that are indirect as well as direct.

   b Now review the nonprofit theory charts in Chapter 3. Select the theory that best explains the existence of the nonprofit. What theory most closely matches the organization's message about why it exists? Write a paragraph that explains why this theory is a better match than the others.

2. Based on the knowledge you have gained about other theories of nonprofits, can you think of additional explanations for the organization's existence that may not be communicated to the public? If so, what are they and what is the basis of your argument?

ACTIVITY

Below is a list of five nonprofit organizations (you might need to do a little bit of research to learn more about these organizations). Look at this list and identify a theoretical explanation that might best explain the existence of each organization and the implications for work in that organization. What theoretical lens best explains the existence of each nonprofit organization, and why?

continued

1. **Greenpeace**[19]

    Mission: Greenpeace is the leading independent campaigning organization that uses peaceful protest and creative communication to expose global environmental problems and to promote solutions that are essential to a green and peaceful future.

    About: A group of thoughtful, committed citizens came together in 1971 to create Greenpeace. A handful of determined activists leased a small fishing vessel, called the *Phyllis Cormack*, and set sail from Vancouver for Amchitka Island in Alaska. Their mission was to protest US nuclear testing off the coast of Alaska with a brave act of defiance: to place themselves in harm's way. Despite being intercepted by the US Coast Guard, these daring activists sailed into history by bringing worldwide attention to the dangers of nuclear testing.

2. **American Red Cross**[20]

    Mission: The American Red Cross prevents and alleviates human suffering in the face of emergencies by mobilizing the power of volunteers and the generosity of donors.

    About: The American Red Cross exists to provide compassionate care to those in need. The network of generous donors, volunteers, and employees shares a mission of preventing and relieving suffering, at home and around the world, through five key service areas: (1) Disaster Relief, (2) Supporting America's Military Families, (3) Lifesaving Blood, (4) Health and Safety Services, and (5) International Services.

    History: Clara Barton and a circle of her acquaintances founded the American Red Cross in Washington, DC on May 21, 1881. The Red Cross received its first congressional charter in 1900 and a second in 1905, the year after Barton resigned from the organization.

3. **Boy Scouts of America**[21]

    About: The Boy Scouts of America is one of the nation's largest and most prominent values-based youth development organizations. The BSA provides a program for young people that builds character, trains them in the responsibilities of participating citizenship, and develops personal fitness. For over a century, the BSA has helped build the future leaders of this country by combining educational activities and lifelong values with fun. The Boy Scouts of America believes— and, through over a century of experience, knows—that helping youth is a key to building a more conscientious, responsible, and productive society.

continued

4. **Los Angeles Mission: The Crossroads of Hope**[22]

    Mission: Providing help, hope, and opportunity to men, women, and children in need.

    About: Founded in 1936, the Los Angeles Mission is a non-profit, privately supported, faith-based organization that serves the immediate and long-term needs of homeless and disadvantaged men, women, and children. The Mission is among the nation's largest service providers to the homeless.

5. **Carnegie Endowment for International Peace**[23]

    About: The Carnegie Endowment for International Peace is the oldest international affairs think tank in the United States. Founded in 1910, it is known for excellence in scholarship, responsiveness to changing global circumstances, and a commitment to concrete improvements in public policy. The *Endowment* conducts programs of research, discussion, publication, and education in international affairs and US foreign policy.

Additional Reading

Young, D. 2000. Alternative Models of Government-Nonprofit Sector Relations: Theoretical and International Perspectives. *Nonprofit and Voluntary Sector Quarterly* 29(1): 149–172.

Samuelson, Paul A. 1954. The Pure Theory of Public Expenditure. *Review of Economics and Statistics* 36(4): 387–389.

Samuelson, Paul A. 1955. Diagrammatic Exposition of a Theory of Public Expenditure. *Review of Economics and Statistics* 37(4): 350–356.

Notes

1 About Habitat for Humanity. Accessed May 24, 2013 at http://www.habitat.org/how/about_us.aspx

2 Habitat for Humanity, Who we are. Accessed May 24, 2013 at http://www.habitat.org/how/about_us.aspx

3 Ott, J. Steven (ed.). 2001. *The Nature of the Nonprofit Sector*. Boulder, CO: Westview Press.

4 Salamon, Lester M. 1995. Partners in Public Service: Government-Nonprofit Relations in the Modern Welfare State. Baltimore: John Hopkins University Press.

5 Hansmann, Henry. 1980. The Role of Nonprofit Enterprise. *Yale Law Journal*, 89: 835–901.

6 Weisbrod, Burton A. 1988. *The Nonprofit Economy*. Boston, MA: Harvard University Press.

7   Miles of Murals: A Rogers Park Project. Accessed May 24, 2013 at http://mileof murals.com/home.html

8   http://rogerspark.com/rp/news_articles/view/tour_rogers_parks_mile_of_murals_-_ sunday/ Accessed May 24, 2013

9   Weisbrod, Burton A. 1975. Toward a Theory of the Voluntary Non-Profit Sector in a Three-Sector Economy, in Edmund S. Phelps (ed.), *Altruism, Morality, and Economic Theory*. New York: Russell Sage Foundation.

10 Salamon (1995).

11 For more reading on this point, see Young, Dennis (2001) Government failure theory, Chapter 16 in Steven J. Ott, *The Nature of the Nonprofit Sector*.

12 Lohmann, Roger. 1989. And Lettuce is Non-Animal: Toward a Positive Economics of Voluntary Action. *Nonprofit and Voluntary Sector Quarterly*, 18(4): 367–383.

13 Lohmann (1989).

14 This chapter does not provide exhaustive coverage of all non-economic nonprofit theoretical perspectives, but rather covers the key non-economic theories most widely accepted within the field of nonprofit studies.

15 Lohmann, Roger A. 1992. A New Approach: The Theory of the Commons, in Roger A. Lohmann, *The Commons: New Perspectives on Nonprofit Organizations and Voluntary Action*. San Francisco: Jossey-Bass, pp. 46–82.

16 Berger, P. L. and R. J. Neuhaus. 1977. *To Empower People: The Role of Mediating Structures in Public Policy*. Washington, DC: American Enterprise Institute for Public Policy Research.

17 http://www.bullypolice.org/ Accessed June 10, 2013.

18 Young, Dennis. 2000. Alternative Models of Government-Nonprofit Sector Relations: Theoretical and International Perspectives. *Nonprofit and Voluntary Sector Quarterly*, 29(1): 149–172.

19 http://www.greenpeace.org/usa/en/ Accessed April 19, 2012.

20 http://www.redcross.org/ Accessed April 22, 2012.

21 http://www.scouting.org/ Accessed May 24, 2013.

22 http://losangelesmission.org/ Accessed June 12, 2013

23 carnegieendowment.org/ Accessed June 13, 2013.

SECTION II
THE NONPROFIT SECTOR IN CIVIL SOCIETY

4

NONPROFITS AND COMMUNITY-BUILDING

CHAPTER LEARNING OBJECTIVES

By the end of this chapter, students will be able to:

1. Explain how nonprofit and civil society organizations contribute to the social fabric of America
2. Define social capital and discuss its importance in building communities
3. Understand how different types of nonprofit organizations contribute to civil society
4. Understand how federated structures of nonprofit organizations have affected community building
5. Discuss the role of technology in civil society and online community-building
6. Provide examples of the "dark side" of civil society and associations in the US and elsewhere

---

Introduction

In the previous chapter we saw that nonprofit and civil society organizations often build communities by supplementing or substituting the goods and services provided by the government and for-profit sectors. But some of

CEASEFIRE

Violence is endemic in American society. Gang violence is spreading. Do these phrases sound familiar to you? Notice how they compare violence to the spread of diseases? Gary Slutkin, an epidemiologist and physician who worked on infectious diseases in Africa, noticed the same thing. He also noticed that violence in many communities mimics infectious diseases, like AIDS or malaria, spreading from individual to individual, within families, households, and communities. Slutkin suspected that maybe we could treat violence the same way we treat infectious diseases[1]—addressing the problem at its source, before it spreads. He put this to the test with the creation of the CeaseFire program in Chicago in 1995. CeaseFire treats violence at the source, where the community is most infected and where action, intervention, and treatment may be most effective at preventing its spread.[2]

With support from government grants and foundations, CeaseFire employs community members, outreach workers, and, most importantly, former gang-members who work as "Interrupters." The job of the interrupter is to stop violence before it starts or before it spreads. Interrupters rely heavily on their connections in the community, their street credibility, to convince individuals engaged in a violent outbreak to stop the violence, to not seek revenge, to break the pattern. Because gang members are more likely to trust former gang members than the police, social workers, pastors, and other outreach specialists, they are better equipped to interrupt (and hopefully stop) violence at its start. Interrupters use their connections in the community (networks and social capital) to detect and interrupt planned violent activity, change the behavior of high-risk individuals (often through mentoring), and change the community norms (shape civil society). Over the years, programs like CeaseFire have effectively stopped individual instances of violence, but also transformed the communities where they work—developing networks of individuals who are called to action when violence breaks out.

CeaseFire was started with the support of federal and state grants. Based on its initial success, the program was refunded with support from state grants and local foundations

continued

and corporations (2005–2007) and from 2007–2012 it was funded with a grant from The Robert Wood Johnson Foundation.[3,4] Formal evaluations of the CeaseFire program have found that it has successfully reduced violent crime in a number of Chicago neighborhoods and reduced shootings and killings.[5,6,7] In addition to the immediate result of reducing violent crime, CeaseFire has played an important role in helping to build personal connections and norms of trust in these neighborhoods. The model relies on former gang members ("interrupters") from the same neighborhoods to establish relationships with gang members who are still immersed in a network that promotes violence. The interrupters build trust with gang members, enabling them to build new social ties outside of the gang and create a bridge for them to exit. Interrupters help to foster positive social connections, and create hope for individuals who may feel like they are caught in an inescapable lifestyle. In short, CeaseFire is helping to build social capital in these neighborhoods.

Relying on former gang members and other community activists to interrupt violent crime activities requires extensive coordination among community members and the interrupters. Additionally, individuals working with CeaseFire receive extensive training, support, and intervention from experts in criminology, social work, psychology, epidemiology, and others areas of study. The partnership between local universities, area hospitals, community members, and CeaseFire employees has enabled the development of networks and partnerships throughout Chicago that extend beyond the original program mission. Moreover, CeaseFire activities help to bring together the neighborhoods where they work, connecting residents to resources and enabling better, more effective responses after violent crime incidents. For example, many interrupters provide emotional and sometimes financial support to families coping with violent crime. In addition to mediating individual crime incidents, interrupters organize community-mobilizing activities including marches, vigils, and funerals.

Today the organization is known as CureViolence. It has branches in Baltimore, London, New York, and South Africa. You can learn more about the program at www. cureviolence.org. The film, *The Interrupters*, which premiered at the 2011 Sundance film festival and was broadcast on PBS Frontline in 2012, follows three interrupters in Chicago—Ameena Matthews,[8] Cobe Williams,[9] and Eddie Bocanegra[10]—and is available for streaming at the PBS Frontline website[11] and on Netflix.

the "goods" that nonprofit organizations provide are intangible. Some types of nonprofits mainly produce social "goods" that we cannot see, but we can feel or experience in ways that simply make life more enjoyable. A neighborhood association, for example, may not provide any direct services to its residents, but thanks to a civic-minded resident volunteering to maintain an online forum, residents can share news, events, and advice, find a babysitter or new tennis partner, and engage in discussions over mayoral candidates and other issues that affect the community. The neighborhood association might also hold meetings throughout the year and social events such as an annual block party so neighbors can interact. Examples of the types of **social goods** created by these kinds of nonprofit organizations are trust, social cohesion, tolerance, fellowship, solidarity, and reciprocity (the willingness to do things for others based on the view that you might someday need them to return the favor). In this chapter, we discuss the ways nonprofit organizations create intangible social goods, which help to support and define our social structure and enhance civil society. Specifically, we explore how nonprofit and civil society organizations contribute to the social fabric of America and examine the relationship between nonprofit organizations and civil society.

Upon initial consideration, the contributions of nonprofit organizations to civil society may seem straightforward. A non-profit organization like CeaseFire reduces violence. A nonprofit pre-school provides childcare for working parents and facilitates early childhood development. A regional food bank aggregates surplus food and redistributes it to local food pantries. An environmental advocacy organization educates the public about climate change and encourages individuals to contact their elected officials. Each organization works in its own way to improve the quality of life in the community it serves. Why not simply aggregate the measurable impact of every nonprofit in a community and say that a community has been "built"? Assessing the aggregate impact of childcare and senior centers, food pantries, hospitals, schools, mental health clinics, recreation programs, affordable housing development corporations, the local civic orchestra, workforce development agencies, and much more, is a good place to begin. These organizations provide services, distribute resources, and offer measurable goods to communities including housing, food, job training, and activities. At the same time, other less tangible but equally important dimensions of community-building are taking place, including feelings of safety and security, increased diversity and tolerance, and a sense of belonging.

In the discussion that follows, we look beyond the direct provision of goods and services to understand the community-building role of nonprofits. First, we identify the inter-relationships of civil society and nonprofit and voluntary organizations, starting from the premise that civil society is the broader social and legal structure that makes it possible for nonprofit organizations to exist. Second, we introduce the concept of social capital and investigate how civil society and social capital relate to one another, nonprofit organizations, and voluntary action. Third, we examine some traditional voluntary associations, civic groups, churches, and service organizations as examples of how these local organizations create common spaces for individuals and communities to organize and strengthen civil society. Fourth, we discuss how many community-based nonprofits are organized through a federation and how this structure affects community-building. Finally, we discuss how digital technology may be changing the relationships between community-based organizations, nonprofit associations, and civil society, including some potential negative impacts upon civil society.

Understanding the Relationship between Civil Society and Nonprofit Organizations

In Chapter 1, we defined civil society as "the macro-level institutional structure of laws, norms, and customs that give rise to the organizations and associations that citizens create (outside of government and the market)."[12] Civil society provides the social and legal structure that makes it possible for nonprofit organizations to exist. At the same time, nonprofit organizations help to foster the norms of tolerance, belonging, equality, altruism, and so on that make our society a better place. But what is it about civil society that makes the creation and growth of nonprofits possible? As we have suggested earlier, civil society is a broad concept, encompassing the inter-related elements of formal structures of society (rules and laws) and the informal parts of society (collective beliefs, cultural norms and values) that give rise to shared ideas, action, and organization created by citizens.

In Chapter 1, we defined the core components of civil society as institutions, ideas and action, and organizations (formal and informal). These three elements are inter-related, and the inter-play between these components creates, sustains, and furthers civil society. At this point, we will flesh out these components, drawing upon Sievers'[13] description of civil society as a "constellation" including philanthropy, rule of law, the common good, nonprofit and voluntary institutions, individual rights, free expression, and tolerance.

Institutions

Douglas North defines **institutions** as "regularities in actions . . . customs and rules that provide a set of incentives and disincentives for individuals" (p. 231).[14] Civil society depends heavily on customs and laws, and indeed legal rules such as tax deductions for charitable giving create incentives for individual action that supports civil society. According to Sievers, the **rule of law**—which he defines as "a body of rules providing an accepted framework for the resolution of disputes and the pursuit of common social aims"[15]—is a foundational pillar of civil society. The rule of law makes the creation of nonprofit organizations possible and promotes a healthier democracy. The rule of law protects an individual's right to organize and create associations and organizations. Without the rule of law, society would be in chaos. Thus, the rule of law creates the conditions for civil society, allowing individuals to freely act and to organize.

Norms are another facet of the institutional structure supporting civil society. Normative traditions, or **norms**, provide guidance about what is good or bad, right or wrong, and what should be done or not done. While norms can vary by cultural context, many basic ideas and beliefs about the **"common good,"** or collective interest of society, transcend national boundaries. Norms are indicative of civil society across cultures and countries, uniting members of a group and helping to guide, control, and regulate acceptable behavior. Norms greatly influence our thinking and behavior, bounding the behavior of our society and groups and individuals within civil society.

Tolerance is a social norm, and a key indicator of civil society.[16] Tolerance supports diversity of beliefs and cultures. Nonprofit organizations are often established to advance the rights or interests of a minority group of individuals, serving the needs of groups that might be marginalized by mainstream society and formal private and government institutions. Consider the work of organizations such as the Arab Community Center for Economic and Social Services (ACCESS), in helping to educate the public about the Arab culture, and working to increase tolerance of a population of Americans that are routinely victims of racial profiling and hate crimes in the post-9/11 era. In addition to providing more than 90 programs and services to low-income citizens of all races and ethnicities, ACCESS serves as the host site for the Arab American National Museum, and has been a key player in facilitating dialogues at both the national and community level that aim to foster cultural understanding and increased tolerance.

Similarly, AIDS organizations in the 1980s and 90s worked to educate the public about HIV and AIDS, shifting public perceptions of the illness from a stigmatized disease to a mainstream public health problem. Today, organizations supporting marriage equality for the LGBTQ community are working to pass legislation and raise awareness of their concerns, while at the same time working to promote tolerance. These examples help us to see the important ways that nonprofit organizations can work to advance the interests of a specific group and increase tolerance to promote a more civil society.

Individual rights and free expression, two important norms in the US, are an institutional component of American civil society and are normative values[17] that are deeply held and widely shared by Americans. Free expression is an important value as noted in the First Amendment of the US Bill of Rights, which promises the Freedom of Speech, Press, Religion, and Petition. Individual rights ensure that citizens are protected by the rule of law and free to pursue individual goals for individual purposes, including organizing to form advocacy groups or nonprofit organizations to pursue a collective agenda. According to Sievers,[18] civil society enables the articulation of individual interests and individual rights protect members of civil society from the state. Some of these norms are codified in the US Constitution and Bill of Rights, others are formalized through legislation and legal rulings (for example Roe vs. Wade, the Civil Rights Act of 1964, Equal Employment Opportunity Act 1972), while others are informal and held as cultural norms. A healthy civil society protects individual rights, while also advancing the common good, making civil society a complex arrangement that seeks to balance a variety of norms and values. The norms, values, ideas, and beliefs that promote civil society are numerous, including (but not limited to) charity, philanthropy, trust and trustworthiness, reciprocity, solidarity, diversity, in addition to those we have discussed in detail in this section.

Ideas, Action, and Organizations

Nonprofit organizations and citizen-driven, organized action serve to bring together the many norms and values of civil society and enable the collective pursuit of goals that advance free expression, individual rights, and tolerance, along with other norms and values within the rule of law. When individuals seek to express their preferences, practice their faith, organize to advance a common cause, or convene to share their cultural heritage, they often do so within the structure of nonprofit and civil society organizations. Associations and voluntary organizations offer the structure within which individuals can unite to contribute to civil society. Individuals may associate or organize to celebrate their commonalities or to advance the interests of their collective identity—consider organizations for the protection and advancement of cultural interests, such as the Chinese Cultural Association, Alpha Kappa Alpha (the African American sorority), the Puerto Rican Cultural Association, or any number of similar organizations. Nonprofit organizations become the vehicles by which cultural values and norms are fostered in civil society.

Nonprofit organizations are a critical element of civil society, providing the organizational infrastructure that helps bond citizens together around beliefs, ideas, causes, conditions, and experiences. Nonprofit organizations are the vehicles by which philanthropy, the rule of law, and normative traditions work in concert to unite citizens who share interests to pursue a common good. Examples are everywhere in our communities, including the Red Cross responding to disasters, Roman Catholic schools serving the educational interests of Catholic families, senior citizen centers caring for the elderly, and animal rescue organizations protecting vulnerable creatures who cannot defend themselves.

At the same time, citizens who join together in pursuit of collective goals or beliefs do not always create formal organizations to pursue their shared interests. In many instances, the common ideas that unite individuals simply lead to voluntary action, sometimes on a massive scale, other times on a small scale. On the large scale, consider, for example, the Occupy Movement. The Occupy Movement, which we shall examine in detail in Chapter 8, was an international protest movement that united citizens to collective action around the shared belief that society's wealth should be more evenly distributed. Local groups throughout the world (more than 95 cities and 82 countries) established camps similar to the ones in New

York City and protested local concerns such as the power of corporations, the global financial system, and income inequality.[19] Despite the Occupy Movement's large scale of organized action by citizens with common values and beliefs, there was no formal organization binding the Occupy participants together or structuring their actions. Indeed, a hallmark of the Occupy Movement was its anti-establishment nature. Each local group had the discretion to determine their own actions, rather than having an agenda dictated to them from higher up the hierarchy, which is the typical approach with formal organizations, including many large nonprofits.

On the opposite end of the spectrum, the MowerGang in Detroit is an example of one of the thousands of citizen-initiated actions that occur on a small scale, or at the community level. The MowerGang is not a formal organization, but rather a group of local volunteers that take turns going to local unkempt playgrounds and ball fields in Detroit to clean them up, with the hopes of providing open spaces for children to play (see Chapter 8 for more discussion of the MowerGang). While many citizen-initiated associations result in the creation of a formal nonprofit organization, it is important to emphasize that many other instances of citizens' shared beliefs or mutual interests lead to action that occurs outside the scope of a formal organization, the Occupy Movement and MowerGang simply being two examples. In short, civil society is a broad space that accommodates a wide range of ideas, citizen actions (large and small scale), and organizations (formal and informal) outside of the market and government. Nonprofit organizations are one example of the ways in which citizens can formally organize and move to action.

Social Capital, Civil Society, and Nonprofits

Nonprofit organizations contribute to civil society in many tangible ways, providing goods and services, bringing about political change (at least some of them), employing thousands of people, and redistributing resources through charitable donations and acts. As discussed earlier, nonprofits also play an important role in advancing the common good, tolerance, and other normative values in society. Moreover, participation in nonprofit and voluntary organizations and associations helps to give people a "sense of belonging." Nonprofits are an important component of community building as they bring people together, connecting them in new ways and generating combined resources that are more powerful than individuals working separately. **Social capital** is one of the intangible dimensions of nonprofit organizations that builds and strengthens civil society. Social capital refers to the collective benefits (economic, emotional, and psychological) derived from the social connections between individuals or groups.

The term social capital shares some similarities with financial capital. Just as we have money and resources that we can accumulate, invest, or spend, we also have social capital (friendships, business partnerships, group memberships) that bring resources to us and can be spent or used to advance our interests. The same way that we can accumulate and spend financial capital, we can invest in relationships, accumulate social connections, and use those connections to our advantage. Individual social capital can be combined in organizations and associations to the greater advantage of the group or community. When social capital is absent or exists at low levels, communities often suffer because individuals have a lack of social resources and connections to call upon and people may experience feelings of isolation and alienation.

Consider the example of CeaseFire highlighted at the start of this chapter. Social capital is present in the communities served by CeaseFire, resting in the organizations and individuals that live and work in these neighborhoods. When CeaseFire began its work, seeking to interrupt the chain of violence, they brought together a variety of individuals with distinct sets of social capital and social networks—including social workers, teachers, community leaders, pastors, and expert public health researchers. Each of these individuals was interested in reducing violence in the community, but one of the key features making CeaseFire different from previous programs is that they also incorporate community members who have strong ties to gang members in these neighborhoods. These "interrupters" bring an important social capital element to the situation —they have personal connections within the communities, making them indispensable to the process of violence intervention. Additionally, by working together, CeaseFire pools individual resources and connections and draws on new resources: for example, the rising expectations from community members that CeaseFire and the interrupters will be available to help when violent situations emerge. CeaseFire is able to provide far greater resources and more effective services as a community organization that draws on the social capital of many than they would as individuals acting alone.

The impact of nonprofit organizations on communities goes beyond the sum of products and services provided. These organizations, both formal and informal, form the "social fabric" of civil society. Countless social networks exist among, across, and within these various organizations. While a person might join a book club to read interesting novels, they might become connected to individuals who know hundreds of different people. In sociological terms, these networks facilitate social capital, or the "connections among individuals in social networks and the norms of reciprocity and trustworthiness that arise from them."[20] Individuals who belong to a variety of voluntary associations will have more access to new networks and more social capital than those individuals who only belong to one organization. And individuals who give of their own time and resources to these organizations will be investing their social capital in these organizations, with the likely result of more social capital accruing to them.

While the term social capital was first used in the early 20th century[21] it was popularized by Robert Putnam (2000) in the best-selling book *Bowling Alone: The Collapse and Revival of American Community*. In his book, Putnam argued that the end of the 20th century was bringing a decline of social capital in the US. He used compelling data and anecdotal evidence to show that Americans' participation in civic associations and community groups, volunteering, and church attendance, which promotes community-building, had declined dramatically from the 1960s to 2000. Putnam blamed the decline in civic activities in the US on technology, longer work hours, dual wage-earning households, and political disenchantment.

A number of critics have objected to Putnam's assessment of the decline of American social capital and communities, noting that technology has changed the ways in which many Americans engage, but it has not necessarily decreased civic engagement.[22] Some have observed that the Internet *adds* to social capital, rather than transforming or diminishing it.[23] Others note that while the entry of women to the workforce had changed the ways in which middle class Americans engaged in civil society (no longer women at home organizing neighborhood meetings, while their husbands visited the local Elks or Moose club), these changes do not undermine civil society. Rather, the women's movement increased the professionalization of women's organizations, enabling women to run nonprofits as full-time careers, not just after-school activities. Moreover, the shifting role of women has meant more equality in civil society and an increase in the voice and contribution of women to such organizations.

Others have argued that civic activity is not declining in the US, but just taking different forms.[24] For example, though Americans are registering for fewer bowling leagues, they are more active in soccer leagues and a variety of online forms of organizing. Critics note that Putnam ignored other important forms of social capital, when lamenting the decline of bowling leagues, and that he romanticized the social capital and civic culture of the 1950s.[25] Specifically, the argument has been made that Putnam failed to acknowledge the faults of the civil society in the 1950s (e.g. less equality and more segregation and sexism), ignoring interpersonal networks and new forms of civic activities (e.g. the Internet).[26]

While Putnam's assessment of social capital at the turn of the century may not have been entirely on the mark, it is important to note the critical role that social capital plays in civil society, then and today. Each generation has its own preferred forms of making social connections, and many people today associate extensively through online mediums such as social networking sites, as well as participate in community activities in person, whether they be church, sports clubs, political groups, or parent meet-ups. Despite the virtues of the Internet for making connections quickly to large numbers of people, our personal connections may still yield a better return on social capital investment. For example, a university student learns about scholarship programs through other students in her study group. Your former professor e-mails information about a job opportunity that could jumpstart your career. A church member recommends an assisted living facility to another family during coffee hour on Sunday. Norms of reciprocity are another important component of social capital. Reciprocity refers to the ways in which people respond to one another, both positively and negatively. If your neighbor offers to take in your mail when you go on vacation, you can reasonably expect to take in his mail when he goes away. Social capital is also channeled through collective action and the formation of broader identities and solidarity. Each of these mechanisms for the development and exchange of social capital serve to build and strengthen civil society. Nonprofit organizations and associations are an important vehicle for such exchanges, serving as a venue for bringing together individuals with shared interests, values, and goals.

The Importance of Social Capital for Community-Building

Nonprofit organizations and associations play an important role in connecting individuals and groups in civil society, and produce intangible social goods such as happiness, social cohesion, and a sense of belonging and purpose. Social capital is a by-product of nonprofit organizations that, when created through networking and building strong interpersonal relationships within the organization and its community, strengthens and reinforces the interpersonal ties and sense of purpose that hold the organization together. Fostering social capital is one of the most important ways that nonprofit and voluntary organizations contribute to communities. According to Schneider (2009), nonprofits fulfill this role in three ways: serving as places where preexisting social capital can be brought together, serving as places where social capital can be built, and enabling local social capital to scale up and result in representation at a larger level (national or international).[27]

Of course, nonprofit organizations do not have a monopoly on social capital; social connections and human bonds that strengthen them are built through a variety of societal institutions and contexts, including some government and for-profit organizations and workplaces. However, nonprofits serve as vehicles for uniting preexisting social capital.[28] Nonprofits are an organizational mechanism for bringing together individuals who have *some* social capital, in order to combine that into a larger force, united for a single purpose. For example, consider the Women's Ordination Conference (WOC), which was founded in 1973 from a group of Roman Catholic women who felt called to the priesthood. The WOC works for women's ordination as priests and bishops in the Roman Catholic Church.[29] Another example is the *September 11th Families' Association*, which was formed to "unite the 9/11 community, present evolving issues, and share resources for long-term recovery."[30] Nonprofits enable individuals to bring together resources where they can be shared and built upon, making the group more powerful than the individuals. For example, the National Resource Defense Council (NRDC) is an advocacy organization made up of attorneys dedicated to promoting enforcement of environmental laws. The organization was founded in the 1970s to bring together group resources where individual efforts would not have been as effective. These organizations were both formed by community residents who sought to pool their social capital (resources, networks, and connections) to advance their shared interest. In each case, a social network already existed when the nonprofit was launched. The social capital within these networks became a resource for serving an expanded circle of people.

Technology has redefined the meaning of community, and nonprofit organizations not only play an instrumental role in building social capital in the traditional sense of community—defined by geographic space—but they also create social capital within virtual communities. Thanks to the Internet, members of various groups are able to interact much more frequently through online organizing forums. Technology has been instrumental in strengthening the ties among members of groups, allowing for more frequent communication as well as the ability for members of groups to connect with others, far beyond the borders of their physical location. For example, leaders of child welfare organizations throughout the nation can convene online for a policy strategy discussion through webinars hosted by the Alliance for Children and Families, or members of the city management profession can seek advice from colleagues through online platforms made available by the International City/County Management Association. In other instances, technology has enabled small grassroots efforts to scale up into global organizations. Below, Box 4.1 provides an example of scaling up with technology, detailing a story of an organization that has relied on technology to spread its message, increase its membership, and build social capital among men around the world.

Voluntary Associations and Local Civic Groups

Much of the nonprofit organizing and activities that take place in American society occur at the local level through voluntary associations, local civic groups, political parties, neighborhood associations, churches, sport and social clubs, Parent Teacher Associations, and other community-based organizations. **Voluntary associations**, defined as groups of individuals who enter into an agreement to form an organization to accomplish some purpose (e.g. unions, trade associations, professional associations), serve an important role in civil society. They enable collective action, protect individual rights, and enable collective negotiation. Nonprofit organizations that serve local communities and group interests are a vital part of civil society, serve a variety of purposes, and come in all shapes and forms including church-based, community-based, and neighborhood-based organizations.

BOX 4.1 THE ROLE OF TECHNOLOGY IN BUILDING SOCIAL CAPITAL, LOCALLY AND GLOBALLY

This is a tale of how a $147 million global charity movement began when a couple of guys in Melbourne, Australia, after drinking a few too many beers on a night in 2003, dared each other to grow moustaches. It is also a tale of how the Internet, combined with the persistence of the organization's founder, enabled a crazy idea for a local fundraiser to evolve into a successful worldwide charity movement.

For Movember, the Qantas Wallabies unveil a Boeing 737–800 aircraft with a giant moustache to raise awareness of prostate cancer and men's mental health

Adam Garone, the charity's founder, describes the night the idea hatched, all in good fun. He and his friends were out at a bar and jokingly schemed of ways to "bring back the moustache." Deciding that perhaps "bringing back the moustache" should have some greater purpose, Garone thought of all the charity efforts focused on breast cancer and realized that there was a lack of initiatives related to men's health. He and his friends decided they would begin the month of November clean-shaven and commit to "grow a mo" (slang for moustache) during the month, at which time they would accept pledges and raise awareness of men's health issues. Thus began the global movement known as Movember.

According to the organization's website: "Movember's vision is to have an everlasting impact on the face of men's health. During November each year, Movember is responsible

continued

for the sprouting of millions of moustaches on men's faces around the world. Through the power of the Mo, vital funds and awareness are raised to combat prostate and testicular cancer and mental health challenges."[31]

Thanks to the Internet, men all over the world now participate in Movember. Those who wish to participate are asked to register on the organization's website Movember.com and then grow a moustache for the 30 days of November. Participants, better known as "Mo Bros," ask family and friends to donate to their efforts. The effort is not only designed to raise funds for men's health, but Mo Bros raise awareness of men's health issues by prompting conversations wherever they go, as people inquire about their moustaches. At the end of the month, Mo Bros and Mo Sistas (who also help to raise funds, and tolerate the moustaches) celebrate their Movember journey by throwing their own Movember party or attending one of the official Movember gala parties held around the world.

Movember was not an instant worldwide success. In fact, Garone had a bit of a challenge getting it off the ground. Initially keeping their efforts local, Garone set out to find a partner such as the Prostate Cancer Foundation in Australia who would endorse the Movember effort and give it greater credibility. While the Prostate Cancer Foundation was happy to accept the tens of thousands of dollars raised by Garone in the initiative's

In 2013, The Reference Centre for Men's Health, a unit of the State Health Department in Sao Paolo, used a blue moustache to promote prostate cancer awareness

continued

early years, the CEO of the Prostate Cancer Foundation told Garone that the organization was "too conservative" to be affiliated with such an unorthodox effort.

That's when Garone started to think bigger. He began contacting leaders of Prostate and Testicular Cancer organizations in other countries to pitch his idea. He began in Canada, where he was able to find his first official partner and legitimize his fundraising. And as they say, the rest is history. Today, Movember describes itself as a global movement "inspiring more than 3 Million Mo Bros and Mo Sistas to participate across 21 countries worldwide." In short, Movember has created a community of men (and women), dedicated to doing something to raise funds and awareness, improve men's health, and have a little fun. In addition to organizing a global community online, fundraising efforts build social capital at the local level as Mo Bros reach out to their friends, families, and neighbors for donations, and later host a party to celebrate their efforts.

The scope and scale of this initiative would not have been possible without the Internet. According to the organization's website, over 1.1 million Mo Bros and Mo Sistas around the world joined the movement in 2012, raising $147.0 million (US dollars). In the US alone, over 209,000 Mo Bros raised $21.0 million.

You can watch the story of Movember's origins and growth as told by the organization's founder, Adam Garone, by accessing this video link:

> http://www.ted.com/talks/adam_garone_healthier_men_one_moustache_
> at_a_time.html

Religious organizations and groups make up a key part of the nonprofit community and make important contributions to civil society. In the US, there is no state-sponsored or publicly-subsidized church. As noted by Alexis de Toqueville,[32] because of the separation of church and state, there is a vibrant religiosity in the US. Researchers note that religious diversity and plurality is more likely where there is dissociation between religion and state.[33] Freed from the state, religious organizations can engage in a free market, competing for membership and support, and ultimately this results in increased religious participation.[34]

Membership in religious organizations often requires behavioral changes and commitments and financial giving. And while members of religious organizations reap direct benefits from their membership, non-members are also beneficiaries of the activities of religious organizations. Religious organizations often require or encourage their members to engage in acts of charity, community development, giving, and community-building. They also host organized activities and deliver services—for example, running a soup kitchen or food pantry, hosting community festivals and events, owning and operating schools and educational facilities, and organizing their members to participate in volunteer activities such as home-building.

Religious organizations contribute to civil society in a number of ways. One of their important influences is on political life. While many individuals might consider nonprofit organizations, especially churches, synagogues, and mosques, as prohibited from engaging in political activities, they are in fact quite influential. According to Beyerlein and Chaves (2003) "although in absolute terms congregations' levels of political activism seem rather low, relative to other nonpolitical organizations they engage in politics in substantial numbers" (p. 229).[35]

Another important way that religious organizations contribute to civil society is by providing services to immigrants and enabling groups to assimilate and integrate into civil society. For example, from 1965–1998 more than one million Muslim immigrants entered the United States following a change in immigration law.[36] These new immigrants were entering a civil society dominated by a Judeo-Christian culture. According to some theorists,[37] this new, ethnically diverse Muslim community (from the Middle East, Southeast Asia, South Asia, and Sub-Saharan Africa) came to the US in search of educational and economic opportunities, in addition to seeking refuge from persecution. These new immigrants were united in their Muslim faith, and through Muslim nonprofit organizations were able to establish mosques, places of worship, schools offering language instruction, and programs promoting cultural outreach and charitable assistance. Additionally, American Muslims have been able to organize themselves through nonprofit organizations to engage in political lobbying, public affairs, cultural development, and education. In these ways, religious organizations contribute to civil society, and the nature of nonprofit organization in the United States enables civil society to absorb new religious groups.

Community-based organizations, similar to other types of voluntary associations and groups, organize around a common interest or to achieve a common goal. Typical community-based organizations include neighborhood watch groups, block clubs, and neighborhood associations. Community-based organizations might also organize to represent the interests of a particular racial or ethnic group—for example, Puerto Rican, Polish, or Ukrainian associations.

Modern community-based social clubs have emerged based on current interests and concerns. For example, community groups have emerged to engage in sporting activities like Ultimate Frisbee and Frisbee golf. Both sports, popularized among high school and college students in the 1960s, now enjoy support from organized sports groups and online communities that meet up to exercise and socialize. Ultimate Frisbee is taught and played at schools, parks and recreation departments, boys and girls clubs, churches, colleges, and youth and adult leagues. From its humble roots at Columbia High School in Maplewood New Jersey, it has grown to become a full-fledged sport through the active organizing of local groups and sporting enthusiasts. Other nonprofit organizations help to track and post information about Frisbee Golf courses (e.g. discgolfcourses.org, a complete and current directory of every disc golf course in the US) and promote the sport through public invitations for community members to participate in sporting activities.

In addition to voluntary associations, religious organizations, and community-based groups, **civic organizations** are a vital component of the nonprofit sector. Historically, local civic organizations such as the Rotary Club, Benevolent and Protective Order of Elks (BPOE), Moose, Masons, and the Junior League were important groups for organizing local interests and social capital. The Junior League (formally the Association of Junior Leagues International, Inc.) was formed in New York City in 1901 to organize women in the settlement movement, which we learned about in Chapter 2. Today the Junior League includes 293 chapters in Canada, the United Kingdom, Mexico, and the US, which organize women to build member's civic leadership skills and improve their communities through volunteerism.

Many civic organizations function at the local, national, and international levels. For example Rotary International, an international service organization, operates at the local and international level. Over 34,000 local clubs meet weekly for breakfast, lunch, or dinner, to build social and professional ties and organize service goals. Meanwhile the organization works across cities, states, and national borders to provide humanitarian services and build goodwill and peace in the world. To advance their motto "Service above Self" Rotary Clubs sponsor international exchange programs for students and professionals and support development projects through international sister city programs. Rotary Clubs serve an important function at the local level, creating a common space for members to engage in social and professional networking, community service, volunteerism, and philanthropy. The local chapters of the Rotary Club connect individuals with their communities through service activities and community outreach.

As we learned in Chapter 2, Rotary Club is an example of a community-based organization that operates in a **federated structure**. In a federated structure there is a strict hierarchical structure from local to international, with state, regional, and national levels in between. The PTA is another example of a federated structure, where intermediate levels of regional and council levels lie between state groups and the national level.[38]

In the 19th century and up till the 1950s, these large federated organizations were quite common in the United States, though their popularity has been declining since the 1960s. Some note that the federated structure was ideal for transferring information from the local to the national level and setting policies at the national level that could filter down to the local level. Individuals liked that they could belong to their local Shriner's Club or PTA and feel an affinity with members across the country. Moreover, the federated structure allowed local clubs to collect dues and target efforts directly to the community, while benefitting from the overall leadership and structure of the larger organization. One might argue that this type of structure becomes less necessary when individuals can organize, communicate, share information, and transfer funds and make payments more quickly, and sometimes instantaneously, because of advancements in information and communication technologies.

As social and political life in the US has become more diverse and technology has enabled faster information flow, there has been an increase in bottom up organizing and horizontal information sharing. Organizations can now coordinate directly with members, amass large amounts of information about public opinion, and mobilize people and resources in ways unthinkable in the 1950s. Additionally—for example, in the case of the PTA—the increase of women in the workforce, full-time working mothers, and female-headed households has left the PTA without the manpower of volunteer stay-at-home mothers.[39] Others note that large federated nonprofit organizations grew to a size and girth that required more professionalized leadership. Today, many of these nonprofit associations are run by professionals who lobby Congress and are less connected to the local communities that support the national organization.[40] These social and political changes have shifted the ways in which associations and civic organizations operate in the US.

While civic organizations are credited with strengthening the social bonds among their membership, within and across families, neighborhoods, and communities, they are not without controversy. For example, consider the BPOE, which was founded in 1868 and currently reports a membership of over one million in the US. The BPOE, also known as the "Elks," was originally founded as a private club to evade the New York City laws limiting the operating hours for public taverns. It later evolved to become a major fraternal, charitable, and service organization. Upon its establishment, the BPOE denied membership to blacks and women. In the 1970s, the BPOE amended its membership rules to admit African Americans, though the Winter Haven, Florida Elks Club remained segregated until 1985. Women were granted BPOE membership in the mid-1990s. Today the BPOE continues to restrict its membership to US citizens over the age of 21 who believe in God—atheists are excluded. Thus, while the Elks strengthen the social bonds of members and provide important services to their communities, they have also done so while excluding portions of society.

Of course, we might explain the evolution of membership at the BPOE as a sign of the times, becoming more egalitarian as society has become more egalitarian. But it is important to note that nonprofit associations and civil society organizations are often founded on characteristics that unite a set of individuals, which may at the same time be a set of characteristics that exclude another group of individuals. So as this fraternal order works to benefit its membership and contribute to civil society, it may simultaneously create or reinforce divisions in civil society.

The Role of Technology in Modern Civil Society

Technology has made it easier for people to connect based on shared beliefs and interests regardless of geographic location. Individuals who might have felt isolated because of their beliefs, interests, or illnesses can now find

BOX 4.2 SORORITIES AND FRATERNITIES: BUILDING SOCIAL CAPITAL OR CREATING DIVISIONS?

Though today they often carry a reputation of being centers for partying, collegiate fraternities and sororities have a long history on North American campuses—a history of organizing, service, and philanthropy. Fraternities and sororities (also known as Greek letter organizations) are considered mutual aid societies that engage in philanthropic activities, provide academic and social activities for their membership, and sometimes provide residential and dining facilities for their members.

The first Greek letter organization, Phi Beta Kappa, was a secret organization founded in 1776 at The College of William and Mary in Virginia. Membership to Phi Beta Kappa was limited to upperclass men and those who become members of the faculty would remain active members of the fraternity, leading it to become an influential association of faculty and select students on several college campuses. The first general fraternity (that was not a secret society), Kappa Alpha Society, was established at Union College in New York in 1825. And the first "national" fraternity, expanding its membership to multiple colleges in 1831, was Sigma Phi. The first sorority, Alpha Delta Pi, was established in 1851 at Wesleyan College. While the first sorority modeled after the male model of the fraternity, Pi Beta Phi, was created in 1867 at Monmouth College in Illinois.

Greek letter organizations have, historically, organized under some shared principle of membership—for example, this shared principle might be "building character." Others serve as communities for engineers (Theta Tau), students of agriculture (Alpha Gamma Rho), or particular ethnic and racial groups. But of course, these organizing characteristics can mean excluding others. In response to the exclusionary aspects of early fraternities the first black fraternity, Alpha Phi Alpha, was founded in 1906. Alpha Kappa Alpha, the first black women's sorority, was established in 1908 at Howard University. In 1931, the first Latino fraternity was founded—Phi Iota Alpha. Sigma Chi Omega was the first multicultural fraternity (1993) and in 1994 Iota Nu Delta was established as the first South Asian interest fraternity. Most recently, the first Muslim fraternity was established at the University of Texas in 2013.[41]

continued

Members of Alif Laam Meem, a national Muslim fraternity based at the University of Texas at Dallas, during a demonstration against domestic violence, 2013

Many would argue that by focusing their efforts on a particular group, sororities and fraternities are able to provide an important support system for marginalized groups in the collegiate system. For example, Alpha Kappa Alpha, the first black women's sorority, was established to support African-American women where they lacked the power, authority, or opportunities to advance their interests.[42] Alpha Kappa Alpha has helped improve the social and economic conditions of their membership and their communities through service programs that focus on education, health, family, and business. They also participate in Congressional lobbying to advance the interests of their members and other marginalized communities. These types of activities certainly speak to the power of these types of associations.

However, others argue that the exclusionary (and sometimes elitist) nature of Greek letter organizations makes them inappropriate for college campuses. Oberlin College has banned Greek letter organizations and secret societies since 1847 and many Quaker colleges and universities have banned fraternities and sororities because they violate the Quaker principle of equality. More recently, fraternities have been banned from Williams College, Middlebury College, and Amherst College.

Sororities and fraternities on campus are a good example of private, nonprofit associations that seek to pool the collective will, ideas, and resources of their members to advance the interests of their members. But are these democratic forms of organizing?

continued

Do these associations contribute to the common good? Or do they serve to advance the interests of a few? Are they elitist? Given their policy of excluding outsiders, do these associations strengthen social capital and civil society, or undermine it? Given your responses about sororities and fraternities, do you feel the same about associations off campus, such as Rotary International or the Girl Scouts of America?

Additional Reading and Video Links:

"Meet Alif Laam Meem, America's First Muslim Fraternity, AKA Alpha Lambda Mu." The Huffington Post. Yasmine Hafiz. http://www.huffingtonpost.com/2013/09/05/alif-laam-meem-america-first-muslim-fraternity_n_3865722.html
Upworthy—Muslim America Rocks. http://www.upworthy.com/muslim-america-rocks

support from similar individuals. Technology has also enabled persons and groups to mobilize resources in short periods of time. Consider the speed with which donations were collected following the earthquake in Haiti, or the private fund set up to raise money for the three victims of a tragic kidnapping in Cleveland, Ohio. In the two months after their rescue in May 2013, donors had given over one million in funds to the three victims.[43]

Social media and organizing online have replaced many traditional forms of face-to-face organization. Many elderly play bridge and Scrabble® online, keeping their minds sharp and maintaining connections to friends and relatives who might not live nearby. Similarly, individuals network for jobs, romantic relationships, and new friends online. These changes have altered the ways that we think about social capital and also the ways in which nonprofit organizations interact with civil society. Today, many thriving nonprofit organizations require an online presence, a website to post activities and events, a Facebook page to attract and inform community members, Twitter activity to quickly disseminate short highlights about important events and accomplishments of the organization, and Smartphone applications to help clients locate services or support.

As we have noted throughout this chapter, nonprofit organizations and associations can provide important venues for organizing and mobilizing individuals to advance community interests, care for individuals, or provide support for groups that might otherwise remain outside or marginalized in our communities. While nonprofit and civil society organizations can have strong positive outcomes for our society, they can be vehicles for the organization of hate groups or anti-social movements. Robert Putnam notes that while social capital can sound like a wonderful outcome of organizations and associations, "it can be directed toward malevolent antisocial purposes just like other forms of capital."[44]

This "dark side" of associations and civil society refers to the negative consequences, whether they are intentional or not. Associations and organizations based on narrow interests might work to reinforce social stratification.[45] For example in the 1950s many of the neighborhood and community-based associations that helped communities thrive were typically exclusionary, often "along racial and gender and class lines."[46] In fact, the community-based structure of these organizations helped to reinforce the segregated structure of our neighborhoods. Some argue that excessively strong ties in groups can actually threaten the larger, collective good. These "Superglued" groups can be so focused on what unites them that, at the same time, they become destructive toward non-members. Consider extremist groups that have organized based on a shared value, such as a belief in the superiority of their own race (e.g. NeoNazis) or the extreme views about women and education (e.g. the Taliban in Afghanistan). In attempts to protect their own values and interests, these groups become destructive toward other segments of society.

Just as the civil rights and immigrant rights organizations serve to advance the interests of marginalized groups in our communities, other organizations might seek to advance beliefs that conflict with mainstream values and social norms. For example, consider the Westboro Baptist Church (WBC),[47] an unaffiliated Baptist church known for its extreme ideologies, in particular its efforts against gay people. The church is often described as a hate group, but at the same time serves as an organizing mechanism for a set of individuals who believe they are advocating for their own religious beliefs. The same social structure and set of legal rules that make it possible for Rainbow/PUSH to organize to advance the interests of those seeking social justice and civil rights also set the stage for the Westboro Baptist Church to mobilize its resources against gay people, including protests at Federal courthouses performing same-sex marriages and the funerals of gay individuals, such as Matthew Shepard, the college student who was beaten to death in 1999 by two men because he was gay.[48]

The Westboro Baptist Church demonstrates to promote their beliefs, but often draw larger crowds in opposition to WBC viewpoints

The examples discussed here highlight the tension between a civil society where all individuals and groups have the ability to organize and have their views heard, and a civil society that is limited to a "good society," or some collective notion of what is good for society. The modern system of civil society in the United States allows voice for all marginalized groups, even those with which we might disagree. But what happens when hate groups gain power and become legitimized? Who determines which values are most vital to civil society and which are no longer acceptable? Do hate groups have the same rights as charitable organizations? And what defines a hate group? These are many of the questions that challenge a thriving, pluralistic civil society.

Summary

In addition to providing tangible goods and services, nonprofit organizations also provide a great deal of intangible "social goods" benefitting society such as increasing levels of trust, social cohesion, tolerance, fellowship, and solidarity, among others. By offering spaces and places—both physical and virtual—for citizens to interact, associate, and contribute personal resources, nonprofit organizations help to build social capital, or social ties that bind members of a community together. Nonprofit associations play a critical role in building communities, contributing products and services to our communities, but more importantly generating social capital, uniting individual social capital for larger purposes, and providing opportunities for members to develop more social capital.

Civil society is a broad concept that links together institutions, ideas and action, and organizations (both formal and informal). Civil society includes the social and legal structures that make it possible for nonprofit organizations to exist. At the same time, nonprofit organizations help to foster the norms of trust, tolerance, belonging, equality, altruism, and so on, which make society a better place. A small percentage of nonprofits, however, are exclusionary or promote anti-social messages. Whether these organizations are a part of civil society or undermine civil society remains a topic for debate. Regardless of the view on this point, the US enjoys a relatively strong civil society compared to other countries. Technology has re-defined the meaning of community, enabling like-minded people to more easily find each other and build and maintain social ties. While participation in traditional associations, churches, and community-based initiatives has declined in recent years, the Internet has strengthened social capital in new ways.

KEY TERMS

- Civic organizations
- Common good
- Federated structure

- Institutions
- Norms
- Rule of law

- Social capital
- Social goods
- Voluntary associations

DISCUSSION QUESTIONS

1. How are the concepts of nonprofit organizations and civil society related? Provide an example to illustrate your response.

2. What are some examples of nonprofit organizations or community groups in your neighborhood or city that are working to build social capital? How

do these organizations or groups go about building social capital? What indicators do you have that social capital is being "built" by an organization or group?

3. Given the ways that technology has redefined communities and networking, are old-fashioned civic groups such as the PTA and Rotary Club still relevant today?

4. What are some of the possible negative outcomes of free speech and the right to establish nonprofit organizations or groups that are based on extreme ideologies, such as exhibiting hatred toward a particular segment of the population? Are these groups also a part of civil society, or do they undermine it?

ACTIVITY

Building Social Capital in College—A Thought Exercise

Consider your own social capital and networks. Who do you know? Who do they know? Are there people in your network to which you have "strong ties" and others to which you have "weak ties"? Who are the people that have the most resources in your network? Consider the social capital you have based on your hometown, from your time in high school, through your family, through your extracurricular activities, online, and now in your college life.

College is a perfect time to expand your social networks and build social capital. Here is an environment full of new opportunities and people, colleagues, graduate students, faculty, and an abundance of support staff and activities intended to build a community on campus. Are you a member of a sorority or fraternity? Do you participate in intramural sports? Do you have an active study group? Do you participate in a club based on a hobby or interest? Each of these activities is an opportunity for building social capital and investing in yourself and your community. Your social capital becomes a safety net in times of need, serving as a resource throughout your life.

Consider the different people in your network and how they might bring different forms of social capital to your life. If you needed help, where would you go? Who would you ask for assistance with homework, with a financial problem, or with a personal problem? If you are planning to go to graduate school, you will want to access different

continued

parts of your social network—the advising office, faculty, graduate students that you know, and friends of your parents who went to graduate school. If you decide to take a summer volunteering in Vietnam, you will want to access other parts of your network. Now consider how much of your network is supported by nonprofit organizations—the university, your church, the nonprofit sports and social club, your sorority.

As you consider your own personal network, partner with a classmate and discuss the following questions:

1. How do you contribute to social capital in your own community? Community can be defined as where you live, or more broadly as a community of interest or a group to which you feel a sense of belonging.

2. What are some things you could do to build more social capital in your community? What, if any, are the barriers for you to build more social capital?

Additional Video Teaching Materials for CeaseFire Example

Title: "The Interrupters" Ameena Matthews on The Colbert Report. February 2, 2012

Link: http://www.colbertnation.com/the-colbert-report-videos/407605/february-01–2012/ameena-matthews

Description: CeaseFire's Ameena Matthews explores how her tough inner-city upbringing informs her work as a peacemaker among Chicago's gangs. (06:57)

Title: CeaseFire—Rogers Park/Chicago Promo Video

Link: http://www.youtube.com/watch?v=tc-Sqg3uFFQ

Description: CeaseFire's Tio Hardiman described what he'd tell the president's new commission on gun violence. (33:23)

Title: Gary Slutkin: Can violence be cured?

Link: http://www.youtube.com/watch?v=9IwDellYqZE

Description: Gary Slutkin explains his ideas about violence as a public health issue and starting the CeaseFire program. Presentation at TEDMED presentation 2013. (15:35)

Title: Safe Streets Baltimore

Link: http://www.youtube.com/watch?v=RtjU2w3F4n0

Description   In response to a recent shooting, SAFE STREETS Baltimore organizes a Community Response March with other members of the Baltimore community in order to make their presence heard as a force against local violence. (2:12)

Title: Operation SNUG and the King of Kings Foundation on location

Link: http://www.youtube.com/watch?v=-8COMo-JBVE

Description: What is SNUG? SNUG is "Guns" spelled backwards. Snug—modeled after the
highly effective Chicago CeaseFire program—provides a coherent series of interventions
to address violence, particularly among youth and in economically disenfranchised
neighborhoods. The SNUG Coalition consists of community organizations in ten urban
neighborhoods across NY State. (5:01)

Title: Chicago CeaseFire Works With Families, Gangs to Stop Violence—ABC News

Link: http://www.youtube.com/watch?v=KlfiNz-ikNg

Description: News report about crime epidemic in Chicago. (7:11)

Title: Cure Violence Partners with Groupon Grassroots

Link: http://www.youtube.com/watch?v=k7gZR4Uw1BM

Description: This Mother's Day, you can give the gift that EVERY mother wants—a safe
neighborhood for her children. Because we CAN stop shootings and killings. Cure
Violence is doing it—in Chicago, in Baltimore, in New York City, in New Orleans, in
Kansas City—in 16 cities in 45 neighborhoods across the United States. Go to
http://www.groupon.com/deals/cure-violence to support the Cure Violence national
Groupon Grassroots campaign starting April 25–May 1. 100% of donations help
Violence Interrupters curb neighborhood violence around the country by detecting and
mediating potentially lethal conflicts. [An interesting example of fundraising.] (1:40)

Title: Ameena Matthews—The Interrupters in Oakland

Link: http://www.youtube.com/watch?v=hB_H_ACjoKo

Description: The Interrupters was previewed at the Oakland Museum of California on February
9th. Ameena Matthews, an outreach worker for CeaseFire, discusses the similarities
between Oakland and Chicago and the importance of teaching our history to our youth.
(9:04)

Title: The Interrupters

Link: http://www.pbs.org/wgbh/pages/frontline/interrupters/

Description: Frontline website with access to documentary "The Interrupters." Full length
film. (114:36)

Notes

1   Kotlowitz, Alex. May 4, 2008. Blocking the Transmission of Violence, *New York
Times*. Accessed Sept 13, 2013 at http://www.nytimes.com/2008/05/04/magazine/
04health-t.html?pagewanted=all&_r=0

2   Skogan, Wesley G., Susan M. Hartnett, Natalie Bump, and Jill Dubois. May, 2008. Executive Summary: Evaluation of CeaseFire-Chicago. Accessed September 13, 2013 at http://www.ipr.northwestern.edu/publications/papers/urban-policy-and-community-development/docs/ceasefire-pdfs/executivesummary.pdf

3   Bonner, Heidi S., Sarah J. McLean, and Robert E. Worden. October, 2008. CeaseFire Chicago—A Synopsis, Finn Institute. Accessed September 13, 2013 at http://finn institute.org/uploads/CeaseFire-Chicago.pdf

4   CeaseFire: Chicago Violence Prevention Program. Treating violence like an infectious disease. July 15, 2009. Robert Wood Johnson Foundation. Accessed September 13, 2013 at http://www.rwjf.org/en/about-rwjf/newsroom/newsroom-content/2009/07/ceasefire-chicago-violence-prevention-program.html#grants

5   Binlot, Ann. August 4, 2011. Violence, Redeemed: "The Interrupters" Follows Reformed Felons Driven Back to Crime—to Stop It.

6   Skogan et al. (2008).

7   Ritter, Nancy. 2009. CeaseFire: A Public Health Approach to Reduce Shootings and Killings. National Institute of Justice, *NIJ Journal* 264. Accessed September 13, 2013 at http://www.nij.gov/journals/264/ceasefire.htm

8   Ameena Mathews is the daughter of Jeff Fort, a major gang leader in the 1970s in Chicago. As a teenager Ameena was involved in a gang. She now works to promote community-building and keep kids from engaging in violence and gang activity.

9   Ricardo "Cobe" Williams served three terms in jail for drug-related charges and attempted murder.

10 Eddie Bocanegra committed murder when he was 17 and then spent 14 years in jail. He now works with CeaseFire to keep other young people from making the same mistakes he did.

11 http://www.pbs.org/wgbh/pages/frontline/interrupters/ Accessed September 13, 2013.

12 Anheier, Helmut K. 2005. *Organizations: Theory, Management, Policy*. New York, NY: Routledge Press.

13 Sievers, Bruce R. 2010. Civil Society, Philanthropy, and the Fate of the Commons (Civil Society: Historical and Contemporary Perspectives). Tufts Press.

14 North, Douglas C. 1987. The New Institutional Economics. *Journal of Institutional and Theoretical Economics,* 142: 230–237.

15 Sievers (2010).

16 Sievers (2010).

17 Sievers (2010).

18 Sievers (2010).

19 Derek Thompson (15 October 2011). "Occupy the World: The '99 Percent' Movement Goes Global." *The Atlantic*. Accessed 15 October 2011 at http://www.theatlantic.com/business/archive/2011/10/occupy-the-world-the-99-percent-movement-goes-global/246757/.

20 Putnam, Robert D. 2000. *Bowling Alone: The Collapse and Revival of the American Community*. New York, NY: Simon and Schuster, p. 19.

21 Putnam (2000), p.19.

22 Fischer, C. S. (1992). *America Calling: A Social History of the Telephone to 1940*. Berkeley, CA: University of California Press; Fischer, C. S. (2001). Bowling alone: What's the score? Paper presented at the American Sociological Association, Anaheim,

CA, August 17–21; Anabel Quan-Haase and Barry Wellman. 2004. How does the Internet Affect Social Capital. In Marleen Huysman and Volker Wulf (eds), *IT and Social Capital*. Cambridge, MA: MIT Press.

23   Quan-Haase, Anabel and Barry Wellman. 2004. How does the Internet Affect Social Capital, in Marleen Huysman and Volker Wulf (eds), *IT and Social Capital*. Cambridge, MA: MIT Press.

24   Lehmann, Nicholas. 1996. Kicking in Groups, *The Atlantic Online*, April 1996, http://www.theatlantic.com/past/docs/issues/96apr/kicking/kicking.htm. Accessed July 15, 2013.

25   Bunting, Madeleine. 2007. Capital Ideas, *The Guardian*. Wednesday 18 July, 2007.

26   Fischer (2001).

27   Schneider, Jo Anne. 2009. Organizational Social Capital and Nonprofits. *Nonprofit & Voluntary Sector Quarterly*, 38(4): 643–662.

28   Schneider (2009).

29   http://www.womensordination.org/content/view/3/37/ Accessed July 7, 2013.

30   http://911families.org/about-us/ Accessed July 7, 2013.

31   http://us.movember.com/about/ Accessed September 19, 2013.

32   De Tocqueville, Alexis. 1838. *Democracy in America*. New York: George Dearborn and Co.

33   Chaves, Mark and David E. Cann. 1992. Regulation, Pluralism, and Religious Market Structure: Explaining Religion's Vitality. *Rationality and Society*, 4: 272.

34   Iannaccone, Laurence R. 1991. The consequences of religious market structure: Adam Smith and the economics of religion. *Rationality and Society*, 3: 156–177; Martin, David. 1978. *A General Theory of Secularization*. New York: Harper Colophon; Martin, David. 1991. The Secularization Issue: Prospect and Retrospect. *British Journal of Sociology*, 42: 465–474.

35   Beyerlein, Kraig and Mark Chaves. (2003). The Political Activities of Religious Congregations in the United States. *Journal for the Scientific Study of Religion*, 42(2): 229–246.

36   Nimer, M. 2002. *The North American Muslim Resource Guide: Muslim Community Life in the United States and Canada*. London: Routledge.

37   Gill, Anthony J. and Steven K Pfaff. 2010. Acting in Good Faith: An Economic Approach to Religious Organizations as Advocacy Groups, in Aseem Prakash and Mary Kay Gugerty (eds), *Advocacy Organizations and Collective Action*. Cambridge University Press, pp. 58–90.

38   Crawford, Susan, and Peggy Levitt. 1999. Social Change and Civic Engagement: The Case of the PTA, in Theda Skocpol and Morris Paul Fiorina (eds), *Civic Engagement in American Democracy*. Washington, DC: Brookings Institution Press.

39   Crawford and Levitt (1999).

40   Skocpol, Theda. 2003. Diminished Democracy: From Membership to Management in American Civic Life. Norman, OK: University of Oklahoma Press.

41   Barrow, Jo. 2013. Inside America's First Muslim Frat House, *The Independent*. September 3, 2013. Accessed July 15, 2013 at http://www.independent.co.uk/student/student-life/inside-americas-first-muslim-frat-house-8796828.html

42   Brown, Tamara L., Gregory Parks, and Clarenda M. Phillips. 2005. *African American Fraternities and Sororities: The Legacy and the Vision*. Lexington: University Press of Kentucky, p. 342.

43 http://www.latimes.com/news/nation/nationnow/la-na-nn-cleveland-kidnapping-victims-fund-20130709,0,2192264.story. Accessed July 15, 2013.

44 Putnam (2000), pp. 21–22.

45 Putnam (2000), p. 358.

46 Putnam (2000), p. 358.

47 http://www.godhatesfags.com/ Accessed July 15, 2013.

48 Murder charges planned in beating death of gay student, *CNN*. October 12, 1998. Accessed July 15, 2013 at http://web.archive.org/web/20000607204809/ http://cnn.com/US/9810/12/wyoming.attack.03/index.html

5

COMMUNITY SERVICE AND VOLUNTARY ACTION

CHAPTER LEARNING OBJECTIVES

By the end of this chapter, students will be able to:

1. Explain how volunteering helps build social capital and promotes civil society

2. Distinguish between formal and informal volunteering

3. Describe some basic facts about who volunteers in America

4. Describe key motivations that explain why people volunteer

5. Identify some critical ways technology is re-shaping volunteerism

6. Locate an appropriate volunteer opportunity to suit one's own personal needs and interests, using one or more volunteer matching resources

---

Introduction

Volunteering and community service strengthen the social fabric of America, and are a critical component (the "action" component) of civil society. As we learned in Chapter 1, volunteers constitute a critical resource in the nonprofit sector. This extensive reliance on people who donate their

MAKING A DIFFERENCE AS A MENTOR: BIG BROTHERS/BIG SISTERS PROGRAM

Twenty-two-year-old Garrett Smith sat at his desk on the first day of his "real" job as a public relations and social media specialist for the state's chapter of the Autism Society of America. As Garrett looked around his new workplace, he couldn't help but feel overwhelmed by his good fortune in finding a job so quickly after college, and not just any job, but one in an organization that would allow him to "give back." You see, Garrett had not always been so lucky.

Growing up it was just him and his mom, Tina, who worked long hours waiting tables to support them. Beginning in fifth grade, Garrett was on his own after school till he went to bed at night. It worked okay at first, but by middle school he fell in with a bad crowd and the long hours of unsupervised time after school led to trouble. He stopped doing his homework, his grades plummeted, and he was regularly in detention. After school he roamed the streets with his friends, smoking marijuana, harassing other kids, and causing trouble. When he was in the 5th grade, he was caught shoplifting from a local corner store, but the owner chose to let it go rather than get the police involved. Things reached the breaking point, however (literally), when Garrett and two of friends were arrested for breaking some windows and vandalizing a home in the neighborhood.

Garrett had officially entered the juvenile justice system at the age of 13. He was charged with vandalism and breaking and entering. Since it was a first offense, he was put on probation, assigned a case worker, and ordered to pay towards the damage he had done to the vandalized house. Tina felt angry, frustrated, and disappointed in her son. She could barely afford to pay rent, let alone pay for new windows on a house that was not even hers. While she couldn't just quit her job to stay home to supervise her teenage son every night, she decided that Garrett needed additional support and guidance in his life. He needed someone other than his mom who could be a positive influence. He needed a role model, someone he could look up to.

Tina called Big Brothers/Big Sisters (BB/BS) and explained the situation. After a few weeks of searching for the right match for Garrett, a BB/BS staff member called Tina to set up an appointment to bring a possible mentor out to meet Garrett. The mentor was Dave, a 27-year-old guy who worked as an engineer. Dave had some extra time on his hands and a desire to make a difference. At first, Garrett did not like the idea but he had no choice but to go along with it. Dave had made a commitment to see his mentee or "little" for roughly 3 hours a week, for one year. They set up an initial arrangement in which Dave would come over every Wednesday evening, and he and Garrett would work on homework or school assignments, make dinner, and eat together, and if there was time left, they could play video games or watch TV.

continued

It took a few weeks, but Garrett began looking forward to Wednesday evenings. It turned out that Dave was a pretty cool guy. He was quite a talker and told Garrett about college, his job, his own family, and his social life. Garrett actually found Dave pretty interesting, and they got along well. Over time, Garrett's grades began to improve. Dave played in a soccer league and Tina allowed Garrett to go with Dave on Saturday mornings to watch the games. After the games, they would hang out for a while or do some kind of activity. By the end of Dave's one-year commitment, the two had formed quite a bond. Garrett was a pretty bright kid, and he began making much better choices even when Dave or his mother were not around. Although Dave could not be sure that Garrett's improvement had anything to do with the mentoring, he liked to think he had made a difference. He told Garrett, Tina, and the BB/BS staff that he would volunteer another year as Garrett's "big."

That second year turned into a third, fourth, fifth, and so on. Although Dave saw Garrett less frequently in those subsequent years, Garrett knew he could always count on Dave, whether it was talking about girl problems, finding an after-school job, or asking for advice on college applications. Garrett graduated in the top 25% of his high school class and opted to go to a state college about two hours from home. Garrett excelled in his college courses, and found that so many years of being on his own throughout high school made him very disciplined in college. Dave encouraged him to do internships and get involved in extracurricular activities on and around campus in order to build his networks. Dave's advice was good as usual, and Garrett found his current job at the Autism Society through his boss at his former internship.

Although Garrett doesn't see Dave on a regular basis anymore, the two are still in touch and Garrett considers him a lifelong friend. He wonders where he'd be right now if it hadn't been for Dave's steady presence in his life over the past eight years. He feels thankful and is anxious to make his own contributions to society now.

Why do you think Dave volunteered to be a Big Brother? What motivated him? Why would he spend time doing something completely for free (and perhaps even on occasion spending his own money) when he could have used that time doing something more productive—perhaps at a second job? Who benefitted more from Dave's volunteer service, Dave or Garrett?

time not only to carry out the mission of organizations but also to govern them is one of the key features that distinguishes the nonprofit sector from the public and for-profit sectors. Moreover, nonprofits organize volunteers for strategic action toward problems or causes in communities. Some nonprofit organizations, such as the Red Cross or Big Brothers/Big

Sisters, rely almost entirely on volunteers to carry out their missions while others rely only partially or occasionally on volunteers for fundraising or other clearly defined tasks, such as designing a website, or sorting clothing and other donated items. Even those nonprofits that employ a highly professionalized paid staff and do not use volunteers in the day-to-day work of their organization still rely on volunteers to serve on their boards of directors, where they offer their skills, knowledge, and unique perspectives to help govern and direct the organization toward its mission.

Volunteers play a vital role in helping to create civil society. The act of contributing time to a cause helps to build social capital, as volunteers personally interact with staff, clients, other volunteers, and members of the public more broadly, through nonprofit organizations and voluntary groups. This chapter examines volunteering and community service in America, primarily through the lens of the nonprofit sector and civil society organizations. First, we examine the link between volunteering and social capital, with an eye toward ways volunteering contributes to community-building. Next, we look at some statistics on volunteering in America to better understand who volunteers. Then, we examine some theories about individual motivations for volunteering. We then discuss the important role of intermediary organizations, which are special types of nonprofits that help individuals find and connect with volunteer opportunities that match their skills and interests. Finally, we look at some of the ways that technology has broadened the structure of opportunities for volunteers.

Volunteering and Social Capital

As we learned in the previous chapter, social capital arises from the norms of trust and reciprocity created from individuals' interpersonal relationships and social networks. Individuals build these social networks through their communities—in whatever ways a particular individual defines their community. Contributing one's time to the community helps to strengthen social ties between both the volunteer as well as the recipient of the giver's time. Social capital is built and strengthened by both informal volunteering and formal volunteering. For example, raking a neighbor's leaves because they are recovering from surgery is as much an act of volunteering as reporting for duty each Friday to the local senior center to deliver hot meals for elderly shut-ins. *Formal* volunteering generally refers to volunteer work carried out through an organization, while *informal* volunteering is defined as time donated on an individual basis, outside of an organizational context.[1] Both types of volunteering contribute to social capital, community-building, and civil society, and there is evidence that those who volunteer informally are more likely to also volunteer in formal capacities as well.[2] And, while our discussion here has emphasized the benefits that accrue to the community and to organizations as a result of volunteering, there is some evidence to suggest volunteering also has some positive psychological benefits for the individual donating his or her time.[3]

Many types of nonprofit organizations and voluntary groups rely on the individuals who make up the group to produce a "social good" that not only strengthens social ties within and among its members, but creates social capital for the larger community. Consider Alcoholics Anonymous (AA) and other twelve-step programs. Alcoholics Anonymous is a voluntary, worldwide movement with approximately 114,000 groups and over 2,000,000 members in approximately 170 countries.[4] Describing itself as a "society of peers," AA members volunteer their time by providing support to other members of the community struggling to maintain sobriety through group meetings, while they themselves benefit from the support of the group. In this case, the volunteer, or person donating their time, is simultaneously the beneficiary of donated time. The efforts of the group members not only create benefits for one another, but for the larger community in minimizing the negative effects that alcohol dependence can have for family members and others who interact with alcoholics.

Other types of nonprofit organizations and community groups engage volunteers in ways that help to create social capital in neighborhoods suffering from low levels of social capital. For example, the nonprofit organization, Growing Home, runs an organic urban farm in Chicago's high poverty Englewood neighborhood, an area recognized as a "food desert." Neighborhood residents come to volunteer in the gardens, attend classes on cooking and healthy eating, and purchase low-cost, fresh produce at the neighborhood farm stand each week. The organization hosts a variety of community events and conducts outreach within the neighborhood in order to get as many residents engaged as possible in the organization's neighborhood health efforts. By creating a place residents can gather, learn new things, build relationships, and work together toward the collective

Growing Home's neighborhood farm stand, Englewood, Chicago, 2013

effort of improving neighborhood health, Growing Home provides an organizational vehicle through which social capital can be built by the residents of Englewood.

Who Volunteers?

How many Americans volunteer? Where do they volunteer? And who are these people who contribute their time without pay in an effort to benefit society? The Corporation for National and Community Service (CNCS), the Federal government agency that runs the Americorps program, makes it easy for us to answer the question of who volunteers. The CNCS partners with two other Federal programs, the Bureau of Labor Statistics (BLS) and the Current Population Survey (CPS), to report data on the

THE CORPORATION FOR NATIONAL AND COMMUNITY SERVICE (CNCS)

The CNCS was created in 1993 to engage more than 5 million Americans in service through the core programs of Senior Corps, AmeriCorps, and the Social Innovation Fund. CNCS is the largest grant-maker for service and volunteering and aims to strengthen America's nonprofit sector by harnessing the energy and talent of Americans by increasing service in local communities.

The mission of CNCS is to improve lives, strengthen communities, and foster civic engagement through service and volunteering.

http://www.nationalservice.gov

percentage of Americans that volunteer by age, race, gender, state, region, and other demographic characteristics. They measure volunteerism in US society as a **volunteer rate**, which notes the percentage of people from a particular group who engage in volunteering. The CNCS produces a report each year on Volunteering and Civic Life in America with an interactive website that allows users to find all kinds of interesting data on volunteering, in each of the 50 states and in aggregate: http://www. volunteeringinamerica.gov/national.

According to the 2012 report of Volunteering and Civic Life in America, 64.3 million Americans volunteered in a formal organization, with volunteerism reaching its highest level in five years. This amounts to 26.8% of the adult population engaging in formal volunteering, while a much larger proportion, an estimated 65.1% (143.7 million persons), engage in informal volunteering such as helping a neighbor. Table 5.1 lists the volunteer rates in the US by state, including the District of Columbia. Rates of volunteering in America vary quite a bit from as high as 43.8% in Utah to as low as 20.4% in Louisiana. The average volunteer rate is around 28.5% . Altogether, Americans engaged in approximately 7.9 billion hours of formal volunteering in 2012, with the value of this time estimated at $171 billion.[6] The overall rate of volunteering among Americans has remained relatively steady over the last decade, with 25–30% of American adults engaged in formal volunteering each year.

America is a diverse society and its citizens have diverse priorities and preferences for causes to which they devote their time. Figure 5.1 offers

TABLE 5.1 Volunteer Rates in the United States, by State, 2012

State	Volunteer Rate (%)	State	Volunteer Rate (%)	State	Volunteer Rate (%)
Utah	43.8	Montana	29.9	California	25.1
Minnesota	37.7	Wyoming	29.9	Alabama	25.1
Idaho	36.5	Dis. Columbia	29.1	Tennessee	24.8
Kansas	36.4	Virginia	28.5	Delaware	24.8
Nebraska	36.0	Maryland	28.5	Rhode Island	24.5
Iowa	36.0	New Hampshire	28.4	Georgia	24.3
South Dakota	35.7	Indiana	28.0	Arizona	24.2
Wisconsin	35.6	Michigan	27.9	Texas	24.0
Washington	34.5	Oklahoma	27.7	Kentucky	23.7
Vermont	34.4	Illinois	27.4	West Virginia	23.1
Oregon	34.1	Ohio	27.4	Hawaii	23.0
Alaska	33.2	New Mexico	26.7	New Jersey	22.9
Colorado	32.8	Pennsylvania	26.7	Arkansas	21.8
Maine	32.5	Massachusetts	26.5	Florida	21.4
Missouri	30.7	Mississippi	26.0	Nevada	20.7
North Dakota	30.4	North Carolina	25.8	New York	20.6

Source: Corporation for National and Community Service.[5]

a breakdown of the various fields in which American adults volunteer. Churches and religious institutions capture the majority of American volunteers, with 34.4% donating their time in these religious institutions, followed by educational organizations in which 26.6% of Americans volunteer. The large proportion of Americans volunteering in the education sector can be attributed to the fact that many parents volunteer in their children's schools.

Volunteering is more popular among some groups than others. Typically, middle aged Americans are the most engaged in formal volunteering, women volunteer more than men, and education is positively related to volunteering.[8] Approximately 31.6% of those aged 35–44 volunteer, and the volunteer rate tends to decline after the age of 45. Contrary to some perceptions that younger people lack an inclination toward civic engagement, the volunteer rate is particularly high among teens (16–19-year-olds) at 27.4% , and somewhat lower among those in the 20–24 age

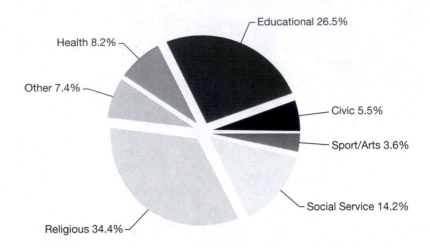

Numbers in the chart may not add up to 100% because of rounding

FIGURE 5.1 Where Do Americans Volunteer?

Source: Reprinted from Volunteering and Civic Life in America, 2012. Corporation for National & Community Service.[7]

bracket (18.9%). It is possible that the higher rate among the teen group can be explained by the increasing tendency of high schools to require community service hours, high school students having more free time to volunteer, or the trend of volunteering to increase resume material for college applications, a topic which we will examine more closely later in the chapter.

Women tend to volunteer in higher rates than men. Almost 30% of women volunteer in the US compared with 23% of men. The higher rate of volunteering among women holds across all age groups, educational levels, and other major demographic characteristics. Those with children also tend to volunteer more, a factor that is likely linked to the high percentage of volunteers in the education sector as shown in Table 5.1. The volunteer rate among parents (adults with children) is seven percentage points higher than the national average, with 33.7% of parents volunteering. And, there is evidence to suggest that it is not just stay-at-home moms who volunteer. Almost four out of ten working mothers (38%) volunteer in some capacity within their communities.

Figure 5.2 illustrates adult volunteer rates in the US by education level. Education is directly linked to higher rates of volunteering. Among those

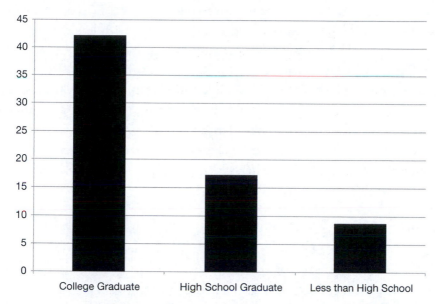

FIGURE 5.2 Volunteer Rates by Education in the US among Adults Age 25 and Over, 2012.

Source: Volunteering and Civic Life in America, 2012. Corporation for National and Community Service. http://www.volunteeringinamerica.gov/national

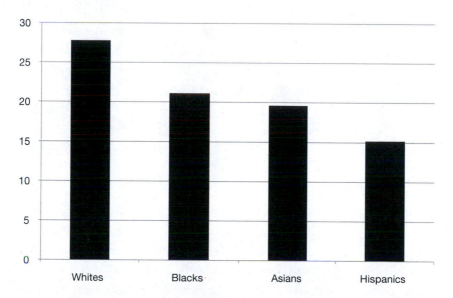

FIGURE 5.3 Volunteer Rates by Race and Ethnicity in the US among Adults Age 25 and Over, 2012.

Source: Volunteering and Civic Life in America, 2012. Corporation for National and Community Service. http://www.volunteeringinamerica.gov/national

age 25 and over, 42.2% of college graduates volunteered, compared with 17.3% of high school graduates, and 8.8% of those with less than a high school diploma. American volunteer rates by race and ethnicity are shown in Figure 5.3. Among major race and ethnic groups, whites formally volunteer at the highest rate (27.8%), followed by blacks (21.1%), Asians (19.6%), and Hispanics (15.2%). It is important to note that since these percentages reflect *formal* volunteering only, they may not be an accurate reflection of total volunteering, including informal volunteering, social support, and informal caregiving which are quite high within black and Latino family and friend networks.[9]

Motivations for Volunteering

Now that we have a picture of who volunteers in America, and where they volunteer, we can begin to examine the reasons people might choose to give of their time. As some have pointed out, volunteering (at least in the formal sense) requires some planning and initiative.[10] A person must seek out volunteer opportunities. Assuming the person is choosing to volunteer of his or her own free will, they have probably spent some time thinking about it and perhaps even talked to others who volunteer, in the process leading up to the decision. The prospective volunteer must invest time in searching for volunteer opportunities and considering the right fit for their interests.[11] Why do people go through all this effort just so they can give away one of life's most precious commodities—time? That is, why do people volunteer? While scholars have proposed many theories, most of these explanations can be grouped into three categories: altruistic explanations, egoistic (or instrumental) explanations, and coercive explanations.

Altruistic Explanations

Altruism is defined as "a social behavior carried out to achieve positive outcomes for someone other than self."[12] A person who describes their reasons for volunteering as "to give back to society," "to make a difference," "to help the less fortunate," or "to help others in need" is someone who can be said to have altruistic concerns motivating their decision to volunteer. Individuals often volunteer to express or act upon important values like humanitarianism or because they feel that it is important to help others.[13] Some others who volunteer may have been personally affected by a cause or issue and wish to reciprocate the help they received by giving of their own time toward the cause.

As we learned earlier, women are more likely to volunteer than men. Is this because women are biologically predisposed to be nicer, kinder people? Or is it because girls are more likely to be socialized from a young age to serve others? Or is it because women used to stay home and had more time to volunteer, so now that more women work they still feel this obligation? A major debate among altruism scholars has to do with the question of whether altruism is a trait that is "hard-wired" into us (behavioral theory of altruism), or whether altruistic behavior is something that can be learned from the social environment (environmental theory of altruism).[14] While there remains a lot of disagreement over these theories, many would suggest that altruism is complex and is present within human beings in different degrees. Thus, perhaps it is possible that a person is partly born with a disposition toward altruistic action, but this tendency can be nurtured over time through encouragement by, and observation of, parents, peers, religious traditions, and other role models or important influences in our environment.

Egoistic Explanations

Egoism is defined as the notion "that individual self-interest is the actual motive of all conscious action."[15] The notion of egoism has its basis in the economic model of man, which views human beings as rational, self-interested, "utility maximizers" seeking to advance one's own interests in any given situation. Those motivated by egoism or instrumentalism may cite building or strengthening one's professional network, gaining professional experience, getting a foot in the door at a place they'd like to work, or opportunities to socialize as their reasons for volunteering. Another set of reasons people may volunteer that align with the theory of egoistic motivations relate to protection of oneself or reducing negative feelings such as guilt, alleviating personal problems, or to escape from one's own troubles.[16]

However straightforward these theories may seem on paper, in reality we cannot neatly separate these motivations. Human beings are complex and it is likely that some combination of altruistic and instrumental motivations is responsible for the decision to either start or continue volunteering. Or as one altruism theorist summed it up "people are by nature, neither saints nor sinners."[17] A person who is regarded as altruistic and chooses to volunteer for a local domestic violence shelter out of pure concern for battered women and their children may also find that she derives some professional benefit, as she plans to go to law school and, based on her experiences at the shelter, now plans to specialize in women's interest law or divorce law. College students may volunteer at the local soup kitchen because it makes them feel good, looks good on a resume, and also helps them meet people. People may be simultaneously driven to volunteer by a mixture of altruistic and egoistic motives, and in fact there is evidence that the majority of people cite more than one reason in their decision to volunteer.[18]

Coercive Explanations

A newer set of explanations for volunteering would suggest that individuals are not intrinsically motivated to volunteer, but, instead, required to do so by persons or institutions that hold power over the individual. The two most visible contexts in which mandated or **compulsory volunteering** exists in the US are in high schools and in local judicial and corrections systems. Parochial high schools and private colleges and universities, particularly those based on a religious faith, have a long history of requiring volunteer hours in order for students to graduate, but the trend has spread in recent years to many public high schools, particularly in more affluent communities. The state of Maryland, for example, mandates volunteering among all of its high schools.[19] In some cases, nations require service as an alternative to conscription (required military service). For example, in Germany and Finland young men are required to serve in the military but can choose an alternative civilian service, or honorary service. Proposals for required national service are often discussed in the US system, though they have never been passed by the Congress. The second group of persons influenced by compulsory volunteering are those who are found guilty of a minor crime and, rather than receiving a jail or prison sentence, the person is placed on probation and sentenced to community service.

These two scenarios rely on somewhat different logics for requiring volunteering. On the one hand, the case for requiring students to volunteer is typically based on rationales such as character development, fostering empathy for those who are less fortunate, and, most importantly, instilling a sense of citizenship and civic duty at an early age. On the other hand, when the judicial system mandates volunteering it is with the intent of creating a consequence for the individual who committed unlawful behavior, or, put another way, as punishment for wrong-doing. Although some might argue that community service for offenders serves a secondary purpose, which is that the offender has an opportunity to experience the intrinsic rewards of productive labor and a sense of community belonging based on the notion of accountability and restitution,[20] there remains some concern that mandatory service is not voluntary and therefore takes away the notion of doing good, being altruistic, or contributing to a common good and civil society.

Proponents of mandated service for high school and college students argue that it is important to impart of sense of duty and responsibility to society at a young age, because it increases the likelihood that young people will adopt the habit of volunteering over their lifespan. There is in fact some evidence that those who volunteer as teenagers are more likely to remain engaged in volunteering as adults. Yet other research has found that among those with prior volunteer experience, those exposed to external control (mandate to volunteer) express lower intention to volunteer in the future than those that volunteered freely.[21] Similarly, there is some evidence that students subjected to mandatory service do not have more positive attitudes or feelings toward civic engagement later in life, as compared to those who volunteer but were not required to do so.[22] With regard to mandatory community service for offenders on probation, there is little evidence that such service works to reduce recidivism rates.[23]

For these and other reasons, mandated volunteering remains a contro-versial topic. One critical reason has to do with the fact that mandatory volunteering is an oxymoron. To volunteer means to give freely of one's time. Mandated community service requires one to do something one did not come to the conscious decision to do on one's own. While many of those who are required to perform volunteer service surely find satisfaction in their efforts, and some of them perhaps would have chosen to volunteer on their own, the fact remains that others who are forced to volunteer will resent it, and thus may lack the necessary attitude, decorum, and commitment to have any impact in their volunteer role.

In short, the act of requiring someone to volunteer stands at odds with the spirit of voluntary action, at least when we think of voluntary service as being inspired by altruism. This point has been made by some high school administrators whose districts have entertained the idea of instituting a formal volunteer requirement for graduation, but ultimately rejected it. For example, Geoffrey N. Gordon, former superintendent of the Port Washington school district in New York, said "I don't believe in mandatory community service, I believe in volunteerism."[24] Another New York school district (Great Neck) has also declined to mandate community service despite the fact that roughly 40% of its high school student body already volunteers, because according to the superintendent, "It just seemed to the faculty that, when you mandate it, you lose the joy of volunteering."[25] Thus, while many high schools and colleges will continue to adopt service requirements, others will take the approach of simply encouraging it, perhaps even incentivizing it, but will stop short of requiring it. Probation courts for their part will continue to mandate community service, as part of a broader movement toward restorative justice in the criminal system.

Arguments that mandatory volunteering goes against the very meaning and intent behind the action have not deterred some from trying to extend service requirements to a new population: those receiving welfare or other types of public benefits. See Box 5.1 for a discussion of this emerging issue.

Finding the Right Fit

While we have examined some of the key reasons why people might choose to volunteer including giving back to society, helping the less fortunate, gaining new skills, and meeting new people, we have given less consideration up to this point to questions of why people *stay* in their volunteer positions. While some, or perhaps even all, of the reasons that compel people to make the initial choice to volunteer will likely play a role in keeping the volunteer in the position over time, a key factor increasing the likelihood that volunteers *stay* is ensuring the right fit. The work associated with the volunteer position must align closely with the specific needs, goals, and interests of the volunteer, and should make the best possible use of the skills and abilities the volunteer has to offer.

Many volunteers leave volunteer positions because they are assigned tasks that are boring, trivial, not well-thought out, or fail to make use of the volunteer's skills and abilities. A former track coach may volunteer for Special Olympics thinking he will be making a difference by spending

BOX 5.1 COMPULSORY COMMUNITY SERVICE: AN ISSUE FOR DEBATE

Under a bill passed in 2013 by the state Senate in Michigan, more than 100,000 Michigan residents receiving welfare benefits will soon be required to do community service. State agencies encourage welfare recipients to find jobs and caseworkers meet with them regularly to check on their progress. Those unable to find work will be expected to perform community service and risk losing welfare benefits if they fail to complete the minimum required service hours.

The bill has been met with mixed support. On the one hand, some are criticizing this law, noting that "mandatory community service" amounts to a punishment for being poor, while others argue that it will place too large a burden on the nonprofit organizations, as many lack capacity to effectively manage and oversee volunteers.[26] On the other hand, proponents of the law argue that community service offers unique opportunities for welfare recipients to learn new skills and build networks and relationships that might lead to a job. Many citizens within the more conservative ranks of the public have argued that welfare recipients should not be allowed to sit idle and collect an income at the taxpayers' expense, especially if they are able-bodied and can perform a service.[27]

In a similar scenario, the Georgia state legislature has recently considered a bill that would require volunteering for those who are out of work and collecting unemployment in the state. The "Dignity for the Unemployed Act" would require those receiving an unemployment check to volunteer at least 24 hours per week in order to earn/maintain their benefits. At roughly 10% , Georgia currently has one of the higher unemployment rates in the nation. Republican state Senator, John Albers, who proposed the bill, views the mandatory service as a solution to reducing unemployment. The logic behind the proposal is that those out of work may feel defeated, but going out into the community to volunteer helps job-seekers find motivation, build a resume, network, and feel good about serving others. However, opponents of the law argue that the service hours pose a hindrance to job search efforts, as one has fewer hours in the week to search for and apply for jobs, as well as reduced availability for interviewing. Some have also argued that requiring volunteering places an economic burden on those already struggling, as many nonprofit organizations and volunteer sites are spread out geographically requiring long drives and recipients will not be compensated for gas money or travel expenses.[28]

It is unclear whether or not the kinds of bills proposed in Michigan and Georgia will take hold, however there seems to be a growing interest as Florida and North Carolina have recently begun considering similar laws to extend community service requirements to recipients of public assistance.[29]

continued

Questions: Should service be mandated? Do your attitudes and feelings toward mandatory volunteering differ according to whether the population being required to serve are high school students, college students, criminal offenders, or recipients of public assistance? Do you think these laws are designed with the intent of helping the individual and civil society, or is the service more like a punishment or a deterrent to keep people from receiving welfare and unemployment benefits?

time coaching kids with disabilities, but then gets assigned the task of making calls to locate practice facilities. Needless to say, this volunteer is likely to experience great disappointment and not stick with it. Others may have specific skills but do not wish to use them in their volunteer role. For example, a person who is an accountant in her day job may want to volunteer with a local animal shelter because she loves animals. If she is assigned the task of reviewing the organization's financial statements, she may not be a fully committed volunteer, since she volunteered to spend time with animals.

Nonprofit organizations have made some mistakes over time with regard to matching volunteers to tasks. Some still make these mistakes, but many others have grown more sensitive to the need to create a good experience for the volunteer. Many organizations now take more time orienting and training volunteers, and trying to find out what the volunteer hopes to get out of the experience. Technology has also played a key role in increasing the likelihood of a good fit between the volunteer's interest and the organization's needs. Whereas before the prospective volunteers may have had to go door-to-door inquiring about volunteer positions or make phone calls, they can now use a variety of websites and search engines to find volunteer opportunities that align with their availability and interests. These opportunities can range from searching the "volunteer" want-ads on Craigslist, or utilizing the highly sophisticated search engines of nonprofit **intermediary organizations** that are designed specifically to match volunteers and their skills to available opportunities.

Some of these intermediary organizations may be familiar to you, such as the United Way. In addition to their roles as fundraising entities and grant-makers, the United Way has had a long history of promoting volunteerism, evident in its modern tagline "Give, Advocate, Volunteer."

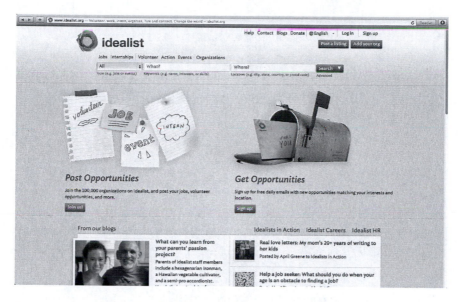

IMAGE 5.1 Screenshot of the idealist.org website.

For some interesting facts on United Way's leadership in promoting volunteerism in America and abroad over the last 125 years, see the chronology on the organization's website: http://www.unitedway.org/pages/history/.[30] Today nearly all local United Ways have a "volunteering" tab on their main website that routes users to another page where they can create a volunteer profile or search for available volunteer opportunities in their community. Another key intermediary organization that helps match prospective volunteers to nonprofit organizations is idealist.org. Image 5.1 shows a screenshot of the Idealist website, which enables individuals to find volunteer opportunities, jobs, and internships. The prospective volunteer can search Idealist by keyword, plugging in words or phrases that indicate their interests or skills, as well as location (city, state, country, or zip code). Idealist is well-linked to other social media platforms and allows registered users to sign in via their Facebook, Twitter, LinkedIn, or Google+ accounts.

Intermediary organizations that link prospective volunteers to organizations and causes have proliferated with the rise of the Internet, and the United Way and Idealist represent only two examples. There are many more of these kinds of organizations, including volunteermatch.org, greatnonprofits.org, and serve.gov among others. Many cities have their own local or regional volunteer matching sites. The goal of all of these organizations is generally the same, which is to help prospective volunteers find the best possible match for their interests, skills, and availability. One of these intermediary organizations, the Taproot Foundation, has specialized in pairing high-skill volunteers with nonprofits that need business expertise. See Box 5.2 for an interesting story about the Taproot Foundation.

Aside from being matched with the wrong position or role, another reason volunteers may leave a volunteer positions is they feel a lack of connection to anyone at the organization. This is particularly problematic for people who volunteer during the evenings and on the weekends. A volunteer who reports for duty outside the "normal" work hours may arrive

BOX 5.2 CAN YOU SPARE SOME TIME (PRO BONO)?: THE TAPROOT FOUNDATION

For some volunteers, stuffing letters into envelopes for the nonprofits' annual campaign is not going to cut it. A large and growing number of white-collar professionals with specialized skills are seeking to volunteer their time and talents for social good. The Taproot Foundation offers the perfect vehicle for linking up these prospective volunteers with nonprofits in their communities who need their services.

Taproot Foundation offers an online marketplace for matching up professionals who wish to donate their skills "**pro bono**" or free of charge to nonprofit organizations with specific skill and technical needs. The organization's website is divided into two frames: "Get Pro Bono" and "Do Pro Bono." Nonprofit organizations in need of technical skills or that have specific projects can apply to Taproot for managed team-based pro bono projects through the "Get Pro Bono" feature or browse pre-scoped project templates for independent use. Taproot simplifies infrastructure needs for nonprofit organizations by grouping areas of possible support into common categories such as financial management, fundraising, legal, marketing and communications, strategic planning,

continued

human resources, information technology, public relations, real estate, and so on. Nonprofits can then take these scoped templates to a pro bono consultant or team of consultants source through their personal or LinkedIn network to execute specific projects that are realistic and produce impactful results. Professionals wishing to volunteer their professional skills through Taproot's team-based Service Grant program can register through the "Do Pro Bono" link. They complete a profile about themselves, indicating their areas of skill and expertise, and identify the types of projects they wish to work on. Taproot then matches the pro bono professionals with nonprofit organizations according to location, expertise, and project interest. Additionally, professionals can take the "pro bono pledge," committing to giving back via pro bono within their communities.

The Taproot Foundation was founded in 2001, based on a decade-old although less widespread pro bono movement in the US, in which socially-conscious businesses encouraged their employees to donate their time and expertise to the community. This tradition has been particularly visible in the legal field, with lawyers donating their time to nonprofit organizations including free legal aid clinics. Although Taproot's headquarters is located in San Francisco, it currently operates an online marketplace, connecting nonprofits with pro bono professionals in major cities across the US and also offers opportunities to perform pro bono work in some locations abroad.

Funded in large part by corporate sponsorships with major US firms such as Pfizer, American Express, and Deloitte (just to name a few) and foundation partners, the Taproot Foundation is an example of a highly successful and effective intermediary organization. The website boasts of 15,000 professionals in the US currently donating their time, through connections facilitated by Taproot. With the growing confidence and interest in pro bono services, new pro bono providers are emerging quickly. These range from formal corporate programs (over 30 of which have been designed in partnership with Taproot), to new standalone providers worldwide, to traditional volunteerism and capacity-building programs expanding into pro bono service. The largest institutional source of pro bono is professional services firms (e.g. consulting firms, design firms, etc.). Bain & Co., for example, delivered $40 million in pro bono in 2011. While the supply of pro bono services and programs is rapidly growing, the need in the nonprofit sector remains significant. Taproot offers a constantly-updating figure at the top of its website revealing the dollar value of pro bono services donated to date which read $122,620,927 at the end of 2013. The organization has a goal of reaching $1 billion in donated services by 2020. Do you think they will get there?

For a short video on Taproot's origins and current work, visit: http://www.taprootfoundation.org/

at the work site to find that there are very few staff present with whom they can interact. Others may leave their volunteer posts because they feel as if their efforts are not recognized or appreciated by the nonprofit organization.

Each of these scenarios highlights the importance of having a good volunteer management program in place within the organization that is accepting volunteers. While some nonprofits have learned the bitter lesson of high volunteer turnover, and many have gotten better over time about building in resources for recruiting, training, and overseeing volunteers, many nonprofits still under-invest in volunteer management programs. It may be tempting for nonprofit leaders to think of volunteers as "free labor" without recognizing the costs associated with having volunteers. Organizations that understand the value of volunteers will invest the resources necessary to develop an appropriate volunteer screening and selection process, provide proper training and orientation of volunteers, ensure adequate supervision, oversight, and support of volunteers, and will have established routines for rewarding, recognizing, and expressing appreciation for volunteers. Each of these is an essential component of an effective volunteer management program. The nonprofit organizations that have figured this out and develop the capacity to create a positive volunteer experience will have the competitive edge in attracting and retaining the best and brightest in today's competitive market for good volunteers. Having a good volunteer management program may be optional for some nonprofits, but it is essential for those that rely on volunteers to carry out their mission, such as Big Brothers/Big Sisters profiled earlier in the chapter.

In sum, the factors that keep volunteers engaged in nonprofit organizations depend on the individual. Two people can engage in the same volunteer activity but may be motivated by completely different reasons.[31] Therefore it is important that the nonprofit receiving the gift of a person's time invests the effort in finding out what the person hopes to gain from the experience, and then takes steps (to the extent possible, and within reason) to ensure that the volunteer's expectations are met.

The Role of Technology in Volunteering

As we discussed in Chapter 4, technology has altered the ways in which we view and define community. In this same way, technology has changed the landscape of volunteering. In addition to technological resources we have already considered such as search engines and volunteer matching sites run by intermediary organizations, the Internet has broadened the structure of opportunities in such a way that individuals no longer need necessarily to report for duty at an organization, or commit for any period of time, in order to volunteer. With the advent of **virtual volunteering**, those who wish to donate their time can now do so at their leisure and in the comfort of their own homes.

Virtual volunteers (a.k.a. online volunteers) complete their volunteer tasks, either wholly or in part, off-site from the organization for which they are volunteering, using the Internet and a home, school, or work computer, or other Internet-connected device, in order to benefit a nonprofit organization.[32] What kinds of tasks do virtual volunteers perform? Online volunteers perform an incredibly wide array of tasks including translating documents, creating web pages, editing or writing proposals, press releases, or newsletter articles, developing material for a curriculum, designing a database, designing graphics, scanning documents, providing legal, business, or medical expertise, moderating online discussion groups, creating podcasts, editing videos, monitoring the news, tagging photos and files, and managing other online volunteers, among other things.[33] Knowledge contributions to Wikipedia, for example, provide an illustration of the way that people might engage in virtual volunteering. Wikipedia is the free online encyclopedia which claims 71,000 active editors, or people who voluntarily contribute content in their specialized areas of expertise or knowledge.[34]

Since virtual volunteers work remotely, many more people may find it possible to donate their time. The Internet has enabled anyone with the time, desire, skills, and an Internet connection the opportunity to become a volunteer. Aside from the ability to volunteer from home, or a location of one's own choosing, another attractive feature of virtual volunteering is that one need not make a long-term commitment. **Micro-volunteering** is a form of virtual volunteering that engages the volunteer in a task that takes only minutes or a few hours to complete, and does not require an ongoing commitment by the volunteer.[35] Micro-volunteering is similar to **episodic volunteering** in that it offer volunteers a low-commitment option to give of their time. Episodic volunteering usually refers to a one-time volunteer experience, or volunteering that occurs on a very limited time basis. An example of this would be a Girl Scout troup that volunteers to pick up trash along a designated stretch of public land one Saturday, through the Adopt-A-Highway program.

But micro-volunteering requires even less time and effort than a typical episodic volunteer experience, which one must plan for, travel to, and invest a day or at least several hours to complete. Micro-volunteering can be limited to minutes or even seconds, conducted via a regular computer or through a wide array of smartphone applications. Through these apps, and other micro-volunteering platforms, people are asked to give of their time by commenting on blogs, giving opinions, sharing ideas, tagging photos, tweeting or re-tweeting messages, or sharing information via Facebook or social media utilities. **Crowdsourcing** could be considered another common way that people might engage in micro-volunteering. Crowdsourcing involves soliciting contributions in the form of ideas or content for a decision or project from a large group of people, usually from an online community.[36]

Some have praised the concept of micro-volunteering, recognizing that it is yet another way that nonprofits and social change organizations might tap into the human desire to help, albeit among those with very limited time, or who are unwilling or unable to make a long-term commitment. Indeed, intermediary organizations have begun developing handbooks and tool kits for nonprofit organizations on how to structure micro-volunteering projects in order to get the maximum benefit from them.[37] Critics, however, point to the deficiencies in technology, in particular the mobile phone apps, and argue that we have a long way to go before this trend catches on. It is safe to say at this point that micro-volunteering is an emerging area of voluntary action and only time will tell if this trend will take hold, and whether or not it will have a discernible impact on the nonprofit sector.

Summary

Voluntary labor is a critical resource for nonprofit organizations and one of the distinguishing features of the nonprofit sector. Volunteering is a form of civic engagement, and helps to foster social capital between and among individuals and organizations within communities, and strengthens civil society. There are many reasons individuals might choose to volunteer, but most people are compelled to volunteer by some combination of altruistic and instrumental motives. However, there are some who engage in community service because they are mandated or coerced to do so by a person or institution who holds power over the individual, as in the case of high school students being required to volunteer in order to graduate. Mandated volunteering is somewhat controversial because volunteering is generally understood as giving freely of one's own time, and when an individual is forced to give of their time, the motivation, helpful attitude, and intent to "do good" may be absent which can create problems for the organization receiving the person's time.

Finding the right fit is critical to ensuring the volunteer experience will be rewarding. If volunteers are to stay in their roles for any length of time, the volunteer position must be suited to each person's interests and availability. Nonprofit intermediary organizations such as the United Way and Idealist have helped to bridge the gap between nonprofit organizational needs and individuals searching for suitable volunteer opportunities. Both nonprofit organizations and volunteers have benefitted from technological advances, as nonprofits can advertise their volunteer positions on their websites and dozens of intermediary organizations have sophisticated search engines that allow for precise matching of volunteers' searches to organizational opportunities. Today, many people also engage in virtual volunteering, which allows individuals to perform volunteer work from the convenience of their home or any other location with an Internet connection. Virtual volunteers often contribute their knowledge and skills to specific projects that nonprofit organizations need done, such as website development, or graphic design, that the organization lacks the staffing capacity or expertise to accomplish on its own. While the role of technology in volunteering is still emerging, it is fair to say that the Internet has dramatically broadened the structure of opportunities for volunteers.

KEY TERMS

- Altruism
- Compulsory volunteering
- Crowdsourcing
- Egoism
- Episodic volunteering
- Intermediary organization
- Micro-volunteering
- Pro bono
- Utility maximizer
- Virtual volunteering
- Volunteer rate

DISCUSSION QUESTIONS

1. Do you currently volunteer? If so, what are the reasons you chose to volunteer? Why did you choose the particular volunteer opportunity? For those who do not volunteer, what are the reasons you choose not to volunteer?

2. Do your parents volunteer? Do you think your decision to volunteer or not volunteer has been shaped by their example?

3. If you have volunteered in the past but left a volunteer job, what are the reasons you discontinued the service? Could the organization have done anything differently to ensure you were having the optimal volunteer experience?

4. Do you think altruism is more like something people are born with, or more a product of learning from their environment? Explain why you think it is more one or the other.

5. When service is mandated and not performed at the initiative of the individual, how does that change the volunteer experience for the individual and for the recipient organization?

6. What are the advantages of intermediary organizations matching volunteers to organizations? Are there any disadvantages to this approach? When you finish your college degree, would you consider doing pro bono work for a nonprofit organization?

Websites

Corporation for National and Community Service—The CNCS produces a report each year on Volunteering and Civic Life in America with an interactive website that allows users to find all data on volunteering in the 50 states: http://www.volunteering inamerica.gov/national

Idealist: www.idealist.org

Volunteer Match: www.volunteermatch.org

Great Nonprofits: www.greatnonprofits.org

Corporation for National and Community Service: www.serve.gov

Notes

1   Lee, Young-Joo and Jeffrey Brudney. 2012. Participation in Formal and Informal Volunteering: Implications for Volunteer Recruitment. *Nonprofit Management & Leadership*, 23(2): 159–180.

2   Lee and Brudney (2012).

3   Cunniffe, Eileen. 2013. Study Underscores the Health, Wellness and Career Benefits of Volunteering. *The Nonprofit Quarterly*, October, 22, 2013. Accessed March 8, 2014 at https://nonprofitquarterly.org/policysocial-context/23113-study-underscores-health-wellness-and-career-benefits-of-volunteering.html

4   Alcholics Anonymous (AA) At-A-Glance. Accessed October 23, 2013 at http://www.aa.org/pdf/products/f-1_AAataGlance.pdf

5   Corporation for National and Community Service. Volunteer Rates—States. Accessed February 26, 2014 at http://www.volunteeringinamerica.gov/rankings.cfm

6   Volunteering and Civic Life in America. 2012. Corporation for National and Community Service. Accessed October 23, 2013 at http://www.volunteeringinamerica.gov/national

7   Volunteering and Civic Life in America (2012).

8   All statistics reported in this section were obtained from the 2012 report on Volunteering and Civic Life in America.

9   Dominguez, Siliva and Celeste Watkins. 2003. Creating Networks for Survival and Mobility: Social Capital Among African-American and Latin-American Low-Income Mothers. *Social Problems*, 50(1): 111–135

10 Clary, E. Gil and Mark Snyder. 1999. The Motivations to Volunteer: Theoretical and Practical Insights. *Current Directions in Psychological Science*, 8(5): 156–159.

11 Clary and Snyder (1999).

12 Rushton, J. Phillippe. (1980, p. 8). *Altruism, Socialization, and Society*. Englewood Cliffs: Prentice Hall.

13 Clary and Snyder (1999).

14 Wolfe, Alan. 1998. What is Altruism?, in Walter W. Powell and Elisabeth S. Clemens (eds), *Private Action and the Public Good*. New Haven, CT: Yale University Press.

15 Merriam-Webster Dictionary. 2013. Accessed October 24, 2014 at http://www.merriam-webster.com/dictionary/egoism

16 Clary and Snyder (1999).

17 Wolfe (1998).

18 Clary and Snyder (1999).

19 Stewart, Ain. 2003. The Logic of "Mandatory Volunteerism," New York Times, March 23, 2003. Accessed October 26, 2013 at http://www.nytimes.com/2003/03/23/nyregion/the-logic-of-mandatory-volunteerism.html?pagewanted=all&src=pm

20 State of Illinois Circuit Court of Cook County. Accessed October 26, 2013 at http://www.cookcountycourt.org/ABOUTTHECOURT/OfficeoftheChiefJudge/ProbationDepartments/ProbationforAdults/SocialServiceDepartment/CommunityServiceProgram.aspx

21 Stukas, Arthur A., Mark Snyder, and E. Gil Clary. 1999. The Effects of "Mandatory Volunteerism" on Intentions to Volunteer. *Psychological Science*, 10(1): 59–64.

22 Henderson, Alisa, Steven D. Brown, S. Mark Pancer, and Kimberly Ellis-Hale. 2007. Mandated Community Service in High School and Subsequent Civic Engagement: The Case of the "Double Cohort" in Ontario, Canada. *Journal of Youth & Adolescence*, 86: 849–860.

23 Schneider, Anne L. 1986. Restitution and Recidivism Rates of Juvenile Offenders: Results from Four Experimental Studies. *Criminology*, 24(3): 533–552.

24 Stewart (2003).

25 Stewart (2003).

26   Cohen, Rick. 2013. Michigan: Let's Make Benefit Recipients Volunteer for Non-profits. *Nonprofit Quarterly*. 24 September 2013.

27   Dignity for the Unemployed Act Requires Jobless To Volunteer For Benefits. 2011. First Posted: 12/12/11 09:27 AM ET. Updated: 12/12/11 11:54 AM ET. Huffington Post. Accessed October 26, 2013 at http://www.huffingtonpost.com/2011/12/12/dignity-for-the-unemploye_n_1139447.html

28   Dignity for the Unemployed Act Requires Jobless To Volunteer For Benefits (2011).

29   Wheatley, Thomas. 2011. Lawmaker wants jobless to perform mandatory community service to receive unemployment benefits. Accessed October 27, 2013 at http://clatl.com/freshloaf/archives/2011/11/30/lawmaker-wants-jobless-to-perform-mandatory-community-service-to-receive-unemployment-benefits

30   United Way of America. Accessed March 8, 2014 at http://www.unitedway.org/pages/history/

31   Clary and Snyder (1999).

32   Cravens, Jayne. 2007. Online Volunteering Enters Middle Age—And Changes Management Paradigms. *Nonprofit Quarterly*, 4: 65–68.

33   Service Leader. Virtual Volunteering Resources. The University of Texas at Austin. Accessed October 27, 2013 at http://www.serviceleader.org/virtual

34   http://www.serviceleader.org/virtual/examples. Accessed October 27, 2013.

35   Weeks, Linton. 2009. The Extraordinaries: Will Microvolunteering Work? National Public Radio. July 01, 200912:01 AM. Accessed October 28, 2013 at http://www.serviceleader.org/virtual

36   http://www.merriam-webster.com/dictionary/crowdsourcing and http://www.cbsnews.com/news/what-is-crowdsourcing/ Accessed October 28, 2013.

37   How to Develop a Microvolunteering Action. Help from Home. Accessed October 27, 2013 at http://www.helpfromhome.org/microvolunteering-project.pdf

6

PHILANTHROPY, FOUNDATIONS, AND GIVING

CHAPTER LEARNING OBJECTIVES

By the end of this chapter, students will be able to:

1. Describe some of the key functions of foundations
2. Explain the relationship of foundations to the rest of the nonprofit sector
3. Describe some basic facts about giving patterns in the US
4. Explain some of the reasons that people give their money to charity
5. Describe the role of technology in giving to nonprofit organizations and social causes

---

Introduction

Americans give roughly $300 billion per year to charity.[4] Despite the high-profile wealthy figures described in the anecdote below, one does not need to be a billionaire, millionaire, or even earn six figures in order to be a philanthropist. As we noted in Chapter 2, **philanthropy** is a fundamental value underlying the nonprofit sector, defined as "an act or gift done or made for humanitarian purposes." While the term philanthropy, is often

THE GIVING PLEDGE

Giving it All Away, the Modern American Philanthropist

The Giving Pledge is an effort to help address society's most pressing problems by inviting the world's wealthiest individuals and families to commit to giving more than half of their wealth to philanthropy or charitable causes either during their lifetime or in their will.

In June 2010, a group of billionaires came together to pledge to give away at least 50% of their wealth to philanthropy and charity. As of 2013, the pledge, first proposed by Warren Buffet and Bill Gates, has gained the support of 112 other billionaires including Michael Bloomberg (business magnate and politician), Sara Blakely (creator of Spanx), Ted Turner (media mogul), Lyda Hill (granddaughter of Dallas oil industry tycoon H. L. Hunt), George Lucas (filmmaker), Mark Zuckerberg (Facebook co-founder), and John Paul DeJoria (John Paul Mitchell Systems co-founder). "The Giving Pledge" has a website listing all those who have committed to the pledge: http://www. thegivingpledge.org

Some of these billionaires give because they can. Others give because they do not intend to leave their wealth for their children. In 2006, Warren Buffet committed to give away 99% of his wealth before dying. In his pledge, T. Bonne Pickens writes "To date, I've given away nearly $800 million to a wide-range of charitable organizations, and I look forward to the day I hit the $1 billion mark. I'm not a big fan of inherited wealth. It generally does more harm than good."

Michael Bloomberg, who as of March 2013 has a net worth of over $30 billion ranking him as the 13th richest person in the world,[1] has also signed the pledge. As a self-made billionaire, Bloomberg has long noted that he does not plan to leave his wealth to his daughters. Instead, he has given millions of dollars to philanthropy with a focus on public health, government innovation, the environment, education, and the arts.[2] In a commencement address at Bard College in 2006, Bloomberg stated, "I am a big believer in giving it all away and have always said that the best financial planning ends with bouncing the check to the undertaker."[3]

The Giving Pledge is not legally binding and does not involve pooling money or supporting a particular organization or cause. Instead, individuals and families are asked to pledge to give away their wealth and make a public statement and commitment about how they will engage in that giving. The Giving Pledge asks members of the group to make a public statement of how they will engage in philanthropy, expecting that being explicit about giving intentions will help "inspire conversations, discussions,

continued

and action, not just about how much but also for what purposes/to what end and bring together those committed to this kind of giving to exchange knowledge on how to do this in the best possible way."

The public statement also serves to raise awareness about philanthropy in general, creating an atmosphere of giving. The pledge is a "moral commitment to give" and a venue for billionaires to share their ideas and develop innovative ways to give. The website notes that "We live in an exciting time for philanthropy where innovative approaches and advances in technology have redefined what's possible. Grassroots movements are proving every day how a single individual, regardless of wealth, can make a lasting impact on the lives of others."

Word Map from the Text of 2011 Giving Pledge Letters

Questions: What do you think of The Giving Pledge? Are these billionaires being particularly generous? Should they give away all their wealth? If you were worth millions, what would you do? What types of organizations would you give your wealth to?

associated with the Warren Buffets of the world, it is widely embraced among Americans. In fact, the vast majority of American households—88% —gave to charity in 2012.[5] Private giving constitutes a vital resource for the nonprofit sector, enabling charitable organizations of all kinds to further their missions. Similar to their reliance on voluntary labor, non-profits' dependence on monetary contributions is a key feature distinguishing the nonprofit sector from the for-profit and public (government) sectors.

This chapter examines this fascinating aspect of human behavior— giving away one's hard-earned money to help someone else or to further a particular cause. Private giving to nonprofit organizations comes from two main sources: **foundations** and individual donations. The chapter is organized around these two topics. We will briefly consider the origins of foundations in the US, followed by a discussion of the contemporary foundation subsector in America, identifying the number and types of these institutions. We then describe some of the major purposes and functions of foundations and consider some of the questions surrounding these organizations. After summarizing the foundation landscape in the America, we turn our attention to individual giving, examining some basic facts about who gives, followed by a look at some of the reasons, or motives, that compel giving. Finally, we consider the role of technology in giving, looking at the ways that the Internet, social media, and mobile technology have altered the landscape of giving in recent years.

Foundations

Foundations are a small but critical subset of the US nonprofit population. The vast majority of foundations are grant-making organizations, meaning that they exist to finance the work of other nonprofit organizations whose missions align with the foundations' giving priorities. This financing occurs by giving **grants**. Grants are financial awards that are given from one party (the grant-maker) to another (the grant recipient), with no requirements for repayment. Grants are typically given to fund a project or activity. In 2011, foundations gave away $46.9 billion and comprised roughly 13% of all private giving to nonprofit organizations.[6] Thus, foundations are a critical source of funding to the nonprofit sector and individual organizations, helping to supplement the revenue nonprofits receive from government, individual donors, corporations, and other sources. In this section, we will examine foundations, beginning with a brief history of foundations, followed by a look at the number and types of foundations in the US today. Lastly, we examine some of the key functions and purposes of foundations.

The History of Foundations

The origins of US foundations began with Andrew Carnegie. Perhaps the most famous philanthropist of all time, Carnegie was a European immigrant of modest means who made his fortune in the steel industry in the late 1800s. Described as a **pragmatist**, a person who believes decisions should be made based on evidence and practical knowledge of how to adapt and control reality, Carnegie lived a modest lifestyle and believed in hard work, rugged individualism, and the right to accumulate wealth.[7] However he also believed strongly in education and elevating the human experience. To this end, Carnegie not only gave away his entire fortune, but he also called upon other men of means to do the same in his published manifesto *The Gospel of Wealth*. In this work, Carnegie called on the rich to use their wealth to improve society by redistributing their fortune, living a moderate lifestyle, and not leaving large sums of money or material possession to heirs, believing it encouraged laziness and a sense of entitlement. Carnegie's manifesto was highly influential among other wealthy industrialists of his time, and although his **paternalistic** views (the belief that a person or organization should protect people, make decisions for them, and give them what they need, eliminating their own freedom to choose what is best for themselves) have been somewhat controversial, his words remain relevant today and serve as a guiding force for many of the most wealthy philanthropists of modern times.

Not only did Carnegie's financial gifts help to expand public infrastructure such as libraries (see Box 6.1) and catalyze a more formalized aid system, it also encouraged subsequent men of wealth such as John D. Rockefeller and John D. MacArthur to embrace his ideas. These early pioneers, and others such as Edsel Ford and Ewing Marion Kaufman, helped to shape the concept of modern philanthropy and giving. The work of these early philanthropists in the 19th and 20th centuries paved the way for growth of the foundation sector and served as the template for modern foundations, which today invest heavily in **social programs** throughout the US and abroad. Box 6.1 provides an in-depth look at the life of Andrew Carnegie, father of the modern American foundation sector, and his motivations for giving away his vast fortune.

The Modern US Foundation Sector

In the more than 100 years that have elapsed since Carnegie's *The Gospel of Wealth* was published, the US foundation sector has grown dramatically, developing into a robust set of institutions that invest billions of dollars each year into social programs administered by public and nonprofit organizations. As Table 6.1 shows, there are more than 88,000 foundations in the United States today. Among those 88,000 organizations, the majority (62.5%) report asset levels less than $1 million; they are small, private

BOX 6.1 AN AMERICAN PHILANTHROPIST—GIVING THEN, LIBRARIES NOW

Andrew Carnegie, American businessman and philanthropist, 1913

Andrew Carnegie (1835–1919), the son of a handloom weaver, came to the US from Scotland in 1848, built a steel empire, became the richest man in the world, and then gave it all away to fund 1,689 public libraries. Carnegie envisioned his libraries as a means for advancing the lives of the poor, a critical source for education and knowledge. In 1903, his donation of $300,000 built Washington DC's oldest library, open to women, children, and all races. Carnegie's libraries were a refuge and knowledge center for the marginalized in American society. "During the Depression, D.C.'s Carnegie Library was called 'the intellectual breadline.' No one had any money, so you went there to feed your brain" (Stamberg, 2013).[8]

Why Libraries?

At the age of 13, in Allegheny City, Pennsylvania, Carnegie started his first job in a textile mill as a bobbin boy. He was determined to work his way out of poverty, but he could not afford the $2.00 subscription to the local library that was available to apprentices. He sent a request to the library asking for permission to use the library. When his request was denied, Carnegie sent his letter to *The Pittsburgh Dispatch*. Raising this public awareness of his inability to access the library led the library to open to working men and bobbin boys, not just apprentices. Carnegie believed that education was the key to advancing his life.

continued

Self-educated and determined, Carnegie went on to telegraphs, railroads, iron, and steel. When he sold Carnegie Steel to J. P. Morgan for nearly half a billion dollars, J. P. Morgan called Carnegie "the richest man in the world." He then gave away about $350 million of his earnings—mostly to libraries.

Then, and now, Carnegie libraries are some of the most beautiful buildings in town. More important, they provide services beyond just books including computers, job training, and other community services. Public libraries, first funded by Carnegie, are of central importance to community-building in many towns around America and in some cases provided communities with the first and only public access to books and knowledge. Ben Loftis, director of the Union County Carnegie Library in South Carolina, notes that Carnegie's gifts ensured that libraries "went from being for just the wealthy elite landowners and planters to actually being a service for the entire county that everybody has access to" (Stamberg, 2013). Carnegie changed libraries from exclusively institutions for the rich to important, community institutions for the public.

Carnegie's Views of Philanthropy

By the time of his death in 1919, Carnegie had given away most of his wealth, including around $60 million to fund 1,689 public libraries. Carnegie believed he was responsible for giving back to the society that helped to create his wealth. According to Carnegie, "The man who dies thus rich dies disgraced" (1889).[9]

But Carnegie's view of philanthropy was not one of blind charity. He expected the poor to work for themselves, noting that "In bestowing charity, the main consideration should be to help those who will help themselves" (Carnegie, 1889). Carnegie believed that free and public access to knowledge (e.g. libraries) would provide the self-motivated to advance their lives. Carnegie viewed philanthropy as an obligation of the rich: that the rich should give so that the poor could improve their lives and ultimately society. For Carnegie, giving was "a code of honor" (Stamberg, 2013).

While Carnegie saw philanthropy as his civic duty, his generosity might also be characterized as paternalism—acting to make decisions and take care of others while taking away their responsibility or ability to choose for themselves. Carnegie envisioned himself as a shepherd of his wealth, responsible for doing what he thought was best and right for others. He argued that "the man of wealth thus becoming the mere trustee and agent for his poorer brethren, bringing to their service his superior wisdom, experience, and ability to administer, doing for them better than they would or could do for themselves" (Nasaw, 2007, 350).[10] During the Homestead Steel Strike of 1892, Carnegie fought against workers' demands for better pay and working conditions. Carnegie believed that it was better to use his wealth to build libraries and public

continued

institutions for the working class, rather than raise their wages and trust them to invest in their own futures. He is quoted as having said, "If I had raised your wages, you would have spent that money by buying a better cut of meat or more drink for your dinner. But what you needed, though you didn't know it, was my libraries and concert halls. And that's what I'm giving to you" (Stamberg, 2013).

Carnegie was one of the greatest philanthropists in American history. We have him to thank for many public libraries that stand in large cities and small towns throughout the United States—testaments to learning and ambition. However, libraries that have benefitted Americans for over 100 years may have come at the expense of workers at the turn of the century.

While Carnegie's business success and subsequent generosity and investment in public goods remain an example for wealthy Americans today, we are left with many questions. Is it the obligation of the rich to give back to society? Should those who achieve great wealth determine the best way to advance society? Would Carnegie's wealth have been better spent improving factory conditions for his workers—reducing their work hours so they would have had time to read a book, instead of investing in books for future generations? If Carnegie hadn't built libraries around the US, would the government have done it? Would we have libraries in many towns in America without Carnegie's philanthropic giving?

foundations. Only 2.8% of private foundations in the US in 2010 reported assets of more than $25 million.

Types of Foundations

There are four main types of foundations: grant-making, operating, corporate, and community. In the US, **grant-making foundations** are by far the most numerous, comprising roughly 90% of the foundation subsector.[11] As their name implies, these organizations exist primarily to issue grants to other nonprofit organizations and, to a lesser extent, government organizations whose programs, services, projects, and initiatives align with the foundations' goals and mission. The assets of these foundations vary from billions of dollars to small family foundations with only a few thousand dollars. Examples of well-known grant-making foundations include the Bill and Melinda Gates Foundation, the Ford Foundation, Kellogg Foundation, and Rockefeller Foundation.

TABLE 6.1 Number of Private Foundations in the United States, 2010

Total Asset Level	Number Filing with IRS in Past 2 Years	Total Revenue ($)	Total Assets ($)
Under $1 million	55,591	3,298,926,031	15,363,736,867
$1–10 million	27,625	7,781,948,867	73,466,872,946
$10–25 million	3,132	5,215,044,056	48,813,229,630
More than $25 million	2,531	27,525,260,093	444,933,691,884
Total	88,879	43,821,179,047	582,577,531,327

Source: IRS Business Master File 04/2010 (with modifications by the National Center for Charitable Statistics at the Urban Institute).

There are several varieties of **corporate foundations,** but the most common type is the company-sponsored foundation.[12] As the name implies, corporate foundations are established and often governed by members of the corporate leadership or by individuals the corporation chooses. Well-known examples of large corporate foundations include Target Corporation, Coca-Cola, Verizon, Exxon, General Mills, and the Wells Fargo Foundation. As these names suggest, corporate foundations can be found in nearly every industry including retail, food and beverage, telecommunications, oil and gas, and the banking and finance industry. Many pharmaceutical manufacturers have corporate foundations as well—such Merck, Abbott, Eli Lilly, and Novartis—through which these companies make special grants to healthcare organizations to help sponsor indigent patients' treatment and facilitate access to needed medications. While the financial gifts made by these corporations through their foundations amount to a relatively small fraction of the corporations' total profits, these funds can nevertheless be quite substantial and of significant value to the nonprofit organizations that receive the funds. Walmart, for example, ranks fifth on the list of corporate foundations in terms of total annual giving—in 2010 it gave away $2 billion in cash and in-kind donations in the food area alone as part of its "Fighting Hunger Together" initiative.[13] These monies were dispersed to community-based nonprofit organizations throughout the country in communities where the corporation has local stores.

Community foundations are a special type of grant-making foundation that "pools revenue and assets from a variety of sources (individual, corporate, and public) for specified communal purposes."[14] Community foundations are different from grant-making foundations and corporate foundations in that they operate with a conglomerate of funding sources. The world's first community foundation was the Cleveland Foundation, which was established in 1914 by banker, lawyer, and former mayor Frederick H. Goff. Goff wanted to pool the resources of Cleveland's philanthropists into a single permanent fund that could be endowed and used for the betterment of the city in perpetuity.[15] Goff's model for community giving caught on, and today there are more than 700 community foundations in the US, and an estimated 1,700 community foundations worldwide.[16] The largest of these in terms of assets is the Tulsa Community Foundation (assets of $3.8 billion as of 2011), followed by the Silicon Valley Community Foundation ($2.9 billion) and the New York Community Trust ($2 billion).[17] These and hundreds of other community foundations across the US make grants for causes as diverse as promoting local economic development, strengthening public education, supporting arts and cultural institutions, creating scholarship funds, financing local pageants and festivals, and supporting numerous other local priorities and initiatives.

Another type of foundation, albeit a relatively small slice of the foundation sector, is the **operating foundation**. In contrast to grant-making foundations that give away their funds to other organizations working towards the same goals as the grant-making foundation, operating foundations use their funds to pursue their goals directly. Foundations that engage in scientific or social science research are a common example of operating foundations. Well-known examples of operating foundations include the Russell Sage Foundation, which is solely dedicated to funding research in the social sciences; the Open Society Institute, founded and funded by liberal billionaire George Soros, with the aim of promoting democratic governance, human rights, and economic, legal, and social reform; the Henry J. Kaiser Family Foundation, which develops and runs its own research, journalism, and communication programs focused on major healthcare issues facing the US; the Lincoln Institute of Land Policy, a think tank that aims to provide education and research on issues related to the use, regulation, and taxation of land; and the Commonweal Foundation, which supports and operates educational programs and projects assisting underserved children and youth. Operating foundations come in all shapes and sizes and seek to solve a variety of social problems in the US through their own research, programs, and activities.

Two organizations in the US serve as important authorities on foundations: The Foundation Center and the Council on Foundations. These organizations assemble data on the number and types of foundations in the US and provide rank-ordered lists of foundations by asset size and annual giving. They simplify and streamline the grant-search process for nonprofit organizations seeking funding, as their websites allow users to search by state, zip code, and program area, as well as find useful practical information and training resources on writing grant proposals and applying for foundations funds. Table 6.2 provides a list of the top twenty US foundations by asset size, based on data compiled by the Foundation Center. The largest is the Bill and Melinda Gates Foundation with assets over $34 billion, followed by the Ford Foundation, a corporate foundation with assets over 10 billion.

The Functions of Foundations

Foundations primarily serve as vehicles for enabling large sums of privately owned money to be invested and saved without penalty of tax payment, for the purpose of producing some type of social benefit. While their main purpose might be seen as **redistribution,** or the transfer of wealth from one individual or group to another, foundations serve several other important purposes in US society.

Another key purpose of foundations is **stimulating innovation.** Foundations invest money into creative new programs or ideas that involve risks. The John D. and Catherine T. MacArthur foundation for example makes annual awards of $625,000 to 20 to 40 individuals who hold promise for increasing creative capital in society. Known as "genius grants" these awards are "not a reward for past accomplishment, but rather an investment in a person's originality, insight, and potential"[18] and are awarded to people in fields as diverse as chemistry, poetry, mathematics, medicine, theatre, film-making, law, and statistics, among many others. Similarly the Herman and Frieda L. Miller Foundation funds efforts to enhance empowerment and civic engagement among the diverse communities throughout the greater Boston and Eastern Massachusetts area. The Miller Foundation invests in innovative solutions for community-organizing, field- and movement-building efforts, strengthening alliances between

TABLE 6.2 **Top 20 US Foundations by Asset Size**

Rank	Foundation Name (State)	Assets ($)	Type	
1.	Bill & Melinda Gates Foundation (WA)	34,640,122,664	Grant-making	A
2.	Ford Foundation (NY)	10,984,721,000	Corporate	B
3.	J. Paul Getty Trust (CA)	10,502,514,302	Grant-making	B
4.	The Robert Wood Johnson Foundation (NJ)	8,967,712,917	Grant-making	A
5.	The William and Flora Hewlett Foundation (CA)	7,735,372,000	Grant-making	B
6.	Lilly Endowment Inc. (IN)	7,281,773,872	Corporate	B
7.	W. K. Kellogg Foundation (MI)	7,256,863,114	Grant-making	B
8.	The David and Lucile Packard Foundation (CA)	5,797,424,139	Corporate	A
9.	The John D. and Catherine T. MacArthur Foundation (IL)	5,703,076,554	Grant-making	A
10.	Gordon and Betty Moore Foundation (CA)	5,366,672,508	Grant-making	A
11.	The Andrew W. Mellon Foundation (NY)	5,262,632,426	Grant-making	A
12.	The Leona M. and Harry B. Helmsley Charitable Trust (NY)	4,062,077,909	Grant-making	B
13.	Tulsa Community Foundation (OK)	3,828,264,000	Community	A
14.	The California Endowment (CA)	3,660,548,000	Grant-making	B
15.	The Rockefeller Foundation (NY)	3,507,144,871	Grant-making	A
16.	The Kresge Foundation (MI)	3,025,786,097	Grant-making	A
17.	Bloomberg Philanthropies (NY)	2,991,369,695	Grant-making	A
18.	The Duke Endowment(NC)	2,948,446,116	Grant-making	B
19.	Robert W. Woodruff Foundation Inc. (GA)	2,841,725,477	Grant-making	B
20.	Carnegie Corporation of New York (NY)	2,764,431,433	Grant-making	B

Source: The Foundation Center: www.foundationcenter.org

Notes: Data last updated from financial data in the Foundation Center's database as of January 25, 2014. A:12/31/2011; B:2012.

and action plans of advocacy groups, and helping grass roots leaders and organizations build capacity to participate in larger social change efforts. The foundation uses the following description of innovation as a guide in their grant-making decisions: "An innovation is a new approach to address a problem or need, or an approach used to address a new situation or context, which warrants experimental application, learning or development."[19] As this definition suggests, creative ideas involve risks, and risk sometimes involves failures. Unlike governments, which must be cautious about expenditures so as not to attract criticism from the public about wasteful spending, foundations involve private money that can be spent however its leaders choose, making foundations an ideal source of funding for investing in innovative and riskier endeavors.

Foundations articulate a vision for change, and develop a targeted, but systematic strategy for achieving that vision. This involves intensely **targeting resources** toward specific, but multi-faceted and complex problems that no single organization can solve on their own. Foundations target resources by determining their priorities, or vision for society, and then create broad "programs" under which they make grants to help pursue their goals. Foundations carefully select nonprofits and, to a lesser extent, government organizations and individuals who apply for grants under these program areas, to obtain funding to carry out new ideas or programs that might help to fulfill the foundations' vision. In many instances, these visions relate to solving deeply entrenched and seemingly unsolvable social issues, such as ending poverty, climate change, or crime. For example, the Charles Stewart Mott Foundation has a program area called "Pathways Out of Poverty" in which it makes grants to organizations that seek to improve community education, expand economic opportunity, and build organized communities.[20] Similarly, the Rockefeller Foundation aims to achieve its vision through four key focus areas: to advance health, revalue the ecosystem, secure livelihoods, and transform cities.[21] By targeting the roughly $132 million in grants Rockefeller gave away last year into these four areas, they might be able to have a greater impact by concentrating their spending on these specific issues. Thus, foundations use their wealth to target large-scale social issues by granting funds to nonprofit organizations.

Lastly, foundations play an important role as **policy change agents**. Although foundations do not lobby directly for specific policies or political agendas, foundations invest heavily in social science research and policy analysis institutes that evaluate specific government programs and policies and recommend new policy solutions. For example, the Brookings Institution is a nonpartisan organization with a strong reputation for producing credible research that has helped to shape government policy in numerous areas including business and finance, defense and security, energy and the environment, law and justice, international affairs, metropolitan issues, social policy, and technology, among others.[22] The Brookings Institution receives the majority of its support from private foundations including the Ford Foundation, the Gates Foundation, the Pew Charitable Trust, MacArthur, Carnegie, and a few corporate foundations such as Bank of America and Exxon Mobile. By providing on-going operating support for Brookings and similar types of think tanks, foundations are able to have a significant impact as policy change agents, investing in research that influences political decision-making and in organizations that help to shape policy.

While foundations help to benefit US society in numerous ways, there remain several controversies and questions surrounding their work and their special nonprofit status. Among these questions are whether their investments benefit all in society or just elite interests and whether foundations are sufficiently transparent in their spending and decision-making. Other concerns relate to the lack of diversity in foundation leadership, and whether foundation giving is effective, or, put another way, whether it achieves the desired impact. The first issue relates to redistribution and investments in particular types of outreach. Critics question whether redistribution is a legitimate label for foundation activities, particularly when we consider that billions of dollars are invested each year in areas such as the arts, which typically count wealthier persons among their patron bases. Some question if foundations help all of society, or just the wealthy and those who are least in need of foundation assistance. For example, human services receives only about 15% of all foundation funds,[23] causing some to question whether a larger percentage should be invested in social programs and efforts to advance all of society, not just elite interests.[24] Ultimately, as private organizations, individual foundations set their own giving priorities and retain the discretion and privilege to invest in programs as they wish.

Another on-going question with regard to foundations relates to the issue of accountability. Although these institutions are often privately created and run, they are still afforded nonprofit status under the presumption that they will create public value. Much of their operation and decision-making occurs outside of the public view, with little justification or rationale provided for their grant-making decisions. The lack of transparency in these institutions might be regarded as problematic from an accountability standpoint. Foundations are given the public benefit of nonprofit status (e.g. no taxation), but are not accountable to public oversight or scrutiny. As nonprofit organizations and foundations work to bring social change or invest in creating social good, there is little to no oversight of these activities. Who is ensuring that these investments really are best for society? Accountability and oversight for the large investments that foundations make in society typically fall to the donating organization itself.

Foundations have been further criticized for their lack of diversity.[25] Today, the individuals in charge of making grant-giving decisions are overwhelmingly white and male. Some argue that the limited diversity in grant-making organizations and large philanthropies limits the impact of giving. Advocates for diversity note that more diverse philanthropies can better advance the common good, increase their effectiveness by adding diversity to problem-solving and leadership, and increase impact in the communities they seek to serve. Foundations that are more representative of the populations that they seek to serve will likely have more buy-in from communities and see more successful outcomes from their philanthropic efforts. For many foundations, this means recruiting more women, minorities, and community members to their boards and on their staff.

Finally, questions endure with regard to foundations' effectiveness. To what extent does foundation-spending result in changes in the social problems the foundations seek to address? While foundations have raised the bar somewhat in recent years with requests for their grantees to measure and demonstrate performance, by no means do foundations systematically make grants or continue to invest in organizations or programs based on outcomes. Many foundations choose to become ongoing partners with a nonprofit organization, providing general operating support year after year with little expectation of continuous improvement or performance reporting. This speaks to the somewhat unpredictable and idiosyncratic preferences of foundations, and the reality is that they fund what they want, regardless of any demonstrable social return on investments.

This discussion has painted a picture of institutionalized giving in America. Equipped with a basic understanding of foundations, we will now shift our attention to examine giving by individuals—that is, giving that occurs not through foundations, but directly from private citizens or households to nonprofit organizations.

Giving in the US

Who Gives?

"Almost everyone" is the short answer to the question "Who gives?" As mentioned earlier, the vast majority of American households (88%) give to charity each year. In fact, although the foundations discussed earlier give large amounts of money to particular causes, individuals are a larger source of giving than foundations. According to The Giving USA Foundation, in 2009 individuals accounted for the largest proportion of private giving to public charities, 75% of giving ($227.41 billion) came from individuals compared to 13% from foundations ($38.44 billion), 8% from bequests ($23.80 billion), and 4% from corporations ($14.10 billion).[26]

Giving patterns vary by income level, age, religious affiliation, and region of the country. Giving varies in ways that might come as a surprise. For example, simple logic might suggest that the wealthy give more because they have more to give. However, middle-class Americans give a much larger share of their discretionary income to charities than do the rich. According to a 2012 report by the *Chronicle of Philanthropy*, households that earn $50,000 to $75,000 give an average of 7.6% of their discretionary income to charity, compared with an average of 4.2% for people who make $100,000 or more.[27] Other researchers note that the lowest income groups in the US give a larger proportion of their income to others than do higher income groups, and that, during economic downturns, charitable giving among richer donors declines more than among lower income givers.

These data tell only half the story however, because they capture only those households that itemize their federal tax returns, which allows for receiving the tax benefits of charitable contributions. Recall that in Chapter 2 we learned that lower income households are far less likely to itemize their tax returns, meaning that charitable giving by this group is not rewarded with tax breaks like it is for those in the wealthier groups who more often itemize their returns. While the total dollars donated by those in the upper-middle class and wealthy households amounts to more than that donated by lower income groups, the middle and lower income groups donate a larger percentage of what they have to give, meaning that they are ultimately more generous with their giving. Data from the US Bureau of Labor Statistics indicates that the poorest fifth of American households give 4.3% of their income to charitable organizations, compared to 2.1% among the fifth richest households.[28]

There are also some interesting trends with regard to charitable giving by age. Contrary to the often-heard claims that young adults are apathetic and disengaged, giving is common among those in Generation Y, also called Millennials (ages 18–32; born 1980s–2000s), and their collective contributions amount to 11% of total giving in the US today. A 2013 report by Blackbaud shows that 60% of this group gave an average of $481 per year across 3.3 organizations. While Generation Xers (ages 23–48; born 1960s–1980s) give more money than Gen Yers in total, they actually lag slightly behind Gen Y in total participation with 59% in this cohort giving an average of $732 across 3.9 charities. Among Baby Boomers (ages 49–67), 72% gave an average of $1,212 across 4.5 charities. Figure 6.1 shows the distribution of total giving in the US by generation. The largest share of giving comes from Baby Boomers (43%), followed by older Americans, or "Matures" (aged 68 and above). A large number of Matures give; for example, 88% of all people in this cohort donate an average of $1,367 to 6.2 charities.[29] As these numbers would suggest, both the likelihood of giving and the size of the gift increase with age, as individuals become more financially secure.

Religion is an important factor in giving. As we learned in Chapter 2, charity and philanthropy are deeply embedded values underlying all of the main religions of the world. In 2013, roughly 75% of people who frequently attend religious services also gave to congregations, and 60% gave to religious charities or nonreligious ones. By contrast, less than half of people who said they did not attend faith services regularly supported any charity.[31] One of the explanations for increased giving among the religious is that many organizations' religions advocate formal tithing. A **tithe** is a one-tenth of something, but the term is often used to refer to the 10% of giving that many religious groups recommend for their members. In the US, patterns of giving based on religiosity tend to correspond with regional patterns of giving. Areas of the country that are deeply religious give more to charity than those that are not religious. For example, when we rank

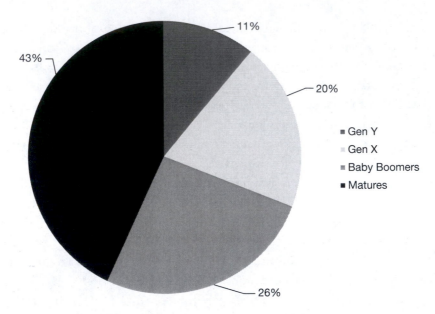

FIGURE 6.1 Total Giving in the US by Generational Cohort, 2013.

Source: Blackbaud, 2013. *The Next Generation of American Giving* Report.[30]

the states by giving as percentage of household income, two of the top nine states are Utah and Idaho, which have high numbers of Latter Day Saints (Mormon) residents who have a strong tradition of tithing at least 10% of their income to the church. All the remaining states in the top nine of charitable states are located in America's "Bible Belt."[32]

Patterns of charitable giving in the US are also noticeable by political ideology. People living in more politically conservative states tend to rank higher than those in more liberal states when it comes to giving as a share of household income. According to the *Chronicle of Philanthropy*, the eight states where residents gave the highest share of income to charity voted for the Republican presidential candidate (John McCain) in 2008, while the seven-lowest ranking charitable states supported the Democratic candidate (Barack Obama).[33] These patterns of giving, by state and political party, are related to the distribution of religiosity and poverty in the US and likely regional and state culture. Giving by region of the country is somewhat complex, as there are a number of ways to look at this, including total contributions, discretionary income by household, giving as a percentage of income by household, and so on. The *Chronicle of Philanthropy* offers an updated, interactive website that allows users to compare giving not only by state but by neighborhood (zip code), and offers interesting facts for each jurisdiction including median donation, percentage of population that donates, median household contribution, and many other interesting giving facts. Examine patterns of giving in your zip code, city, state, or region by visiting their website: http://philanthropy.com/section/How-America-Gives/621?cid=megamenu

Who Benefits from Giving?

A long-standing controversy with regard to giving in the US is that the legal rules for charitable giving benefit the wealthy, who are more likely to itemize their federal tax returns and are able to obtain tax write-offs from their charitable contributions. At the same time, there is evidence that the wealthy give the largest share of their donations to nonprofits representing arts and culture, health, and educational institutions, including elite private colleges and universities, and not to organizations that provide help to the poor. Thus the question of "who benefits from giving?" can be answered in terms of which individuals personally benefit the most from the tax write-offs afforded to citizens in the US who itemize, and the question can also be answered in terms of which types of organizations and groups within the nonprofit sector benefit most as recipients of giving. Let us address this latter part of the question first, by looking at some facts that are presented in Figure 6.2.

Figure 6.2 shows how donors allocate their contributions by income group and type of organizational recipient. The pie chart in the lower right hand corner shows where the wealthiest households, those with incomes of $1 million and up, donate their contributions. The largest share of donations made by the wealthiest households goes to health organizations (25%) and education (25%), which includes alumni giving to elite private colleges and state universities. The next largest groups to benefit from giving by the wealthy include religious institutions (17%) and arts and culture (15%). Of all income groups represented in Figure 6.2, the wealthiest households give the least to organizations that serve the poor (4%). By contrast, households with incomes of less than $100,000 per year allocate their donations very differently. The pie chart in the top left corner of Figure 6.2 shows that these middle and working-class households give

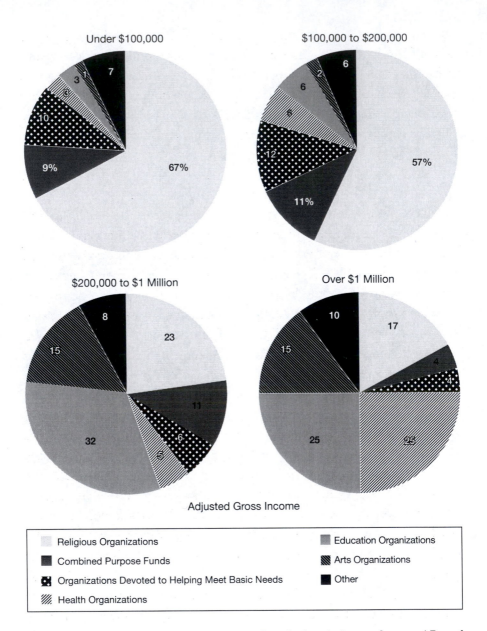

FIGURE 6.2 How Donors Allocate Their Charitable Contributions by Income Group and Type of Recipient, 2005.

Source: Congressional Budget Office based on data from the Center on Philanthropy at Indiana University, Patterns of Household Charitable Giving by Income Group, 2005 (Indianapolis: Indiana University/Purdue University, 2007).

Note: Combined Purpose Funds, such as the United Way, receive contributions and allocate them to many different types of charities.

a much larger proportion to religious institutions (67%) and organizations serving the poor (10%), and much less to education (3%) and arts and cultural institutions (1%). In sum, higher income households donate more dollars to health and educational organizations, while middle and lower income households donate to religious organizations. And when we look at donations to the poor, 4% of higher income household donations go to the poor compared to 10% from lower income households.

Researchers argue that donations to the poor are higher among lower income households for a few reasons. First, members of lower income households are more likely to know and interact with poor people who need donations. Second, lower income individuals are more likely to be members of religious organizations that promote giving, either formal tithing or through beliefs that giving will enrich their lives.[34] Third, higher income households are more likely to be approached by alumni organizations (where they attended college) and arts and cultural institutions seeking charitable donations. These are a few of the explanations that can help us to make sense of the stark differences in charitable contributions by income group illustrated in Figure 6.2.

As suggested by the robust charitable giving by the wealthy to private educational institutions, healthcare, and arts and culture organizations, the well-off seem to have an advantage in the US system of charitable giving. A scholar of philanthropy, Teresa Odendahl, once argued that the US nonprofit sector was ineffective at redistributing wealth because "the philanthropy of elites is not a system whereby the fortunate redistribute resources to the less fortunate. Instead, philanthropy is primarily a system whereby the wealthy help to finance their own institutions" (Odendahl, 1989, p. 242).[35] She further argued that this creates double loss for the poor. Not only do organizations that help the poor get the tiniest fraction of private giving, but of even greater consequence is that this detail gets masked in public discussions of "philanthropy" when total philanthropic giving figures are used as a rationale against greater investment of government funding to address social needs. The long-standing controversy over this reality has led to some proposals for reforming the charitable deduction policy (as we learned about in Chapter 2), but it is unclear whether these proposals will gain the political traction needed to make changes in how deductions are allowed for those who itemize their charitable giving.

Why Do People Give?

The same theories that aim to explain why people choose to volunteer (Chapter 5) also help to explain why people donate money to charity. Both altruistic and egoistic motives underlie reasons for giving. Altruistic reasons might include helping those who are less fortunate, giving back to society, or because one feels called to help remedy economic injustice and inequality. For example, many of the donors highlighted in the opening example of The Giving Pledge note that they want to benefit society and make a lasting impact on their communities, countries, or the world. Egoistic, or instrumental, reasons for giving might include positive feelings generated for the giver, also known as the **warm-glow giving** effect, increased status, public recognition, tax benefits, to leave a legacy, or even be immortalized.

In their book, *The Seven Faces of Philanthropy: A New Approach to Cultivating Major Donors*, Russ Alan Prince and Karen Maru File argue that there are seven types of donors: the Communitarian, the Devout, the Investor, the Socialite, the Altruist, the Repayer, and the Dynast.[36] The authors argue that Communitarians give because they believe that giving makes sense for the community: they do it to make their community, city, or country a better place to live. The Devout give because they believe it is God's will or their obligation as a member of a particular community of faith. The third type of giver is the Investor. This person is giving, or being philanthropic, because it is good for business or personal reputation. Some corporate givers might fall into this category. The Socialite refers to people who do good because it is fun or as a mechanism for raising their social status. Socialites might organize parties or galas to raise money for a charity or a particular cause, but they are more motivated by the party or event itself than the actual cause. The fifth category is the Altruist, a person who is giving because it feels right. Sixth is the Repayer, a person who gives because they are returning some good that they received. Alumni giving often falls into this category, where someone who becomes a successful lawyer or businesswoman might donate to the school where she got her training. Similarly, a cancer survivor might bequeath his estate to a hospital or clinic that provided exceptional care and support to him while he was sick. The final type of giver is the Dynast, a person who is giving because it is a family tradition, or a means to maintain a family legacy.

There may also be an element of coercion underlying some decisions to donate. Coercion refers to persuading a person to do something by using force or threats. **Coercive giving** can range from a subtle pressure to give, to a requirement to volunteer their time. Coercive reasons for giving might include social pressure, or desire for conformity, which occurs when your friends or family ask you to donate to a cause. Social pressure plays an important role in giving, as evidenced by the classic study in which people are more likely to put money in the Salvation Army bell-ringer's bucket when they see others do it first.[37] Organizations that appeal to donors in ways that make them give because they feel guilty, bad about themselves, or at risk of harm (i.e. contracting cancer or some other illness, etc.) if they do not give are illustrative of ways that subtle coercion might compel giving.

As we learned in the last chapter, selflessness and self-interest are not mutually exclusive, and people may give for some combination of these reasons. However, the most commonly cited reason that people donate to charity is the "joy of giving":[38] that is to say that giving brings them personal satisfaction, or a "warm glow." The theory of warm-glow giving suggests that instead of being motivated by an interest in the welfare of the recipient, individuals are also motivated by "impure altruism," or a desire for the positive feeling an individual gets from helping others.[39,40] James Andreoni, the economist who developed the warm-glow theory, suggests that donors derive utility from giving, the way in which consumers derive utility from consumption. In the case of charitable giving, the utility comes in the form of a "warm glow." There is physiological evidence of the warm glow, as researchers have found that the "reward centers" of the brain are activated by charitable giving.[41] As the warm-glow theory ultimately suggests, the reasons people give are complex and instrumental reasons for giving probably cannot be neatly disentangled from more purely altruistic reasons.

The Role of Technology in Giving

Technology has had nothing short of a revolutionary impact on private giving in America, and has also dramatically changed the way that nonprofit organizations are appealing to the giving public. Thanks to an ever-proliferating number of online fundraising platforms, anyone can raise funds for any cause they choose. "**Crowdfunding**" is the broad term given to these fundraising initiatives, and is defined as "the practice of funding a project or venture by raising many small amounts of money from a large number of people, typically via the Internet."[42] Individuals can set up pages and make personal fundraising appeals for causes as wide-ranging as paying for medical treatment or sending their child to college. While these appeals for donations may be compelling and their creators can reach their goals very quickly, the donor is not entitled to a tax deduction when making a contribution to an individual.

Many formally incorporated nonprofit organizations use these personal fundraising pages as well, including the Leukemia & Lymphoma Society's "Team in Training" and Susan G Komen's 3-day "Walk for the Cure," enabling participants to create their own personal pages for obtaining pledges, and allowing donors the benefit of the tax deduction for their contribution. The Movember fundraiser for men's health that we discussed in Chapter 4 has individual participants create web pages to track their moustache-driven fund raising activities. In other instances, established organizations rely on crowdfunding methods to raise money for a special project or infrastructural need. For example, the Chicago-based urban farming nonprofit, Growing Home (that we also highlighted in Chapter 4), set a goal early in 2013 of raising $20,000 for a new hoop greenhouse. Titling the project "Harvesting Hope", Growing Home successfully raised the money within a matter of months with 339 backers through the online platform Kickstarter.[43]

Social media has also had a dramatic influence on giving, as individuals can now quickly and easily make donations via Facebook, Twitter, and other social media platforms. And nearly all crowdfunding platforms link to these social media sites as well. Moreover, nonprofit organizations have recognized the importance of becoming visible through social media in order to maintain their relevance and continue to attract donations. Research suggests that the vast majority of medium-to-large registered nonprofits are hooked into at least one form of social media, the most common of which is Facebook.[44]

Mobile technology has also had an influential role in changing the nature of giving. Within the last decade, there has been a dramatic rise in giving via SMS (short-message service), also known as **text giving** or **mobile**

giving. This form of fundraising has been particularly useful for raising large sums of money to address immediate needs. Humanitarian relief organizations, such as The American Red Cross and Oxfam, have partnered with mobile carriers to raise money quickly in order to respond to catastrophic natural disasters such as the 2010 Haiti earthquake, the 2011 Japanese Tsunami, and the 2013 typhoon in the central Philippines. When raising money after the Haiti earthquake, the American Red Cross set a record for mobile donations in 2010, raising $7 million US dollars in 24 hours when they allowed people to send $10 donations by text message.[45] Moreover, giving by cell phone is not limited to raising money for disasters or emergent needs. Organizations such as GiveDirectly allow donors to make direct cash transfers to the poor in Kenya, to use however the recipient deems necessary, and the program will soon be expanded to several other high-poverty countries. Donors simply place money into a mobile account and then distribute those funds to individuals around the world who have cell phones. For more information on the GiveDirectly program and some of the challenges associated with this model of giving, see Box 6.2.

Mobile applications represent yet another emerging vehicle for giving. Google's "One Today" app, for example, profiles a new charity every day and allows users to donate a dollar.[46] The logic behind such applications is that they create efficiencies for donors, who can save time searching for causes to donate to and do not have to think about the amount of the donation since the app limits giving to $1 each day. Google's app and similar charity apps such as JustGive can be highly useful in providing information shortcuts for prospective donors, and help to increase the visibility of high-performing but under-capitalized organizations. Mobile apps as giving vehicles may be particularly useful for engaging younger people in giving, as young people rely extensively on smartphones, may not have a lot of knowledge about the universe of worthy organizations, and do not necessarily have a lot to give. Research indicates that when asking Generation Y (i.e. younger people) about giving, 47% had given through organization websites and 62% would give via mobile phone if that option were available.[47] Moreover, younger people are using social media to promote giving among their friends and family, with 50% sharing information about charities with their friends on Facebook and 56% viewing online videos about charities that they support.[48]

BOX 6.2 WHAT IS THE BEST WAY TO GIVE?

What is the best use of charity? How can nonprofits best make a difference in society? If you have $500 to donate, what is the best way to make the most impact with your donation? What charity is making the biggest difference—where will your $500 be the most effective? These are questions that confront individuals and organizations all over the world.

The founders of GiveDirectly asked these questions and decided maybe the best way to help others is to give them money to help themselves. GiveDirectly describes their goal as "providing a global alternative to orthodox philanthropy,"[49] using mobile banking as a format for distributing charitable donations directly to individuals in developing countries. The GiveDirectly founders know that cash transfers to the poor is an unpopular form of philanthropy, but they argue it is the most efficient, transparent way to give.

Cash transfers are unpopular for a number of reasons. First, there is the threat of corruption. Second, many organizations do not trust individuals to spend the money wisely. They worry that people will spend the money on drugs, sex, cigarettes, alcohol, weapons, gambling, and other wasteful activities. Third, some argue that "hand-outs" don't work because they create a sense of dependency. Fourth, giving money to some individuals, and not all members of the community, may further inequity in society. Fifth, some argue that giving money is a temporary solution, but does not give poor people long-term solutions to their problems, such as better healthcare, jobs, or education.

In response to these criticisms (and stereotypes), GiveDirectly notes that many studies show that cash transfers do work. On their website, GiveDirectly notes that there is an abundance of evidence about how the poor use cash transfers. The UK Department for International Development notes that cash transfers are "one of the more thoroughly researched forms of development intervention." Cash transfers enable the poor to have the flexibility to pursue their own financial goals including increasing health of children,[50,51,52,53] improving educational opportunities for children and reducing child labor, [54,55] and increasing annual income, investments, and savings.[56,57] GiveDirectly recipients have used funds to upgrade the roofs of their homes, purchase beds, pay a dowry, send their kids to school, and buy cows and other livestock to feed their families and generate income.

With improvements in technology, GiveDirectly can give away money without physically delivering cash. Mobile phones in many countries now serve as mobile bank accounts. A donor can place $20.00 into a mobile account and then distribute those funds to

continued

individuals around the world who have cell phones. Transfers can be made to hundreds of people within seconds.

Give Directly is a simple organization that distributes giving as follows: (1) donors give money through the GiveDirectly webpage; (2) GiveDirectly locates poor households in Kenya; (3) GiveDirectly transfers the donation electronically to the recipient's cell phone in Kenya; (4) the recipient uses the donation to pursue his or her own goals.

GiveDirectly operates under three values:

1. Efficiency—Put at least 90% of every donated dollar in the hands of the poor.
2. Transparency—Do one, easy-to-understand thing with every donated dollar; do it ourselves without subcontractors; and clearly explain what it costs to do it.
3. Respect—Empower the poor to set their own priorities.

GiveDirectly is doing something very few charities do—they are giving money directly to the poor. And they believe this is the best, most efficient way to end poverty. Because GiveDirectly has developed an approach to development that is uncommon, they have felt the need to prove the effectiveness of their approach.

First, they chose this approach because of the overwhelming evidence that cash transfers work. Additionally, they wanted to ensure that the organization would have very low administrative costs to ensure that the bulk of donations went directly to the poor. For example, GiveDirectly does not offer micro-loans. They note that there is little empirical evidence that micro-loans lift households out of poverty, there are high administrative and monitoring costs associated with micro-loans, and the high interest rates associated with micro-loans often make them unattainable for the poorest households.[58]

GiveDirectly also chooses cash transfers without conditions because they want to empower the poor to make their own decisions about advancing their lives, and placing conditions on how the funds are used requires costly monitoring and enforcement structures.[59] For GiveDirectly, cash transfers are the highest impact, lowest cost mechanism for alleviating poverty in developing communities. GiveDirectly does extensive analysis of their programs and takes an evidence-based approach to their work, to ensure that their programs are the best way to help people.

GiveDirectly's success has been widely noted. In 2012, GiveDirectly received a $2.4 million Global Impact Award from Google, with the goal of increasing donations to poor families and also to underwrite some of the costs of expanding the program to a second country. In 2013, Give Well ranked GiveDirectly the #2 Charity on its list of Top

continued

Charities[60] because it delivers 90% of its expenses directly to extremely low-income people in the developing world, has documented its success, has high levels of transparency, and is committed to self-evaluation and improvement.

What do you think? Is this the best way to give to the poor? What are the limits of this approach? Could this work in your local community, town, or neighborhood? How important is it that the majority of a donation goes to the poor and not to the organization's overhead?

More Information

Listen to Planet Money reporters David Kestenbaum and Jacob Goldstein discuss GiveDirectly on *This American Life*. http://www.thisamericanlife.org/radio-archives/episode/503/i-was-just-trying-to-help?act=1

Summary

Philanthropy is an important concept in American society, helping to fund and shape the work of nonprofit organizations in civil society. Philanthropic giving occurs in two forms: foundation giving and individual donations. Foundations account for both large and small amounts of giving to all types of nonprofit organizations, including arts and cultural institutions, education institutions, and nonprofit organizations serving local communities. Many foundations are associated with the wealth of individuals or corporations. They make grants to nonprofit organizations and, in some cases, pursue their own activities to shape civil society.

While many nonprofit organizations rely on the important financial support of foundations, many also rely on individual giving. As noted in this chapter, Americans of all types regularly make private donations to nonprofit organizations. Giving varies by gender, age, income, and religious affiliation. As society evolves so do giving patterns. And, of course, with the development of new technologies, giving mechanisms change. Today people donate by handing a dollar to an individual on the street, through their religious organizations, via direct withdrawals from their paychecks, through matched employer donation efforts, through social media, through the fundraising efforts of their individual friends, and via text message. As the nonprofit sector continues to grow and evolve, so too will the philanthropic efforts of foundations, groups, and individuals in America.

KEY TERMS

- Coercive giving
- Community foundations
- Corporate foundations
- Crowdfunding
- Foundations
- Grants
- Grant-making foundations

- Mobile giving
- Operating foundations
- Paternalistic
- Philanthropy
- Policy change agents
- Pragmatist
- Redistribution

- Social programs
- Stimulating innovation
- Targeting resources
- Text giving
- Tithe/tithing
- Warm-glow giving

DISCUSSION QUESTIONS

1. What role do foundations serve in society? Do we really need them? Why don't people with a lot to give away just give directly to agencies and causes they care about?

2. Odendahl stated that "philanthropy is primarily a system whereby the wealthy help to finance their own institutions." To what extent do you think this is true? Are there some examples from your own city or regional community that seem to support this statement, or to refute it?

3. Do you find it surprising that red states give a greater share of their household income to charity than blue states? If we were to take out giving to religious institutions do you think we would see different giving patterns by region?

4. Think about the last time you donated money to any cause, whether by text, Internet, or simply handing someone money on the street. Why did you choose to give money to that cause? Among the factors discussed in this chapter that compel people to give, which ones played a role in your giving decision?

Websites

The Giving Pledge: http://www.thegivingpledge.org

Chronicle of Philanthropy: http://philanthropy.com/section/How-America-Gives/621?cid=megamenu.

GiveDirectly: http://www.givedirectly.org

Stamberg, Susan. 2013. How Andrew Carnegie Turned His Fortune Into a Library Legacy. Aired August 01, 2013 3:00 AM, National Public Radio. Available online at http://www.npr.org/2013/08/01/207272849/how-andrew-carnegie-turned-his-fortune-into-a-library-legacy?ft=1&f=

Planet Money reporters David Kestenbaum and Jacob Goldstein discuss GiveDirectly on *This American Life*. http://www.thisamericanlife.org/radio-archives/episode/503/i-was-just-trying-to-help?act=1

Additional Reading

Carnegie, Andrew. 1889. Wealth. *North American Review*, No. CCCXCI, June 1889. Accessed July 31, 2013 at http://www.swarthmore.edu/SocSci/rbannis1/AIH19th/Carnegie.html

Gordon, John Steele. 2006. The Sunny Steel Baron and His Bootstraps Fortune. Book review. Published: October 30, 2006. Available online at http://www.nytimes.com/2006/10/30/books/30gord.html?_r=0

Nasaw, David. 2007. *Andrew Carnegie*. Penguin Group (USA) Incorporated. ISBN-13: 9780143112440

Notes

1   Forbes Profile—Michael Bloomberg. Accessed Sept 17, 2013 at http://www.forbes.com/profile/michael-bloomberg/

2   Pappu, Sridhar. 2011. What's Next for Michael Bloomberg, *Fast Company*, August 8, 2011. Accessed Sept 17, 2013 at http://www.fastcompany.com/1769004/whats-next-michael-bloomberg

3   Bloomberg. Michael R. Commencement Address. Bard College. May 26, 2007. Accessed Sept 17, 2013 at http://www.bard.edu/commencement/2007/bloomberg_speech.shtml

4   http://www.npr.org/2011/11/25/142780599/why-we-give-not-why-you-think Accessed November 16, 2013.

5   http://www.nptrust.org/philanthropic-resources/charitable-giving-statistics. Accessed November 26, 2013.

6   http://nccs.urban.org/faq/ Accessed November 16, 2013.

7   Ott, J. Steven and Lisa A. Dicke. 2012. *The Nature of the Nonprofit Sector*, 2nd edition. Boulder, CO: Westview Press.

8   Stamberg, Susan. 2013. How Andrew Carnegie Turned His Fortune Into a Library Legacy. Aired August 01, 2013 3:00 AM, National Public Radio. Accessed at http://www.npr.org/2013/08/01/207272849/how-andrew-carnegie-turned-his-fortune-into-a-library-legacy?ft=1&f=

9   Carnegie, Andrew. 1889. Wealth. *North American Review*, No. CCCXCI, June 1889. Accessed July 31, 2013 at http://www.swarthmore.edu/SocSci/rbannis1/AIH19th/Carnegie.html

10   Nasaw, David. 2007. *Andrew Carnegie*. Penguin Group (USA) Incorporated. ISBN-13: 9780143112440

11   Anheier, Helmut. 2005. *Nonprofit Organizations: Theory, Management, and Policy*. Routledge Press.

12   Anheier (2005).

13   Cohen, Rick. 2013. Walmart's Mixed Generosity: Great for Nonprofits, Not So Much for Employees. *The Nonprofit Quarterly*, Friday, September 6, 2013. Accessed: November 17, 2013 at http://www.nonprofitquarterly.org/policysocial-context/22862-walmart-s-mixed-generosity-great-for-nonprofits-not-so-much-for-employees.html

14   Anheier (2005), p. 306.

15   http://www.clevelandfoundation.org/about/history/ Accessed November 17, 2013.

16   http://www.clevelandfoundation.org/about/history/ Accessed November 17, 2013.

17   Foundation Center. 25 Largest Community Foundations by Asset Size. Accessed February 10, 2014 at http://foundationcenter.org/findfunders/topfunders/top25assets.html.

18   http://www.macfound.org/pages/about-macarthur-fellows-program/ Accessed November 19, 2013.

19   http://millerfoundation.grantsmanagement08.com/?page_id=31. Accessed November 17, 2013.

20   http://www.mott.org/FundingInterests/programs/pathwaysoutofpoverty.aspx Accessed November 19, 2013.

21   http://www.rockefellerfoundation.org/ Accessed November 19, 2013.

22   http://www.brookings.edu/about#research-programs/ Accessed November 19, 2013.

23   http://data.foundationcenter.org/ Accessed November 17, 2013.

24   Eisenberg, Pablo. 2012. The Misplaced Giving Priorities of America's Wealthy. *Chronicle of Philanthropy*, January 24, 2012. Accessed March 9, 2014 at http://philanthropy.com/article/Misplaced-Giving-Priorities-of/130436/

25   D5, Growing Diversity, Equity, and Inclusion in Philanthropy. Accessed November 17, 2013 at http://www.d5coalition.org/

26   http://nccs.urban.org/faq/ Accessed February 10, 2014

27   http://philanthropy.com/article/America-s-Generosity-Divide/133775/ Accessed November 26, 2013.

28   Greve, Frank. 2009. America's Poor Are Its Most Generous Givers. *McClatchy Newspapers*, May 19, 2009. Accessed February 10, 2014 at http://www.mcclatchydc.com/2009/05/19/68456/americas-poor-are-its-most-generous.html#storylink=cpy

29   All statistics reported in this paragraph are from the *"Next Generation of American Giving"* report produced by Blackbaud (2013). Accessed November 20, 2013 at https://www.blackbaud.com/nonprofit-resources/generational-giving-report-infographic

30   Blackbaud. 2013. *The Next Generation of American Giving*. Accessed November 17, 2013 at https://www.blackbaud.com/nonprofit-resources/generational-giving-report-infographic

31   Daniels, Alex. 2013. Religious Americans Give More, New Study Finds. *Chronicle of Philanthropy*, November 25, 2013. http://philanthropy.com/article/Religious-Americans-Give-More/143273/ Accessed: November 26, 2013.

32   *Chronicle of Philanthropy's* "How America Gives" interactive map "Percentage of Income by Household." Accessed November 26, 2013 at http://philanthropy.com/article/Interactive-How-America-Gives

33   Gipple, Emily and Ben Gose. America's Generosity Divide. *Chronicle of Philanthropy*, August 19, 2012. Accessed: November 26, 2013 at http://philanthropy.com/article/America-s-Generosity-Divide/133775/

34   Greve, Frank. 2009. America's poor are its most generous givers. McClatchy Newspapers, May 19. Accessed February 10, 2014 at http://www.mcclatchydc.com/2009/05/19/68456/americas-poor-are-its-most-generous.html#storylink=cpy

35   Odendahl, Teresa. 1989. The Culture of Elite Philanthropy in the Reagan Years. *Nonprofit and Voluntary Sector Quarterly*, 18: 237–248.

36   Prince, Russ Alan and Karen Maru File. 2001. *The Seven Faces of Philanthropy: A New Approach to Cultivating Major Donors*. Jossey-Bass Pfeiffer.

37   Krebs, Dennis L. 1970. Altruism—An Examination of the Concept and Review of the Literature. *Psychological Bulletin*, 73: 258–302.

38   Mount, Joan. 2001. Why Do People Give? In Steven J. Ott (ed.), *The Nature of the Nonprofit Sector*. Boulder, CO: Westview Press.

39   Andreoni, James. 1989. Giving with Impure Altruism: Applications to Charity and Ricardian Equivalence. *Journal of Political Economy*, 97(6): 1447–1458.

40   Andreoni, James. 1990. Impure Altruism and Donations to Public Goods: A Theory of Warm-Glow Giving. *Economic Journal*, 100(401): 464–477.

41   Harbaugh, W, U. Mayr, and D. Burghart. 2007. Neural Responses to Taxation and Voluntary Giving Reveal Motives for Charitable Donations. *Science*, 316(5831): 1622–1625.

42   http://www.forbes.com/sites/tanyaprive/2012/11/27/what-is-crowdfunding-and-how-does-it-benefit-the-economy/ Accessed November 26, 2013.

43   http://www.kickstarter.com/projects/15862127/harvesting-hope. Accessed November 27, 2013.

44   Kanter, Beth, Allison Fine, and Randi Zuckerberg. 2010. *The Networked Nonprofit: Connecting with Social Media to Drive Change*. San Francisco: John Wiley & Sons.

45   http://www.prnewswire.com/news-releases/red-cross-raises-more-than-32-million-via-mobile-giving-program-84117617.html. Accessed November 27, 2013.

46   http://venturebeat.com/2013/08/10/google-one-today/#cybR7hmm8a0PeKPy.02 Accessed November 27, 2013.

47   https://www.blackbaud.com/nonprofit-resources/generational-giving-report-infographic. Accessed February 10, 2014.

48   https://www.blackbaud.com/nonprofit-resources/generational-giving-report-infographic. Accessed February 10, 2014.

49   http://www.givedirectly.org/blog.php. Accessed August 15, 2013.

50   Cunha, Jesse. 2010. Testing Paternalism: Cash vs. In-Kind Transfers in Rural Mexico. Technical Report, Stanford University, March 2010.

51 Baird, Sarah, Richard Garfein, Craig McIntosh, and Berk Ozler. 2012. Effect of a Cash Transfer Programme for Schooling on Prevalence of HIV and Herpes Simplex Type 2 in Malawi: A Cluster Randomised Trial. *Lancet*, February 15, 2012.

52 Paxson, Christina and Norbert Schady. 2007. Does Money Matter? The Effects of Cash Transfers on Child Health and Development in Rural Ecuador. World Bank Policy Research Working Paper 4226, May 2007.

53 Amarante, Veronic, Marco Manacorda, Edward Miguel, and Andrea Vigorito. 2011. Do Cash Transfers Improve Birth Outcomes? Evidence from Matched Vital Statistics, Social Security and Program Data. National Bureau of Economic Research Working Paper 17690, December 2011.

54 Edmonds, Eric. 2006. Child Labor and Schooling Responses to Anticipated Income in South Africa. *Journal of Development Economics*, 81.

55 Baird, Sarah, Craig McIntosh, and Berk Ozler. 2011. Cash or Condition? Evidence from a Cash Transfer Experiment. *Quarterly Journal of Economics*, 126.

56 Sadoulet, Elisabeth, Alain de Janvry, and Benjamin Davis. 2001. Cash Transfer Programs with Income Multipliers: PROCAMPO in Mexico. *World Development*, 29(6): 1043–1056.

57 Rubalcava, Luis, Graciela Tereul, and Duncan Thomas. 2004. Spending, Saving, and Public Transfers Paid to Women. On-Line Working Paper Series CCPR-024-04, California Center for Population Research 2004. Accessed Nov 13, 2013 at http://www.escholarship.org/uc/item/95m9f476

58 Fernando, Nimal. 2006. Understanding and Dealing with High Interest Rates on Microcredit. Asian Development Bank, May 2006.

59 Caldes, Natalia and John Maluccio. 2005. The Costs of Conditional Cash Transfers. *Journal of International Development*, 17: 151–168.

60 http://www.givewell.org/charities/top-charities. Accessed August 23, 2013.

SECTION III

POLITICAL, SOCIAL, & ECONOMIC ASPECTS OF THE NONPROFIT SECTOR

7

THE INFLUENCE OF NONPROFIT ORGANIZATIONS ON THE POLITICAL ENVIRONMENT

CHAPTER LEARNING OBJECTIVES

By the end of this chapter, students will be able to:

1. Describe the legal limitations faced by public charities in the political arena

2. Identify specific types of nonprofit organizations involved in the political arena and how they influence policy-making

3. Identify and explain specific activities and strategies associated with nonprofits' political mobilization role

4. Describe specific activities and strategies used by nonprofits in their political representation role

5. Describe ways in which nonprofit organizations provide political education for citizens

---

Introduction

Nonprofit and civil society organizations are influential actors in American policy-making and politics. These organizations shape policy-making and the electoral process at all levels of government in the form of lobbying groups, service organizations, political parties, and policy research institutes

LANDMINES—WORKING WITH VICTIMS AND ADVOCATING FOR CHANGE

George has been working for over two years now in Cambodia with the Association for Aid and Relief (AAR), a Japanese nongovernmental organization that works to empower people with disabilities so they can fully participate in society. The AAR runs two programs that teach landmine victims work skills. The Vocational Training for the Disabled (AAR–VTD) teaches people how to build and repair sewing machines which they can then take back to their villages to build small-scale textile businesses. The Wheel Chair for Development program teaches landmine victims how to build and repair wheelchairs, important devices in a nation with around 40,000 amputees.

Landmines are a major problem in Cambodia. After a three-decades-long war, the Cambodian Mine Action Centre (CMAC) estimates that there are still four to six million mines and other unexploded ordnance in Cambodia, and more than 200 people each year fall victim to these explosives—one of the highest casualty rates in the world.[1,2] Because landmines were scattered throughout the countryside, no one knows where they are located, resulting in numerous victims each year, one-third of which are children.[3]

When George first arrived in Cambodia, he worked with the Landmine Relief Fund, a US based 501(c)3 charity, that has grants from the US Department of State and raises funds from donors to support the work of the Cambodian Self Help Demining (CSHD), a Cambodian group that works to eradicate landmines, the Cambodian Landmine Museum, and children living at the Landmine Museum Relief Center. He worked at the Cambodian Landmine Museum to learn more about the problem. He then volunteered for Mines Advisory Group (MAG)[4] as a community liaison. MAG works to remove landmines, but since George had no training to remove explosive devices, he instead focused on helping MAG to educate communities, development agencies, and local authorities about landmines. Then, after about 6 months of working with MAG, he decided he wanted to directly help the victims of landmines. This brought him to AAR, where he offers English language classes in the mornings and spends the afternoons teaching landmine victims how to maintain and repair sewing machines—important tools for creating textiles to be sold at the market to help landmine victims earn a living and support their families.

George has found his time in Cambodia very rewarding. He has helped to improve the lives of a number of individuals, their families, and, in some cases, their communities. But the more he has worked at AAR and MAG the more he has begun to understand the root problem—the production and placement of landmines. Rather than provide landmine victims with training, wouldn't it be better to eliminate landmines altogether? The problem on the ground might be living without an arm or a leg, but the source of

continued

that problem is a world where governments, armies, and rebel groups place landmines in civilian communities. The problem is 3 million mines in Bosnia-Herzegovina, many of them shaped like "kinder eggs," ice-cream cones, and helicopters, so as to attract children. The problem is a world where private companies produce and sell these landmines that kill and maim civilians and make it too dangerous to plow fields.

George is happy to help landmine victims, but he wants to make a bigger difference. He wants to end the production and use of landmines. After doing some research, George is becoming more active with political activist organizations, working as an advocate for the International Campaign to Ban Landmines (ICBL), the International Committee of the Red Cross, and the United Nations to lobby the US government to sign the Ottawa Treaty (Convention on the Prohibition of the Use, Stockpiling, Production and Transfer of Anti-Personnel Mines and on their Destruction) which aims to eliminate anti-personnel landmines (AP-mines) around the world. The Ottawa Treaty asks signatories not to manufacture, stockpile, or use anti-personnel mines. It has been signed by 161 states, but not the United States. Although the US stopped manufacturing landmines in 1997, it has one of the largest stockpiles in the world. George believes that, as a world leader, the US has an obligation to sign the Ottawa Treaty and work to eliminate these dangerous devices. He hopes that lobbying the US government will have more long-term effects on reducing landmine victims than the work he was doing in Cambodia.

George wants to help landmine victims. Are his efforts best spent working for nonprofit organizations that are on the ground training workers and caring for victims? Or are his efforts best spent lobbying to change the national and international laws that govern the production of landmines? Can he do this as a volunteer? Can he do this as a nonprofit employee? Is a nonprofit organization the best way for George to bring social and political change to the world? Should nonprofits stay out of politics and stick to helping people?

or "think tanks." In addition to these types of organizations that have a more direct role in the policy and politics arena, many other types of non-profit organizations, including associations, human service organizations, and churches provide outlets for political dialogue, social networking, and volunteerism. Thus, these latter groups also contribute to American political life by serving as vehicles for promoting civic engagement, political discourse, and furthering democratic ideals.[5]

This chapter examines three critical roles that nonprofit organizations play in shaping public policy and politics in the US: political representation, political mobilization, and political education. These roles are inter-related. Some nonprofit organizations perform all three roles in their efforts to influence policy or election outcomes. We will examine not only the types of nonprofit organizations that perform political roles, but also the many ways in which these organizations help to shape American democracy by promoting connections between ordinary citizens and their government. When the timing is right for dramatic political change, nonprofit organizations engaged in political representation, mobilization, and education can be catalysts in the process for creating broad-based social change. Because the topic of social movements warrants its own discussion, we will examine the role of nonprofits in social movements in the next chapter; here we focus on their political role.

Before moving into our discussion of nonprofits' political representation, mobilization, and education roles, there are some fundamental differences in the laws governing the political activities of public charities and other types of nonprofit organizations that are important to understand. The next section examines the key distinctions between public charities (501(c)3 organizations) and social welfare organizations, labor and business league organizations, and other lobbying organizations (501(c)4 and 501(c)6 organizations) that fall under other sections of the tax code. We then discuss how nonprofit organizations shape the political environment through political representation, mobilization, and education activities.

Critical Differences in Nonprofits' Political Activities

As we learned in Chapter 2, the vast majority of the nonprofit organizations registered with the Internal Revenue Service (IRS) are 501(c)3 organizations (otherwise known as public charities) including arts, education, science, healthcare and social service organizations. Despite their large proportion of the nonprofit universe, prevalence in society, and thus their collective impact on the political landscape, many people carry the misconception that public charities are not involved (or should not be involved) in the political arena.[6] Although public charities can engage in political activities, they are required by law to do so on a more limited scale, which includes strict prohibitions on supporting or endorsing political candidates.

Because the primary mission of public charities is to provide a particular service or public good, rather than influence policy, the federal government places strict legal limits on the political activities (and lobbying) of public charities. These legal limits often cause confusion and misconceptions about the ways in which nonprofit organizations are allowed to participate in public policy. Tax-exempt nonprofit organizations are allowed to lobby, but there are limitations on how that lobbying can work. First, in general, they cannot use federal funds or contract funds to lobby on legislative matters or for electioneering purposes. But, 501(c)(3) organizations can use general-purpose funds to lobby and community foundations can ear-mark grants for lobbying. Second, 501(c)(3) nonprofits cannot endorse candidates. But nonprofits can lobby within a set of limits. Public charities, 501(c)3 organizations, can choose between two sets of rule to follow: the **Substantial Part Test** or the **Expenditure Test**, known as the 501(h) election.

The Substantial Part Test governing public charities requires that organizations that wish to maintain their public charity status (and the financial benefits that come with it) cannot engage in "substantial" lobbying and must carry out their political activities in a **nonpartisan** fashion. Nonpartisan means that the organization cannot adopt the position, or express the views, of a particular political party or candidate. Substantial lobbying is a somewhat ambiguous legal rule that says lobbying or advocacy cannot consume a "substantial part" of the organization's activities or expenditures. The vast majority (98%) of 501(c)3 nonprofits fall under the Substantial Part Test since the bulk of their work is charitable and not political. But the remaining 2% of 501(c)3 organizations opt for the Expenditure Test designation, known as the "H election," which establishes a clearer limit on how much agencies can spend on lobbying: up to 20% of their total annual budget on "lobbying related activities," up to a flat $1 million for organizations with total revenues in excess of $17 million. For example, a $2 million organization can spend up to $250,000 on lobby-ing. Additionally, cost-free activities including volunteer time do not count in the measure of lobbying activities—only the budget amount counts. Those under the 501(h) test can engage in direct lobbying, including communications with legislators and expressing vies on specific legislation. They can also spend 25% of their lobbying limit on grassroots lobbying, which includes communications to the public, expressing views on specific legislation, and making calls to action. H-electors also benefit from other rules that make it easier to participate in the political process including

TABLE 7.1 Rules for Lobbying among Public Charities

	Substantial Part Test	Expenditure Test 501(h)
Allowable Amounts of Lobbying	Allowable amount of lobbying expenditures are not clearly defined.	A formula defines the amount of lobbying expenditures: 20% of the first $500,000 of annual expenditures; 15% of the next $500,000; up to $1 million a year.
Result of Rule Violations	A single year violation can result in the loss of tax-exempt status.	A single year violation does not affect tax-exempt status. A four-year violation can result in the loss of tax-exempt status.
Auditing	IRS auditors determine if a lobbying activity has the existence, nature, powers, or tax-exempt status of the organization.	IRS auditors do not consider the issue as a factor in measuring possible lobbying activities.
IRS Reporting	IRS requires a detailed description of activities to determine if there is excessive lobbying.	The IRS requires that organizations report the amount of funds spent on lobbying and grassroots lobbying.

Source: Drawn from Texas Commission on the Arts: Investing in a Creative Texas. Accessed February 13, 2014 at http://www.arts.texas.gov/resources/tools-for-results/advocacy/lobbying-and-the-law-for-nonprofits-under-section-501c3/

provisions that allow nonprofit leaders to help draft legislation. Table 7.1 compares some of the rules and IRS auditing practices for nonprofits that fall under the Substantial Part Test or the Expenditure Test.

Public charities cannot carry out political activities in an ideological, or **partisan**, fashion; they must be nonpartisan, meaning they cannot endorse candidates for office, make political contributions to candidates or parties, or advocate in favor of or against the platform of a particular candidate or party.[7] For example, most religious organizations in the US are registered as 501(c)3 organizations, precluding them from making political contributions to candidates or parties or advocating for a particular political party. But, many churches, synagogues, and mosques do advocate for or against particular policies: for example, supporting pro-life initiatives or encouraging policies that end the use of the death penalty. Many congregations and religious leaders work diligently to walk the fine line between advocating for political policies that support their religious beliefs, while refraining from supporting particular candidates. In fact, there are many mechanisms by which public charities can and do engage in political representation, mobilization, and education activities within the legal limits, and we shall soon look at a number of examples. But before discussing those activities, we first turn to nonprofit organizations that are free to engage in political activities, including direct support of candidates and partisan policies.

Lobbying Groups and Interest Groups: 501(c)4, 501(c)5, and 501(c)6 Organizations

In comparison to public charities, there are classifications of nonprofit organizations that are allowed to lobby for and advance the political interests of a particular cause or group of individuals. "Social welfare" organizations 501(c)4, such as the Sierra Club and National Rifle Association, and 501(c)5 and (c)6 labor and business league organizations, such as the AFL-CIO and the Chambers of Commerce, are all allowed to engaged in political activities, endorse candidates, and partake in partisan activities. These organizations, often referred to as **lobbying groups** or **interest groups**, are created specifically for the purpose of representing a particular cause or the needs and interests of their members. They constitute a much smaller share of the US nonprofit sector, as compared to 501(c)3 public charities, but play a critical role in the American political process. These organizations can more or less engage in as much lobbying as their resources enable, and they are free to be partisan in their messages. In other words, they can publicly endorse candidates for office, encourage their followers or members to vote for particular candidates, create and fund advertisements designed to help bolster or undermine a candidate with regard to a particular issue. As we shall examine shortly, organizations that fall within these categories of the nonprofit sector are the "heavy hitters" of political influence in Washington D.C., and they can also be powerful forces in state-level policy-making and elections.

Some leaders of public charities (e.g. service-providing nonprofit organizations) would like to benefit from the political activism that is allowed for 501(c)4, 501(c)5, and 501(c)6 organizations. They want to more aggressively pursue political goals and advocate for policies that would benefit their organizations and their clientele. This has led some 501(c)3 organizations to create partner or sister organizations that have an alternative legal status (lobbying or interest group), enabling them to engage more directly in the political process. By creating linked 501(c)3

BOX 7.1 **PUBLIC CHARITIES, "SISTER" ORGANIZATIONS, AND TRANSPARENCY**

For nonprofit leaders that want to get involved in politics and policy, the choice of incorporating with 501(c)4 status is a double-edged sword. On the one hand, this status allows the organization to make a clear statement about which political candidates it supports and to freely encourage its members to vote for those candidates, and allows the organization to engage in unlimited lobbying. On the other hand, 501(c)4 status poses a clear disadvantage from the perspective of fundraising and sustaining a base of paying members since organizations with this status cannot offer donors or members a tax write-off in exchange for their membership dues or any additional donations made to the organization, a benefit which is reserved exclusively for 501(c)3 organizations, or public charities.

Many nonprofit leaders have found a way to "have their cake and eat it too." It has become increasingly common for strategic nonprofit leaders to create multiple nonprofit organizations of different types under one corporate umbrella. One common arrangement is to have a 501(c)3, a related 501(c)4, a connected Political Action Committee, and a 527 organization.[8] Consider The Sierra Club, for example. The Sierra Club is a 501(c)4 membership organization whose primary purpose is lobbying in the interest of environmental issues. The Sierra Club Foundation, which is a 501(c)3, is its related charitable and educational arm, while the Sierra Club PAC was set up to make political contributions, and the Sierra Club Voter Education Fund is its related 527 organization created to get-out-the-vote for environmentally friendly candidates.

Although organizations that choose a complex corporate structure such as this cannot actually combine or share day-to-day operations, they can have overlapping members on their boards of directors, share advocacy plans, collaborate on strategies of action, and manage their resources in ways that allow for maximizing their political goals. While all of this is perfectly legal, it is not particularly transparent to the public. More importantly, government regulators within the IRS and Federal Elections Committee may find it difficult or impossible to track which organizations are connected to one another, and how money moves between the organizations.[9]

According to one expert on this matter,[10] there are many potential concerns with these arrangements. The little bit of information that is required on the IRS reporting form may make it difficult to determine "who is really behind an organization" and how the various inter-connected nonprofit entities are related for political purposes. This lack of transparency also has implications for donors and members, who might be concerned about whether their contribution is being put toward its intended purpose. Finally,

continued

those in charge of overseeing these organizations within the government may not even be able to detect whether funds have been diverted to purposes that are inconsistent with an individual organization's tax status, or whether political activities have been financed with inappropriate donations.

Should nonprofit organizations be allowed to "have their cake and eat it too," by creating multiple tax-exempt organizations and taking advantage of all different benefits that each form permits? For the average member of a 501(c)4 such as the Sierra Club (paying around $35 per year), is transparency an important issue? Should it matter to those who donate to a service-providing public charity that the charity has a sister organization that engages in lobbying and political action? For example, Planned Parenthood exists to provide preventive health services and family planning for low-income women but also has sister organizations that lobby for reproductive rights and financially support political candidates whose views and records align with that of Planned Parenthood's mission and agenda. Do most donors know the difference between the public charity and the lobbying organization? Should they? Are these inter-connected nonprofit organizational arrangements problematic? What evidence suggests that they are problematic? And if they are problematic, what should be done?

and 501(c)4 organizations, as well as associated Political Action Committees (PACs) and other organizational vehicles to pursue their political goals, many leaders of public charities have found a way to work within the confines of the law and enjoy the best of both worlds. Although this allows public charities to maximize their political impact while still pursuing their service missions, it does raise some questions about the transparency of these arrangements. See Box 7.1 for further discussion and an illustration of this scenario.

Shaping the Political Environment: Nonprofits and Political Representation

Representation is a key component of the political system in the United States. As a representative democracy, Americans are continually asked to elect representatives or entrust representatives to elect officials on their behalf (consider the Electoral College, where our representatives cast electoral votes for the American president). Just as politicians represent districts and citizens, organizations can represent our interests in the political system. Professional **lobbyists**, people whose business is to influence legislation on behalf of the group of individuals who hire them, work on behalf of private interests (e.g. oil companies), nonprofit interests (e.g. universities), and public interests (e.g. protection of public lands or better air quality).

The **political representation** role requires nonprofit organizations "to speak for, act for, look after the interests of respective groups."[11] Nonprofit organizations primarily carry out their representation role through lobbying and advocacy activities. Whether it is a critical-care physician paying membership dues to the American Medical Association to support lobbying for higher Medicare reimbursement rates, or a homeless family whose need for safe and affordable long-term housing is represented through the advocacy efforts of the National Coalition for the Homeless, lobbying and advocacy organizations act *on behalf of* those they represent, giving voice to the needs of their members and clients in the political system. In the US there seems to be a group to represent everyone, and, for most us, there are multiple nonprofit groups that represent our personal interests and the social causes we care about. In the discussion that follows, we will examine some of the strategies and tactics nonprofit lobbying and advocacy groups use in their efforts to provide political representation for their group members.

The term lobbying often carries a negative connotation within the general public. What exactly is lobbying? Is it different from advocacy, and if so, how? Why do we even have or need lobbying and advocacy groups? Does lobbying and advocacy only benefit the wealthy and powerful? Let us briefly consider each of these questions as we explore how these groups provide political representation for their members, clients, and service populations.

What is Lobbying and Advocacy?

Lobbying can be defined as "attempts to influence legislation or government spending plans in order to achieve an outcome more favorable to a group's agenda or objectives."[12] These attempts to influence legislation or government spending are also frequently referred to as **advocacy**, especially when performed by certain kinds of nonprofits, such as public charities. While the terms lobbying and advocacy are often used synonymously, some have suggested there are differences, with advocacy encompassing a broader set of activities. For example, Anheier defines advocacy as "the act of pleading for or against a cause, as well as supporting a position, point of view, or course of action,"[13] whereas he describes lobbying as "a specialized form of advocacy that is largely the domain of 501(c)4 organizations seeking to impact public policy and issue-making functions of an administrative, regulatory, or legislative body."[14] In general discourse, the term lobbying is used when describing business, labor, or industry groups' attempts to influence policy or politicians while the term advocacy is more frequently used to describe attempts to influence policy by public charities or public interest lobbying groups, such as the American Association of Retired Persons (AARP).

The terms lobbying and advocacy are often used interchangeably. At other times, they are used to imply different types of agendas as groups work to advance a cause or proposal. In popular language, lobbying often implies promoting private corporate interests, while advocacy implies promoting social or public interests. Merriam Webster defines a lobby as "an organized group of people who work together to influence government decisions that relate to a particular industry, issue, etc." while advocacy is "the act or process of supporting a cause or proposal: the act or process of advocating something."[15] In this chapter, we use the term lobbying to refer to organizational efforts to directly influence legislation, administrative rules, or budgetary decisions; lobbying aims to influence political decisions. By contrast, we use advocacy as a broader set of activities that includes direct lobbying of political decision-makers on behalf of members or clients as well as *some* activities aimed at educating members or clients about a cause or issue (educating), and *some* activities that encourage direct political participation by clients and members (mobilizing), such as asking them to contact their elected officials about a specific bill or budget issue. Lobbying is concerned with influencing government and policy, while advocacy advances an agenda in both the political arena and society at large. Both lobbying and advocacy are mechanisms for representation in the political system, but advocacy also sometimes includes mobilization and education roles as well.

Lobbying and advocacy organizations employ a wide range of strategies and tactics to influence public policy, and these efforts can be targeted at local, state, or federal levels, or any combination thereof. The pressure for change exerted by groups may be directed toward elected political officials—lawmakers, administrative agencies, or both—depending on whether the organization is (a) taking a stand on a proposed or pending piece of legislation, (b) trying to influence administrative rules for a bill or ordinance that already exists, (c) trying to influence the budget process, or (d) simply trying to increase awareness of the organization's cause or needs of its members or service population. Common activities carried out by non-profit lobbying and advocacy groups include: testifying before legislative bodies; advocating on behalf of, or against, proposed legislation; making a statement during the public comment portion of government meetings; submitting amicus briefs or statements in court; informally talking and meeting with policy-makers about their organizations and the needs of a group's membership or service population; and participating in government planning or advisory groups.[16]

Although advocacy involves a few more strategies and tactics than lobbying—those aimed at educating and mobilizing—the goals of these activities are ultimately the same. Lobbying and advocacy has four goals[17]: (1) influencing legislation or regulations; (2) improving governmental service programs; (3) securing government funds; and (4) obtaining special benefits for members or clients. Of course these goals are not mutually exclusive, as the pursuit of one may lead to the accomplishment of others. For example, nonprofit hospitals or health centers may successfully lobby against proposed changes to state Medicaid rules that call for eliminating or reducing certain reimbursable services, but in the process they would also accomplish the goals of influencing regulations and protecting benefits for their clients (patients).

Why Do We Need Lobbying and Advocacy Groups?

Sometimes lobbying and advocacy groups are presented in a negative light, with a bad reputation as power-wielding organizations with too much influence over public officials. Given this reputation, one might wonder whether our society would simply be better off without them. Would our democracy work better if we eliminated lobbyists? Instead of lobbyists, citizens could just contact their elected officials individually to express their views. Instead of responding to lobbying groups with excessive resources to advance a special interest, political officials and representatives would need to respond to individual citizens. Pluralist theory and collective action theory, which we examined in Chapter 3, help to provide some insight into the role of lobbyists in American representative democracy.

From the pluralist perspective, an abundance of interest groups representing all segments of society is good for democracy and ensures that no single group or interest can become all-powerful, nor can the public become victims of government tyranny. Pluralists argue that multiple, competing groups vying for political influence, public resources, and greater expression of their values in the public arena contribute to a more robust democracy and ensure a fairer and more just distribution of public resources. This system of competing interest groups, along with ever-changing political leadership in both the executive and legislative branches of government, ensures that all groups get their way on some issues some of the time, but not on all issues all of the time.

Collective action theory argues that citizens organized and working together as a group around a common cause or issue are a more efficient and effective way to exert influence over policy and politicians than citizens working alone as individuals. As we discussed in Chapter 3, collective action theory views nonprofit groups—especially lobbying and advocacy groups —as emerging to accomplish what one person cannot do alone. Collective action theory portrays nonprofits as organizations arising to express group interests—members of a group share common values, beliefs, preferences, or goals. By uniting together around these shared values, beliefs, preferences, or goals, individuals can pool their resources, establish coordinated strategies and action plans, and be more effective at getting the attention of legislators. Moreover, when acting as a group or through lobbyists, individuals are able to support multiple causes or political interests without exhausting all of their time and resources on a single issue. Many of us do not have the motivation to spend our time calling and sending e-mails to our city officials, state representatives, and congressional representatives. Moreover, acting as a group increases the likelihood that elected officials will be responsive to our interests. While elected officials might not be inclined to listen to the views of any one particular voter, most want to be re-elected and therefore cannot afford to ignore or alienate large groups of voters.

Does Lobbying and Advocacy Disproportionately Benefit the Existing Power Elite?

Not all lobbying and advocacy groups are the same. Some groups, such as Greenpeace and the AARP, are described as "public interest" lobbying groups because they advocate for policies that the group believes are of benefit to society as a whole—the environment and care for retired people respectively. These groups would argue that by achieving their goals they create benefits for all of society. By lobbying to protect the environment, Greenpeace's activities result in policies that create healthier oceans and air for all people. Similarly, by protecting the interests of retired people, AARP creates benefits for the families that might support retired individuals and all those who will someday retire themselves. The legislative victories of these public interest lobbying groups create benefits (or consequences, depending on your views) that cannot be limited only to those who pay dues or contribute to the organization. In essence, nonmembers and regular citizens become "free riders," benefitting from the activities of these organizations without being burdened with the cost of supporting those activities.

Of course, that which constitutes the "public interest," and benefits or costs, lies in the eye of the beholder. Consider the National Rifle Association (NRA), a well-known and influential public interest lobbying group. The NRA was founded in 1871 with the mission of promoting firearm competency, safety, and ownership. The NRA provides training and firearm proficiency courses for many police departments. It is a 501(c)4 with four 501(c)3 charitable subsidiaries: NRA Civil Rights Defense Fund, NRA Freedom Action Foundation, NRA Foundation Inc., and the NRA Special Contribution Fund. The NRA has a century long history of lobbying for the protection of the Second Amendment right to keep and bear arms and against firearm legislation that might threaten or limit that right.

The NRA is one of the most powerful and politically influential public interest lobbying groups in the US,[18] with a budget of $231 million and a membership over 5 million in May 2013.[19] But some Americans do not believe that the NRA serves the public interest; they disagree with the NRA's mission and have organized their own groups, such as Moms Demand Action for Gun Sense and the Brady Campaign to Prevent Gun Violence. These organizations are also working in the public interest, but with an opposing mission to that of the NRA. One might argue that each of these groups serves the public interest, since they ensure that two sides of the issue are represented in our political system. But, at the same time, the outcomes of their activities might injure or threaten the interests of one or more opposing groups. For example, if Moms Demand Action was successful in its efforts to get a federal bill passed requiring universal background checks for gun-buyers, the entire public might be made safer as fewer persons with criminal records would be allowed to obtain guns. The potential benefit of living in a safer society as a result of this policy change is something that extends to everyone—it is not a benefit that can be limited only to that small percentage of the population that chooses to become a member of Moms Demand Action or support the organization with a financial contribution. However, the NRA would argue that this type of legislation limits the rights of lawful gun owners, while doing little to prevent criminals from having guns, thus making all of us less safe while violating our rights. Whose public interest is more important, that of NRA members or those on the side of Moms Demand Action?

Public interest lobbying groups exist to represent a wide variety of issues and populations in the US including many organizations that advocate on behalf of underrepresented groups. There are lobbying groups that represent ethnic and racial minorities such as the National Association for the Advancement of Colored People (NAACP) and the Hispanic 100 Policy Committee, and organizations representing several vulnerable populations such as the Disabled American Veterans Foundation and Americans for Children's Health. These advocacy groups work on behalf of populations that have traditionally been marginalized in the political system. The Human Rights Campaign, for example, is a national nonpartisan organization with a mission to lobby lawmakers and educate the public to ensure the rights of lesbian, gay, bisexual, transgender, and queer (LGBTQ) individuals are protected. This organization "engages in direct lobbying, provides grassroots and organizing support, and educates the public to ensure that LGBTQ individuals can be open, honest, and safe at home, at work, and in the community." Given the existence of these types of organizations serving underrepresented and marginalized groups, it is fair to say that the wealthy and powerful are not the only groups that benefit from political representation offered by lobbying and advocacy groups.

Many public interest advocacy groups tend to rely upon grassroots mobilization strategies and national leadership to build a broad membership base by identifying committed members to create and lead state and local chapters to expand their influence around the country. Thus, the power of these advocacy groups is often found in their numbers. Large memberships enable the mobilization of resources to engage in direct phone call or mailing campaigns, marches, and demonstrations. Modern technologies, including the Internet and social media, have made it incredibly fast and simple for these organizations to mobilize members to contact their legislators via text, e-mail, and phone (see Box 7.2 for an example). A simple tweet or Facebook post can quickly mobilize hundreds of members, and potentially reach thousands of nonmembers who are connected to members through social media.

As we noted earlier in the chapter, in addition to nonprofit organizations whose main purpose is lobbying and advocacy, public charities and human service organizations also engage in lobbying and advocacy (with some legal constraints). Since public charities (501(c)3 organizations) must carefully balance their service delivery roles with their political representation roles, rather than lobby directly they often work in conjunction with lobbying organizations.

Some human service organizations join coalitions or intermediary groups that function as advocacy "umbrellas," taking on the representation role for public charities. For example, public charities that provide child welfare services may choose to join another nonprofit, The Alliance for Children and Families, which is a national organization that provides advocacy on behalf of nearly 350 nonprofit child welfare service providers throughout the United States. The Alliance for Children and Families works to represent the political interests of the human service organizations and their clients through lobbying and advocacy work, leaving the public charities to focus on service provision and their charitable missions. Advocacy umbrellas enable human service organizations to ensure that they have a voice in the political process, without requiring them to directly engage in lobbying activities. Clients of organizations serving children, persons with severe disabilities, the frail, elderly, and critically ill, and immigrant and refugee populations, who are often prevented from direct political participation by citizenship status or language barriers, are just a few of those who may benefit from the lobbying and advocacy efforts of their service organization.

While it is true that the wealthy and powerful are not the only ones to benefit from lobbying groups, it is also true that they probably benefit disproportionately. There is a famous saying by E. E. Schattschneider that "the flaw in the pluralist heaven is that the heavenly chorus sings with a strong upper-class accent."[20] Translated into plain English, the most powerful and well-funded lobbying groups tend to be those representing corporate America—business and industry groups. In contrast to public interest lobbying groups, labor and industry lobbying groups exist to represent the interests of prestigious and wealthy professionals such as doctors, lawyers, and realtors, as well as businesses such as hospitals, restaurant owners, and beer distributors. While these types of lobbying groups may also have large numbers of members to mobilize, their real power is in their financial resources and their ability to persuade elected officials that the health of the American economy rests on the legislators' support of spending decisions (and sometimes laws or rules) that benefit the industry group. Table 7.2 provides a list of the most powerful lobbying groups in America, as rated by members of Congress, their staffs, and senior White House officials. The list is from 2001, but is important because it was based on reports from members of Congress about the lobbyists that they paid the most attention to and those that they felt had the greatest influence in Congress. As you examine this list, consider whether or not Schattschneider's comment carries truth: Are the most powerful lobbyists advancing the interests of a strong upper-class, corporate America, or working people?

In sum, nonprofit lobbying and advocacy groups play a critical role in the American political system representing the interests of American businesses, private citizens, underrepresented groups, marginalized populations, and the public interest. Sometimes, lobbying groups with the most resources and the most professional staff have the greatest influence and are more skilled at navigating the policy process. In other cases, groups with the largest membership are best equipped to mobilize their resources to influence the policy processes. Lobbying groups, though they seek to advance the interests of their membership, often advance legislation and policies that have beneficial effects for others in society, creating public outcomes for nonmembers. And while some nonprofit organizations are

TABLE 7.2 Most Powerful Lobbying Groups in America, 2001

	Total Revenues, 2012 ($)	IRS Designation*
1. National Rifle Association	218,983,530	501(c)4
2. American Association of Retired People	16,124,327	501(c)4
3. National Federation of Independent Business	95,350,055	501(c)6
4. American Israel Public Affairs Committee	66,862,011	501(c)4
5. Association of Trial Lawyers of America		
6. American Federation of Labor & Congress of Industrial Organizations	168,123,814	501(c)5
7. Chamber of Commerce of the United States of America	147,372,355	501(c)6
8. National Beer Wholesalers of America	11,604102	501(c)6
9. National Association of Realtors	157,065241	501(c)6
10. National Association of Manufacturers	35,558,576	501(c)6
11. National Association of Homebuilders of the United States	55,510,961	501(c)6
12. American Medical Association	247,052,700	501(c)6
13. American Hospital Association	11,050,608	501(c)6
14. National Education Association of the United States	376,500,845	501(c)5
15. American Farm Bureau Federation	28,213,261	501(c)5
16. Motion Picture Association of America	60,800,518	501(c)6
17. National Association of Broadcasters	47,906,831	501(c)6
18. National Right to Life Committee	5,549,712	501(c)4
19. Health Insurance Association of America	11,109,808	501(c)6
20. National Restaurant Association	91,400,324	501(c)6
21. National Governors' Association	19,511,194	501(c)3
22. Recording Industry Association of America	28,971,171	501(c)6
23. American Bankers Association	85,072,792	501(c)6
24. Pharmaceutical Research and Manufacturers of America	204,851,231	501(c)6
25. International Brotherhood of Teamsters	174,851,880	501(c)5

Source: Fortune Magazine "Power 25 Survey for 2001." Accessed July 1, 2013 at http://www.thefree library.com/National+Rifle+Association+Ranked+No.+1+on+FORTUNE+Power+25+List.-a074485661

Note: Data for the Association of Trial Lawyers are unavailable for 2012. Methodology: Fortune Magazine collaborated with scientific polling experts to survey and interview approximately 2,200 Washington insiders, including members of Congress, their staffs, and senior White House officials, to identify and rank the groups they perceived to wield the most power and hold the greatest sway over federal lawmakers. Respondents were also asked their views of which tactics were most and least effective in influencing legislators. *501(c)4 = Civic Leagues & Social Welfare Organizations; 501(c)5 = Labor, Agriculture & Horticulture Organizations; 501(c)6 = Business Leagues, etc.

established with the sole purpose of engaging in lobbying and advocacy, other types of nonprofits, specifically public charities, often find mechanisms for engaging in lobbying, either through umbrella organizations or through coalitions with advocacy groups. The complex political system in the United States gives ample opportunities for nonprofit organizations to engage in the political system and represent the interests of their membership or the public at large.

Shaping the Political Environment: Nonprofits and Political Mobilization

While the representation role involves nonprofit organizations speaking *on behalf of* the needs and interests of clientele groups, nonprofits' **political mobilization** role encourages citizens to *directly participate* in the political process. Mobilization activities include encouraging members or clients to attend public hearings or meetings to express their views; persuading or assisting members in writing, calling, e-mailing, or contacting via social media their legislators at local, state, or congressional levels; registering members to vote and encouraging their participation in elections; and, sometimes, encouraging participation in a demonstration, rally, boycott, or protest. Types of nonprofit organizations that perform mobilization activities include advocacy organizations, political parties, voter engagement organizations, and a wide variety of public charities, although not all of these organizations perform all of these functions. Moreover, the strategies and messages these organizations use to mobilize members and affiliates vary a great deal, depending on whether the organization is limited by the nonpartisan rule.

Nonprofits Mobilizing Public Voice

Many local chapters of advocacy organizations mobilize members and the general public to attend state or local public hearings or legislative sessions to express their support or opposition to a proposed ordinance or bill. For example, as the Illinois state legislature debated a bill in 2013 that would allow concealed carry of firearms in the state, the Illinois and Chicago chapters of the gun control group Moms Demand Action worked to turn out citizens at the state capitol speaking out in opposition to the bill, some of whom shared personal testimony about family members who had been victims of gun violence. The Chicago chapter of the organization also worked to mobilize residents of area municipalities considering local gun control ordinances to attend city meetings and speak out in support of these measures. As a result of the pressure put on city governments by members of this group, many suburban communities such as Evanston, Hazel Crest, and Homewood adopted their own gun control measures, including assault weapons bans, giving them local control over the issue before the state legislature passed the concealed carry law. Another frequent scenario involves human service organizations mobilizing clients to give personal testimony at budget hearings or debates, to express opposition to proposed cuts or to plead for expanded services. Many nonprofit mental health organizations, for example, have been successful in staving off or minimizing cuts to Medicaid services by turning out staff, clients, family members, and caregivers in large numbers to protest these cuts at the state budget hearings and county commission meetings.

Contacting elected officials to express opinions on policy issues, pending legislation, or budgetary matters is one of the oldest forms of political participation in the United States. However, most people have busy lives and very few would go out of their way to contact an elected official to express their dissatisfaction without some prompting. Historically, those with the highest incomes and education have dominated political participation in the US. While the relationship still exists to some extent, nonprofit organizations have played a critical role in making democracy more inclusive and widening the scope of political participation. The Internet has also been instrumental in this regard, dramatically enhancing the mobilization function of nonprofits. Every major advocacy organization (and many public charities as well) now enables members, clients, and other interested parties to subscribe to "action alert" listservs in order to receive e-mails about specific bills and budget issues that encourage them to contact elected officials and express their views. For example, one organization that has played a prominent role in the national debate over immigration reform—the Illinois Coalition for Immigrant and Refugee Rights (ICIRR)—displays an invitation to sign up for action alerts on the main page of their website, alongside an unflattering photo of an Illinois state legislator with a caption reading *Time for the House Deputy Whip to Remember November & Back Immigration Reform.*

Moreover, the process of contacting legislators has been simplified as many nonprofits performing the mobilization role allow visitors to their websites to search for their representatives by zip code and to send e-mails with pre-filled messages just by clicking on a button. Based on the zip code entered, the site generates a listing of all federal and state representatives for the user with boxes alongside the legislators' names that the user can check off in order to compose one letter that can be sent to all selected representatives. Some of the largest and most well-funded advocacy organizations, such as The Christian Coalition, offer mobile apps that enable users to obtain and act on their legislative alerts more quickly through a smartphone. Advocacy organizations and other types of politically inclined nonprofits are also increasingly relying on social media such as Facebook and Twitter to advance mobilization efforts. These new technologies have proven particularly useful in expanding the scope of political participation as individuals unaware of a cause or issue may see the "likes" and online posts of a friend and decide that they too wish to become involved in the cause. For an example of a nonprofit advocacy organization both founded and operated largely through social media, see Box 7.2.

Community-organizing groups are a specific type of organization that embodies the political mobilization role of nonprofits. While community-organizing groups may also press for legislative change and social reform using some of the same approaches as advocacy organizations, community-organizing groups differ in that they seek to empower residents and promote the general well-being of entire communities rather than specific interest groups. These objectives are typically accomplished by identifying and training community leaders to become activists, facilitating coalitions, mobilizing community members to vote, pressuring local lawmakers and government administrators for reforms that will benefit the community, developing issue campaigns, and organizing protest activities if conventional strategies fail to bring about the desired social change. For example, the People Improving Communities through Organizing (PICO) National Network is a federated system of faith-based communities organizing efforts that work to create social change in low-income communities throughout the US. Typical of other community-organizing groups, PICO uses the strategy of empowering community members through leadership training and civic capacity-building so that they may pursue needed local reforms related to housing, healthcare, economic security, school improvement, youth development, and immigration reform.

BOX 7.2 USING SOCIAL MEDIA FOR POLITICAL INFLUENCE: MOMS DEMAND ACTION

On the morning of December 14, 2012 in the quaint suburban community of Newtown, Connecticut, an emotionally disturbed young man shot and killed his mother with an assault rifle, and proceeded to shoot his way into nearby Sandy Hook elementary school, killing twenty first-graders and six more adults. The day after this tragedy unfolded, the seed of a new nonprofit organization was planted when an Indianapolis mother of five by the name of Shannon Watts started a Facebook page called *One Million Moms For Gun Control*. Mrs. Watts shared the page with her 175 Facebook friends, and, as it turned out, one of her friends had another Facebook friend in New York—unconnected to Watts—with the same idea. The two worked together to build their network of followers through Facebook, and simultaneously took steps to formalize their efforts into an organization, which was subsequently named *Moms Demand Action for Gun Sense in America*.[21]

Moms Demand Action compares itself to "Mothers Against Drunk Driving" which was created in 1980 to lobby for stricter drunk driving laws. With lobbying and policy change also at the heart of its mission, Moms Demand Action was created "to demand action from legislators, state and federal; companies; and educational institutions to establish common-sense gun reforms."[22] The organization describes itself as "a non-partisan grassroots movement" and makes clear that their aim is not to infringe on responsible gun-owners' second amendment rights. According to the organization's website: "Moms Demand Action is not asking our government to ban guns . . . We simply support common-sense solutions to the overwhelming and increasing epidemic of gun violence in America." The organization's goal is to pursue policy change in the following six areas:

1.   require background checks for all gun and ammunition purchases;
2.   ban assault weapons and ammunition magazines that hold more than 10 rounds;
3.   track the sale of large quantities of ammunition, and ban online sales;
4.   establish product safety oversight of guns and ammunition, and require child-safe gun technology;
5.   support policies at companies and public institutions that promote gun safety;
6.   counter the gun industry's efforts to weaken gun laws at the state level.[23]

What has set Moms Demand Action apart from other gun control groups is that the organization originated through social networking, has harnessed the power of social media to build its membership base, and has amassed an impressive cadre of committed activists in a very short amount of time. Despite the fact that the organization

continued

is not yet officially registered or recognized as a formal nonprofit organization, as of 2013 it has more than 104,000 members and nearly 100 chapters in 40 states. The organization uses its main Facebook page, and affiliated chapter Facebook pages, to mobilize members in support of laws promoting gun safety. The organization's leadership uses Facebook to organize local demonstrations, publicize facts about gun violence, broadcast updates about gun legislation, endorse candidates who support their agenda, and provide for quick and easy petition signing and contacting of elected officials. Moreover, the Moms Demand Action website enables visitors to quickly find and contact their Congressional representatives via Twitter or e-mail. Users can choose from a variety of pre-written messages to Tweet, e-mail, or write their own messages. Additionally, Moms Demand Action (whose membership also includes many Dads) publicizes its legislative victories through the Facebook pages, which helps to sustain the activism of its followers and reinforce their commitment to the cause.

By using social media as its primary organizing mechanism, Moms Demand Action has achieved widespread visibility not only in cyberspace and on capital steps throughout the US, but has also captured the attention of the mainstream media. In the first six months of its operation, leaders of the organization appeared on MSNBC, and were interviewed or mentioned in national news outlets including the Huffington Post and NPR, as well as numerous local newspapers such as the Chicago Tribune.

In April of 2013, Moms Demand Action launched a PSA (public service announcement) campaign titled "Choose One," featuring the photo series displayed below, depicting children holding assault weapons alongside children holding innocuous objects that have been banned in American public schools. Unlike conventional PSAs, which are posted via television, radio, billboards, and newspapers, Moms Demand Action launched its PSA by encouraging its membership to "share this page on Facebook, by email, or through your other social networks," and offers a link for website visitors and members to "fast-Tweet" the photo campaign.

Compare the Moms Demand Action PSAs with NRA advertisements and materials.

Activity

Visit the main page of Moms Demand Action's website: http://momsdemandaction.org/ Now visit the main page of the National Rifle Association's website: http://home.nra.org/ What are the major differences between these two pages? Membership has different meanings in these two organizations—what are the key differences? In what ways do Moms Demand Action and the NRA make it easy for citizens to interact with their respective organizations? What are the sources of political power in these two organizations?

continued

Little Red Riding Hood   Source: Moms Demand Action

Dodgeball   Source: Moms Demand Action

Kinder Eggs   Source: Moms Demand Action

continued

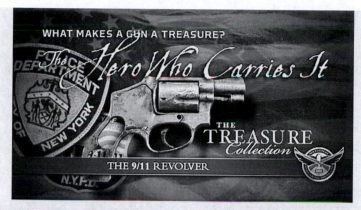

Treasure Collection   National Rifle Association

New NRA   National Rifle Association

Colt   National Rifle Association

Nonprofits Mobilizing Voters

The mobilization of voters in the United States is an important activity of both partisan and nonpartisan nonprofit organizations. Political parties are one of the most important partisan groups seeking to encourage voting in the US. If you took a poll among the students in your class right now, probably every person has experienced at least one knock on the door or been stopped on the street by a representative of a political party or advocacy group, wanting to know if they were registered to vote. They may have even asked you whom you plan to vote for. The two major political parties in the US—the national Republican Party, the Democratic Party—and with other smaller political party organizations such as the Green Party and Tea Party are tax-exempt organizations. These organizations work around the clock during election seasons to register voters and **get-out-the-vote (GOTV)** for candidates who are members of their party, and also work in hopes of persuading undecided voters. Political parties generally do this work through door-to-door canvassing to register voters or asking them to sign pledge cards promising to vote for a particular candidate or slate of candidates. These same organizations also use phone canvassing to mobilize voters, especially for reminding people to get to the polls. Political parties have become very sophisticated in their methods for targeting their efforts at prospective voters, by partnering with private research firms to obtain data that allows them to focus canvassing efforts on neighborhoods where they are most likely to persuade voters in their favor. Many lobbying and advocacy organizations also engage in voter registration or get-out-the-vote work typically with a partisan agenda, going door-knocking or phone-calling, or holding community-based voter registration drives.

Along with political parties, many other types of nonprofits are playing an increasingly influential role in the American political landscape by mobilizing clients, members, and the general public to participate in elections. A wide range of nonprofit organizations participate in elections by holding voter registration drives and working to ensure that registered voters show up to the polls on election day through *nonpartisan* GOTV efforts. Many community-organizing groups, churches, voting rights groups, ethnic and immigrant service organizations, and human service agencies work to mobilize voters regardless of particular political issues or views.

While political parties, labor unions, and lobbying groups of all types have a long history of working to get-out-the-vote for their preferred candidates, the widespread involvement of nonpartisan groups in elections is a more recent phenomenon. Some nonpartisan groups, such as the League of Women Voters, have worked to encourage voter turnout for many decades. However, it was not until the passage of the National Voter Registration Act (NVRA)—also known as the "Motor Voter" law—in 1993 that nonpartisan voter registration and GOTV efforts spread to other types of nonprofit organizations. Signed into law by President Clinton, the goal of the NVRA was to reduce historic disparities in voter turnout rates that fall along lines of race, income, age, and disability.[24] The law set out to accomplish this by requiring public welfare agencies and all offices of state-funded programs providing services to persons with disabilities (including nonprofits providing these services) to make voter registration forms available on site, to assist clients in completing the forms if they wish to register, and to transmit completed forms to the appropriate state official. It is often referred to as the "Motor Voter" law because it requires Departments of Motor Vehicles around the country to offer voter registration along with motor vehicle services, like getting a driver's license. The law also explicitly encourages all other "nongovernmental entities" to offer nonpartisan voter registration opportunities as well. While not all nonprofit organizations that are eligible choose to engage in election activities, most lobbying and advocacy groups offer links to the national voter registration form on their websites during national election years, as do the major political parties.

Many community-organizing groups, such as the PICO National Network mentioned earlier, and community-based organizations such as Headcount[25] or Voice of the Ex-Offender (VOTE) in New Orleans,[26] organize events and assign staff and volunteers to go door-to-door with voter registration forms during election season, in an effort to register new voters, but not to persuade them to vote for any particular candidate. These groups often make phone calls or go door-knocking again in the final days before the election (and on Election Day) to remind people to get to the polls. Other organizations offer "agency-based" voter registration opportunities on-site at the service delivery agency, such as Health Access, or do some combination of agency-based voter registration and door-to-door registration in the community, such as the Arab Community Center for Economic and Social Services.

Through agency-based voter registration, nonprofit human service organizations play an important role in electoral mobilization. Even after voter registration opportunities were expanded through the 1993 National Voter Registration Act, registration rates remained disproportionately lower among low-income citizens and racial minorities. By performing nonpartisan voter registration and get-out-the-vote (GOTV) activities, human service organizations help to make democracy more inclusive by engaging low-income citizens and marginalized populations in the voting process. In addition to their frequent contact with low-income clients, nonprofits are often more highly trusted by clients than services provided by government voter registration offices. For example, one study shows that black and Hispanic citizens (and citizens from Spanish-speaking households) are more than twice as likely to register to vote via third-party nonprofit groups than white citizens and those from English-speaking households.[27]

Some organizations that offer voter registration go a step further in their voter mobilization efforts by providing information on voter registration deadlines, candidate policy positions and voting records, ballot measures, polling locations, and any other nonpartisan activity intended to increase the likelihood of voting and casting informed votes.[28] Some of these organizations even work to reduce physical barriers to voting, such as providing rides to the polls or helping people obtain absentee ballots, particularly organizations serving elderly persons, or persons with disabilities who may have difficulty getting around in the community. At least with regard to human service organizations, there is strong evidence that nonpartisan voter registration and voter mobilization efforts make a big difference in increasing voter turnout rates of low-income voters.[29]

Nonprofits Mobilizing Public Action

Finally, some nonprofit organizations mobilize their clients for direct participation in the political process through demonstrations, rallies, protests, or boycotts. While these activities constitute more "unconventional" political participation,[30] their potential to politically empower groups can be exceedingly effective, particularly when they are linked to broader social change efforts as we shall see in the next chapter. Mobilizing members to action is typically done by lobbying and advocacy groups and informal organizations, but is relatively rare among public charities who face tighter legal restrictions on their political activities. Additionally, the leaders of many public charities do not want to attract attention to political activities that might distract from their service missions, or become involved in a political process that might threaten their access to government funding and support.

Some political scientists and organizers would argue that political action (through protest, march, or demonstration) and defiance against government laws or authority and protests that lead to mass disruption are a true source of political power, particularly for the poor who have limited means to effect policy change in other ways. It has been argued that protest forms of political participation are the only actions that have ever produced large-scale dramatic policy reforms.[31] One need only to consider the organized actions of citizens and community-based organizations engaged in the Labor Movement or the Civil Rights Movement to see the merit in this argument. Consider the powerful effects of lunch counter sit-ins, bus boycotts, and marches during the segregation era.

Most organizations that pursue political action strategies to mobilize their members or clientele use them as a limited part of a more comprehensive approach to their advocacy, rather than the main tactic. For example, environmental groups devote most of their resources to direct lobbying, grassroots mobilization, and shaping public opinion through political education, but on occasion determine that a rally or protest is deemed the best strategy for influencing policy. For example, early in 2013 the leaders of roughly 90 environment groups, including the Sierra Club, 350.org, National Resource Defense Council, Waterkeeper Alliance, and the Rainforest Action Network (just to name a few), collaborated to stage the "Forward on Climate" rally outside the White House in opposition to President Obama's plan to go forward with the Keystone XL Pipeline. The rally drew more than 40,000 participants, including many celebrities, and constituted the largest gathering of environmental activists in history. As a testament to the rarity of this event, Sierra Club's Executive Director Michael Brune stated, "For the first time in the Sierra Club's 120-year history, we have joined the ranks of visionaries of the past and present to

Vancouver Critical Mass

engage in civil disobedience, knowing that the issue at hand is so critical, it compels the strongest defensible action."[32] Echoing these sentiments and speaking to the rarity of the protest tactic, Natural Resources Defense Council President Frances Beinecke stated, "The time is right for this rally."[33]

In comparison, some organizations are centered on political action. Consider the Critical Mass. The primary activity of Critical Mass is a monthly bike ride. Critical Mass has a decentralized structure with no leadership and no membership: it is simply an event to which all are invited. Some consider the monthly ride to be a protest against the car-centric, oil-dependent culture, while others view it as an awareness-raising exercise. Critical Mass is a cycling event that is held the last Friday of every month in more than 300 cities around the world. Cyclists meet at a set location and time and then travel through the city or town demonstrating the power of cyclists. These "biketivist" groups often stop traffic and take over whole city streets, arguing that they are traffic, raising awareness of cyclists, the need for bicycle-friendly streets, and the associated health and fitness

World Naked Bike Ride, London, 2008

outcomes of cycling. The first political-protest ride was held in 1992 with the aim of reclaiming the streets of San Francisco. Today these events are viewed as a celebration of cycling, a social movement, and a public nuisance. In the spirit of Critical Mass, other organizations have developed to protest and raise awareness for political issues via mass bicycle rides. The World Naked Bike Ride (WNBR) is an international clothing optional bike ride where individuals meet to ride in demonstration of "a vision of a cleaner, safer, body-positive world,"[34] while others ride in protest against oil-dependent forms of transportation. Both of these examples represent non-profit organizations that act primarily to mobilize members, or affiliates, using action and protest strategies over more conventional forms of political engagement. See the photo opposite of Critical Mass bike riders in Vancouver.

In order to avoid some of the stigma associated with the term "protesting," some nonprofit organizations have developed alternative terminology. The grassroots pro-life public charity Bound4LIFE organizes "Silent Sieges" through its local chapters across the country, indicating in bold print throughout its website and print materials: "It's not a protest. It's a prayer meeting!"[35] Chapter leaders are required to organize volunteers to participate in Silent Sieges at least monthly to stand outside Planned Parenthood and courthouses with red tape over their mouths bearing the word "life." Although for most organizations (particularly public charities) these types of activities would be rare and part of a broader social change strategy, in the case of Bound4LIFE these public demonstrations are the primary activity of the organization whose stated mission is: "Bound4LIFE exists to mobilize the nation to Fast and Pray for the ending of abortion. We stand outside Court Houses and abortion clinics with red LIFE tape on our mouths."[36] Similar mobilization activities include Take Back the Night walks or marches, where groups walk the streets at night to raise awareness about sexual assault, domestic violence, and the physical safety of women in our communities.[37]

Some nonprofit organizations are attempting to put a positive spin on political demonstrations by "reverse protesting" or assembling in groups in public to demonstrate their appreciation for legislators whose votes align with the group's mission. For example, the grassroots group Moms Demand Action, which we learned about earlier, organized a series of "stroller jams" outside the district offices of US Senators voting in favor of background checks for gun buyers in 2013. The stroller jams involved mothers and their children congregating in large numbers with signs that read "thank you" and "we've got your back" signs. The stroller jams are organized as recurring events to support not only federal lawmakers, but also state legislators, and local public officials who have demonstrated support for stricter gun laws with their votes or initiatives in sponsoring legislation in this area.[38]

It is clear that nonprofit organizations play a critical role in mobilizing groups and individuals to become more engaged in the political process, through direct contact with political officials, voting, and political action. Mobilization activities include encouraging members to contact political officials, enlisting people to register to vote, supporting efforts to get individuals to vote, and inspiring individuals to organize toward political action, be it a march, a bike ride, or a silent sit-in. Each of these activities enables nonprofit organizations to engage in the political system and mobilize their membership and others toward some political goal. How nonprofit organizations mobilize their members and the ways in which they approach the political system are conditioned by their organizational status, mission, and goals, but, regardless of the means for mobilization, it is apparent that nonprofit organizations of all types play an important role in shaping the political environment in the United States and mobilizing individuals and groups to participate in the public policy process.

Shaping the Political Environment: Nonprofits and Political Education

The third way that nonprofit organizations engage in the political environment is through **political education**. One type of nonprofit organization that plays a critical role in advancing political education is the public policy research institute, also known as "**think tanks.**" These organizations employ professionals, including economists and policy analysts, who conduct research on policy issues and produce reports that are informative for both policy-makers and others inside the political decision-making world, but are also a useful source of information for the public. Think tanks seek to influence policy by providing information to citizens, voters, activists, the media, and policy-makers. While many think tanks claim to be nonpartisan, most of them operate from an ideological perspective, which is often apparent in the policy issues they choose to focus upon, as well as the policy recommendations issued by these organizations. For example, a think tank that focuses on freedom from government interference, tax policy, and gun rights might be assumed to be conservative, while a think tank focused on urban education, poverty, and social justice might be considered liberal.

Some think tanks are more overt in their political leanings than others, and clearly aim to support policies aligned with a distinct ideology. For example, organizations such as the Cato Institute and Heritage Foundation make clear in their mission statements that they work to promote conservative policies, while, at the liberal end of the spectrum, the Center for American Progress and Demos engage in research that supports progressive policies. On the other hand, some nonprofit think tanks have a reputation for being more nonpartisan and generating information that is more objective and politically neutral. Examples of these organizations include Rand Corporation, Brookings Institution, and the Urban Institute. Box 7.3 highlights the mission statements of some prominent public policy research institutes (or think tanks) in the US.

BOX 7.3 MISSION STATEMENTS OF PROMINENT PUBLIC POLICY RESEARCH INSTITUTES IN THE UNITED STATES

Heritage Foundation

Mission: To formulate and promote conservative public policies based on the principles of free enterprise, limited government, individual freedom, traditional American values, and a strong national defense.

http://www.heritage.org/about

Cato Institute

The mission of the Cato Institute is to originate, disseminate, and increase understanding of public policies based on the principles of individual liberty, limited government, free markets, and peace. Our vision is to create free, open, and civil societies founded on libertarian principles.

http://www.cato.org/mission

Center for American Progress

The Center for American Progress is an independent nonpartisan educational institute dedicated to improving the lives of Americans through progressive ideas and action. Building on the achievements of progressive pioneers such as Teddy Roosevelt and Martin Luther King Jr., our work addresses 21st-century challenges such as energy, national security, economic growth and opportunity, immigration, education, and health-care. We develop new policy ideas, critique the policy that stems from conservative values, challenge the media to cover the issues that truly matter, and shape the national debate.

http://www.americanprogress.org/about/mission/

Demos

Demos is a public policy organization working for an America where we all have an equal say in our democracy and an equal chance in our economy. Our name means "the people." It is the root word of democracy, and it reminds us that in America, the true source of our greatness is the diversity of our people. Our nation's highest challenge is to create a democracy that truly empowers people of all backgrounds, so that we all have a say in setting the policies that shape opportunity and provide for our common future. To help America meet that challenge, Demos is working to reduce both political and economic inequality, deploying original research, advocacy, litigation, and strategic communications to create the America that the people deserve.

http://www.demos.org/about-demos

continued

Rand Corporation

The Rand Corporation is a nonprofit institution that helps improve policy and decision-making through research and analysis. Rand focuses on the issues that matter most such as health, education, national security, international affairs, law and business, the environment, and more. With a research staff consisting of some of the world's preeminent minds, Rand has been expanding the boundaries of human knowledge for more than 60 years.

http://www.rand.org/about/history.html

Brookings Institution

The Brookings Institution mission is to conduct high-quality, independent research and, based on that research, to provide innovative, practical recommendations that advance three broad goals: (1) strengthen American democracy; (2) foster the economic and social welfare, security, and opportunity of all Americans; and (3) secure a more open, safe, prosperous, and cooperative international system.

http://www.brookings.edu/about#research-programs/

Urban Institute

The Urban Institute gathers data, conducts research, evaluates programs, offers technical assistance overseas, and educates Americans on social and economic issues—to foster sound public policy and effective government.

http://www.urban.org/about/

Government **watchdogs** are another type of nonprofit that performs political education. These organizations play an important role in the political landscape by making more transparent for the public everything from lawmakers' voting decisions, to campaign financing, and government rule-making. These organizations not only provide helpful and unbiased information for citizens trying to better understand their government, but they keep legislators and government bureaucrats more accountable to the public. As we learned in Chapter 2, some types of government watchdog groups such as the League of Women Voters have been around since the reform movement took hold in America in the early 20th century. However, the Internet has dramatically increased the impact of nonprofit watchdog organizations, making it simple for the average citizen to obtain information on his or her elected officials quickly and at no cost (other than the price of monthly home Internet). Organizations such as Project Vote Smart provide comprehensive information on the voting records of every US Senator and Representative in Congress, as well as the voting records of state lawmakers on key votes in each of the 50 states. The information produced by Project Vote Smart allows prospective voters to familiarize themselves with the positions and values of their legislators, so that the voter can become more informed and decide at election time whether or not they want to re-elect that person to represent them, or whether another candidate might do the job better.

Other government watchdog organizations serve to publicize financial contributions to political campaigns and officials. For example, Opensecrets.org educates the public on the source of campaign funds for federal lawmakers, including the President. Opensecrets.org has a search engine that allows users to find politicians by name and view how much funds were raised for each campaign, as well as the amounts contributed by individuals, Political Action Committees, and lobbying groups. Alternatively, users can also search Opensecrets.org to find contributions and financial activities of specific lobbying organizations. Suppose you are a hunter and long-term NRA member and want to make sure your organization is supporting candidates who will defend Second Amendment rights. You could enter the National Rifle Association into the Opensecrets.org search engine and a list of all the elected officials and candidates who received campaign funds will be returned, along with the amount of money given to each candidate by the NRA.

Other types of nonprofit watchdog groups focus their efforts on educating the public about proposed rules that are developed by bureaucrats within federal agencies. For example, the Center for Effective Government is a watchdog group whose goal is to ensure "government reflects the needs and priorities of the American people, as defined by an informed, engaged citizenry"[39] and aims to make transparent the workings of government in a limited number of priority areas including Citizen Health and Safety, Revenue and Spending, and Openness and Accountability. While government rule-making may seem like the nitty-gritty details of laws that few would care about, many issues the Center for Effective Government works to educate the public about have direct consequences for the average citizen. For example, the organization recently worked to publicize (and build support against) a controversial rule proposed by the US Department of Agriculture's (USDA) Food Safety and Inspection Service (FSIS) that would have shifted responsibility for poultry inspections away from government inspectors, allowing employees of the slaughtering plants to do their own inspections of the chickens they prepare for market.[40] The rationale behind the proposed change was cost-savings, as the federal government hoped to cut costs by eliminating this function from government. The Center urged citizens to contact the FSIS to oppose this rule, citing facts about the sharp rise in salmonella poisoning and other illness that had already occurred since budget cuts had been made to the FSIS over the preceding years. The organization cautioned citizens that if the rule was finalized, inspectors would have one third of a second to examine each chicken carcass and the public would be at risk of consuming more contaminated meat and more widespread outbreaks of food-borne illness would follow.[41]

Some of the other types of nonprofit organizations we have discussed in the chapter also engage in political education activities. Many lobbying and advocacy organizations provide "fact sheets" with statistics and data designed to persuade citizens of the importance of an issue and why they should support it. Lobbying and advocacy organizations rarely conduct the research themselves that is used to build their fact sheets, but more often cull their information from reports published by think tank and academic studies. Using Moms Demand Action as an example, the facts in the box overleaf are published by the organization in an attempt to educate the public about gun violence, and of course in hopes of convincing citizens or prospective members that the cause is important.

Finally, many types of public charities engage in political education activities. Human service organizations play a particularly important role in this regard because many of them provide services to lower-income citizens, who are, statistically speaking, the least likely to be politically engaged.[42] Low-income citizens are often disadvantaged by insufficient education and information needed to participate in the political process. Nonprofit human service organizations play an important role in helping to make democratic participation more inclusive by providing clients with education about the legal apparatus of government, how it impacts them, and how to navigate it.

Informational resources provided by nonprofit agencies may compensate for a client's lack of formal education or supplement existing knowledge

MOMS DEMAND ACTION FOR GUN SENSE IN AMERICA: FACT SHEET

- Every day, eight children are killed by guns.
- Between 1980 and 2012, 300 people have been killed in gun violence in schools.
- 100,000 people a year are shot in America.
- Nearly 3,000 kids every year will die from gun murder, suicide, accidental death, or police intervention.
- Of the 62 mass shootings carried out in America since 1982, the killers obtained weapons legally in 49 cases. Of the 142 weapons in the killers' possession, 68 were semi-automatic weapons, and 35 were assault weapons.
- Many critics will say that arming more people is the way to stop shootings. There were armed guards at Columbine High School, but 15 people still died. In other examples where armed citizens were able to thwart an attack, most of the responders were trained police officers or armed services members.
- Stand Your Ground laws do not deter violent crime. In fact, there is a clear increase in homicides in states that have these laws, resulting in up to 700 more shooting deaths nationwide each year.

Moms Demand Action for Gun Sense in America, 2013. Fact sheet: http://momsdemandaction.org/facts-about-gun-violence/. Date accessed: July 16, 2013.

of legal rules. Nonprofits educate their clients about the rights granted to them under state and federal laws. This may include education related to entitlement programs, due process rights, rights within a particular service system, or basic citizenship rights. Human service organizations also educate their clients about proposed laws and regulations that have the potential to affect them. Many nonprofit women's health and family planning clinics educate their clients, who are often on low incomes, about proposed laws and judicial rulings that may threaten their reproductive freedoms. These types of organizations may also provide clients with education on the positions taken by candidates running for office, including judicial candidates who are prospective appointees to the state and federal bench.

Nonprofit human service organizations also provide political education for their clients by structuring opportunities for them to learn about democratic deliberation and effective political participation. Human service organizations help their clients develop democratic participation skills by providing opportunities for them to serve on client advisory boards and committees, participate in program planning, and serve on ad hoc agency work groups or policy development committees within the organization. By participating in the work of a service agency, clients can acquire the experience and skills required for participation in a democratic society.

In sum, nonprofit organizations play an important role educating citizens, clients, activists, political officials, and the media about the political process and important policy issues. From think tanks to neighborhood associations, nonprofit organizations use education to engage in the political process. The educational activities of nonprofit organizations can range from providing nonpartisan information to specific information about how to act or vote on a particular policy or issue. And, of course, tax status (public charities as compared to lobbying groups), mission, and partisan affiliations help to shape the ways in which nonprofit organizations engage in the educational aspects of the political system.

Summary

Nonprofit organizations are an important fixture in the American political landscape, engaging in political representation, mobilization, and education roles. Nonprofit organizations fulfill the representation role by lobbying government officials, sometimes in the interests of corporate industries or narrowly defined groups, while other organizations engage in policy advocacy that is aimed at the broader public interest. Through their mobilization roles, nonprofit organizations encourage citizens to become active participants in the political process, by facilitating contact with elected officials or government agencies, registering voters, and encouraging voter participation. Many types of nonprofits provide political education, both partisan and nonpartisan, including think tanks, and policy research institutes, advocacy groups, and many types of public charities provide nonpartisan political education. Lobbying and advocacy groups play a particularly prominent role in the American political arena. While public charities engage in all of these three key roles of political representation, mobilization, and education, these activities cannot comprise a substantial part of their activities and they must be carried out in a strictly nonpartisan fashion.

KEY TERMS

- Advocacy
- Expenditure Test
- Get-out-the-vote (GOTV)
- Interest groups
- Lobbyists / lobbying / lobbying groups

- Nonpartisan
- Partisan
- Political education
- Political mobilization
- Political representation

- Representation
- Substantial Part Test
- Think tanks
- Watchdogs

DISCUSSION QUESTIONS

1. What are the goals of lobbying and advocacy organizations? How do nonprofit organizations achieve these goals?

2. What is the role of lobbyists in the political process in the United States? What are some of the positive aspects of lobbying? What are some of the negative aspects of lobbying?

3. Many public policy research institutes, or think tanks, have partisan agendas. Should these public policy research institutes be nonpartisan in order to qualify for nonprofits status? Do you think the public can tell the difference between partisan and nonpartisan think tanks? Does it matter?

4. Do you think that nonprofit organizations should be allowed to directly lobby political officials? Should they be able to participate in the political process by lobbying for or against particular types of legislation? What are the costs and benefits of nonprofit lobbying in the American system?

5. If you were planning to pursue a career in public policy and wanted to have the greatest effect on a policy area, what type of job would you pursue: a government job, a position at a think tank, a position at a lobbying firm, or a role in an advocacy organization? Explain your reasoning for working for that type of organization. What type of impact would you hope to have? What would be the limitations of working with that type of organization?

Websites

Open Secrets: www.opensecrets.org
Project Vote Smart: http://votesmart.org/
Bolder Advocacy: Change the world with advocacy. Navigate the Rules
    http://bolderadvocacy.org/navigate-the-rules

Notes

1   http://www.mineaction.org/resources/project?search_type=country&c=6. Accessed July 26, 2013.

2   http://www.seasite.niu.edu/khmer/Ledgerwood/Landmines.htm. Accessed July 26, 2013.

3   Carmichael, Robert. 2010. Fewer Casualties From Mines in Cambodia, but Reduced Funding Means Risk Remains. Phnom Penh 23 February 2010. Accessed July 26, 2013 at http://www.globalsecurity.org/military/library/news/2010/02/mil-100223-voa04.htm

4   http://www.maginternational.org/cambodia/ Accessed July 26, 2013.

5   Skocpol, Theda. 2003. *Diminished Democracy: From Membership to Management in American Civic Life.* Norman, OK: University of Oklahoma Press.

6   Berry, J. M. and D. F. Arons. 2003. *A Voice for Nonprofits.* Washington, DC: Brookings Institution Press.

7   They can, however, publicly adopt a position on a specific issue.

8   Reid, Elizabeth. 2001. Nonprofit Advocacy and Political Participation, in E. T. Boris and C. E. Steuerle (eds), *Nonprofits and Government: Collaboration and Conflict.* Washington, DC: Urban Institute Press, pp. 291–325.

9   Reid, Elizabeth. 2001.

10 Reid, Elizabeth. 2001.

11 Pitkin, H. F. 1967. *The Concept of Representation.* Berkeley, CA: University of California Press, p. 117.

12 The Business Dictionary. Accessed July 11, 2013 at http://www.businessdictionary.com/definition/lobby.html

13 Quoting Hopkins (1992), in Anheier's 2005 text (see Note 14).

14 Anheier, Helmut K. 2005. *Nonprofit Organizations: Theory, Management, Policy.* Routledge; Hopkins, Bruce R. 1992. *Charity, Advocacy and the Law.* New York, NY: Wiley & Sons.

15 http://www.merriam-webster.com/dictionary/lobby and http://www.merriam-webster.com/dictionary/advocacy. Accessed February 11, 2014.

16 LeRoux, Kelly and Holly Goerdel. 2009. Political Advocacy by Nonprofit Organizations: A Strategic Management Explanation. *Public Performance and Management Review,* 32(4): 514–536; Berry, J. M., and D. F. Arons. 2003. *A Voice for Nonprofits.* Washington, DC: Brookings Institution Press; Ezell, M. 1991. Administrators as Advocates. *Administration in Social Work,* 15(4): 1–18.

17 Kramer, Ralph M. 1981. *Voluntary Agencies and the Welfare State.* Berkeley, CA: University of California Press.

18 Fortune Releases Annual Survey of Most Powerful Lobbying Organizations, *Timewarner.com,* November 15, 1999. Accessed February 12, 2014 at http://archive.is/vni2b

19   Korte, Gregory. 2013. Post-Newtown, NRA membership surges to 5 million, *USA Today*. Accessed February 12, 2014 at http://www.usatoday.com/story/news/politics/2013/05/04/nra-meeting-lapierre-membership/2135063/

20   Schattschneider, E. E. 1960. *The Semi-Sovereign People*. New York: Holt, Rinehart and Winston.

21   Belkin, Lisa. 2013. One Million Moms for Gun Control: The Origins of a Movement, *The Huffington Post*, January 25, 2013. Accessed July 3, 2010 at http://www.huffingtonpost.com/2013/01/25/one-million-moms-for-gun-control_n_2549452.html

22   http://momsdemandaction.org/about/ Accessed July 1, 2013.

23   http://momsdemandaction.org/about/ Accessed July 1, 2013.

24   Piven, Frances Fox and Richard A. Cloward. 1977. *Poor People's Movements: Why They Succeed, How They Fail*. Vintage.

25   HeadCount provides voter registration assistance on a strictly nonpartisan basis to any US citizen age 18 or over without regard to political affiliation, race, religion, or age. HeadCount does not endorse, support, or coordinate with any political party or candidates for elected office, or take positions on any ballot initiatives. Accessed August 15, 2013 at http://www.headcount.org/mission-statement/

26   VOTE (Voice of the Ex-Offender) is a grassroots, membership based organization founded and run by Formerly Incarcerated Persons in partnership with allies dedicated to ending the disenfranchisement and discrimination against FIPs in New Orleans and throughout Louisiana. Accessed August 15, 2013 at http://vote-nola.org/aboutus

27   Donovan, Megan K. 2011. States Move to Restrict Voting: What Nonprofits Can Do to Defend the Right to Vote. Webinar given by the Fair Elections Legal Network, October 27, 2011.

28   See IRS Revenue Rule 2007–41 for specific examples of non-permissible activities and cases illustrating their application. Accessed at http://www.irs.gov/pub/irs-drop/rr-07-41.pdf

29   LeRoux, Kelly and Kelly Krawczyk. 2012. Can Nonprofit Organizations Increase Voter Turnout? Findings from an Agency-Based Voter Mobilization Experiment. *Nonprofit and Voluntary Sector Quarterly*, 43(2): 272–292.

30   Patterson, Thomas. 2004. *We the People. A Concise Introduction to American Politics*. New York, NY: McGraw-Hill; Reeser, L. and I. Epstein. 1990. *Professionalization and Activism in Social Work: The Sixties, the Eighties, and the Future*. New York: Columbia University Press.

31   Piven and Cloward (1977).

32   Dozens Arrested at White House Protest of Keystone XL Pipeline, *Environment News Service*, February 13, 2013. Accessed July 12, 2013 at http://ens-newswire.com/2013/02/13/dozens-arrested-at-white-house-protest-of-keystone-xl-pipeline/

33   Gerken, James. 2013. "Forward on Climate" Rally brings Climate Change Activists to the Mall in Washington D.C., *Huffington Post*, February 17, 2013. Accessed July 12, 2013 at http://www.huffingtonpost.com/2013/02/17/forward-on-climate-rally_n_2702575.html

34   http://www.worldnakedbikeride.org/ Accessed July 12, 2013.

35   https://bound4life.com/the-silent-siege/ Accessed July 12, 2013.

36   http://www.guidestar.org/ReportOrganization.aspx?ein=20–8293287. Accessed July 12, 2013.

37   takebackthenight.org/ Accessed July 25, 2013.

38   http://momsdemandaction.org/stroller-jam/ Accessed July 12, 2013.

39   Center for Effective Government. http://www.foreffectivegov.org/what-we-do. Accessed July12, 2013.

40   Greenhaw, Katie. 2013. President Obama's Budget Proposal Assumes Flawed Poultry Inspection Rule Will Be Finalized, *Center for Effective Government*, April 11, 2013. Accessed July 17, 2013 at http://www.foreffectivegov.org/node/12438

41   Greenhaw (2013).

42   Brady, H. E., S. Verba, and K. L. Schlozman. 1995. Beyond SES: A Resource Model of Political Participation. *American Political Science Review*, 89(2): 271–294.

8

NONPROFIT AND VOLUNTARY ACTIVISM

SOCIAL MOVEMENTS AND PROTEST POLITICS

CHAPTER LEARNING OBJECTIVES

By the end of this chapter, students will be able to:

1. Describe the general characteristics of social and political movements

2. Identify the circumstances that can lead to social movements

3. Describe the role of nonprofit organizations in political and social movements

4. Describe social change organizations and some of their activities

5. Provide examples of historic social movements that have shaped modern US society as well as current social movements

6. Discuss the role of technology in shaping modern social movements

---

Introduction

Individuals have a number of mechanisms for engaging with the policy process, including voting, contacting political representatives, donating funds to support a cause, joining groups to lobby or advocate for change, and contesting policies and legal rules through boycotts and public protests. But how do people without voting rights engage in the political process

THE RIGHT FACE AT THE RIGHT TIME FOR A SOCIAL MOVEMENT

In 2009, Windsor's partner and wife of more than 40 years, Thea Spyer, died. Windsor and Spyer were a happy couple—completely devoted to one another. They met in 1962, got engaged soon after, travelled the world together, and eventually got married in Canada in 2007, near the end of Spyer's life.

When Thea Spyer died, Edith Windsor learned she was not eligible for the exemption on estate tax that applies to husbands and wives. Windsor would be required to pay $363,053 in taxes to the federal government and $275,528 to New York State to take over their shared assets. Because the Defense of Marriage Act (DOMA), signed into law in 1996 by President Bill Clinton, did not recognize their legal marriage as legitimate, Edith Windsor was subject to estate taxes that husbands and wives are exempt from paying. Windsor did not think this was fair. She hired an attorney, Roberta Kaplan, and filed a lawsuit against the US government—Edith Windsor vs. the United States of America.

The Gay Rights Movement had been organizing for decades—from Harvey Milk, the first openly gay American politician elected to public office in 1977, to increased coverage of important gay rights issues (e.g. the groundbreaking 1993 movie Philadelphia, the first mainstream Hollywood film to acknowledge HIV/AIDS, homosexuality, and homophobia), to the increased representation of homosexual characters on TV shows, to heterosexual and homosexual Americans participating in organized marches and protests for equal rights regardless of sexual orientation. Nonprofit and civil society organizations such as Gay & Lesbian Advocates & Defenders (GLAD), a nonprofit legal rights organization in the United States, the Lambda Legal Defense and Education Fund, the ACLU, and hundreds of local lesbian, gay, bisexual, transgender, or queer (LGBTQ) organizations in cities, towns, and campuses across the US have played a critical role in supporting and advancing this social movement, providing support to individuals and coalescing interests to advocate for social, political, and economic change.

Federal laws like the Defense of Marriage Act (DOMA) and states with constitutional amendments prohibiting same-sex marriage (as of 2013, 29 states ban same-sex marriage; 15 have formal legislation allowing same-sex marriage) created multiple fronts in the Gay Rights Movement—with different groups and organizations focusing on different legal, social, political, and economic components of the movement.

When Edith Windsor decided to file a lawsuit requesting that the state of NY and the US government recognize her marriage and grant her the same estate tax exemption as given to husbands and wives, a number of law firms and gay rights organizations told her "it was not the right time." Others noted that there was a need for the right

continued

representative and the right time—some thought a bankruptcy case would be better suited as a challenge to DOMA, while others hoped a class action suit representing a diversity of gay couples would be more effective at challenging DOMA.[1] Roberta Kaplan took the case. She noted that Windsor was an ideal candidate to represent the social movement. The time was right and the case was right.

What made Windsor the ideal candidate to challenge DOMA? She is an older woman, well-educated, attractive, had worked as a programmer for IBM, and was dedicated to her partner, Thea Spyer. In addition to being in a committed relationship for over 40 years, Windsor had cared for Spyer as her chronic multiple sclerosis progressed, providing care and comfort until her death.

In describing Windsor as an ideal candidate to formalize social change within this social movement, some compared her to Rosa Parks, an ideal candidate to formalize action in the Civil Rights Movement. Levy reports in her comparison of Windsor and Parks that Rosa Parks told an interviewer in 1956, "I was not the only person who had been mistreated and humiliated."[2] Claudette Colvin, a 15-year-old, had been forcibly removed from a bus when she wouldn't give up her seat, but local NAACP leaders deemed Colvin too feisty and uncontrollable to be used as a test case for the Civil Rights Movement. Instead, they selected Rosa Parks, who had all the right credentials: a quiet middle-aged seamstress, religious, brave, and known and respected in the community.[3] Just like Rosa Parks, Windsor could be presented as a harmless, older woman who did her duty, loved and cared for her spouse, and was now being unfairly treated by the government. Thousands of people participated in the bus boycotts, but Rosa Parks embodied the movement. Similarly, thousands had participated in the Gay Rights Movement, but Windsor embodied the legal challenge to DOMA.

Both of these cases, though different in many ways, are similar in other ways: they illustrate how social movements develop and emerge over time. While many people may be discontent with the system, marginalized, or treated unfairly, a social movement is a complex endeavor that requires good timing, strategic thinking, legal strategy, mass protests, movement of large groups of people (not just the marginalized but also mainstream society), charismatic leaders, others willing to sacrifice their individual security to take a risk and work for social justice, and of course a little luck. Not all social movements achieve large-scale change, but some do. What predicts social change? What makes some social movements successful and others not? What is the role of nonprofit organizations, associations, and civil society groups to help support and mobilize social movements?

To learn more about Edith and Thea, see the documentary film "Edie and Thea: A Very Long Engagement" directed by Susan Muska and Gréta Ólafsdóttir, 2011.

and bring change to their communities? How do those without the resources to donate money to support a cause participate in the political process? How do marginalized individuals and groups change society so that they are no longer marginalized?

When individuals come together to advocate for some large-scale social reform, we often refer to these as **social movements**. Some social movements rise up among people and organize into formal nonprofit organizations. Other social movements are initiated and supported by nonprofit organizations. Still other social movements are a combination of individual and collective action and the efforts of formal organizations. Social movements are emergent collections of discontented individuals and are often characterized by informal collective action with a focus on a specific political, social, or economic issue.[4] Social movements often rely on the kinds of political action, lobbying, and advocacy groups that we discussed in the last chapter, but are broader in their impact in that social movements are typically challenges to elites and the mainstream power structures and political process. Social movements have the potential to reform and reshape civil society, since they are collective challenges to legal structures and to established political, social, and economic systems, carried out by people who share a common purpose.[5] Civil society provides the larger context or background in which social movements and voluntary activism occurs. Social movements and social change are enabled by each of the components of civil society, including institutional rules and laws such as free speech rights and rights to assemble, common interests which lead to collective action, and organizations both formal and informal that work to bring about the desired change. At the same time, civil society is strengthened by the activism and organizations that build and sustain social movements and social change efforts.

A number of social movements in the 20th century have led to widespread change in civil society: for example, the women's rights and the civil rights movements. In both of these examples, people who lacked political power and the right to vote successfully organized to advance their group interests and gain traction in the political process. In some cases, nonprofit organizations play a critical role in supporting and advancing social movements, serving as vehicles for organizing like-minded people, pooling resources and social capital, and mobilizing large numbers of disenfranchised or marginalized people for a common cause. In other cases, nonprofit organizations are a result of social movements – the formalized institutions that are left after a mass movement.

This chapter highlights social change movements in the US, paying particular attention to protest movements as a strategy for social change. As we learned in Chapter 1, institutional rules and laws are a key component of civil society, and in the US protest movements are a reflection of a robust civil society, enabled by the constitution and legal frameworks that allow for citizens to organize, openly engage in protest, and exercise free speech to challenge authority. We begin our discussion by describing what we mean by the terms social movements and social change movements. We then discuss some of the theories that explain social movements. We discuss the role of nonprofit organizations in social change movements, starting with social movements from the turn of the century (labor rights movement), midcentury (Civil Rights Movement), and then discussing contemporary social change movements (Occupy). We then discuss international examples of social change and protest politics in Burma, Iran, and India.

Social Change Movements—Nonprofits and Voluntary Activism

Social movements are broad efforts by citizens to achieve change when the government or society is not responsive to their needs or interests.[6] Social movements are distinguished from other forms of political organizing by their ability to force large-scale change through disruptive political and social actions such as protests, marches, and civil disobedience. Social movements, also referred to as **protest** movements or protest politics, are often the only mechanism by which a disenfranchised group can engage in the mainstream system. Some researchers argue that social movements are separated from institutional politics because they embody the interests of the alienated and oppressed. Other researchers view social movements from the perspectives of individual activists, leadership strategy and organization, and the role of politics and the state.[7] Early examples of protest politics include the Boston Tea Party, in which colonists protested Britain's tea tax and unfair policy of "taxation without representation" by destroying an entire shipment of tea that arrived into the Boston Harbor. Other examples of social movements include protests and sit-ins during the Vietnam War and the 1963 March on Washington which brought together a huge number of individuals advocating for civil rights, relying on the coordination and participation of both organized groups and the mass participation of individuals who supported the movement. While Americans pride themselves on valuing their right to free expression and the ability to organize and protest, Patterson (2002) notes most Americans never participate in protest movements. Protest politics and social movements are an important element in civil society, but they are relatively unpopular in the mainstream US. Protesters are typically younger and more idealistic, and they make up a small proportion of the population; in fact, many Americans report having never attended a protest. Still, social movements have played an important role in shaping civil society and continue to do so.

Social movement theory has its roots in the fields of sociology and political science. Although we have examples of social movements throughout US history, from the Boston Tea Party to the Women's Suffrage Movement, the 1960s mark an important era for social movements as women, students, blacks, farm workers, and other groups organized to change the political and economic structures of society. Charles Tilly, a sociologist, political scientist, and historian, describes social movements as displays and campaigns by which ordinary people organize to take collective action and make collective claims on society.[8] In most cases, social movements are the primary vehicles for ordinary people to participate in the policy process and bring about social change. Research on social movements typically focuses on issues of collective behavior, and understanding the political, social, and organizational factors that enable social movements to develop and progress to shape civil society. Successful social movements mobilize resources and take full advantage of the political process, expanding political opportunities and building political power. When political institutions are in flux or under stress, there are more opportunities for underrepresented or marginalized groups to use protest politics and other actions to alter the political power structure.

There are a number of theories about what causes social movements. The **classical model** of social movements argues that they are a reaction to strain in society, the political, economic, and social system. Critics of the classical model note that there is always strain in society, discontent or inequality, so it is unclear what level of strain would lead to a social movement. John Wilson notes that "societies are rarely stable, in equilibrium, or without strain because change is constant, the forces which have the potential of producing social movements are always present in some degree."[9] So what explains the emergence of a social movement? When do the conditions arise that make it optimal for people to organize and act for social change?

Some researchers argue that social movements are driven by individual discontent. The problem with this type of model is that it assumes that individuals who engage in social movements are not average, and in many cases describes them as having some sort of abnormal psychology, when in fact many social movements have achieved their goals because they include the participation of average Americans. A social movement relying only on the extremely discontent might not be a very effective movement at all, since it would rely on such a small number of individuals. Consider the Immigrant Rights Movement or the Gay Rights Movement. While undocumented immigrants and Gay, Lesbian, Transgender, and Bisexual (GLTB) individuals will partake in the movement, it is when citizens and mainstream members of society participate that the movement gains even more momentum. Related to this theory is the idea that socially marginalized individuals drive social movements. However, empirical research has found that many social movements are driven by well-integrated members of society who report high levels of organizational membership, education, and occupational prestige.[10] For example, research on the black-student protest movement during the Civil Rights era found that the majority of the social movement members were well-integrated students in the college community.[11]

Some researchers argue that individuals participate in social change movements because of **resource deficiencies** (Jenkins and Perrow, 1977);[12] organizing and joining the movement enables the collection of resources required to participate in advancing the goals of the movement. For those who support the resource mobilization model to explain social movements, individual discontent is insufficient for explaining collective action;[13,14] the aggregation of individual discontent does not fuel the social movement, instead the rise of social movements and insurgency is explained by the aggregation of resources to challenge the elite. Critics of the resource mobilization model note that although the theory does explain *some* movements, it cannot explain all social movements, in particular those that involve mass protest but not resources, or those social movements that include the resources and power of the economic or political elite.

In some cases social movements are motivated by elite interests, where elite institutions provide social movements with the resources needed to achieve their goals.[15] For example, the Farm Workers Movement benefited from the financial support of organized labor and contributors, while the Civil Rights Movement benefited from formal civil rights organizations, church groups, liberal groups, and financial support of individual contributors. Although many times elite political, economic, and social institutions are pivotal in supporting social movements, elite institutions can also prevent the success of social movements. Because social movements often involve an **insurgency**, a rebellion or uprising that threatens existing power relationships, some elites may work to squelch such movements. Researchers note examples of elite institutions co-opting social movements or supporting them in order to dissolve the movement's momentum.[16,17]

While some movements might be driven by elite interests and require vast resources and organization, other large-scale social movements have emerged among groups without resources (political, economic, or social). The movements, which often threaten elite interests, rely instead on mass movement and the mobilization of nonmaterial resources such as social capital, moral commitment, trust, friendship, authority, and so on.[18] Movements driven by people, not resources, are sometimes the most powerful and successful movements of all. Examples include the popular uprisings in the Arab world from 2009–2013. These ongoing efforts of people to organize and protest for political freedom and freedom of expression have greatly destabilized the elite interests of the state, foreign actors, and militaries.

Douglas McAdam (1982) argues that the motivating force behind social change movements is individual discontent, usually resulting from feeling alienated or isolated from the policy process, but that individual motivation is not sufficient for catalyzing social movements because it ignores the collective nature of social movements.[19] He argues that social movements are defined by the process by which individual discontent is transformed and mobilized into collective action and that social movements can be explained through a political process model.[20] According to McAdam, individuals who feel marginalized and discontent will be more likely to join an organized movement working for social change. Movement participants are thus distinguished from mainstream society by their social marginality; the social movement gives them an opportunity to organize and engage in civil society. In McAdam's political process model, power is institutionalized in the hands of a few groups and social movements occur when marginalized interests coalesce to challenge the mainstream political process. For McAdam, social movements enable widespread political change by organizing collective action that threatens political stability. McAdam describes leaders of social change movements as radicals, indigenous protesters, and insurgents because they are marginalized by the mainstream political system and must act in aggressive, radical ways to bring about social change. For example, individuals who are denied access to the political process (e.g. voting) might engage in protests, sit-ins, take-overs, civil disobedience, arrests, and other activities that may be deemed disruptive by the main stream, in order to gain access to the political process. McAdam highlights these types of activities in his book *Political Process and the Development of Black Insurgency, 1930–1970*, which analyzes the black social movement that drove the Civil Rights Movement.

While McAdam explains social movements from the perspective of the political process model, others have investigated social movements as movements for economic change, environmental reform, and social and cultural change: not just an organized challenge to the political process, but as an uprising of the masses that effectively disrupts the status quo.[21] Piven and Cloward focus on what they label "Poor People's Movements," social movements of the poor and disenfranchised. Piven and Cloward note that successful US protest movements have erupted among lower-income groups as a response to the political economy in the US.[22] They note that it is widely understood that while power resides in two systems of power, one based on wealth and the other on votes, the pluralist system is far from an accurate representation of power distribution in the US. Votes and power through the electoral system are not as effective as wealth, and in many cases votes and the distribution of electoral power are driven by wealth. Instead, elite interests are advanced by both the economic and the electoral system in the US. According to critics of the pluralist model, participation and nonparticipation are predicted by class, where elites hold most, if not all, of the power while lower-income groups are excluded. In the 1960s, social movements of students and minorities sought to alter this structure. According to Piven,[23] social movements occur when (1) numerous members of society perceive "the system" as losing legitimacy; (2) people who normally believe that they cannot change the system, and it will always be this way, suddenly view an opportunity for change; and (3) people who previously viewed themselves as helpless develop a sense of efficacy—they believe they have the ability or capacity to produce a desired change or result.

Sidney Tarrow, a political scientist and sociologist, argues that social movements often occur through protest cycles, or "cycles of contention." In his book, *Power in Movement*, Tarrow argues that cultural, organizational, and personal resources power social movements toward some political struggle.[24] He notes that there are five political opportunities that can enable social movements: (1) increased access; (2) shifting alignments; (3) divided elites; (4) influential allies; and (5) repression and facilitation. Tarrow notes that the power in social movements is less obvious, but can be very strong, occurring in cycles of protest. He notes that social movements can affect personal lives, policy reform, and civil society. According to Tarrow, social movements require political opportunities, diffuse social networks, familiar forms of collective action, and cultural frames that appeal to a broad swath of society. Tarrow's work indicates that social movements, though cyclical and dependent on particular conditions, can be powerful forces in the political and cultural environment.

In summary, a variety of characteristics help to describe and define social movements. Some social movements are thought to emerge as a result of stress or strain on ordinary people. In other cases, movements are the expression of discontent among individuals and the socially marginalized. Social movements might also be the result of resource mobilization or resource deficiencies that lead people to action. Social movements may represent elite interests, or be co-opted by elite interests, or in other cases may be driven by the interests of non-elites, the poor, and the disenfranchised. Next we will discuss the role that nonprofit organizations play in social movements and then present examples of historic and modern social movements in the United States and abroad.

Nonprofits in Social Movements

For researchers and theorists interested in social movements, there is some disagreement about the role of nonprofit organizations in social movements.

Some argue that nonprofit organizations provide an important organization and mobilizing vehicle for coalescing interests and effectively engaging the political process to demand social change. Others argue that nonprofit organizations inhibit true social change by formalizing the movement, bringing together a wide array of social demands and watering down the radical elements of more spontaneous mass movements. Still others note that truly effective mass movements, once they achieve the attention of elites and gain a position in the political process, will inevitably shift toward formal organization and the creation of nonprofit organizations.

The history of social movements in the US often recalls the important role of formal organizations for mobilizing group interests: for example, the important role of the NAACP during the Civil Rights Movement, the AFL-CIO for the Labor Movement, GLAD in the Gay Rights Movement, and so on. While it is true that formal organization, often done through nonprofit organizations, serves to coalesce and mobilize economic and political resources, there are also examples of mass protests and movements occurring without this formal leadership. Piven and Cloward argue that although formal organizations play an important role in advancing social movements, or result from the activities of social movements, truly successful social movements require mass mobilization, which is often difficult to organize and control. They note the importance of popular insurgency, mass disruption, and protest as important factors in the advancement of political and social movements. Thus, while the formal organization and power of organized nonprofits is important for formal recognition and interaction with elites and the political process, there remains a critical place for popular movement and mass protest.[25]

Nonprofits in American Social Movements: The Labor Movement and the Civil Rights Movement

One of the early social movements in the US was the **Labor Movement** in the 1930s. At the time, this social movement greatly challenged the political, economic, and social situation in the US. Today, the achievements of that social movement are common features in the American workplace, including hourly limitations on the workweek, reasonable wages, support for the unemployed, restrictions on child labor, and more humane workplaces. What we take for granted as basic rights in the workplace today were far from commonplace at the turn of the 20th century. While workplace rights and support for unemployed Americans were limited for decades, it was the Great Depression that brought discontent to the masses and served as a motivation for many marginalized people to mobilize and demand economic and social change. As the economic situation worsened for farmers, urban workers, and people throughout the US, political efforts to alleviate the effects of the Depression were insufficient.

As more Americans found themselves unemployed and suffering, they began to share their stories and blame "the system" for failing them. The first social mobilization came in the form of looting, as protestors marched on stores demanding food. By 1930, workers were organizing and marching in cities throughout the United States under Communist banners that read "Work or Wages." Marches in San Francisco numbered more than 2,000, in Chicago more than 4,000. The unemployed could no longer afford their rents, leading to rent riots in urban areas. Others mobilized to protest at relief offices, demanding rent support, food, money, and goods. The Labor Movement continued to gain momentum. In many cases, people mobilized out of frustration and a loss of resources—people had nothing else to lose. In other cases, organized groups helped to mobilize workers and the unemployed. Communist organizers effectively mobilized people to mass action, helping to marshal and channel their energy. The National Executive Committee of the Socialist Party created groups to lobby for old age benefits, unemployment insurance, and the end of child labor. Groups organized at the national and the local levels, including the Conference for Progressive Labor Action, the AFL, the Community Trade Union Unity League, the Chicago Workers League, the Pittsburgh Unemployed Citizens' league, and others.

The major achievements of the Labor Movement included the Social Security Act of 1935, the Works Progress Administration, and millions of dollars distributed and jobs created under the New Deal. While these outcomes were seen as victories of the Labor Movement, many organizers and activists did not believe that the government had sufficiently responded to the demands of the movement. By 1933, the movement had started to lose momentum, overwhelming support for relief measures had subsided, the economy was recovering, businesses were improving, and the national crisis had evaporated. Some argue that President Roosevelt's programs in response to the Labor Movement—the Wealth Tax Act, the Social Security Act, etc.—helped to moderate the demands of the social movement and served to neutralize some of the demands of the movement and dissipate its momentum.

The history of the labor rights movements is often told as one in which factory workers mobilized into large, stable organizations, and then effectively influenced the political and economic situation. In contrast, Piven and Cloward argue that the most influential time of the Labor Movement was when the masses were mobilized, but before they were organized into formal organizations.[26] The workers' power was not in organized labor, but in their ability to disrupt the status quo. Piven and Cloward note that when workers mobilized and exerted force on the political system, it was through mass strikes. These strikes compelled the government to establish a framework for protecting unions. And with the creation of unions and the formal organization of workers, unions did not promote disruption of the system. In this example, nonprofit organizations brought legitimacy to the process, enabling unions to negotiate directly with the government, but at the same time helped to bring an end to the social movement and mass disruption. According to Piven and Cloward, social movements benefit most when they are less organized, destabilize the system, and draw upon the fear of the masses about the legitimacy and stability of the political, economic, and social establishment.

A Political Process Model—McAdam's Analysis of the Black Insurgency

One of the classic examples of a social movement in the US is the **Civil Rights Movement**. Douglas McAdam argues that the black insurgency is an example of the political process model of social movements where the movement emerges over a long period of time and the political processes enabled a structural opportunity for collective action. He argues that the Civil Rights Movement happened when it did because of the confluence of three factors: expanding political opportunities, mobilization of organizational resources, and shared cognitions and discontent in the minority community.[27] Many of the movement participants were well integrated in the established organizations in the minority community and that this integration and organization enabled collective action in the face of an oppressive political, social, and economic situation.

McAdam notes that the Civil Rights Movement did not emerge from a vacuum or erupt on a single day. Instead, the social movement was the result of decades of strain and oppression. He argues that the span of years from 1876 to 1954 set the conditions for the black insurgency. While the 1954 Brown vs Topeka Board of Education was a significant event that marked the emergence of an organized black movement, political and economic constrictions and events prior to that set the stage, including debt bondage (which bound blacks to the land in ways similar to slavery), general disenfranchisement, exclusion from political and economic gains, violent control against blacks, and the elimination of blacks as an electoral force. As economic constraints in the south triggered the great migration north, blacks then faced economic and political constraints there.

While the widespread discrimination and disenfranchisement of black Americans continued, there were important changes occurring at the Federal level. The NAACP pushed a legal assault against Jim Crow and Truman appointed a Committee on Civil Rights (1946). Moreover black communities began to organize through chapters of the NAACP, churches, colleges, and other groups that could mobilize discontented individuals with shared interests. McAdam also notes that the economic resources of individual black families were improving, enabling individuals to contribute to indigenous organizations that were demanding social, economic, and political change. The black insurgency emerged in 1954 as a result of economic changes (declining cotton prices) and political (US Supreme Court rulings in factor of black rights) and social changes (institutional growth of NAACP and churches). McAdam's empirical research shows that although discontent was present for decades, it was the confluence of these institutional opportunities that made the social movement possible.

But what was the role of nonprofits in this important social movement? The NAACP, churches, and colleges provided a critical organizational base to the Civil Rights Movement. In an analysis of the New York Times Index 1955–1960, McAdam shows that of the 487 movement actions, 50% were initiated by churches, the NAACP, and student groups.[28] These nonprofit and civil society organizations served as a mechanism for recruiting movement participants and organizational collective action. Interestingly, McAdam notes that these organizations did not serve simply as recruiting grounds; instead, participating in protest activities became a defining component of membership. Church members were not necessarily recruited for the bus boycott, but rather participating in the bus boycott came to define church membership. People didn't go to mass gatherings because they were members of the church, but instead saw these gatherings as an extension of church services.[29] Similarly, participation in the social movement came to define the role of being a student in a black college. Thus, in this case, participation in the movement was part and parcel with organizational membership. The social movement was integral to membership in these civil society organizations

Because McAdam describes the black insurgency as a process, he also notes the end of the social movement, or at least its decline. He notes that when the political opportunities contract and organizational strength within the movement subsides, there is a decline in the salience of the movement's issues, and an increased repression by the movement's opponents.[30] Additionally, he notes that with the decline of the social movement comes a decline in organizational strength (1966–1970). He notes that the NAACP, Congress on Racial Equality (CORE), student Nonviolent Coordinating Committee (SNCC), and Southern Christian Leadership Conference (SCLC) all show a measurable decline in membership and

The Civil Rights March on Washington, attended by around 250,000 people, was the largest political demonstration in Washington, DC.

activity initiation by the late 1960s, as there is growing disagreement about the proper goals and methods of the movement at the national level. During the 1970s, these nonprofit organizations shifted to separate goals and missions and became more focused on local issues, instead of being organized toward a unified national agenda, largely in response to a collapse of consensus on major issues and tactics and the diffusion of interests among movement participants.

The Civil Rights Movement offers a classic example of social movements in the US. We see the critical role that nonprofit organizations can play in mobilizing interests and resources toward collective action. We also see the limitations of nonprofit organizations to sustain large-scale social movements over time. Instead, they are important institutions for organizing when a social movement ignites, but likely not the driving force of social movements—which emerge at times when constraints, discontent, and political, social, and economic opportunities align.

Social Change Organizations—Grassroots and Local Change

While most of the social movement literature is focused on large-scale political protest movements that result in major shifts in society, some researchers have used social movement theory to understand smaller scale social change initiated by grassroots organizations. Chetkovich and Kunreuther discuss these types of social movements in their book *From the Ground Up: Grassroots Organizations Making Social Change*.[31] They argue that **social change organizations**, small organizations focused on social change but unaffiliated with a broader social movement, play an important role in social change. They note that in comparison to larger scale social movements these organizations are focused on the local community and a narrower, specific agenda. Their research investigates the leadership, staffing, decision-making structures, constituents, and resource strategies of social change organizations. These authors conclude that social change organizations provide an important mechanism for bringing important social change to local communities. Chetkovich and Kunreuther note that social change organizations complement larger social movements by fulfilling the needs of their local membership. Additionally, social change organizations, with a smaller number of members, can have more

BOX 8.1 THE MOWERGANG—A LOCAL CHANGE ORGANIZATION

The MowerGang has no employees and no money; they simply organize people to action with the hopes of improving their communities and seek to improve the lives of people in Detroit. The MowerGang refuses "to allow bureaucracy and tightened city budgets get in the way of children playing outside." The MowerGang does not build anything new, but simply has picked up where the government has failed to maintain public facilities. The MowerGang goes to local playgrounds that are unkempt and in a state of disrepair, with the hopes of providing open spaces for children to play. The MowerGang describes its work as "one-part biker rally and one-part cleanup." Their website tells more stories of their accomplishments and includes photos of the many transformations they have brought to Detroit area parks: http://www.mowergang.com

focused goals, more motivated membership, and adapt more quickly to the changing needs of local communities. For example, small social change organizations such as Dare to Dream provide services and support to homeless and low-income families, while Advocates for the People organizes and advocates political action on behalf of Latino members and communities.[32] Box 8.1 provides an example of one local change organization, comprised of community volunteers in Detroit who informally organized and mobilized action in order to address a local problem.

Local social change organizations work to affect the immediate lives of individuals and communities, thus supporting and facilitating social, political, and economic change, but social change organizations are not typically considered a motivating factor in social movements. Some scholars of social movement theory, including Piven and Cloward (1977), argue that small, independent organizations detract resources and energy from large-scale social movements and can hinder the ability of social movements or protests to mobilize.[33] Thus, while social change organizations are an important mechanism for nonprofit and civil society organizations to shape individual environments and local communities, there is not agreement as to whether these are examples of social movements, or simply smaller scale changes. Nevertheless, social change organizations are a manifestation of civil society, enabled by the same laws that permit political activism within social movements, and representing both the action and organization components of civil society.

Nonprofits and Contemporary Social Change

Economic Justice and the Occupy Movement—Insurgency or Disorganized Mess?

The Occupy Movement is an international protest movement against economic and social inequality. Specifically, it aims to make society's wealth more evenly distributed. While it is considered an international movement, most of the focus on the Occupy Movement in the US was in Zuccotti Park in New York City, where the Occupy Wall Street protest camp received wide media coverage starting in September 2011. Local groups throughout the world (more than 95 cities and 82 countries) established similar camps and protests based on local concerns regarding corporations, the global financial system, and income inequality.[34,35,36] The movement continued for over a year, until the last high-profile sites in Washington DC and London were shut down in February 2012.

While the Occupy Movement may not have been effective at bringing widespread economic change to society, it mobilized groups and individuals behind their rallying cry "We are the 99%." This slogan focused on the unequal distribution of income in the US, specifically, the concentration of income with the top 1% of earners. The "99%" was in direct reference to a recently released US Congressional Budget Office (CBO) report that noted that between 1979 and 2007 the incomes of the top 1% of Americans grew by an average of 275%, while the increase among middle-income earners, the next 60%, was around 40% and only 20% growth for the lowest 18% of income earners.[37]

Many critics argue that, as a social movement, the Occupy Movement was ineffective because of its lack of leadership, failure to organize into formal organizations, and inability to articulate a shared set of goals. However, others would argue that these are the signs of a true social movement—a gathering of momentum and outcry based on individual discontent coalescing into an aggregated demand for social, political, or economic change. Participants in the Occupy Movement had varying issues of discontent that led them to the movement, including rising unemployment, staggering college and personal loans, frustration with the corrupt banking practices, and the extreme income inequality in the US. As we have noted in previous examples of social movements, nonprofit organizations can play varying roles in activating, coalescing, or co-opting

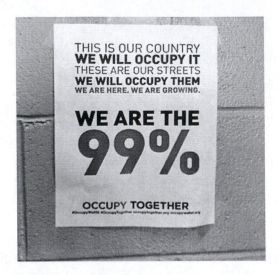

Poster summarizing a key message of the Occupy Movement

the movement. In the case of Occupy, many local nonprofit organizations helped to support local camps and efforts, nonprofits provided resources, food, and equipment to protesters, but, in the end, no large nonprofit or group of nonprofits formalized the movement to carry it forward.

While a lack of leadership might be an indication of a weak movement, it was a defining characteristic of the Occupy Movement. The Occupy Movement was characterized by its participatory nature, modeling a true **participatory democracy**, where each protestor had the same ability to participate and speak in the process. Decisions were made at General Assemblies using a **consensus model** of direct democracy, based on the consent of all participants. Consensus models for decision-making seek to find an acceptable resolution for all involved. The General Assemblies relied on a system of hand signals and a *stack*, a queue of speakers that anyone could join, to enable participation of all who wanted to comment. These processes for organizing and mobilizing groups can slow the decision-making process, but at the same time they ensure that all participants feel heard and are active members of the movement. Thus, while not formalized into a formal organization, the Occupy Movement is an example of the diverse ways in which Americans contribute to and build civil society.

The Occupy Movement was able to gain and maintain momentum partly because of its ability to use social media and technology to harness the

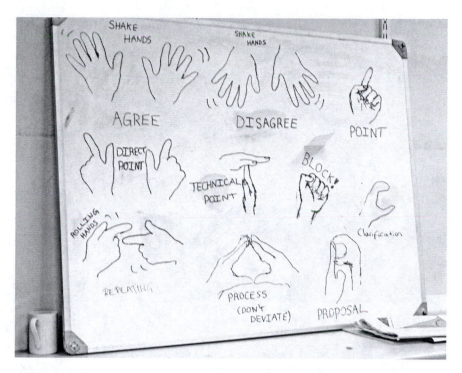

Hand signals used during General Assemblies in the Occupy Movement

support of people from across the US. Occupy activists used Facebook, Twitter, and Meetup to coordinate events and mobilize interested groups and individuals, and they also used Skype to host conference calls across Occupy camps. Protestors used social media to keep their protests alive, noting when supplies were short, such as the need for batteries, generators, foods, and other items on site. They also took full advantage of modern technologies to provide media coverage for their activities, posting live streams of events on the Internet. Subgroups organized online to raise funds to help homeowners facing foreclosure, while others have used the Occupy online movement to organize groups such as Occupy Sandy, which provided relief in the New York area following Hurricane Sandy. As compared to social movements of the past, information and communication technologies enabled Occupy activists to organize faster, broadcast their message more effectively, and harness the support of mainstream members of society who were not interested in joining the protest movement, but wanted to lend their support. At the same time,

Protestors gathering for Occupy Wall Street

these quick, immediate communication tools may have contributed to the diversity of activities and efforts that prevented the movement from narrowing to formal organization.

While the Occupy Movement was able to mobilize support from around the country and generate a great deal of media coverage and attention to issues of income inequality, it was less effective at generating long-term social change. The movement was not particularly effective at articulating its demands and working within the political, social, and economic system to effectively achieve widespread social or economic change. Some might argue that this was the result of a lack of leadership and a failure to articulate well-defined goals. It might also have been the result of the movement losing momentum, as people tired of the energy and resources required to maintain Occupy camps. Others note that as elite institutions began to accept the criticisms from the movement, the movement lost its sense of urgency and importance. For example, in October 2011, the Los Angeles City Council adopted a resolution informally supporting the Occupy Movement and the Executive Director of Financial Stability at the Bank of England noted that the protesters were right to criticize bankers and politicians who were acting immorally.[38] While these examples are an indication of support from mainstream institutions, there was little to no tangible change (social, economic, or political) as a result of the Occupy Movement.

The Occupy Movement demonstrates the resources and effort required to sustain a social movement. As the public loses interest in the movement, it becomes less salient. Other issues emerge on the political agenda and the media horizon, so people begin to support other movements or shift their support to more formal nonprofit organizations working toward economic justice and change. Social movements, while powerful mechanisms for mobilizing popular support and achieving social change, also require extensive effort and energy. The need for sustained effort often necessitates the creation of formal nonprofit organizations and associations to ensure that the movement does not dwindle.

The Role of Technology in Modern Social Movements

Today social movements have the advantage of communication technologies that can increase the speed by which people organize and mobilize. Technologies enable us to mobilize and organize across vast distances and through political barriers. Consider the major effect of cell phone video footage in garnering economic, political, and social support for the protests in Burma (Myanmar) in August 2007, also referred to as the Saffron Revolution. For decades, the Burmese government had maintained tight control of its citizens by banning the use of the Internet. This oppressive regime has been accused of creating economic distress, keeping wealth for itself while the people live in poverty (Burma is among the 20 poorest countries in the world), and overspending on the military at the expense of the people's welfare. With its closed borders and restrictions on Internet use, it is difficult for those outside of Burma to provide support for an insurgency, uprising, protest, or social movement.

In 2007, the State Peace and Development Council, the ruling junta or military group that leads the country, announced that it would end fuel subsidies, causing a rise in prices of 66% in less than one week's time. The Burmese were outraged and took to the streets. The initial mass protest included political activists, women, students, and average citizens. It was nonviolent in nature and consisted mostly of gathering in the streets and walking in protest. The protest was one of the first in the nation for ten years; in 1988 the government had engaged in a brutal crackdown of a

One of the many images of monks and civilians protesting in the streets of Rangoon, Burma, 2007

protest that left 3,000 protesters killed and thousands more imprisoned and tortured.

In response to the 2007 protest, the government began arresting and beating protestors, including prominent Burmese dissidents. In the process of breaking up peaceful demonstrations, the Burmese military injured three monks. This attack on the monks was recorded and shared among dissidents in the country. The Burmese public was outraged and in the following days, more people took to the streets, this time joined by large numbers of Buddhist monks demanding a stop to the violence and a removal of religious services for the military. Within days, more Buddhist monks joined the popular protests against the government's treatment of the people, resulting in what is now referred to as the Saffron Revolution because of the saffron-colored robes worn by the monks. The government allowed the protests to proceed for around ten days, but soon the military took action against the peaceful monks. Cell phones captured much of the protest activity in Burma; video and still images illustrated the brutality of the military junta. Images of Buddhist monks being beaten by armed, uniformed military men flooded the Internet. Public opinion, both inside Burma and throughout the world, turned against the Burmese leadership and quickly led to international intervention and calls for reform and an end to the violence.

Nonprofit organizations in Burma and abroad played an important role in the Saffron Revolution. Inside Burma, organizations, like the Human Rights Defenders and Promoters, helped to mobilize protestors. Local nonprofit organizations also helped to move cell phones and photos across Burmese borders to be published abroad. International nonprofit organizations, including Amnesty International, called for investigations of the government's behavior and protection of the citizens of Burma. Other organizations worked to advance Burmese issues in the media, including Burma Campaign UK which helped to raise awareness of the social movement and violence and mobilize resources outside of the country to pressure the military junta to stop the violence. Other nonprofits worked to raise awareness of the Burmese social movement. For example, the US Campaign for Burma website posted an audio message from Burma that included crying crematorium workers who reported that soldiers forced them to burn injured protesters and civilians on the outskirts of Yangon.

The support and pressure provided by these international organizations was greatly advanced by the digital images that emerged from Burma. With instant, online publication of images of monks being brutalized, nonprofit organizations were able to draw upon popular outrage to raise material and nonmaterial support for their goals and missions. The Burmese government worked to block all websites and services, barring access to web-based e-mail, but the protesters worked around these barriers. Burmese activists and citizens hacked Internet services, transferred photos and digital files across the border to Thailand, blogged about events, and posted pictures and videos whenever they found a window of Internet access. These new, more advanced technologies enabled protestors to provide real-time information about what was going on inside a historically closed off country—resulting in some of the highest levels of international coverage of Burma in history.

Technology is increasingly playing an important role in social movements around the world. While some would argue that technology, like in the case of Burma, is enabling the spread of information and mobilization of groups and resources, others note that social movements continue to require face-to-face interactions and traditional social organizing activities. Consider the role of Twitter in the Iranian Green Revolution, also nicknamed the "Twitter Revolution." Following the 2009 elections in Iran there was a series of protests in support of the opposition candidates in the disputed election of Mahmoud Ahmadinejad.

Following the Iranian election, the opposition candidates claimed that the elections had been rigged and votes manipulated. Iranians took to the streets to protest the election outcomes. Although the protests were peaceful, the police and Basij (a paramilitary group) attacked protestors with batons, pepper spray, and live ammunition. When a young woman by the name of Neda Agha-Soltan was shot by a Basij, a video of the shooting was e-mailed to friends, forwarded to *Voice of America* and *The Guardian* newspaper, and posted to Facebook and YouTube where it was broadcast to the world.[39] Once Iranians and people throughout the world saw the murder of this young woman, even more people took to the streets of Iran, including those who had previously not been politically active.

During the political protests, thousands of protesters were arrested and some reported being tortured in prison. At the same time, Iranian leadership closed the universities in Tehran, banned rallies, and blocked access to websites, cell phone transmissions, and text messaging. Despite these efforts to halt the social movement, the people mobilized using Twitter and other technologies to connect with one another and the rest of the world.

Some argue that Twitter was influential and preferable to other technologies in this case because it is free, public, highly mobile, and quick,[40] making it especially practical for mass protest movements. Additionally, it is difficult for central authorities and governments to control Twitter—"While the front pages of Iranian newspapers were full of blank space where censors had whited-out news stories, Twitter was delivering information from the street level, in real time."[41] But some note that Twitter, like other technologies, is not a silver bullet to mobilize a social movement against dictators, especially since it remains possible for oppressive regimes to block IP addresses and SMS networks. Moreover, some argue that although Twitter was being used in new ways in Iran, the real story remained the widespread social movement that mobilized hundreds of thousands of people and resulted in what some considered the largest social change in Iran in decades, the beginning of the end of the Islamic Republic.[42,43,44]

Burma's Saffron Revolution and Iran's Twitter Revolution are examples of modern social movements that have effectively used information and communication technologies to mobilize average citizens, share information about their demands, and raise awareness among those outside of their countries. One might easily argue that the use of photos, images, and real-time Internet reporting all enable faster mobilization and more effective organizing, creating a more robust civil society. But, at the same time, it remains true that social movements require the mobilization of masses of ordinary people. Both of these social movements were powerful and sustainable because they included average citizens and, in some cases, groups of people who do not normally engage in political protest or criticize the regimes (e.g. Burmese monks, elderly Iranians). The power of the people, though supported and mobilized by technologies, continues to reside in the people and the movement of the people toward a common goal or change.

Contemporary International Social Change Movements

Comparing the political protests in Burma and Iran, we can see similarities with important social movements in the US. In fact, international social movements are much like those in the United States, but of course social, economic, and political institutions of the environment shape the role of nonprofit organizations and the ways in which groups mobilize and engage in the political process. For example, in the Republic of China the organization of labor unions will be different than in the United States, and the movement for workers' rights may be different in Bangladesh. Similarly, political engagement and speaking out against the government will take different forms in a dictatorship or Communist state than in a democratic society such as the US, where the institutional component of civil society allows for the freedom of speech. Moreover, the role of international and domestic nonprofit organizations will depend on the political, legal, and economic structures that regulate the organization of groups.

Still, we know that social movements occur in all societies. Marginalized groups form to demand participation in the political process or to demand social and economic change. And in the rest of the world, just as in the

US, mass mobilization has the effect of disrupting mainstream economic, social, and political activities, forcing elite groups and the politically powerful to acknowledge the concerns of the movement and respond. Some examples of the power of mass social movements include the emerging Women's Rights Movement in India and the Arab Spring. Both of these movements are examples of marginalized groups in society organizing to advocate for their rights. They exemplify popular movements among the general population to demand political and social change. In the case of India, men and women took to the streets to demand a change to the culture of violence against women and the state's unwillingness to protect women and prosecute men who sexually harass and assault women. In the case of Egypt and the Arab Spring, people from all walks of society—youth, men, women, students, elderly, conservatives, and liberals—took to the streets to demand political change, advancement of democratic processes, and economic improvements.

In India, there has been a growing concern about the sexual harassment and assault of women. Harassment of women has become increasingly common in India; many women do not travel alone, do not travel at night, and, when they do, travel in fear. While these assaults have been occurring for years, recent, particularly horrifying attacks have drawn international attention to the issue of safety of women in India and the general neglect of police authorities and the legal system to protect women. In October 2013, a 13-year-old girl was gang raped and then burned alive in Uttar Pradesh, after she and her sister were returning from an area farm.[45] In a separate incident, another 13-year-old girl was attacked and sexually assaulted and murdered by three villagers. These incidents might have gone unnoticed in 2012 or 2010, but the rape and murder of a young woman traveling by bus in December 2012 resulted in a major social movement and fury over the chronic sexual violence facing women in India. According to Jacqueline Bhabha, director of research for the François-Xavier Bagnoud Center for Health and Human Rights at the Harvard School of Public Health, sexual assault is not a new issue in India and there is no shortage of groups dedicated to studying the issue and advocating for womens rights.[46] The difference is that there is now a great deal of national and international attention being devoted to the issue and the social movement.

Most of the current social movement aimed at advancing the rights and protection of women in India has been sparked by the December 2012 attack of a woman and her male friend who were traveling on a private bus. The 23-year-old woman was beaten and gang raped. She died in a hospital two weeks after the attack. The attack generated public outrage and widespread media coverage and sparked a national debate on the treatment of women. Following news of the attack, people throughout India organized to protest against the governments of Delhi and India. Protests took place throughout India: at India Gate, Raisina Hill, in front of the Parliament of India, and at the official residence of the President. More than 600 women protested in Bangalore and thousands of people participated in a silent march at Kolkata.[47] Others signed an online petition showing their outrage at the treatment of women and others replaced Facebook profile images with a black dot symbol, to show their solidarity with the women of India.[48] As a result of these protests, in March 2013, the government passed tough new laws to allow the death penalty in cases of rape. A year after the attack, the four men who carried out the bus attack were put on trial and sentenced to death. After trying the case, Judge Khanna noted that the attack "shocked the collective conscience" of India, and that "courts cannot turn a blind eye" to such crimes.[49]

In this example, the widespread coverage of the bus attack helped to spark a large protest movement in India that has resulted in initial changes to the ways in which rape victims are treated, sexual assault perpetrators are punished, and has raised the national and international conversation about women's rights and sexual assault in India and elsewhere. Nonprofit organizations, women's groups, and individuals have played a critical role in bringing about these changes. Many of them were active before the December 2012 attacks. The emergence of the protest movement was not a new idea, but rather a confluence of organizational efforts, tragic events, and frustration and discontent among a large number of disempowered individuals. This is just one example of many of the modern social and political movements that are bringing change in society.

Summary

Social movements and voluntary activism such as protests are important mechanisms for bringing about social, political, and economic change. They are particularly important for enabling the less powerful or disempowered to communicate discontent and a desire for change. Civil society provides the larger context, or background, in which social movements and voluntary activism occur. Social movements and social change are enabled by each of the components of civil society, including institutional rules and laws such as free speech rights and rights to assemble, common interests which lead to collective action, and organizations both formal and informal that work to bring about the desired change. At the same time, civil society is strengthened by the activism and organizations that build and sustain social movements and social change efforts.

Examples of protest movements include the Civil Rights Movement—to bring political and social change for a large group of Americans who were excluded from the political process—the Green and Saffron Revolutions in Iran and Burma—where protest was used as a tool of dissent for the oppressed—and the modern day Occupy, Gay Rights, and Immigrant Rights Movements. Each of these examples represent different types of movements demanding varying levels of social, economic, and political change. In each example, nonprofit and civil society organizations play important, but varying, roles in shaping the development, process, success, and dissolution of the movement. In some cases, nonprofit organizations serve as organizing mechanisms for developing social movements—bringing together people who have a shared interest in change. In other cases, nonprofit organizations help to mobilize the movement—providing a venue for protest and organization, for example when attending church services includes participating in a march or a protest. And, of course, as social movements lose momentum, they often formalize their efforts into nonprofit organizations that continue to advance the social justice, equality, and other missions and goals of the movement.

KEY TERMS

- Civil Rights Movement
- Classical model
- Consensus model
- Insurgency / insurgencies

- Labor Movement
- Participatory democracy
- Protest
- Resource deficiencies

- Social change organizations
- Social movement

DISCUSSION QUESTIONS

1. What are some of the traditional mechanisms for being involved in the political process in America?

2. What are some of the ways in which social movements mobilize resources and people to engage in the political process?

3. In your opinion, what is the most influential social movement in the US today? If you wanted to become involved in this movement, what would you do?

4. In your opinion, are social change organizations examples of social movements? Why or why not?

5. Do you think that technology will significantly change the ways in which social movements organize and mobilize in the future? Or will in-person, face-to-face activities including protests, sit-ins, and organized meetings remain critical to effective social movements?

   Twitter's Impact On Iran Protests Examined.
   All Things Considered. NPR.

   June 19, 2009 4:00 PM. Audio Clip Available at:
   http://www.npr.org/templates/story/story.php?storyId=105685422

   A common observation in the protests in Iran is that demonstrators are using Twitter and other social media to communicate in the face of government censorship of traditional media. Ethan Zuckerman, a senior researcher at Harvard's Berkman Center for Internet and Society, says though some protesters used Twitter, most of the organizing happened the old-fashioned way.

6. What is the role of nonprofit organizations in mobilizing, supporting, organizing, and managing popular social movements?

7. Consider our discussion from the last chapter about the reluctance of many nonprofits to get involved in the political process. Do nonprofit organizations prevent the development of true social movements and uprisings?

8. Do some Internet research to learn more about the Arab Spring. What type of social movement is occurring in different countries in this region? How have nonprofits influenced the Arab Spring, if at all? What role do nonprofits play in advancing or supporting these movements?

Additional Reading

Jenkins, Joseph Craig and Charles Perrow. 1977. Insurgency of the Powerless. Farm Worker Movements (1946–1972). *American Sociological Review*, 42(2): 249–68.

McAdam, Doug. 1982. *Political Process and the Development of Black Insurgency, 1930–1970.* Chicago, IL: University of Chicago Press.

McAdam, Doug, Sidney Tarrow, and Charles Tilly. 2001. *Dynamics of Contention.* Cambridge, UK: Cambridge University Press.

McCarthy, John D. and Mayer N. Zald. 1973. *The Trend of Social Movements in America: Professionalization and Resource Mobilization.* Morriston, NJ: General Learning Press.

Tarrow, Sidney. 1994. *Power in Movement: Collective Action, Social Movements and Politics.* New York: Cambridge University Press.

Additional Media

To learn more about modern day international social movements, watch the 2013 film *The Square*, directed by Jehane Noujaim and Karim Amer. http://thesquarefilm.com; also available on Netflix.com

Synopsis: *The Square* is a revolutionary film about change and the power of people. The revolutionary events from 2011 through 2013 that aimed at ending political and military oppression in Egypt are documented in this film, from the overthrow of one regime to the overthrow of the new president, a member of the Muslim Brotherhood. Cairo's Tahrir Square is the center of the film, the gathering place for protesters and the center of a social movement. *The Square* tells the personal and political stories behind the revolution. It is an inspirational story of claiming rights and struggling to advance society through the organization of multiple political, social, and religious forces.

Notes

1   Levy, Ariel. 2013. The Perfect Wife—How Edith Windsor fell in love, got married, and won a landmark case for gay marriage, *The New Yorker*, Monday, September 30, 2013. Volume 89, Issue 30, p. 54.

2   Levy (2013).

3   Theoharis, Jeanne. 2013. *The Rebellious Life of Mrs. Rosa Parks.* Boston: Beacon Press.

4   McAdam, Doug. 1982. *Political Process and the Development of Black Insurgency, 1930–1970.* Chicago, IL: University of Chicago Press.

5   Tarrow, Sidney. 1994. *Power in Movement: Collective Action, Social Movements and Politics.* Cambridge University Press.

6   Patterson, Thomas E. 2002. *The Vanishing Voter.* New York: Knopf.

7   Klandermans, Bert and Sidney Tarrow. 1988. Mobilization into Social Movements: Synthesizing European and American Approaches. *International Social Movement Research*, 1: 1–38.

8   Tilly, Charles. 2004. *Social Movements, 1768–2004.* Boulder, CO: Paradigm Publishers.

9   Wilson, John. 1973. *Introduction to Social Movements.* New York: Basic Books Inc., p. 55.

10 Wolfinger, Raymond et al. 1964. America's Radical Right. In David Apter (ed.), *Ideology and Discontent.* Glencoe, IL: The Free Press, pp. 267–275.

11 Orum, Anthony M. 1966. A Reappraisal of the Social and Political Participation of Negroes. *American Journal of Sociology*, 72(1): 32–46.

12 Jenkins, Joseph Craig and Charles Perrow. 1977. Insurgency of the Powerless. Farm Worker Movements (1946–1972). *American Sociological Review*, 42(2): 249–268.

13 Jenkins and Perrow (1977).

14 McCarthy, John D. and Mayer N. Zald. 1973. *The Trend of Social Movements in America: Professionalization and Resource Mobilization.* Morriston, NJ: General Learning Press.

15 McCarthy and Zald (1973); Jenkins and Perrow (1977).

16 Allen, Michael Patrick. 1974. The Structure of Interorganizational Elite Cooptation: Interlocking Corporate Directorates. *American Sociological Review*, 39(3): 393–406.

17 Alford, Robert R. and Roger Friedland. 1975. Political Participation and Public Policy. *Annual Review of Sociology*, 1:429–479.

18 Piven, Frances Fox and Richard A. Cloward. 1977. *Poor People's Movements: Why They Succeed, How They Fail.* Vintage.

19 McAdam, Doug. 1982. *Political Process and the Development of Black Insurgency, 1930–1970.* Chicago, IL: University of Chicago Press.

20 McAdam (1982).

21 McAdam (1982).

22 Piven and Cloward (1977).

23 Piven, Frances Fox. 2006. *Challenging Authority: How Ordinary People Change America.* Rowman & Littlefield Publishers.

24 Tarrow (1994).

25 Piven and Cloward (1977).

26 Piven and Cloward (1977).

27 McAdam (1982), p. 61.

28 McAdam (1982), pp. 125–126.

29 Watters, Pat. 1971. *Down to Now: Reflections on the Southern Civil Rights Movement.* New York: Pantheon Books.

30 McAdam (1982), p. 63.

31 Chetkovich, Carol and Frances Kunreuther. 2006. *From the Ground Up: Grassroots Organizations Making Social Change.* Ithaca, NY: Cornell University Press.

32 Chetkovich and Kunreuther (2006).

33 Piven (2006).

34 Thompson, Derek. 2011. Occupy the World: The '99 Percent' Movement Goes Global, *The Atlantic.* Accessed October 15, 2011 at http://www.theatlantic.com/business/archive/2011/10/occupy-the-world-the-99-percent-movement-goes-global/246757/

35 Adam, Karla. 2011. Occupy Wall Street protests continue worldwide, *The Washington Post.* October 16, 2011.

36   Walters, Joanna. 2011. Occupy America: protests against Wall Street and inequality hit 70 cities | World news, *The Observer* (UK). Accessed October 13, 2011 at http://www.theguardian.com/world/2011/oct/08/occupy-america-protests-financial-crisis

37   Congressional Budget Office. Trends in the Distribution of Household Income Between 1979 and 2007. Congress of the United States. Washington, DC. PDF available at http://www.cbo.gov/publication/42729

38   Wilson, Simone. 2011. City Council Unanimously Passes Occupy L.A. Resolution— Protesters Struggle to Distance Themselves From Democrats, Unions, *Los Angeles News, The Informer*. Accessed October 11, 2013 at http://blogs.laweekly.com/informer/2011/10/city_council_passes_occupy_la_resolution_democrats_unions.php

39   Stelter, Brian and Brad Stone. 2009. Web Pries Lid of Iranian Censorship, *The New York Times*. Accessed October 11, 2013 at http://www.nytimes.com/2009/06/23/world/middleeast/23censor.html?hp&_r=0

40   Grossman, Lev. 2009. Iran Protests: Twitter, the Medium of the Movement, *Time*, Wednesday, June 17, 2009. Accessed October 11, 2013 at http://content.time.com/time/world/article/0,8599,1905125,00.html#ixzz2hQxCLgLz

41   Grossman (2009).

42   Iran's Twitter revolution. Editorial, *The Washington Times*, Tuesday, June 16, 2009. Accessed October 11, 2013 at http://www.washingtontimes.com/news/2009/jun/16/irans-twitter-revolution/

43   Taheri, Amir. 2009. The fight for Iran's future is far from over, *The Times* (London).

44   All Things Considered. Twitter's Impact On Iran Protests Examined, *National Public Radio*, June 19, 2009. Accessed Oct 11, 2013 at http://www.npr.org/templates/story/story.php?storyId=105685422

45   Class 8th UP girl burned alive after gang rape by 3 villagers, *Times of India*, October 23, 2013. Accessed October 26, 2013 from http://articles.timesofindia.indiatimes.com/2013–10–23/lucknow/43323537_1_3-villagers-minor-girl-elder-sister

46   Singal, Jesse and Rachel Bishop. 2013. Gang rape, burning of teen stir outrage in India, *USA Today*, October 25, 2013. Accessed October 26, 2013 at http://www.usatoday.com/story/news/world/2013/10/24/india-girl-raped-fire/3178689/

47   Kolkata walks in silence to protest Delhi gangrape, *IBNlive.in.com*, December 23, 2012. Accessed October 26, 2013 at http://ibnlive.in.com/news/kolkata-walks-in-silence-to-protest-delhi-gangrape/311865-3-231.html

48   When words fail, a dot speaks volumes, *The Times of India*, December 21, 2012. Accessed October 26, 2013 at http://articles.timesofindia.indiatimes.com/2012–12–21/chandigarh/35952817_1_delhi-gangrape-city-student-dot

49   Delhi gang rape: Four sentenced to death, *BBC News*, September 13, 2013. Accessed October 26, 2013 at http://www.bbc.co.uk/news/world-asia-india-24078339

9

ECONOMIC CONTRIBUTIONS OF NONPROFIT ORGANIZATIONS

CHAPTER LEARNING OBJECTIVES

By the end of this chapter, students will be able to:

1. Describe the nonprofit sector's contributions to the US economy relative to other major industries

2. Identify the major employers within the nonprofit sector

3. Explain some of the factors that have contributed to nonprofit employment growth in recent years

4. Describe some of the ways that job training and community development organizations promote local economic development

5. Describe how business attraction, development, and promotion organizations help to fulfill local economic development goals

6. Compare and contrast job training and community development organizations with nonprofits in the business attraction, development, and promotion field and identify the key differences between the nonprofits that fall into these categories

---

Introduction

Employment is key to a strong economy and a healthy modern society. When people are employed they earn income which gets re-circulated into the economy as spending on housing, groceries, education, utilities,

INSPIRING JOB TRAINING IN CHICAGO

Quantrell was a young man without a job. He had little hope that he would ever land one. As a convicted felon with no high school diploma, employers did not want to hire him. The odds of ever getting his foot on the ladder of economic opportunity seemed nearly impossible. But things began to change for Quantrell after he enrolled in the free culinary training program at Inspiration Corporation.

A nonprofit focused on job training, housing, and poverty, Inspiration Corporation bills itself as a "catalyst for self-reliance." A signature program of the organization is the 13-week foodservice training program that prepares participants for careers in the hospitality industry through both hands-on and classroom learning. The curriculum includes basic culinary skills and concepts, reading and converting recipes, nutrition education, following and taking direction, teamwork, sanitation and safety, restaurant service, employment and life skills classes. The hands-on portion of the program is carried out through Inspiration Kitchens, the successful social enterprise arm of the organization that operates two restaurants that are open to the public. Working in these restaurants gives culinary students practice to work in the sometimes chaotic environment of restaurants. In addition to serving paying customers and offering catering services, the Inspiration Kitchens' restaurants provide daily free meals to the working poor.

At Inspiration Kitchens, Quantrell met many people who would help to change his future. As his confidence began to grow, he was given more responsibilities in the kitchen. He graduated from the culinary training program and was promoted by Inspiration Corporation to kitchen manager, and later to Sous Chef/trainer, his first full-time job with benefits. He was awarded a partial scholarship to attend Robert Morris College where he earned an Associate's Degree in culinary arts. Having completed his degree, and developing the confidence and skills he needed to be successful in the workforce, Quantrell was hired into a full-time position as a Chef instructor at the Greater Chicago Food Depository, a nonprofit organization that works toward hunger relief and serves as the primary food bank and food distribution center in the city of Chicago.

Quantrell's story is not unique. He is one of thousands of individuals who has gotten on the road to self-sufficiency by a nonprofit workforce development organization.

To read more about Quantrell's story, the work of Inspiration Kitchens, and the history of Inspiration Corporation which was founded by a Chicago Police Officer, visit their website, www.inspirationkitchens.org, or link to their YouTube video to hear the stories of others who have found hope and a career path through this organization: http://www.youtube.com/watch?v=jgpfLJkRHXY

childcare, entertainment, clothing, and a variety of other consumable goods and services. Good jobs are a fundamental pillar of any economic development or economic growth plan.[1] The nonprofit sector plays an important role in the American economy, not only as a provider of jobs for more than 9% of the US workforce, but also as an important subset of organizations that are committed to providing job training and employment development. Many nonprofits help to prepare individuals who face employment barriers (e.g. low skills, criminal background, lack of formal education) to gain job-related skills, known as **vocational skills**, and by working closely with the local business sector to place these individuals in successful jobs. Moreover, another group of nonprofit organizations work in partnership with local governments to help plan and achieve local economic development goals, including everything from plans to reduce the local unemployment rate, to making small business loans, to attracting new businesses to the community. The nonprofit sector plays an integral, yet often understated, role in achieving local economic development objectives in most US communities.

This chapter provides a closer look at the contributions of the nonprofit sector to the US economy. The discussion is organized into two parts. First, we examine the nonprofit sector as a major provider of jobs, comparing nonprofit sector employment to other major industries and identifying the primary sources of employment with the nonprofit sector. Second, we discuss the role of nonprofit organizations in local economic development, including workforce development, vocation and job skills training programs, neighborhood revitalization programs, housing, and multi-service organizations. We note the nonprofit activities and impacts in the community and economic development subsector, in particular how these nonprofit efforts aim to lift those who are stuck, often through no fault of their own, at the bottom of the income and opportunity ladder. We will also take a brief look at nonprofit economic development organizations that work hand-in-hand with local government officials to pursue city or county economic development goals, typically by serving clients that include for-profit firms and business owners.

The Nonprofit Sector as a Major Employer

Nonprofit organizations make significant contributions to the US economy by employing tens of thousands of workers, and producing goods and services that contribute to the nation's gross domestic product (GDP), the market value of all goods and services produced in a country in a year. As we learned in Chapter 1, nonprofit employment has grown steadily over the past several decades, and the sector's contribution to US GDP has risen sharply since 1985, with particularly robust growth in the first decade of the new millennium. In 2010, nonprofit organizations produced goods and services that added $779 billion to the nation's GDP, accounting for roughly 5.4% of GDP. Nonprofit organizations accounted for more than 9% of total employment in 2012 and paid out approximately $576.9 billion in wages to US workers.[2] Perhaps even more interesting is the fact that nonprofit sector growth continued throughout the decade despite two recessions, surpassing the growth rate of both government and the for-profit sector.[3] In fact, nonprofit employment grew every year between 2000 and 2010, while the for-profit sector lost jobs in most of these years.[4] This continued growth of nonprofit employment during the harshest economic times the US has seen in almost a century suggests that the nonprofit sector has indeed become a critical component of the US economy.

> Nonprofits have been holding the fort for much of the rest of the economy, creating jobs at a time when other components of the economy have been shedding jobs at accelerating rates. This striking pattern holds for nearly every state and for most major fields of nonprofit activity.
>
> (Salamon, Sokolowski, and Geller, 2010)

Later in this chapter we will consider some possible explanations for the growth of the nonprofit sector during this tumultuous decade, but first let us consider the more fundamental question of how the nonprofit sector compares to other major industries in terms of size. Figure 9.1 reveals that the nonprofit sector is the third largest employer (10.7 million people) in the private sector, trailing behind only the retail trade (14.5 million people) and manufacturing (11.5 million people).

Of course, nonprofit employment varies by state and region. Figure 9.2 shows the variations in nonprofit employment across the US, illustrating the percentage of private employment that is accounted for by nonprofit organizations. Nonprofit organizations make up the largest proportion of employment in New England (16.2%) followed by the Middle Atlantic

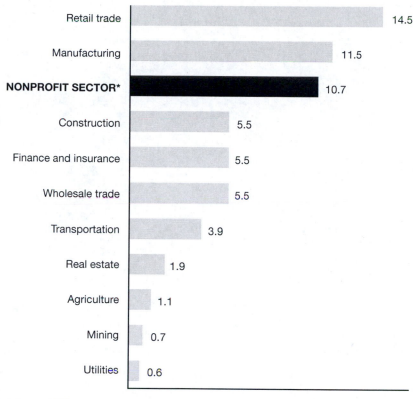

Retail trade — 14.5
Manufacturing — 11.5
NONPROFIT SECTOR* — 10.7
Construction — 5.5
Finance and insurance — 5.5
Wholesale trade — 5.5
Transportation — 3.9
Real estate — 1.9
Agriculture — 1.1
Mining — 0.7
Utilities — 0.6

*50 states and DC   Millions of people

FIGURE 9.1 Employment in the Nonprofit Sector Versus Selected Industries, 2010

Source: Salamon, Sokolowski and Geller. 2012. *Holding the Fort: Nonprofit Employment in a Decade of Turmoil.* The John Hopkins Nonprofit Economic Data Project. Employment Bulletin #39. John Hopkins Center for Civil Society Studies. January 2012.

region (15.4%). Nonprofit organizations make up a smaller portion of employment in the western and southern states, accounting for only 5.8% of employment in the West South Central region and 7.2% in the Mountain region. Perhaps unsurprisingly, older, more well-established parts of the country tend to have more nonprofit organizations per capita, and thus nonprofit employment in these places accounts for a larger share of total private employment. This is likely due to the prevalence of universities and healthcare centers in these communities, and because many nonprofits have their corporate headquarters in major cities in these regions.

As we have learned throughout this book, the nonprofit sector is incredibly diverse and encompasses a wide variety of organizations. This

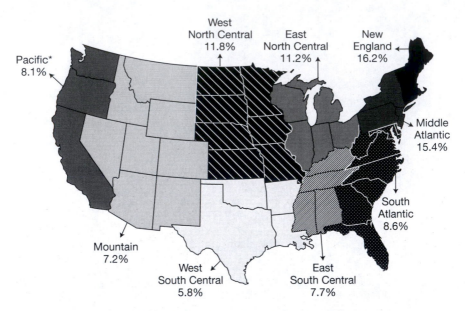

FIGURE 9.2 Nonprofit Employment as a Share of Private Employment by Region

Source: Salamon, Sokolowski and Geller. 2012. *Holding the Fort: Nonprofit Employment in a Decade of Turmoil*. The John Hopkins Nonprofit Economic Data Project. Employment Bulletin #39. John Hopkins Center for Civil Society Studies. January 2012.

diversity raises an important question: Where are the jobs to be found? Who are the major employers within the nonprofit sector? Are there just as many nonprofit jobs in advancing environmental concerns as there are in educating youth in private K–12 schools? These are important questions for college students looking for jobs in public service. Just as nonprofit jobs are unevenly distributed across regions of the US (see Figure 9.2), jobs are also unevenly distributed among industry, or field.

Figure 9.3 uses data from 45 states and the District of Columbia to show the distribution of nonprofit jobs by field in 2010. The pie chart reveals that nonprofit employment is concentrated into three major fields: healthcare, education, and social services. Combining hospitals, nursing homes, and ambulatory care, healthcare is the largest source of nonprofit jobs in the US, employing 57% of the nonprofit workforce. The nonprofit education field, comprised of private elementary and secondary schools along with private colleges, state universities, community colleges, and other educational institutions, accounts for the second largest share of nonprofit employment, at 15%. Many universities and colleges employ not just

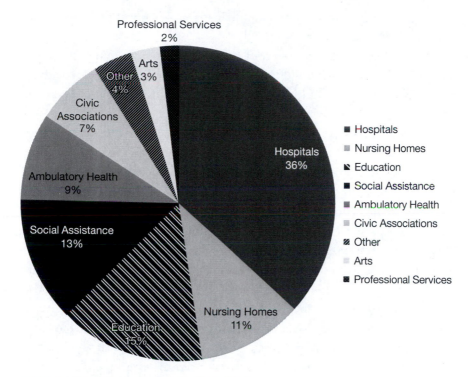

FIGURE 9.3 Nonprofit Employment by Field, 2010.

Source: *Holding the Fort: Nonprofit Employment in a Decade of Turmoil* by Salamon, Sokolowski, and Geller (2012).[5]

professors, but researchers, administrative staff, janitorial and facilities staff, and student workers in addition to running libraries, science labs, hospitals, clinics, agricultural extension offices, and a number of other important offices that provide services to the communities and states where they operate.

The social services field is the third largest employer, accounting for 13% of all nonprofit employment. As we have seen in previous chapters, a wide range of organizations make up the social services field including job training providers (which we shall examine more closely later in this chapter), housing providers, domestic violence shelters, food banks, adoption and foster care agencies, and many others. Collectively, healthcare, education, and social services make up 85% of the paid jobs in the nonprofit sector. Other fields such as public benefit organizations (civic associations) and the arts account for relatively small shares of nonprofit employment, 7% and 3%, respectively.

As mentioned earlier, nonprofit employment clearly outpaced growth in both the government and for-profit sectors from 2000 to 2010 adding more jobs every year during this decade, amounting to an average annual growth rate of 2.1% over the decade.[6] Moreover, nonprofit growth was consistent across all regions of the US; nonprofit employment rose in every single region, while for-profit employment declined in most regions (only the Pacific and Mountain regions added for-profit jobs during this decade).[7] What explains this growth in nonprofit employment during an era in which the rest of the economy was suffering? Salamon, Sokolowski, and Geller (2010) offer several explanations for this phenomenon. First, they suggest that some of the expansion may have been driven by growth in government spending in areas in which nonprofits operate (social services, healthcare, etc.). Additionally, nonprofit jobs may have increased toward the end of the decade by an infusion of federal funding from the American Recovery and Reinvestment Act in local economic development activities. However, a second key factor in nonprofit growth has to do with the fact that nonprofit employment is heavily concentrated in service fields; since the 1940s, the US has been transitioning toward a service economy. When we consider the fact that nonprofit organizations have little to no presence in declining industries such as manufacturing and steel, but a strong presence in service fields, it becomes easier to see why nonprofits have grown in this recent time of economic downturn.

The growth in nonprofit employment and subsequent increase in the nonprofit sector's share of GDP are both indicators that the nonprofit sector occupies a place of importance in the US economy. Whether this level of growth can be sustained, however, remains in question. The nonprofit sector faces a number of threats including uncertainty of future government funding and encroachment from for-profit businesses into service areas that have historically been dominated by nonprofits. Nonprofit organizations in many areas, including social services, education, hospitals, and nursing homes, have recently begun to lose market share to for-profits providing the same services.[8] In the next chapter, we will examine more closely some of the factors that may work to limit nonprofit growth in the future. For now, we turn to the role of nonprofits in local economic development.

The Nonprofit Role in Local Economic Development

Economic development refers to the plans of action made and carried out by public officials and communities to raise the standard of living and economic health of a particular geographic area. Although there are some federal and state policies, programs, and funding sources designed to help local communities in their economic growth and development efforts, economic development is generally believed to be a function best suited for planning and execution at the local level, since each community has different labor market conditions, access to capital, and different geographic features and natural assets to build an economic strategy upon.[9] While economic development planning has traditionally been a service function of local government, much like public safety or parks and recreation services, nonprofit organizations and for-profit businesses are integral parts of these plans. Nonprofit organizations are essential partners to local government in achieving economic development goals.

According to Blakely and Leigh (2010) the goals of regional and local economic development include

> strengthening the competitive position of regions and localities by developing otherwise underutilized human and natural resource potential; improving employment levels and long-term career options for local residents; increasing the participation of disadvantaged and minority groups in the local economy; realizing opportunities for indigenous economic growth by recognizing opportunities available for locally produced products and services; improving the physical environment as necessary to improve the climate for business development and enhancing the quality of life for residents.
>
> (p. 34)[10]

There are many different types of nonprofit economic development organizations that help local governments achieve these goals. We group these nonprofit organizations into two categories: job training and community development organizations and business attraction, development, and promotion organizations. In the next section, we discuss these two types of economic development nonprofit organizations that engage in different types of activities to help local governments work toward economic goals.

Job Training and Community Development

While closely related to economic development, community development is a somewhat broader concept and encompasses a diverse set of activities that often includes not only job training and workforce development, but also education, advocacy, housing services, **microenterprise** (a small business that has five or fewer employees and low levels of capital, less than $35,000) and small business development (especially women and minority-owned businesses), neighborhood revitalization, or some combination thereof.[11] Whereas economic development efforts are intended to improve the local economy overall, community development efforts generally are concerned with improving the well-being and economic circumstances of lower-income individuals and economically distressed communities or neighborhoods. Community development encompasses not just developing the economy, but also the social fabric of the community. **Community development** is defined as "a set of values and practices which plays a special role in overcoming poverty and disadvantage, knitting society together at the grass roots and deepening democracy."[12]

Community development efforts are generally carried out through a special type of nonprofit known as a **Community-Based Development Organization (CBDO)**. Sometimes these are also called **Community Development Corporations (CDCs)**. A CBDO is a "nonprofit organization controlled by residents of low to moderate income areas to help stimulate economic and physical improvement of the community."[13] Some CBDOs are very small, providing only one service, or covering a narrow geographic area, while others are large, multi-service organizations serving an entire city or region. Sometimes CBDOs operate job-training programs, while others focus on advocacy, affordable housing, redevelopment, or other services. See Box 9.1 for a comparison of two different community development organizations, one that provides a full array of services to combat poverty and a second that focuses primarily on housing.

Although all CBDOs work to develop the local economy and improve the community, not all of them directly operate their own workforce development programs. CBDOs that do not have their own job training or workforce development programs generally form partnerships with other community nonprofits that provide these services, linking clients to these critical resources. The problems affecting low-income communities are inter-related, including a lack of financial and social resources, unsafe

BOX 9.1 COMMUNITY-BASED DEVELOPMENT ORGANIZATIONS: TWO DIFFERENT CASES

There are thousands of Community-Based Development Organizations (CBDOs) in the US, many of which are concentrated in urban and metropolitan areas and, to a lesser extent, rural areas. Like snowflakes, no two CBDOs are exactly alike; they come in a variety of shapes and sizes. Some are very small, providing only one service or covering a narrow geographic area, while others are large, multi-service organizations tending to cover an entire city or region. To showcase the diversity of nonprofit organizations engaged in community development efforts, we describe two different CDBOs here: Wayne Metro Community Action Agency and Mission Development.

Wayne Metro Community Action Agency (CAA) is a full service community development organization serving the city of Detroit and surrounding 42 communities that make up Wayne County. Wayne Metro CAA obtained nonprofit status in 1971 and has a mission "to empower low-income individuals and strengthen communities through diverse services, leadership and collaboration." The organization has 16 service locations throughout the county and an annual budget of $27.7 million. It is a highly reputable organization and is recognized by charity watchdog groups as being an exemplary nonprofit.[14] Wayne Metro CAA offers services in five categories: basic needs, homeless and housing services, stability and life skills, youth and family educational services, and community and economic development programs.

The basic needs category includes several programs and services such as food assistance, a mobile farmer's market, community gardens, energy education, Medicaid and Affordable Care Act enrollment assistance, and referrals to other social services. In the housing and homeless services area, Wayne Metro CAA offers a Shelter+Care program, street outreach, a youth and run-away drop-in center, and supportive services for veterans' families. Many services are offered under the category of stability and life skills including a community financial center, free tax preparation, employment and training program, family self-sufficiency program, foreclosure intervention, homeownership programs, and a program called Michigan $aves which enables lower-income individuals and families to learn strategies for saving, form individual development accounts, and begin to build assets. Youth and family educational programs include an after-school youth program, community baby shower, early learning program, Headstart, a homeless youth education project, literacy education and parenting success programs, and summer youth programs. Under the community and economic development heading, the organization provides home weatherization, supportive housing, and new housing construction carried out through its own company, Excellent Construction, which is wholly owned and operated by Wayne Metro CAA.

continued

Wayne Metro CAA is a good example of a broad purpose community development organization that offers its own employment services. One of the employment and training programs provided by the organization includes group skills classes that emphasize pre-employability skills, resume development, establishment of references, tips on job search and follow-up techniques, "soft skills" counseling (how to dress for a job interview, punctuality and appearance, how to conduct oneself, etc.), job leads, access to Internet/e-mail service, fax, copier, and mailing service, and bus tickets and gas money to attend job interviews that can be accessed when needed. Wayne Metro CAA also offers a work experience program that entails eight weeks of on-the-job work to enhance a client's marketability and help them learn new skills. Finally, the organization offers material support to those already working, participating in a vocational/academic skills training or work experience/on-the-job training program, which might include uniforms/clothing for work, tools/supplies for work or training, auto repair, bus pass, driver's license restoration, certifications/licensure, or text books.

In contrast to Wayne Metro CAA's multi-service approach, Mission Housing Community Development (MHCD) was incorporated the same year (1971), but has a much narrower approach to service delivery. Serving the Mission District neighborhood in San Francisco, MHCD's mission is "to develop high-quality, well-managed, affordable, sustainable homes and communities that promote the self-sufficiency of low and moderate income families, seniors, and persons with diverse needs."[15] With an annual budget of about $4.3 million, MHCD works to develop and provide a wide variety of housing options for low-income citizens of the Mission District neighborhood as well as special populations including the elderly and persons with disabilities.

MHCD manages 11 apartment complexes designated for families, one senior housing complex, four hotel-style dwellings that provide single room occupancy, and many scattered site properties including 11 rehabilitated buildings. MHCD is constantly working to develop additional affordable housing options for the community through various efforts. They operate a Neighborhood Stabilization Program, which purchases and redevelops foreclosed and abandoned properties, putting them back into the stock of safe and affordable housing. MHCD has done an impressive job of meeting housing needs in this low-income neighborhood. The organization has been able to accomplish housing goals by creating a subsidiary organization, Caritas Management Corporation, to serve as a property management company. The Caritas Management Corporation manages the day-to-day oversight of MHCD's housing properties, enabling MHCD to focus on administrative aspects such as strategy, growth, and expansion opportunities, ensuring accountability to funders and compliance with legal rules.

To learn more about Wayne Metro CAA and Mission Housing Community Development and their programs, services, and sponsors, visit their websites: http://waynemetro.org/ and http://www.missionhousing.org/

or unaffordable housing, and low levels of **political efficacy**, the belief that one has the power to affect political situations and change the course of city policies or funding decisions. Many CBDOs not only work to create affordable housing, but also to provide education and workforce skills, and help community members find jobs so that they can afford permanent, safe housing. Moreover, they work to clean up neighborhoods, teach skills for democratic participation, instill a sense of ownership among residents, and reignite business investment to bring job opportunities to the community.

Both community development and job training represent areas in which the federal government invests heavily, so nonprofit organizations that provide these services typically receive extensive funding from the federal government, and, sometimes, state and local governments as well. The willingness of the government to invest in these types of services is related to the American value of individualism that we discussed in Chapter 2. Most Americans tend to feel that people should work hard and provide for themselves if they are physically able to do so. American policy-makers and citizens believe that jobs are the best approach to solving problems associated with poverty, viewing income-assistance for healthy working-age individuals an ineffective "hand out." Many Americans view employment as an acceptable solution for combatting poverty, and would thus prefer to have their tax dollars fund job training programs instead of welfare or unemployment checks. For these reasons, there is a great deal of popular support and federal funding for job training and placement programs. Before examining the impact that community development and job training providers have had on alleviating poverty and shaping economic opportunity, we will consider the history of these two fields, including the federal government's role in each, beginning with CBDOs.

The roots of the community development movement in America can be traced back to the 1960s when funding for the Federal War on Poverty was widely available to urban residents to craft self-organized responses to community needs. In fact, many of the more than 3,800 CBDOs in existence throughout the US today were conceived through federal funding made available in the 1960s. Additionally, many of today's CBDOs began as **Community Action Agencies** (CAAs) or **Community Action Programs** (CAPs).[16] One of the unique features of the Community Action Agencies, which has carried forward to some extent to present day

CBDOs, is the value placed on having members of the community who receive the services play a role in agency governance and decision-making. Given the coincidence of the War on Poverty with the passage of civil rights legislation, federal funding for CBDOs came with the mandate for "**maximum feasible participation**," meaning that the federal government required that disadvantaged citizens have a voice in the design of programs and service delivery in their communities. A condition of maximum feasible participation for grant funding means that CBDOs have a strong history of being grassroots organizations that rely on community members as staff and volunteers to carry out their day-to-day work.

Today, although most CBDOs have diversified their sources of income, many remain extensively funded by the federal government. The US Department of Housing and Urban Development (HUD), which was formed in 1965 and helped spur the growth of many CBDOs and nonprofit housing organizations, continues to serve as a critical partner and source of funding for community development nonprofits. One of HUD's longest continuously run programs is the Community Development Block Grant (CDBG) program. Block grants refer to federal payments to states or local governments that occur as "blocks" of money, with only general guidelines as to how the money should be spent. For example, a block grant might be for alleviating poverty, but the local government can determine for itself how to best use that funding: for example, by investing in job training, subsidizing housing, educating youth, or giving cash payments to the poor. Block grants allow local (e.g. city, county, regional, or state) governments to experiment with different programs to address problems or to tailor the spending to their particular, local needs.

The CDBG program is a federal program that distributes money to local governments to address local community development needs. The CDBG program exists "to ensure decent affordable housing, to provide services to the most vulnerable in our communities, and to create jobs through the expansion and retention of businesses."[17] The CDBG distributes federal grants to large cities and urban areas that need investment in housing and programs to increase economic opportunities for low- and moderate-income individuals. It also allocates funds to improve the living conditions in areas hit by natural disasters, and communities hardest hit by housing problems such as foreclosures and delinquencies. Many times, a portion of CDBG monies is passed along from the city to local nonprofits.

For a more in-depth look at the history of HUD, its leaders, and its various funding programs visit the chronology on the organization's website.[18]

Job training and other employment services are an integral part of community development efforts. In addition to the workforce readiness programs housed within community development organizations (like the employment services that exist within Wayne Metro CAA detailed in Box 9.1), there are more than 5,700 registered nonprofit organizations in the US that are focused on employment. These nonprofits offer employment preparation and placement services, job training, vocational counseling, sheltered workshops, and vocational rehabilitation services. Much like community development, the number of nonprofits focused on employment issues has grown over time, especially in the past thirty years, due to steady streams of funding from the Employment and Training Administration (ETA), a part of the US Department of Labor. Nonprofit job training and workforce development organizations share a close relationship with the federal government, since the government is their primary source of funding. They are also strongly tied to local governments who play an important role in coordinating relevant actors and creating a strategy for using federal workforce monies in local communities.

Laura Bush talks with, from left, Gabriel Flores, Archie Dominguez, and Shirley Torres during a discussion at Homeboy Industries in Los Angeles, April 27, 2005. Homeboys Industries is a job-training program that educates, trains, and finds jobs for at-risk and gang-involved youth

The federal government has a long history of sponsoring jobs programs beginning with the **Works Progress Administration (WPA)** of the 1930s. After the Great Depression, the WPA sought to put Americans back to work through government-paid jobs in infrastructure development. As a carry-over from this program, the Comprehensive Employment and Training Act (CETA) of 1973 was passed by Congress to appropriate funding to train workers, primarily those with low incomes and the long-term unemployed, and place them into jobs in public service.

The WPA was replaced in 1982 by the Job Training Partnership Act (JTPA), which created a stronger role for private businesses in hiring workers who had received job training, rather than government jobs. In 1998, the JTPA was replaced by the **Workforce Investment Act (WIA)** which remains in effect today, and provides the largest source of funding for nonprofit organizations providing workforce development services. There are three key programs of the WIA: (1) adult employment and training; (2) youth employment and training; and (3) dislocated workers' employment and training. These programs had a combined budget of $2.8 billion in 2012.[19] Virtually all of this money is funneled down to local communities and organizations that are working to reduce the unemployment rate by helping people with employment barriers get on the path to self-sufficiency. Although the federal government supplies the funding, nonprofit organizations provide the bulk of the job training and employment support services, though for-profit businesses in the community are also important partners in this process. Nonprofit organizations providing employment services work closely with local businesses to create on-the-job training opportunities and to ensure that skills taught in the classroom and center-based programs match the kinds of skills local employers require.

Nonprofit organizations focused on employment issues vary greatly in the types of services they offer and the populations they serve. Despite this variation, these organizations share the common goal of helping individuals overcome employment barriers and find meaningful work opportunities. There are many types of employment barriers that people face in the US. For example, convicted felons who have been released from prison will face very different employment obstacles than a person who has worked for 35 years in manufacturing but recently lost their job due to outsourcing. Persons with physical or cognitive disabilities face different types of employment challenges than do women transitioning from welfare into the workforce, or senior citizens that must re-enter the workforce to supplement their retirement income. Fortunately, there are nonprofit organizations working in most communities and regions in the US that can assist each of these populations with their employment goals.

There is a great deal of creativity in the programs that address employment and workforce issues. Many nonprofit employment organizations use a **social enterprise** model, meaning that although they have a social purpose or goal they also operate like a business, selling a product or service. For example, Employment Connection in St. Louis, Missouri is a nonprofit that runs a social enterprise called Managed Work Services. Employment Connection "breaks down barriers to self-sufficiency for individuals with limited opportunities including the homeless, ex-offenders, US veterans, high school dropouts, women on welfare, and at-risk youth."[20] Through the Managed Work Services program, the organization develops contracts with local businesses (e.g. hotels, industrial firms, retailers, and restaurants) to place their job trainees into temporary, short-term, and in some cases long-term jobs. Employment Connection prepares people to begin jobs with 40 hours of "soft skills" training, and then places participants into temporary or short-term jobs where they receive on-site support, coaching, and feedback to help improve their prospects for permanent employment. All the revenue that Employment Connections receives through these contracts goes back into the organization and its services, funding new training programs, transportation allowances, counseling programs, career assistance, education and literacy programs, and so on. Examples of nonprofit workforce development organizations that operate social enterprises are quite common, including Inspiration Corporations in Chicago, which runs two successful restaurants (see the opening example of this chapter). Another example is Jewish Vocational Services in Southfield, Michigan, which develops contracts with local businesses for cleaning services. Job trainees work in crews with an employment coach to perform these services, for which the organization gets paid. These social enterprises enable the organization to earn income that can be reinvested in activities that further the social mission.

While most nonprofit employment and training organizations originate with a distinctly local focus through the work of a committed social entrepreneur in the community, there is at least one organization that works nation-wide on job training and workforce development services. Goodwill Industries International Inc. is a familiar name in most US households. While many of you may know it as a convenient place to dispose of old clothing and household items, Goodwill is one of the largest providers of job training and workforce development programs in the US. Goodwill is a 501(c)3 organization providing job training, employment placement, and programs for people with disabilities. It has around 370 sites across the country. While there is indeed a lot of variety among the programs and services offered by these several hundred franchises, Goodwill Industries of Central Arizona, located in Phoenix, is a relatively good representation of the types of services Goodwill provides. In addition to operating several re-sale stores throughout the metro area (that employ some of their trainees), the organization offers a variety of programs to assist various populations in finding employment, including job training for those transitioning from welfare to work, a vocational rehabilitation service for persons with disabilities, and a senior work program for persons over the age of 55 seeking employment. The organization also operates 15 career centers throughout the Phoenix metropolitan area, each offering services that include one-on-one career coaching, access to computers, printers, Internet, phones, and fax machines, resume development, on-site hiring events, job leads, labor market information, computer and customer service skills training, job search strategies, on-the-job training opportunities, and career assessments.[21]

An important question facing community development organizations and workforce development agencies is whether or not these organizations make a difference in society. Are community development organizations effective in reducing economic distress? Do workforce development organizations put people in work, and when they do, are those people earning higher wages than if they had not had the program? The successes and failures of modern day Community Action Agencies have been the subject of extensive analysis,[22,23,24] but there has been much less research evaluating the effectiveness of CBDOs in revitalizing economically distressed communities. There are many case studies and anecdotes to suggest that CBDOs have had a transformative impact on economically disadvantaged individuals and communities, but those cases may not represent the experience of all CBDOs.[25] One study of CBDOs in 58 large US cities offers some promising evidence of CBDO effectiveness, showing that for every $100,000 spent by CBDOs, the number of persons lifted above the poverty line increases by roughly 10 people.[26] This same study found that CBDO expenditures also had a small impact on reducing vacant housing, but had no significant effect on reducing the unemployment rate. It is important to note that this study was conducted in 2010, a year in which unemployment was higher than normal in many cities as a result of the aftermath of the Great Recession. In sum, there is mixed evidence on the effectiveness of CBDOs.

In comparison, there has been extensive evaluation of the effectiveness of federally funded job training programs. In exchange for federal funding, nonprofit (and for-profit) job training providers must collect data on the number of program participants who begin their programs, how many program graduates are placed into jobs, how long it took to get the job, and the type of job. Training providers are also required to follow up with program participants at various intervals after job placement (6 months, 12 months, etc.) in order to track job retention rates. As a result of this extensive data tracking, there is more conclusive evidence about the effectiveness of federally funded workforce development programs. While the findings vary from study to study, the cumulative research on these programs suggests that the net benefits of job training programs out-weigh the costs, meaning that they are both beneficial to the people who participate and a worthwhile use of government money. Box 9.2 describes some of the research that outlines the effectiveness of federal funded job training programs. Research evaluating the WIA job training services also finds positive results from job training. The researchers found that results varied across states, but that participants of WIA adult programs (any service) have a several hundred dollar increase in quarterly earnings, as compared to those who do not participate in job training programs.[27]

While participants of job training programs are not likely to become rich or experience a dramatic increase in standard of living, these programs represent an important part of the solution in reducing unemployment and advancing economic development in many local communities. Moreover, they offer a pathway to jobs and economic opportunity for those in society who face the most serious barriers to employment. While neither community development efforts nor job training programs can be described as major engines fueling the nation's economy, they serve critically important functions by producing small, incremental economic gains at

BOX 9.2 EVALUATING THE EFFECTIVENESS OF FEDERALLY FUNDED JOB TRAINING PROGRAMS

A group of researchers investigated the benefits and costs of the Job Training Partnership Act (JTPA) Title II-A programs. The study was a randomized experiment with 21,000 people from 16 JTPA service areas around the country. Half of the people did not receive job training (the control group). The other half received classroom training, on-the-job training, job search assistance, and other services. The results of the research found that adults who participated in the job training program showed clear gains in income after 30 months. The results also indicate that the program had less of an impact on youth earnings. Women had higher gains than men. Women who received job training earned on average 9.6% more per year than comparable women who did not complete the program. Men who received job training earned 5.3% more per year than men who do not receive job training. The study also showed those who received on-the-job training and job search assistance earn substantially more than those who only received classroom-based training. Job training program participants also had higher rates of high school diploma/GED obtainment. Among women job training participants, 32% had a high school diploma or GED at the end of the 30 month evaluation period, while only 20% of women who did not participate in job training obtained a diploma. The results were similar for men, with an 8% increase in HS diploma/GED obtainment for men participants versus non-participants.[28]

Bloom, Howard S, Larry L. Orr, Steven H. Bell, George Cave, Fred Doolittle, Winston Lin, and Johannes M. Bos. 1997. The Benefits and Costs of JTPA Title II-A Programs: Key Findings from the National Job Training Partnership Act Study. *The Journal of Human Resources*, 32(3): 549–576.

the local level, working to repair weak economies from the bottom up. Moreover, they serve an important role in offering hope for a better future to individuals and communities that have been excluded from the benefits of economic prosperity.

Business Attraction, Development, and Promotion

Business attraction, promotion, and development organizations are an important group of nonprofit organizations that are actively engaged in economic development efforts. In contrast to community development and job training nonprofits which aim to spread the benefits of economic development to low-income individuals and communities, business attraction, development, and promotion organizations primarily exist to help corporations, entrepreneurs, developers, and local government officials to attract businesses to a city or region. Local government officials have an incentive to attract new businesses to the city and to maintain existing ones in order to keep and grow jobs within the community and to increase the city's tax base. Local government officials have a number of tools at their disposal to help attract businesses to their communities including **tax abatements** (reductions or rebates in the level of a company's or individual's tax rate), **business improvement districts** (areas where business pay an additional tax to fund projects that serve that district), tax credits, and negotiations about infrastructure building. As such, nonprofits representing business attraction, development, and promotion often work closely with local government officials.

In some cases, local government officials found these business attraction, promotion, and development organizations and then retained a role in the governance or day-to-day operations of the nonprofit. In fact, many business development organizations have been incorporated outside of the public's view, their formation driven through private negotiations between local public officials and private entrepreneurs.[29,30] We shall examine a few examples of nonprofit organizations that focus on business attraction, development, and promotion, beginning with business attraction. It is however, important to note that nonprofits engaged in serving the business community sometimes focus on more than one, or even all, of these tasks.

There are thousands of nonprofit organizations that work directly with local government to attract businesses. A few examples include World Business Chicago (WBC), Winston-Salem Business Inc., and Operation New Birmingham. World Business Chicago's mission is "coordinating business retention, attraction and expansion efforts in order to spur and accelerate economic growth. WBC raises Chicago's profile as a premier business destination and serves as resource for companies."[31] Founded in the year 2000, WBC is a 501c(3) nonprofit organization with annual revenues of about $27.3 million. The current chairman of the board of directors for the organization is Chicago's Mayor, Rahm Emanuel; the rest of the board is comprised primarily of CEOs of Chicago's largest corporations and most prestigious financial firms. The organization is staffed with personnel who are experts in economic development, real estate, finance, and marketing. WBC has a business-friendly website highlighting quality of life in the city, research and statistics on the local labor market, information about financial incentives available to entice businesses into locating in the city, and a site selector map to allow firms to investigate possible locations for their business, including vacant commercial buildings and locations ready for development or redevelopment.[32]

Similarly, Winston-Salem Business Inc.'s (WSBI) mission is "to recruit new businesses to Winston-Salem and Forsyth County to facilitate growth and economic diversification. As new businesses and industries continue to locate in this area, residents will enjoy an enhanced lifestyle *(benefiting from better job opportunities)* and expanding services *(generated from a broader tax base)*."[33] WSBI was founded in 2003 and operates in close partnership with local government. WSBI serves as a business development resource by providing information and linkages to venture capital financing. Another nonprofit founded in 1994 is Operation New Birmingham, a public-private partnership between the City of Birmingham and the private business community. ONB has 501c(3) nonprofit status and its mission is

> the development, historic preservation, and promotion of the city center of Birmingham, Alabama with dual missions of economic development in the City Center and the promotion of racial harmony in the Birmingham community. ONB is working to make the City Center the #1 choice for business, living, healthcare, education and the arts and entertainment in the metro area.[34]

In addition to business attraction, some nonprofit economic development organizations focus on business development. Activities of these nonprofits might include assistance with developing business plans, acting as business incubators, providing technical assistance to businesses, providing small business loans and assistance in accessing start-up capital, managing revolving loan funds, sponsoring individual development accounts, and operating microenterprise loan funds. The Technology, Entrepreneurship, and Development (TED) Center in Delray Beach, Florida illustrates the type of work carried out by business development nonprofits. Founded in 1997, the TED Center has a stated mission of "supporting the successful development of entrepreneurs, small companies, and start-up businesses."[35] The TED Center offers a variety of business support services and resources designed to increase the likelihood that small businesses and start-up companies will be successful. In addition to helping entrepreneurs access venture funding, the TED Center aids business start-ups by providing instruction, training, and technical support. These supports include "direct business assistance, such as website development, the creation of collateral material, marketing and public relations, and financial management services".[36]

The third type of nonprofit economic development organization promotes businesses. Business promoters play an especially important role in tourism and enhancing the experience of visitors to a city or region. Perhaps the most widely known and visible organizations within this category are Chambers of Commerce. There are more than 22,000 registered Chambers of Commerce in local communities throughout the US. Their activities and services vary from place to place, yet share a common purpose to advertise and promote local businesses, and to bring together local business owners to network, strategize, and to speak with one voice on local and state policies that affect the business community.[37] Nonprofit organizations registered as Chambers of Commerce range in number from 72 in small states such as Delaware to as many as 2,142 in California. Nationwide, Chambers of Commerce reported combined revenues of nearly $15 billion in 2013. They provide useful services for both individuals and organized groups planning travel to cities, business conventions, professional association meetings, sporting events, and so on.

With the exception of Chambers of Commerce, business attraction, development, and promotion nonprofits represent a newer generation of nonprofits focused on economic development. Recall that many of the community development and job training organizations that focus on economic solutions for lower-income individuals were founded in the 1970s. In comparison, nonprofits focused on business growth have been founded more recently, in the 1990s and 2000s. The number of these second-generation nonprofit economic development organizations has grown dramatically in the past few decades,[38] and, despite their relative invisibility to the public, they now overshadow community development organizations in terms of economic capacity. While community-based development nonprofits comprise approximately two thirds of all 501c(3) nonprofit economic development organizations registered with the IRS, they account for only 43% of all assets in the nonprofit economic development subsector. The remaining 57% of assets in the nonprofit economic development subsector are collectively concentrated in nonprofits that focus on business and industry, real estate development, and so on.[39] A recent study of nonprofit economic development organizations in six midwestern states documented dramatic growth rates in these second-generation nonprofit economic development organizations.[40]

Many of the activities that business attraction, development, and promotion organizations carry out used to be primarily conducted by local governments. There has been a steady shift of these activities from local governments to these types of nonprofit organizations. One theory suggests that, after the 1970s, these nonprofit economic development organizations emerged as vehicles for institutionalizing the values of private interests and furthering the interests of private developers and business owners.[41] Business attraction strategies such as tax abatements and other location incentives have been the subject of great criticism, as studies show they often do not produce the expected economic gains, and instead divert money away from needed local programs and services.[42] Thus while the use of tax abatements and other location incentives often does not represent a good deal for the public, local government officials typically feel compelled to use these incentives anyway in order to compete with neighboring governments. Since the decision to use these incentives often results in contentious public debate, perhaps local governments are increasingly using nonprofit organizations as vehicles for carrying out their economic development plans without having to face opposition or controversy. Since businesses and developers gain from these policies, they are an instrumental part of the effort to form the nonprofit and may play a continued role in its governance after the organization is established.

Some research suggests, but does not directly prove, that private entrepreneurs create nonprofit development organizations to further their own self-interests. A study of 445 US counties found a significant linkage between the number of new nonprofit development organizations incorporated in a county during the 1990s and the presence of finance, insurance, and real estate firms.[43] Moreover, there is some evidence that wealthier local governments have more nonprofit activity related to business attraction, development, and promotion. While revenues from community-based development organizations remain concentrated in higher poverty cities, wealthier cities have higher concentrations of revenue generated by nonprofit business assistance organizations and nonprofit real estate organizations.[44] A separate study found that cities with higher per capita spending had higher rates of incorporating nonprofit economic development organizations during the 1990s. These studies suggest that wealthier jurisdictions pursue the use of nonprofit organizations to further their economic development goals related to business attraction and development, which has advantages for both local government officials and private entrepreneurs, but may not provide the same advantages to the general public, or the poor and underemployed.

Nonprofit economic development organizations exist to serve a wide variety of interests and diverse constituencies, including both aspiring and already successful business entrepreneurs, commercial, industrial, and residential developers, hotel and restaurant associations, realtors, investors, lenders, and local government officials, among others. Often a city's or state's rationale for granting tax-exempt status is based upon the expectation that a nonprofit will produce public value. Some nonprofit organizations may not provide much public value, but, by mere virtue of their legal status, they are still exempt from paying taxes to the government. The cozy relationship between many development organizations and local governments raises questions for the public. If these organizations are too closely controlled or influenced by private entrepreneurs, then it becomes less likely to be perceived as serving the public interest. Unlike first-generation economic development organizations such as CBDOs and workforce development providers, which have been rigorously evaluated and generally provide services to community members in need, this newer generation of business-oriented nonprofit organizations has not been closely scrutinized. It is unclear to what extent these newer nonprofit economic development organizations produce public value, and therefore it remains important to examine the growth, governance, and outcomes of these organizations in the future.

Summary

Nonprofit organizations make important contributions to the US economy. First, nonprofit organizations employ more than 9% of the nation's workforce, primarily in the fields of healthcare, education, and social services. Second, the nonprofit sector did relatively well during the Great Recession, adding more jobs than both government and the for-profit sectors throughout the first decade of the new millennium. While nonprofit sector employment has grown steadily over time, it is unclear whether this rate of growth will be sustained in the future. Third, the nonprofit sector contributes to local economies and communities through two special categories of organizations: (1) job training and community development organizations; and (2) nonprofits focused on business attraction, development, and promotion.

Nonprofit job training and community development organizations provide a pathway to jobs and economic opportunity for those in society who face the most serious barriers to employment. They receive the bulk of their funding from federal grants for workforce development and job training. While these types of organizations are generally not considered major drivers of local economic growth, they produce small, incremental economic gains at the local level that often have a cumulative effect on local economic conditions, repairing weak economies from the bottom up. Nonprofit organizations carrying out activities related to business attraction, development, and promotion also play an important role in local economies, although their work occurs somewhat outside the view of the general public. Many times these organizations serve as an extension of a local government economic development office, and are sometimes created by city officials perhaps for the purpose of pursuing economic agendas without the interference or debate from the public. Nonprofit business attraction, development, and promotion organizations often exist to serve the interests of business: interests which may or may not be consistent with the interests of community residents at the bottom of the economic ladder.

KEY TERMS

- Business improvement districts
- Community Action Agencies
- Community Action Programs
- Community-Based Development Organization (CBDO)
- Community development
- Community Development Corporation (CDC)
- Economic development
- Maximum feasible participation
- Microenterprise
- Political efficacy
- Social enterprise
- Tax abatements
- Vocational training / vocational skills
- Workforce Investment Act
- Works Progress Administration (WPA)

DISCUSSION QUESTIONS

1. What are the most common types of employment in the nonprofit sector? What are some of the reasons nonprofit health, education, and social services organizations might be losing market share to for-profits providing the same services? How can nonprofit organizations in these industries maintain their place in the service economy?

2. Read Box 9.1, which outlines two different types of CBDOs: Wayne Metro Community Action Agency (CAA) and Mission Housing Community Development (MHCD). What are some of the important differences between these two CBDOs? Which type of CBDO do you think has the potential to be the most successful? If you were developing a CBDO for your community, which approach would you choose? And why?

3. If you were seeking nursing home care for an aging parent with serious health issues, would you choose a nonprofit or for-profit organization to provide the care? What factors would you consider in making your decision? (Hint: You may wish to refer back to the discussion on information asymmetries in Chapter 4.)

4. Do you think it is appropriate for nonprofit organizations to perform activities associated with attracting, developing, and promoting businesses in local communities? Why or why not?

5. What are some of the implications of local governments pursuing their economic development goals through a nonprofit organization, particularly those related to business growth? Why would local governments want to do this? Discuss the pros and cons of this arrangement from the vantage point of three different groups: citizens, businesses, and local government officials (elected or otherwise).

Websites

Inspiration Corporation, founded by Lisa Nigro, a former Chicago Police Officer: http://www.inspirationcorp.org

Inspiration Kitchens: www.inspirationkitchens.org

US Department of Housing and Urban Development: http://portal.hud.gov/hud portal/HUD?src=/about/hud_history

Videos

Inspiration Corporation Video. Uploaded on May 28, 2008. In an atmosphere of dignity and respect, Inspiration Corporation helps people who are affected by homelessness and poverty to improve their lives and increase self-sufficiency through the provision of social services, employment training and placement, and housing. Each year, Inspiration Corporation helps more than 2,000 individuals who are characterized by chronic homelessness, unemployment or underemployment, mental illness or substance abuse, and social isolation.

http://www.youtube.com/watch?v=jgpfLJkRHXY

Notes

1   Blakely, Edward J. and Nancy Green Leigh. 2010. *Planning Local Economic Development: Theory and Practice*, 4th edition. Thousand Oaks, CA: Sage Publications, Inc.
2   The Urban Institute. http://www.urban.org/nonprofits/ Accessed February 18, 2014.
3   The Urban Institute.
4   Salamon, L. M., W. S. Sokolowski, and S. L. Geller. 2012. *Holding the Fort: Nonprofit Employment in a Decade of Turmoil*. The Johns Hopkins Nonprofit Economic Data Project. Employment Bulletin #39. Johns Hopkins Center for Civil Society Studies. January 2012.
5   Salamon, Sokolowski, and Geller (2012).
6   Salamon, Sokolowski, and Geller (2012).
7   Salamon, Sokolowski, and Geller (2012).
8   Salamon, Sokolowski, and Geller (2012).
9   Peterson, Paul E. 1981. *City Limits*. Chicago, IL: University of Chicago Press.
10 Blakely, Edward J. and Nancy Green Leigh (2010).
11 Vidal, Avis C. 2002. *Housing and Community Development*, in Lester M. Salamon (ed.), *The State of Nonprofit America*. Washington, DC: Brookings Institution Press, in collaboration with the Aspen Institute.
12 Bowles, Melanie. 2008. *Community Development Challenge Report*. Produced by Community Development Foundation for Communities and Local Government. Accessed February 19, 2014 at http://cdf.org.uk/content/research/publications
13 Blakely, Edward J. 1994. *Planning Local Economic Development: Theory and Practice*, 2nd edition. Thousand Oaks, CA: Sage Publications, Inc., p. 323.
14 Guidestar.org. http://www.guidestar.org/organizations/38-1976979/wayne-metropolitan-community-action-agency.aspx. Accessed February 21, 2014.
15 Mission Housing Development Corporation. http://www.missionhousing.org/01_about_our-mission.php. Accessed February 21, 2014.
16 Swanstrom, Todd and Julia Koschinsky. 2000. Rethinking the Partnership Model of Government-Nonprofit Relations: The Case of Community Development, Chapter 4 in *Nonprofits in Urban America*, edited by Richard C. Hula and Cynthia Jackson-Elmoore. Westport, CT: Quorum Books.

17   US Department of Housing and Urban Development. Accessed February 21, 2014 at http://portal.hud.gov/hudportal/HUD?src=/program_offices/comm_planning/communitydevelopment/programs

18   US Department of Housing and Urban Development.

19   US Department of Labor. Accessed February 21, 2014 at http://www.dol.gov/dol/budget/2013/bib.htm#eta

20   Employment Connection. Accessed February 22, 2014 at http://www.employmentstl.org/

21   Goodwill of Central Arizona. Accessed February 22, 2014 at http://www.goodwillaz.org/job-training/#career-centers-anchor

22   Morone, James. 1990. *The Democratic Wish*. New York: Basic Books.

23   Marris, Peter and Martin Rein. 1982. *Dilemmas of Social Reform: Poverty and Community Action in the United States*, 2nd edition. Chicago: University of Chicago Press.

24   Browning, Rufus P., Dale Rogers Marshall, and David H. Tabb. 1984. *Protest is Not Enough: The Struggle of Blacks and Hispanics for Equality in Urban Politics*. Berkeley, CA: University of California Press.

25   Rubin, Herbert. 2000. Renewing Hope within Neighborhoods of Despair: The Community Based Development Model. New York: State University of New York Press.

26   Wright, Nathaniel. 2010. Revitalizing American Cities: Do Community Development Corporations Matter? Working paper of the RGK Center for Philanthropy and Community Service at the University of Texas-Austin.

27   Heinrich, Carolyn J., Peter R. Mueser, and Kenneth R. Troske. 2008. Workforce Investment Act Non-Experimental Net Impact Evaluation. IMPAQ International, LLC. Accessed February 22, 2014 at http://wdr.doleta.gov/research/FullText_Documents/Workforce%20Investment%20Act%20Non-Experimental%20Net%20Impact%20Evaluation%20-%20Final%20Report.pdf

28   Bloom, Howard S, Larry L. Orr, Steven H. Bell, George Cave, Fred Doolittle, Winston Lin, and Johannes M. Bos. 1997. The Benefits and Costs of JTPA Title II-A Programs: Key Findings from the National Job Training Partnership Act Study. *The Journal of Human Resources*, 32(3): 549–576.

29   Bauroth, Nicholas. 2008. Explanations for the Proliferation of Economic Development Corporations Across North Dakota and South Dakota. *Online Journal of Rural Research and Poverty*, 3(5): 1–20.

30   Bauroth, Nicholas. 2009. Quietly, A New Institution Arises: The Proliferation of Non-Profit Economic Development Corporations across Six Midwestern States. Paper presented at the Midwest Political Science Association.

31   Guidestar. http://www.guidestar.org/organizations/36–4313685/world-business-chicago.aspx. Accessed February 23, 2014.

32   World Business Chicago. Accessed February 19, 2014 at http://www.worldbusinesschicago.com/services

33   http://www.winstonsalembusinessinc.com/aboutwsbi-overview.htm. Accessed February 19, 2014.

34   http://www.birmingham365.org/org/detail/220157211/Operation_New_Birmingham. Accessed February 19, 2014.

35   The TED Center. Accessed February 23, 2014 at http://www.tedcenter.org/
36   http://www.tedcenter.org/
37   National Center for Charitable Statistics Custom Report Builder. Accessed February 23, 2014 at http://nccs.urban.org/
38   Bauroth (2009).
39   LeRoux, Kelly. 2012. Who Benefits from Nonprofit Economic Development? Examining the Revenue Distribution of Tax-Exempt Development Organizations among U.S. Cities. *Journal of Urban Affairs*, 34(1): 65–80.
40   Bauroth (2009).
41   Bauroth (2009).
42   Reese, Laura A. 1998. Sharing the Benefits of Economic Development: What Cities Use Type II Policies? *Urban Affairs Review*, 33(5): 686–711.
43   Bauroth (2009).
44   LeRoux (2012).

SECTION IV
NONPROFIT SECTOR CHALLENGES & OPPORTUNITIES

10

THE FUTURE OF NONPROFITS
AND CIVIL SOCIETY

CHAPTER LEARNING OBJECTIVES

By the end of this chapter, students will be able to:

1. Identify and describe key demographic shifts underway in America, explaining the implications of these trends for the nonprofit sector

2. Identify sources of fiscal stress and reasons for uncertainty in government spending, and describe how these factors affect nonprofit organizations

3. Describe some public concerns with regard to nonprofit transparency and accountability

4. Explain how increased market competition and pressures for performance may constrain the nonprofit sector in the future

5. Identify some of the factors contributing to a blurring of sector boundaries and future implications of this trend for nonprofits

6. Speculate about some of the ways technology and social media may shape the nonprofit organizations in the future

---

Introduction

In earlier chapters of this book, we learned that the organizations making up the formal nonprofit sector are quite diverse, encompassing groups that

MEETING MENTAL HEALTH NEEDS IN ONE COMMUNITY

Julie McMarty recognized a desperate need in her community—there were many people suffering with mental illnesses who lacked adequate mental healthcare. Public mental health services in her state were so underfunded that the US Department of Justice (DOJ) had sued the state after a number of patients in psychiatric hospitals had died as a result of abuse and neglect. She called together several families of adults suffering from serious mental illness to see if there was something they could do outside of "the system."

A practicing healthcare attorney and administrator, Julie decided it was time to do something about this problem. She formed Sunny Meadows, a nonprofit psychiatric services organization, through which she hoped to bring "best practices" in mental health treatment to her community. Her services started with a monthly electronic newsletter, which grew to a distribution of nearly 2,000 people in two years. Although she had some success in raising money, her lucky break came when she got a phone call from a man whom she had been advising about how to help manage his adult son's difficulties with depression. So grateful was the man for the help Julie had provided, he made a seven-figure donation to Sunny Meadows.

With this investment, Julie was able to take the Sunny Meadows to the next level. Now, Sunny Meadows had the capacity to provide services and operate an outpatient "community mental health center," offering outpatient psychiatric, nursing, and counseling programs. More important, Sunny Meadows was getting results; Julie felt deeply rewarded to see transformative changes in patients, who had been "in the system" for many years, who finally began to make real progress on their road to recovery.

While the private donation money was being used to get these services off the ground, Julie was taking the necessary steps to get registered as a provider with Medicare, which would enable Sunny Meadows to bill private insurance carriers for the mental healthcare services they were providing. Medicare is a government-funded program that guarantees access to health insurance for Americans aged 65 and older and younger people with disabilities. Medicaid, not to be confused with Medicare, is a government-funded program that insures people of all ages who are low-income and lack the resources to pay for healthcare.

Sunny Meadows did a financial analysis, and determined their best course of action was to get Medicare qualified (insurance for people over 65 and disabled persons), and then get reimbursed for the services provided to Medicare-covered clients. Since working with Medicaid (insurance for low-income individuals) proved to be too

continued

complicated, and would not allow the agency to cover its own costs, it was determined that the agency would use its funds, raised through private donations, to cover those with Medicaid or no ability to pay.

Careful financial projections showed this formula would work. However, Julie encountered an unexpected glitch when she could not cut through the red tape with Medicare to get Sunny Meadow's provider billing number. Medicare staff had told her it would take six to eight months to get the provider number. After her application had been pending 18 months, and after being granted a special exception because of the lack of comparable services in the area, Medicare told Julie they would not do any new provider numbers until the DOJ lawsuit with the state mental health system was settled. Without a Medicare provider number, many patients' insurance companies would not enroll Sunny Meadows, leaving the agency to rely exclusively on private donations to operate, which was simply not feasible. Even though Julie was raising about $50,000 a month for "start-up funding" from private sources, the high costs of the kinds of healthcare services Sunny Meadows was providing made the private funding model unsustainable.

Julie and the Sunny Meadows stakeholders agreed it was not a responsible use of charitable resources to continue offering services. In a last ditch effort to save the program that had been so successful in treating persons with serious mental health issues, she approached the three local hospitals that have inpatient treatment programs: a nonprofit teaching hospital, a for-profit psychiatric hospital, and a regional state mental hospital. None of these hospitals offered the kind of outpatient treatment Sunny Meadows provided. Julie took her financial calculations to the nonprofit and for-profit hospitals showing them they could net several hundred thousand dollars per year operating Sunny Meadows' program as a hospital-based outpatient program. With the Affordable Care Act just passed and the future uncertain, none of the potential hospital partners would take the risk. After a few months of these fruitless negotiations, Sunny Meadows was forced to close its doors.

exist to provide mental health, protect animals, save the environment, feed the hungry, conduct scientific research, promote specific religious beliefs, represent the professional interests of lawyers, teachers, doctors, and other types of workers, and an assortment of other purposes. Despite this diversity, nonprofit organizations share a common set of characteristics including distinct legal status, a mission-directed orientation, voluntary governance, reliance on voluntary resources including volunteers as well as charitable donations, and reliance on diverse and changing sources of revenue. Although nonprofit organizations share some similarities with public and for-profit organizations, it is this set of common characteristics that sets nonprofit organizations apart as a distinct sector in our society and in our economy. Additionally, nonprofits fill critical social gaps and unmet service needs that the public (government) and the for-profit sector cannot or choose not to fulfill.

Throughout our discussion, we have examined the multifaceted social, political, and economic roles played by nonprofit organizations in America. In Chapters 4, 5, and 6 we discovered how nonprofit organizations form a key part of the social fabric of American communities, helping to build social capital and providing outlets for volunteerism and giving, all of which promote a more civil society. In Chapters 7 and 8, we saw how nonprofits enhance pluralism and promote a healthy democracy, shaping American public policy, politics, and social movements through political representation, mobilization, and education. In Chapter 9 we learned that nonprofits fill an important role in the economy, not only as employers of millions of Americans, but also through the thousands of job training, workforce development, and economic and community development programs in cities and neighborhoods throughout the country.

As the preceding chapters have suggested, the US nonprofit sector is robust, multifaceted, and a vital fixture in American civil society. Yet perhaps the term "fixture" is not entirely accurate, for it masks the dynamism of the sector. Much like the rest of society, the nonprofit sector is not static, but constantly evolving and ever-changing. There are numerous trends, current and emerging, that will both affect and be affected by nonprofit organizations in the years ahead. This chapter examines six of these trends:

1. Demographic shifts
2. Fiscal stress and uncertainty in government spending
3. Increased demands for transparency and accountability
4. Market competition and pressures for performance
5. Blending and blurring of sector distinctions
6. Rise of technology and social media

These current and emerging trends create both significant challenges and opportunities for nonprofits and civil society that we explore throughout this chapter.

Demographic Shifts

Thanks to the US Census Bureau and related federal agencies responsible for collecting data on the American population, we know that several critical changes are occurring with regard to US demographics—characteristics and qualities of individuals or groups of people including age, sex, race, income, etcetera. Three important demographic shifts are occurring in the US, which will greatly affect the future of the nonprofit sector. These demographic changes include growing diversity and immigration, the aging, or "graying," of America, and rising income inequality along with the suburbanization of poverty. Each of these trends has important implications for the nonprofit sector.

Diversity and Immigration

The American population continues to grow each year, through births and immigration. In the US about four million babies are born each year.[1] In 1991, the highest birthrate was among non-Hispanic blacks, followed by Hispanics, Native American Indians, and non-Hispanic whites. By 2011, Hispanics had the highest birthrate, followed by non-Hispanic blacks. Thus, there has been a slight change in the ethnic distribution of new births in the US. In addition to births, the population in the United States changes due to immigration. At least one million new immigrants come to permanently reside in the US each year.[2] With immigration and higher birthrates among Hispanic Americans, there have been significant shifts in the racial and ethnic composition of the American population. Figure 10.1 illustrates the change in US population by race and ethnicity from 1970 through 2010. According to data collected by the US Census, in 1970 88% of Americans described themselves as white/Caucasian. In 2010, 72% reported being white/Caucasian. The population of African Americans, or blacks, has remained steady at around 12% from 1980 to 2000. In 2010, Asians made up 5% of the population, as compared to only 2% in 1980. The largest demographic shift has been the steady growth of those who identify as Hispanic and Latino, who in 2010 made up 16% of the US population, up from around 4% in 1970.

Figure 10.1 illustrates the changes in the US population among the largest ethnic and racial minority groups: black, Asian, and Hispanic/Latino. While each of these groups make up less than 20% of the US population combined in 1970, by 2010 these groups combined made up closer to 30% of the US population. Figure 10.1 illustrates a steady growth

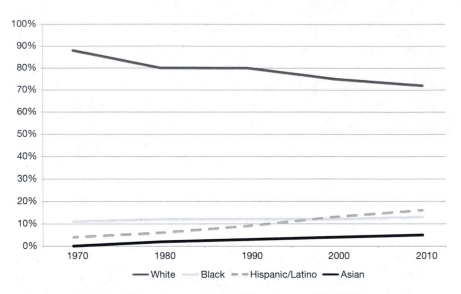

FIGURE 10.1 Racial and Ethnic Composition of US Population, 1970–2010.

Source: US Census, http://www.census.gov/population/www/documentation/twps0056/twps0056.html, http://www.census.gov/prod/2001pubs/c2kbr01–1.pdf, http://www.census.gov/prod/cen2010/briefs/c2010br-02.pdf

in Asian and Hispanic/Latino populations as a proportion of the US population. Based on projections, the US will become "**majority-minority**" by 2042, meaning that current groups now comprising racial minorities will come to make up a majority of the American population: that is, there will be more non-whites than whites in the US, though there will not be one majority ethnic or racial group. Demographers estimate that by 2042, the US will be 30% Latino (almost double today's proportion), while whites will make up 46% of the population, compared with 66% today. As of the 2010 census, whites are no longer the majority in four states (California, Texas, New Mexico, and Hawaii), and 11% of all US counties are majority-minority with another seven very close to the tipping point.[3] Given that white Americans are having fewer children, and many of the live births in the US are born to immigrants each year, the preschool population will cross the "majority-minority" threshold by 2019.[4] In fact, white children are no longer the majority in 31 major metro areas in the US.

Racial and ethnic demographic changes have numerous implications for the nonprofit sector. First, the diversity of American society ensures the need for diverse organizations to service those populations. Second, immigrants often require specialized social services including foreign language assistance and visa and other citizenship services. Ethnic and immigrant service organizations already provide important services for newcomers, helping them to assimilate into American society while celebrating and honoring their heritage and providing a community space for people who share ethnic or national origins to associate and network. Nonprofit organizations like the Asian Counseling and Referral Service, the Polish American Association, and Catholic Charities' Hispanic Apostolate Community Services provide assistance navigating the legal system, English language classes, housing, job placement, along with help applying for citizenship or work visas, registering to vote, accessing transportation, and so on. These organizations will continue to play an important role in aiding new immigrants in their transition into American culture, and are likely to become even more important as the immigrant population in the US continues to grow.

Shifts in racial and ethnic composition also suggest that nonprofit organizations that offer services to the public, from zoos to museums to health and human service providers, must make greater efforts to deliver their services with an eye toward cultural sensitivity and accessibility for a more diverse population of Americans. For example, according to the 2010 US Census, 82% of Americans over the age of five years spoke only English at home. By 2011 this had declined to 79%, indicating an increasing need for foreign-language services in the US.[5] Some nonprofits have already done the necessary work to ensure accessibility of their services to non-English speakers, while many others need to begin taking steps toward converting client and patron communications, including social media, and services into Chinese, Spanish, and other languages, as appropriate. Many nonprofits specialize in providing bilingual services, for their immigrant clientele, but also as a core mission, for example providing bilingual services at emergency rooms, doctor's offices, or at social service agencies. Some nonprofits will also likely need to add or increase the number of bilingual staff in the workplace as the immigrant population grows in the US.

And on that note, perhaps the greatest implication of immigration and the coming "majority-minority" for the nonprofit sector is the need for greater diversity within the nonprofit workforce and among nonprofit leaders and boards. Today's nonprofit workforce is roughly 82% white and only 14% of board members nationwide are people of color.[6] Some argue that the fact that nonprofit staff and boards do not adequately reflect the demographics of the public they serve is problematic. The institutions providing these services are more likely to be viewed as trustworthy and their services more fully utilized when the staff and leadership of these organizations are racially reflective of the communities and clients they serve. At the board level, diversity adds not only substantive value to the decision-making and governance process of nonprofit organizations, but also carries symbolic importance, signaling to clients and community stakeholders the organization's commitment to diversity and representation. Thus, nonprofit organizations may need to make greater efforts to diversify their staff and boards in the coming years if they are to maintain their legitimacy in the eyes of the public.

Nonprofit organizations must evolve to meet the needs of society as it continues to become increasingly diverse along racial and ethnic charac-teristics. Growing numbers of immigrants will challenge nonprofit organ-izations to tailor their services to the variety of clients that they serve. These challenges may include cultural awareness about various groups, but also language barriers. As civil society becomes more diverse, so too must nonprofit organizations, recruiting more diverse employees, leadership, and board members. Successful nonprofits will be those that monitor and anticipate the ever-changing needs of those they serve and the communities in which they work.

Aging of the Population

Thanks to longer average lifespans and decreased birthrates, America will become significantly grayer in the coming years. Already the US population is seeing a slow shift toward aging and retirement. For example, in 1970, 38% of the US population was under the age of 20; by 2010, only 25% of the population was in this youngest group. Meanwhile, the percentage of Americans over the age of 50 has risen from 24% in 1970 to 32% in 2010. Graph 10.2 shows the gradual aging of the American population by decade. Looking at each age group, over time (across the bars), we see that the proportion of Americans in the older age groups is increasing, while the proportion of younger groups is shrinking over time. The shift from a younger population in 1970 toward a larger proportion of older Americans in 2010 is referred to as the graying of America. This trend is

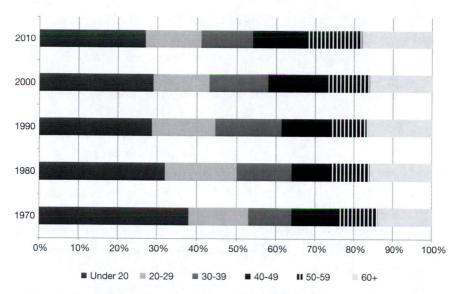

FIGURE 10.2 Percentage of Americans by Age Cohort, 1970–2010.

Source: US Census Notes. 1970 estimates are based on a slightly different formula than 1980–2010, because military persons living overseas are included in the 1970 calculation.

explained by lower birthrates and a steady increase in the life expectancy of Americans. As of 2010, the Centers for Disease Control (CDC) estimates the average American life expectancy to be 78.7 years, which is up from 77.0 in 2000, 75.4 in 1990, 73.7 in 1980, and 70.8 in 1970.[7] It is estimated that the senior population in the US will grow by 36% overall from 2010 to 2020, and by as much as 50% in some of the states during this time period.[8]

"Senior citizens" as a demographic group encompass a wide range of ages and individuals with different kinds of needs. The **Baby Boomers,** people who were born at the end of World War II when there was a great increase in the nation's birthrate, differ from previous retired generations in important ways, including the fact that they possess more education, have had more women in the labor force, and are more likely to occupy professional and managerial positions. This rapidly growing group of "younger" retirees (65–74) need fewer medical and social services, but may present different types of challenges and demands on nonprofit organizations. Among these younger and more "well off" seniors, many are in very good health and have a desire to continue working beyond retirement. These retirees who are not yet ready to retire offer a new set of prospective volunteers for the nonprofit sector. Not only are they eager to be active, they bring with them a set of important professional skills from their time in the workforce. Moreover, these newer retirees come from a generation where both men and women were active in the workforce, thus there are a larger number of retirees that nonprofits can draw upon in volunteer recruitment.

While nonprofits have the opportunity to benefit from these well-educated, active retirees, they also face the challenge of serving a growing elderly population. Individuals over 75 are less likely to be volunteering for nonprofits and more likely to be requiring the services of nonprofit organizations. Seniors over 75 years old made up 6% of the population in 2010 as compared to 4.4% in 1980. Seniors will experience deteriorating health as a result of age, and this is especially true among those over the age of 75. Given the projected growth of the senior population, nonprofit organizations providing services to seniors and the aged are likely to grow over the coming decade, as demand for their services increases along with reliable streams of income from government (Medicare) or other private health insurance carried by seniors. Senior centers, nursing homes, hospice programs, assisted living, long-term care, and adult day care facilities are just a few of the many types of nonprofits that will face increased demand for services in near future. Moreover, growth in the aging population also signals the likelihood of growth in specialized medical services such as geriatric psychiatry, and investment in research on diseases of the aged (dementia, Alzheimers, etc.).

While the aging of the population creates new pressures on certain parts of the nonprofit sector, and creates increased demands for elder services, it also presents an opportunity for the nonprofit sector in terms of increased prospects for charitable bequests and legacy gifts. As the saying goes, the only certain things in life are death and taxes, and while many choose to leave all of their money and possessions to surviving children and relatives, some will choose to make a substantial gift to one or more organizations representing causes they hope to leave a lasting impact upon. Nonprofit organizations that will be successful in the future will adapt to take advantage of the well-educated men and women who are retired but not ready to leave the workforce, provide services to the elderly and aging communities, and work to increase donations and financial contributions from this growing demographic.

Poverty, Inequality, and Suburbanization of Poverty

Suburban America grew in the 1950s, as middle class and upper class families moved to the edges of cities, seeking larger homes, large yards, and distance from the crowds and chaos of the city. The movement to the suburbs continued for decades, often leaving urban areas as centers for those who could not afford to move away: immigrants, lower-income families, and working class Americans. Today, as cities are reviving, there is a reversal of this movement. Now young people, professionals, and even families are moving back to the cities, seeking the diversity and convenience of city living. The resulting influx of people and wealth into American cities has resulted in a new, growing trend of suburban poverty.

The mythical image of the suburbs as a haven to which people escape the social ills of the inner-city has been shattered by 21st century realities of rapidly rising suburban poverty rates. Suburban communities in the country's largest metropolitan areas saw their low-income population grow by 25% between 2000 and 2008, a rate of almost five times faster than the growth of low-income populations in urban areas. As a result, by 2008, large suburbs were home to 1.5 million more people living below the poverty level than the central cities, which are home to almost one third of the nation's poor overall. Between 2000 and 2008, large suburbs saw the fastest growing low-income populations across community types and the greatest increase in the share of the population living under 200% of the poverty level.[9] While this trend accelerated during the **Great Recession** of 2009, demographers note that the growth of poverty in the suburbs was well underway by the turn of the millennium.

A related trend with similar implications for nonprofit organizations is that of rising income inequality in America. By 2008, more than 30% of the nation's population fell below 200% of the **federal poverty level**. The federal poverty level refers to the guidelines set annually by the US government to calculate poverty thresholds for varying family sizes for administrative purposes, including the qualification for government benefits. While the overall poverty rate, the proportion of Americans living below the poverty threshold, for all Americans was reported at 10.5% in the 2010 census, the rate varies across demographic groups, and goes as high as 46.5% for female-headed households with one or more children.[10]

In addition to an increased number of those below the poverty level, those at the bottom of the income ladder seem increasingly likely to stay there. While we often hear people lamenting the "disappearing middle class" in the media or in casual conversation, new evidence confirms that the American population is indeed permanently sorting into two halves: the "haves and have-nots." A 2013 study revealed that over the past two decades there has been a rise in permanent inequality in America, meaning that the advantaged are becoming better off ,while those less fortunate are becoming worse off.[11] It is important to note that these inequalities were studied over two decades, and are not the result of temporary income fluctuations due to loss of a job one year, or temporarily falling on hard times. Rather, a distinct pattern has emerged in which we see greater disparities between upper and lower income American families, a trend that is unlikely to reverse.

The growing number of individuals and families living in poverty in the US has several implications for nonprofit organizations. First, as the number of working poor and those living in poverty increase, nonprofits providing social services will see continued and increased demand for their goods and services. Organizations providing critical services such as Headstart, community health clinics, job training providers, and mental health and substance abuse services may also be confronted with greater demand than they can accommodate. Organizations providing food, clothing, temporary shelter, and other forms of emergency assistance may find it increasingly difficult to keep pace with the growing needs of the poor and may resort to waitlists, **rationing**, and **quality dilution** in order to manage spikes in demand.[12] Waitlists occur when nonprofit organizations can no longer meet the needs of all those seeking their services. In this case, some organizations will create a waitlist, providing services on a first come, first served basis. Rationing involves allocating a set amount of resources and services to each client so that the limited amount of resources available can be distributed to the most people possible. Quality dilution occurs when the nonprofit organization is no longer able to provide high quality services; because of strained resources, the quality becomes diluted. All of these approaches enable nonprofit organizations to distribute resources to more people, or ensure that resources do not run out and can be distributed each day. While these techniques can enable nonprofit organizations to spread resources to more recipients, or over a longer period of time, they are not ideal for addressing increasing needs and demands from the community.

With regard to the growth of poverty in the suburbs, there is likely to be an increased need for affordable and low-income housing options in the suburbs. This demand may create new markets for nonprofit housing providers and opportunities for growth for the nonprofits providing basic social services and emergency assistance. Unfortunately, many nonprofit organizations are based in urban areas, requiring a shift in their infrastructure to suburban locations, where a lack of housing density and public transportation can make it more difficult for low-income families to access services. The current **spatial mismatch**, in which services are available in urban areas but needed in suburban areas, may present major challenges for accessing social services. Evidence has shown that the further people must travel to services, the less inclined they will be to use those services, no matter how badly they are needed.[13] Transportation issues, lack of childcare, time costs of travel, and geographic eligibility restrictions frequently prevent people from accessing services located outside their own communities.[14] As such, nonprofits providing social services and responding to emergency needs may need to develop new strategies to increase outreach efforts and mobile services to those in need.

Fiscal Stress and Uncertainty in Government Spending

As we learned in Chapters 2 and 3, government is a major partner to the nonprofit sector, extensively sponsoring the activity of nonprofit organizations not only through direct funding via contracts and grants, but also through federal, state, and local tax exemptions (income, sales, and property taxes), and reduced postal rates. However, government decision-making with regard to spending and other budget matters has grown increasingly unpredictable due to economic decline and efforts to limit the role of government. Political struggles during the Obama administration, including sharp ideological divisions in the Congress, have prevented lawmakers and the President from finding solutions for economic recovery and agreeing on the appropriate role of government in the economy and in providing healthcare. The challenges of balancing the federal budget, and meeting the competing needs of various political parties, leaves many nonprofit organizations and their employees waiting each year to learn if their programs and salaries will be funded or not.

Given the uncertainty of the federal budget, the fragile state of the economy, and the challenges of continually funding entitlement programs

(programs that guarantee services or payments based on established rights or legislation), there is a need for lawmakers to work closely with the President to find budget solutions that enable a healthy, stable economy. Most economists and budget experts agree that the solutions must include some combination of budget cuts as well as strategies for growing revenue. On both sides of the equation (spending cuts and new revenue) there are potential implications for the nonprofit sector. It is possible that there will be spending cuts for social programs, or spending caps may be put in place, preventing nonprofits that rely on government funding from fully meeting the demands for their services. Two important changes that might affect nonprofit organizations in the future include changes to the Federal law about tax deductions and changes in local and municipal tax codes to hold nonprofits responsible for paying for some of the resources they use.

Several proposals for reforming the tax code are being considered in order to collect more revenue from individual taxpayers and organizations. One of those proposals relates to the charitable deduction. As we discussed briefly in Chapter 2, the Obama administration has put forth a proposal to reduce the value of itemized deductions that are taken by the wealthiest taxpayers. Obama has proposed reducing tax deduction amounts from 39.6% to 28% and limiting the total deductions a person can take to 2% of their adjusted gross income. This change to the tax code would enable the federal government to collect more taxes from wealthy individuals, but might result in reducing the amount of pre-tax dollars that the wealthy decide to give to nonprofit organizations. If enacted, this change would close one tax loophole for the wealthy and generate additional tax revenue for the government treasury. Recall from Chapter 6 that the majority of these donations go to elite private educational institutions, health research, and the arts. While there are many supporters in both political parties for this reform, the issue remains far from resolved as organized interest groups representing the nonprofit sector continue to fight to oppose these reforms, arguing that it will reduce charitable giving to nonprofits.

There have also been proposals at the local level to ensure that municipal governments can raise revenue and are not unduly burdened by tax-exemptions granted to nonprofit organizations. Local, municipal governments have been particularly hard hit by the recession and subsequent housing market crash. Many have sought to manage their fiscal stress using **payments-in-lieu-of-taxes (PILOTS)**, which have direct implications for nonprofit organizations. PILOTS are similar to a local property tax or fee for city services, issued to nonprofits that have historically been fully exempt from paying taxes. Unlike a true tax which organizations and individuals are legally required to pay, PILOTS are (at least in theory) voluntary. The rationale for collecting PILOTS is often framed from the perspective of fairness, as PILOTS offer a way to cover the nonprofit's share of the cost of public services which municipalities normally fund with property taxes, including water usage, street lighting, public safety services, road maintenance, snow removal, and so on. Rather than collect PILOTS, some cities are simply choosing to charge nonprofits a specific tax or fee for municipal services consumed by the organization, such as the case of municipal water use in Chicago that we discussed in Chapter 2. PILOTS as a method of raising revenue among municipalities remains controversial, yet it is on the rise. PILOTS have been used in at least 117 municipalities in at least 18 states in the last few years, and many more are currently taking them under consideration.[15]

Municipalities have had mixed levels of cooperation from nonprofits as they attempt to collect PILOTS. Some cities, like Boston, have established systematic plans that allow them to collect PILOTS from Harvard University and other large tax-exempt organizations within the city limits that can afford to pay.[16] Other cities, such as Evanston, IL, have met with opposition and unsuccessful legal battles when trying to collect these payments.[17] One reason why these programs may or may not work is that the basis for deciding upon an appropriate PILOT amount varies across cities. While there are different methods for determining the amount that should be paid, and there are variations in whether PILOTS are requested on a one-time basis or an on-going plan is established to collect them, this is an important trend that is likely to affect the nonprofit sector to an even greater extent in the future as government budgets remain uncertain.

Nonprofit organizations face an increasingly uncertain environment in which they must manage their finances. While they have historically enjoyed full tax exemptions and relied on government funding and private donations from wealthy individuals seeking tax deductions, this situation may be changing. With the uncertainty of government funding and the possibility of reduced donations and increased local tax payments, many nonprofits are looking to other sources of revenue, including fundraising, earned income, and other more stable sources of funding.

Increased Demands for Transparency and Accountability

When public opinion pollsters and survey experts ask citizens which sector they view as being most trustworthy, or which sector they hold the highest opinion of, the nonprofit sector consistently ranks higher in the public's view than the public and for-profit sectors.[18] In fact, a survey in 2010 found that nearly 95% of wealthy families that support charitable causes year after year report having a great confidence in nonprofit organizations to solve social and global problems.[19] While nonprofit organizations benefit from public confidence, they face the challenges of managing scandal and waste, criticism about executive compensation, appropriate levels of fundraising and investments in the mission as compared to other activities like marketing, and the need to manage oversight and monitoring of their own activities.

Transparency—being open, clear, and visible about business practices— and **accountability**—being accountable or accepting responsibility for one's actions and duties—are critical concepts for ensuring public support for many organizations, but in particular nonprofit organizations which often rely on public funding, donations, volunteers, and aim to provide public goods or services. Transparency requires that organizations operate in a way that is easy for others to see what actions are being performed, including decision-making, management processes, finances, and efficacy and efficiency of services delivered. Transparent organizations are characterized as open and accessible and therefore develop high levels of trust with clients, funders, and supporters. Similarly, being accountable for their actions enables organizations to develop trust and support from external stakeholders.

Unfortunately, the high level of public confidence in the nonprofit sector is shaken with every major scandal that appears in the news headlines. Consider, for example, the story of Greg Mortensen, co-author of the 2007 best-selling book *Three Cups of Tea*, which chronicled the work of his charity, the Central Asia Institute (CAI), in building schools to educate impoverished children in Pakistan and Afghanistan. Mortensen claimed that proceeds from his book and the flood of donations were supporting schools, but later the public learned that he had used roughly $1.7 million in funds from the charity for book-related costs including advertising, events, film and professional fees, and travel, which were never paid back to the charity, despite the fact that the book sold more than four million copies. After coverage of the story on *60 Minutes* in 2011, Mortensen was also accused of lying about CAI's accomplishments in the book in order to increase donations to the organization. After an investigation by the Montana Attorney General's office into how Mortensen ran the charity (Montana is where he founded/operated CAI), he was ordered to reimburse the charity $1 million. Mortensen later admitted to exaggerating some of the stories in the book. So damaging was the scandal to the professional writing career of Mortensen's co-author David Oliver Relin that he ended his own life.[20]

While the *Three Cups of Tea* scandal was particularly visible in the media, it involved offenses that pale in comparison to other nonprofit scandals involving more blatant violations of the law. One need only to peruse the stories in the American Institute of Philanthropy's "Hall of Shame"[21] to get a sense of the outrageous instances of embezzlement, sexual impropriety, public deceit, and abuses of power that have been committed by leaders of nonprofit organizations, including nationally known and trusted brands like the United Way of America. Scandals like these and numerous others threaten to erode public confidence in nonprofit organizations and place pressure on the sector for increased transparency and accountability.

Another major issue facing nonprofit organizations is the issue of executive compensation.[22] As the nonprofit sector has grown increasingly professionalized over the past half century, the scale and complexity of operations have also grown quite dramatically, making the task of managing some of these organizations as challenging as leading a major for-profit corporation. Nonprofit executives' pay has risen in response to these increased requirements for administrative and leadership abilities, but members of the public have, at times, expressed shock and outrage over the six- and seven-figure salaries of nonprofit CEOs. It is not uncommon to find, among the largest and most prestigious US nonprofits, Executive Directors/CEOs making over $500,000 per year. A handful of executives earn salaries in excess of $1 million, a fact that many citizens find outrageous in the context of a charitable organization. The issue of accountability, however, may come down to the question of what is "excessive" compensation, which is generally determined by considering the ratio of the CEO's salary to the organization's total revenue.[23] For example, while the CEO of the Boys and Girls Clubs of America earns $1.85 million, and had roughly $130 million in total expenses, The Metropolitan Museum of Art CEO earns just under $1.5 million, in proportion to $386 million in expenses. In this comparison, the CEO of the Boys and Girls Clubs might be looked at with greater scrutiny as her salary consumes a much larger percentage of the organization's total expenses than the CEO of the Met. Box 10.1 offers a list of some of the most high-paid nonprofit leaders and asks you to consider some of the points in the debate of nonprofit CEO pay.

BOX 10.1 ISSUE FOR DEBATE: WHEN IT COMES TO NONPROFIT CEO PAY, HOW MUCH IS TOO MUCH?

In many ways, managing a large nonprofit is comparable to running a major corporation, and perhaps even more complicated. To be sure, running a large nonprofit organization is a difficult job, involving tasks of complex budgeting, securing, managing, and accounting for multiple sources of funding, not to mention directing programs and services that often employ hundreds, if not thousands, of staff. For the largest nonprofit organizations to continue operating successfully they must invest the resources to attract and retain people with superior administrative skills. While most nonprofit Executive Directors and CEOs earn a more modest salary, public reaction is often one of outrage upon learning that nonprofit CEO salaries sometimes run in the hundreds of thousands, and for a handful of nonprofit executives, even a million or more. According to the Fiscal Times, here is a list of the highest paid nonprofit executives in 2012:[24]

Name & Title	Organization & Location	Compensation Package
Laurence Hoagland Jr., CIO	William & Flora Hewlett Foundation Menlo Park, CA	$2.5 million
John Seffrin, CEO	American Cancer Society Atlanta, GA	$2.1 million
Roxanne Spillett, CEO	Boys & Girls Clubs of America Atlanta, GA	$1.8 million
Reynold Levy, President	Lincoln Center for the Performing Arts New York, NY	$1.4 million
Placido Domingo, General Director	Los Angeles Opera Los Angeles, CA	$1.3 million
Michael Kaiser, President	JFK Center for the Performing Arts Washington, DC	$1.3 million

continued

Name & Title	Organization & Location	Compensation Package
Peter Gelb, General Manager	Metropolitan Opera Association New York, NY	$1.3 million
Glenn Lowry, CEO	Museum of Modern Art New York, NY	$1.2 million
James Willians, CIO	J. Paul Getty Trust Los Angeles, CA	$1.2 million
Edwin Feulner Jr., President	Heritage Foundation Washington, DC	$1.1 million

What are your reactions to seeing this list of highest paid nonprofit administrators? Is it acceptable for those leading nonprofits to earn such large salaries? Why or why not?

Activity

Using Guidestar, Charity Navigator, or annual reports from these organizations' websites, see if you can find the total annual revenues for each of these organizations, and calculate the percentage of the organization's total budget that goes toward paying the CEO. Are there major differences among these ten organizations? Rank them from top to bottom in terms of those whose CEO salaries comprise the lowest share of overall budget.

Successful nonprofit organizations must offer a competitive salaries and benefits package in order to attract and retain high quality leaders with the skills needed to manage these large, complex organizations. According to Dan Pallotta, founder of the AIDS Ride, nonprofit organizations are expected to be thrifty and rely on cheap talent, but do not reward risk-taking, and offer the financial incentives and rewards required to attract and retain talented leaders and workers.[25] Nonprofits must ensure that the salary is appropriate to the job and not too far out of the realm of what comparable other nonprofits are paying. Nonprofit industry groups such as Guidestar have begun producing annual executive compensation reports in order to help nonprofits benchmark their CEO and other high-level executives' pay against other organizations to help ensure that their pay scales align with the "going rate." Nonprofits face the challenges of paying enough to attract and retrain talent, while also being viewed as responsible and not overly wasteful.

A related issue with implications for transparency and accountability is the rise of for-profit fundraising firms and increased concerns over fundraising costs. Some nonprofits are very efficient and conscientious about fundraising costs, while others raise funds in such a way that only a few pennies to every dollar will actually go to the charity or the cause for which the money was raised. For example, some nonprofits hire for-profit fundraising firms to solicit donations on their behalf, with an agreement that the for-profit fundraising agency gets to keep some portion of the monies raised. This is an attractive option for many nonprofits, as they do not have to bear the costs associated with hiring a fundraising professional and they are guaranteed at least some additional funds coming into their organization from the fundraising firm. However, these arrangements become dubious when the for-profit firm solicits donations in the name of a charity, such as the Cancer Survivor's Fund, for example, and fails to tell the donor that only about 11 cents will go to the charity to provide services for cancer survivors, while the paid fund-raiser will be pocketing the other 89 cents.[26]

There are no hard and fast accounting rules about how much of nonprofits' fundraising monies must go toward the cause it was intended to support, and certainly no laws preventing the hiring of a for-profit fundraising firm. While some critics argue that a larger percentage of donations should go to the mission or that nonprofits should not engage in excessive marketing or advertising, there are no real rules about fundraising and little to no official oversight of these accounting decisions. In most cases, the burden of oversight falls to the charities themselves. Nonprofits rely on monitoring from their boards of directors, adherence to codes of ethics, accreditation standards, and other voluntary forms of self-regulation. Nonprofits are subject to less external oversight and regulation than for-profit organizations. There is even some evidence that government organizations monitor their own internal performance at comparable levels of monitoring for-profits' contract partners, but tend to monitor nonprofit contractors much less intensively.[27]

While many nonprofits are subject to external audits from funders or have independent financial audits as a requirement of their funders, these mechanisms are not always sufficient for detecting impropriety or illegal activity. Consider a case that made headlines in 2013—the story of a highly regarded, 40-year-old nonprofit, the Metropolitan New York Council on Jewish Poverty (Met Council). The organization's CEO, William E. Rapfogel, had been conspiring with someone at the insurance brokerage, Century Coverage Corporation, to pad the Met Council's insurance payments by several hundred thousand dollars a year. Despite an annual compensation package in excess of $400,000, Rapfogel pocketed some of this money and gifted the rest to politicians who supplied government grants to the Met Council.[28] These financial indiscretions came to light not through any audit or government oversight, but rather from an anonymous whistle-blower who identified himself as a former employee. Here, the corruption and theft occurring was not captured by formal oversight and monitoring, a concern that some fear may point to an inability to detect and prevent fraudulent behaviors in nonprofit organizations.

In response to the increasing incidence of financial scandals, concerns over executive compensation levels, extraordinary fundraising costs, and generally low levels of government regulation and monitoring of the nonprofit sector, several developments have emerged to help promote transparency and accountability of nonprofit organizations. Perhaps most importantly, nonprofits' main financial form, the 990, which they are required to file annually with the IRS,[29] is made available to the public on websites such as Guidestar. In addition to the 990 form itself, websites such as Guidestar provide the basic financial picture of each registered nonprofit in the US including a simple breakdown of where the organization gets its money, how it spends the money (including fundraising expenditures), names of executive staff and board members, and the salaries of the five highest paid officers for each organization. Users can search by nonprofit organization names, keyword, city, region, and so on, making it easy for prospective donors to compare organizations on a variety of criteria and make more informed decisions about where to donate.

In addition to Guidestar, numerous "charity watchdog" sites have emerged in recent years including Charity Navigator, Charity Watch, and the Better Business Bureau's Wise Giving Alliance. These sites are useful for educating the public and potential donors, providing signals about each organization's quality and credibility through a rating system. Charity Navigator, for example, rates selected nonprofits on a scale of 1 to 4 stars, making it easy for members of the public and potential donors to get a sense of a nonprofit organization's performance. The major drawback to these sites is that they do not offer a rating for every registered nonprofit that exists in the US, only those they choose to rate.

Despite the increased availability of financial information, the presence of charity watchdog groups, and the adoption of voluntary self-regulation programs, breaches of accountability may still occur within nonprofit organizations. Accountability and transparency will remain a key issue for nonprofit organizations into the foreseeable future. Nonprofit boards of directors are ultimately the best mechanism for providing oversight and ensuring accountability of the organization. Unfortunately, board members all too often lack the technical expertise or information to do an adequate job of providing oversight, deferring to the CEO on the basis of trust and blind faith. In addition to adhering to regulatory requirements and participation in voluntary self-regulation programs such as codes of ethics, and accreditation, nonprofits will need to find ways to attract and retain qualified board members who can effectively carry out the oversight and monitoring role.

Market Competition and Pressures for Performance

Although the nonprofit sector in the US has grown dramatically over the past half century, roughly doubling its own size in each decade since 1980, some have begun to question whether this growth is sustainable. As we discussed in Chapter 2, the Internal Revenue Service is quite generous in granting tax-exempt status, approving roughly 70 to 80% of all applications in any given year. While the number of new nonprofit start-ups has continued to flourish, a simultaneous trend of nonprofit "deaths" is occurring, similar to the one we read about with Sunny Meadows at the start of this chapter. By one estimate, a little more than 1 out of every 4 new nonprofits formed today will cease to exist in three years.[30] This "death rate" is largely a result of market saturation. Nonprofit sector experts Lecy and Chisholm (2013) have demonstrated that nonprofit organization entry rates into markets are beginning to converge with exit rates, suggesting that the rapid growth trajectory of the nonprofit sector that we saw in the 1980s is coming to an end. When Lecy and Chisholm studied 313 largest metropolitan areas in the US they found that market saturation, increased competition for limited resources, and consolidation of nonprofit organizations have led to a net loss of the number of nonprofit organizations in some areas.

A key factor in market saturation rates has to do with increased pressures for performance. Today, nonprofit organizations of all types are faced with unprecedented pressures to demonstrate the benefits they are producing. Institutional funders (government and foundations), and increasingly private donors as well, want to know that money given to a nonprofit is yielding a high **social return on investment**, the extra values (e.g. environmental, social, community) that are not normally reflected in conventional financial accounts but are generated by nonprofit activities. Older, larger, wealthier nonprofit organizations clearly have the advantage, as they have the existing staffing capacity and organizational infrastructure to measure performance and publicize their achievements, allowing them to successfully compete for new grants and conduct more effective fund-raising campaigns. Successful, large nonprofit organizations can perpetuate the cycle of capturing larger shares of market revenue, enabling them to strengthen their performance measurement, management, public relations and social media efforts, and so on. Thus, it is becoming increasingly difficult for new nonprofits organizations to enter markets since they lack the experience, reputation, credibility, proven track record of performance, and donor base of older organizations. Thus, new nonprofits, like a new business, face an uphill battle in the competition for scarce resources, as they compete against older, larger, more well-established organizations that represent a "safer" investment for government funders, foundations, and donors. This makes it increasingly difficult for newer and smaller organizations to break into the market and ultimately survive.

Given the increasing difficulty of survival for new nonprofit entrants into the market, organizational mergers, consolidations, and acquisitions within the nonprofit sector are becoming more common.[31] Nonprofit mergers are similar to those that occur in the for-profit sector in that they are an important aspect of corporate strategy that seeks to buy, sell, divide, or combine different companies and similar entities as a corporate finance or management strategy. In the nonprofit sector, generally newer, smaller organizations become "acquired" by a larger organization. These merged organizational arrangements, while initially difficult, especially for the smaller organization which often has to give up its identity and autonomy, can ultimately be beneficial for both organizations. For one thing, **mergers and acquisitions** allow for more efficient use of administrative resources, as there is no longer a need for two Chief Executive Officers, two performance measurement programs, two finance departments, two fundraising and development divisions, and so on. Moreover, merging with a larger organization allows struggling newer nonprofits to continue to "do their thing," offering their programs or services while benefitting from the administrative capacity, resources, and infrastructure of a larger organization.

A study on nonprofit organizational mergers found that the primary motivation for mergers is financial, particularly when small agencies are unable to compete in the market. However, this same study found that good leadership and honest and open communication between both organizations help to ensure a smooth merger process.[32] While there is no reliable data on the number of nonprofit mergers that occur each year, it is generally understood that mergers and consolidations are on the rise, and this trend is likely to continue as long as new nonprofits try to enter markets that are already saturated. Given these realities, it will be very important for future nonprofit entrepreneurs to conduct a thorough market analysis prior to taking any steps to create a new nonprofit organization.

The Blending and Blurring of Sector Boundaries

As we discussed in Chapter 1, the nonprofit sector possesses many characteristics that make it distinct from the public and for-profit sectors. Yet these distinctions have eroded somewhat over time, as nonprofits have grown larger and more professionalized. In some cases, larger nonprofits have taken on behaviors and characteristics of a government bureaucracy. Perhaps this is not surprising, given the extensive reliance of nonprofit organizations on government funding sources and the public serving missions of many nonprofits. Nonprofit organizations have also taken on many qualities of for-profit organizations, as they find themselves increasingly embedded in competitive markets (as discussed above) and must make sound business decisions to survive. Although the blending and blurring of boundaries between the public, nonprofit, and for-profit sectors is nothing new, it is a growing trend that is worth mentioning as one to watch in the future, as recent developments suggest that the line between nonprofit and for-profit organizations will only become murkier.

While nonprofits have always shared some similarities with for-profits, many nonprofit scholars and practitioners would agree that nonprofits are becoming increasingly business-like, treating clients like customers, adopting more profit-driven activities, hiring more employees and leaders with business backgrounds, and in some cases changing their status from nonprofit to for-profit, or low-profit, limited-liability corporations. Variously referred to as the "marketization" or **"commercialization"** of the nonprofit sector, these trends reflect the tendency of nonprofits to adopt principles, practices, and values of the for-profit sector. Many factors have played a role in this trend. One factor relates to a philosophical shift created by managerial reforms of the late 1980s and 1990s such as New Public Management, which calls for government—and their nonprofit contractors—to view public service recipients as "customers" and behave in a more business-like manner focusing on measuring organizational performance and offering financial incentives and rewards for top performers.

Another factor playing into the increasing marketization of the nonprofit sector is that nonprofits have experienced dramatic growth in earned income over the past few decades. The unpredictable nature of private giving, combined with instability in government funding as mentioned earlier, has caused many nonprofit leaders to take proactive and strategic steps towards increasing revenue through earned income. Earned income is a broad term encompassing fees for services, interest from income and dividends, and commercial sales and social enterprises. While private charitable contributions comprised the original mainstay of nonprofit organizations, and later government funds, earned income has eclipsed both of these sources of funding. In fact, earned income has become the largest and fastest growing source of nonprofit income.

The market-based orientation of nonprofit organizations is not "all or nothing" but, rather, marketization exists on a spectrum. A key indicator is the extent to which the organization relies on earned income. Leadership offers another indicator of a nonprofit organization's market propensity. The immense diversity of organizations making up the nonprofit sector has meant that nonprofit leaders themselves come from a wide variety of educational backgrounds including social work, law, theology and religious studies, psychology, sociology, political science, family studies, communications, fine arts, visual arts, and the list goes on. Yet, increasingly, business-trained leaders are coming to dominate the ranks of nonprofit leadership. Boards, charged with the task of hiring and overseeing the Executive Directors/CEO, are setting out to hire individuals with a business degree. Edged out of the private sector job market during the Great Recession and disillusioned with corporate America, many newer MBA grads were welcomed with open arms by nonprofit organizations that were quick to capitalize on finance, marketing, and public relations skills that business trainees bring to an organization.[33] The growth of nonprofit leaders with training in business, as opposed to another field such as social work, has distinct implications for the kinds of values and practices that get embedded into day-to-day operations of the organization. Thus, another indicator of marketization relates to how extensively private sector values are embedded in the organization's key operations including strategic planning, strategic budgeting, financial management, marketing and public relations, hiring and promotion practices, and employee reward structures.

Another new development that has further blurred the boundaries between the nonprofit and for-profit sector is the emergence of the **low-profit, limited-liability corporation (L3C)**. Representing a hybrid between a nonprofit and for-profit, L3C "is a cross between a nonprofit organization and a for-profit corporation"[34] which has a stated goal of performing a socially beneficial service—for example, charitable or educational goals— while not maximizing profits and income. L3Cs are often described as for-profit, social enterprise ventures. An example would be a small, family-owned dairy farm.[35] It is a hybrid structure that combines the legal and tax flexibility of a traditional LLC, the social benefits of a nonprofit organization, and the branding and market positioning advantages of a social enterprise. The biggest concerns about these organizations is that private foundations are allowed to make program-related investments to L3Cs, causing some to worry that they will divert an important share of foundation funds from traditional nonprofits to these for-profit businesses.

Since L3Cs are a relatively new type of organization, it remains to be seen how well this model will fare over time. Legislation allowing for these organizations must exist at the state level, whereas the federal government (IRS) is the gatekeeper for approving tax-exempt status of nonprofit corporations. Currently, nine states have passed laws allowing L3Cs to be created (Illinois, Louisiana, Maine, Michigan, North Carolina, Rhode Island, Utah, Vermont, and Wyoming), and several others have taken it under consideration. As of January 2013, there were 711 active L3Cs in operation among these 9 states, so their overall number is still quite small compared relative to the number of nonprofit organizations.[36]

Nonprofit organizations are facing ever increasing challenges and pressures to compete with one another and other types of organizations, while also trying to balance their budgets, provide oversight of their activities, attract talent, and of course achieve their missions. The blurring of the boundaries between public, nonprofit, and for-profit organizations might be an advantage for nonprofit organizations, as they seek to adopt the financial and accounting practices of for-profit organizations while advancing social missions. In the future, the use of social enterprises, L3Cs, and other organizational forms may help to provide new paths for generating funds that advance social purposes.

The Continued Rise of Technology and Social Media

Over the past 15 years, technology has transformed the operations of nonprofit and civil society organizations, and will continue to play a critical role for the sector well into the future. Beginning with the Internet, this first wave of technology enabled quicker and more efficient advocacy work by nonprofits and civil society groups, allowing them to mobilize stake-holders through action alerts sent via e-mail. It also significantly enhanced fundraising capacity, as the practice of creating an online portal for donations quickly diffused and became a norm among nonprofits at the start of the 21st century, along with the use of e-mail listservs to solicit donations. Nonprofit organizations have also grown to rely extensively on their websites as a key mechanism for publicizing their mission, high-lighting achievements, communicating needs for staffing, donations, and volunteers, and increasingly for interacting with the public and principal stakeholders.

While the use of e-mail and websites has been re-shaping nonprofits' operations and communication for several years, newer technologies of social media are reinventing the nonprofit and civil society sector in even more dramatic ways, and they are evolving at such a rapid pace that the implications of this newer wave of technologies are not yet entirely clear. What is clear, however, is that social media has been widely embraced by nonprofit organizations who employ these new technologies to fulfill a variety of goals including fundraising, cause marketing, volunteer and staff recruitment, policy advocacy, and political change efforts. Results from the 2012 Nonprofit Social Networking Benchmarking Study show that Facebook remains the most widely used social media platform by nonprofits, with 86% of organizations having an active Facebook presence, followed by Twitter (60%), YouTube (48%), and LinkedIn (33%).[37]

Throughout this book, we have considered many examples of the ways nonprofit organizations are exploiting these technologies, from the use of LinkedIn to connect with volunteers in Chapter 5, the use of Facebook and other social media for fundraising in Chapter 6, the use of both Twitter and Facebook to mobilize grassroots political action in Chapters 7 and 8, and the use of nearly all these technologies to help connect nonprofit job seekers to nonprofit employers, as well as promote local economic development, in Chapter 9. Additionally, as we discussed in Chapter 4, social media and social networking platforms offer great promise for strengthening civil society by helping citizens forge new relationships with one another and with organizations and institutions in their communities, however the term community may be defined for the individual. One of the key advantages of social media over one-way forms of technology, such as passive website viewing, is that these platforms are designed for interaction: they enable citizens to form associations, expand their networks, and to quickly engage in the causes and issues they care about.

Social media thus not only allows nonprofits to enhance operations capacity, but it also enables nonprofit organizations to connect more deeply with existing stakeholders, to provide education, and to disseminate information freely. One example of the potential of nonprofit organizations to connect conveniently with current and potential stakeholders (and donors) is found in the online forum Reddit. Reddit is a social news website that allows registered users to submit content in the form of links or text posts. Content is ranked by users who vote each submission "up" or "down," which determines the position of each post on the site's pages. Content is organized into areas of interest known as "subreddits," or subforums, one of which is called the IAmA ("Ask Me Anything") subreddit. In it, people with rare or interesting experiences they're willing to share take part in an online public Q&A session. One such recent session was done by the founder of the nonprofit Multidisciplinary Association for Psychedelic Studies (MAPS), Rick Doblin, Ph.D. and his staff. The purpose of the session was to answer questions from the public pertaining to the role of psychedelic substances in science, medicine, mental health treatment, and spirituality, and to discuss MAPS' research related to these

BOX 10.2 USING SOCIAL MEDIA TO ENGAGE STAKEHOLDERS THROUGH ONLINE DIALOGUE: HOW MAPS EDUCATED THE PUBLIC ON PSYCHEDELICS THROUGH REDDIT

Hey reddit! I am Rick Doblin, Ph.D., Founder and Executive Director of the Multidisciplinary Association for Psychedelic Studies (MAPS). Founded in 1986, MAPS is a 501(c)(3) non-profit research and educational organization that develops medical, legal, and cultural contexts for people to benefit from the careful uses of psychedelics and marijuana.

The staff of MAPS and I are here to answer your questions about:

- Scientific research into MDMA, LSD, psilocybin, ayahuasca, ibogaine, and marijuana
- The role of psychedelics and marijuana in science, medicine, therapy, spirituality, culture, and policy
- Reducing the risks associated with the non-medical use of various drugs by providing education and harm reduction services
- How to effectively communicate about psychedelics at your dinner table
- And anything else!

Our currently most promising research focuses on treating post-traumatic stress disorder (PTSD) with MDMA-assisted psychotherapy.

This is who we have participating today from MAPS:

- Rick Doblin, Ph.D., Founder and Executive Director
- Brad Burge, Director of Communications and Marketing
- Amy Emerson, Director of Clinical Research
- Virginia Wright, Director of Development
- Brian Brown, Communications and Marketing Associate
- Kynthia Brunette, Operations Associate
- Tess Goodwin, Development Assistant
- Ilsa Jerome, Ph.D., Research and Information Specialist
- Bryce Montgomery, Web and Multimedia Associate
- Linnae Ponté, Zendo Project Harm Reduction Coordinator
- Ben Shechet, Clinical Study Assistant
- Berra Yazar-Klosinski, Ph.D., Lead Clinical Research Associate

For more information about scientific research into the medical potential of psychedelics and marijuana, please visit maps.org.

Excerpted from Reddit's IAmA subreddit December 3, 2013: http://www.reddit.com/r/IAmA/comments/1s0mt7/i_am_rick_doblin_phd_founder_of_the. Accessed January 28, 2014.

topics. Box 10.2 features the introductory text of Dr. Doblin and MAPS' IAmA subreddit.

Among those submitting questions were physicians, clinical psychologists, and other healthcare professionals, university researchers, and persons who had experiences using psychedelics either as a patient, research subject, or recreational user. Dr. Doblin and his staff addressed many serious and interesting questions in an accessible language while educating the public. Undoubtedly, this forum raised awareness about the many legitimate uses of psychedelics in science, medicine, and spirituality, but also strengthened ties with and among the organization's stakeholders, who collectively make up a community of individuals with an interest in the seemingly narrow issue area of psychedelics research. Although the goal of such forums is not to raise money, increased donations are often a secondary benefit of this type of social media interaction with stakeholders, as evidenced by the exchange among participants in the MAPS session opposite.

As Reddit counted almost 91 million unique visitors to its website just within the last month, this type of interaction between nonprofit organizations and potential/current stakeholders can be beneficial for both the public and the organizations that "put themselves out there" on social media.

As social media becomes an increasingly important mode of communication in both US and global society, nonprofit organizations have a clear incentive to keep up with this ever-evolving technology and use it in ways that help the organization to maximize its mission. Free social media platforms allow for quickly and easily sharing content and disseminating messages and information to a vast number of users. Moreover they enable nonprofits to expand their fundraising capabilities, policy and social change efforts, and generally maintain closer connections to their stakeholders. That said, exploiting the benefits of social media requires technological capacity in order to manage these platforms, and thus the challenge for nonprofits is maintaining that capacity as they must compete with for-profit firms who often provide better pay and benefits to attract staff with these skills. Indeed, it has been suggested that the lack of clear evidence on the return on investment is likely to be holding nonprofits back from greater use of and financial commitment to social networking, but lack of expertise to manage social media also plays a significant role.[38]

[−]MDMA_Throw_Away 74 points 1 month ago

Top of Form

Keep up the good work, Doc. We're all counting on you.

Bottom of Form

[−]brownestrabbit 24 points 1 month ago

Top of Form

Psst. If you can, throw some dollars (or bitcoins) MAPS' direction.

AND.

Thank you for sharing your story. It is touching and inspiring to hear you had such a beautiful experience.

Bottom of Form

[−]XxionxX 2 points 1 month ago

Top of Form

Sitting here late at night reading this thread and you mention bitcoin. I look over and see that I have my phone next to me (containing btc wallet) and my pants with my wallet are across the room.

There is no way I am going to get out from underneath this blanket, walk across the room, dig out my wallet, and use my credit card to make this donation.

Bitcoin donation it is! Keep being awesome MAPS!

I would like to note that I was the first bitcoin donator. Beat my .02 btc donation if you dare! And none of this nonsense about .021 or .02001 ___ you must beat me by at least a full hundredth of a bitcoin! **Who dare take my challenge!?**

Some early adopter is gonna come by and crush me, I just know it.

Bottom of Form

[−]brownestrabbit 2 points 1 month ago

Top of Form

You are part of this awesomeness.

Bottom of Form

Summary

Nonprofit organizations face a number of challenges at present that will affect the sector well into the future. These trends include major demographic shifts (diversity and immigration, aging of the population, increased poverty and suburbanization of poverty), fiscal stress and uncertainty in government spending, increased demands for transparency and accountability, market competition and pressures for performance, blending and blurring of sector distinctions, the rise of technology and social media. Despite these challenges, we can find reassurance in the fact that the nonprofit sector has shown great resilience throughout its short history,[39] embracing new opportunities and adapting to environmental pressures and changes like no other sector. As the nonprofit sector faces these and other challenges, it will demand a passionate yet competent, skilled, entrepreneurial workforce to lead it into the future. Given the capacity of the nonprofit sector to fulfill a wide variety of social, political, and economic functions in our society, many young people today are attracted to serve in the nonprofit sector. According to a 2010–2011 survey of 12,933 US college students conducted by the National Association of College and Employers, 21% of graduating seniors plan to work for nonprofit organizations or government, up from just 17% in 2009, suggesting an increased desire among young people to serve the public.[40] In the working world these trends can also be seen in the number of applications received by public and nonprofit institutions such as AmeriCorps and Teach for America, who have seen applications triple in recent years.[41] As a new generation of employees, managers, and leaders prepares to enter the nonprofit workforce, it is both an uncertain but an exciting era for the US nonprofit sector.

KEY TERMS

- Accountability
- Baby Boomers
- Commercialization
- Demographics
- Federal poverty level
- Great Recession

- Low-profit, limited-liability corporation (L3C)
- Majority-minority
- Mergers and acquisitions
- Payments-in-lieu-of-taxes (PILOTS)

- Qualitiy dilution
- Rationing
- Social return on investment
- Spatial mismatch
- Transparency

DISCUSSION QUESTIONS

1. What are some of the main reasons nonprofit organizations might fail? Do we need more nonprofit organizations in our communities, or are there already too many?

2. How will an aging population in the United States change the role of nonprofit organizations in civil society?

3. How will changes in immigration patterns in the United States change the role of nonprofit organizations in America? Do you think these changes will be different in rural and urban areas? Or across different states?

4. What is a reasonable salary for a leader of a nonprofit organization? Should salaries be a proportion of the organization's earnings? Should executives be paid what they could make in the private for-profit sector? How much is too much? Who should decide?

5. Are social media and other forms of electronic communication the most important means of contact with existing and prospective stakeholders, or do you think it is important for nonprofits to continue reaching out to the public, donors, and stakeholders through more traditional methods?

6. In what ways do you think technology will shape nonprofit organizations' work in the future? In what other ways might nonprofits use social media? What types of new technological developments do you foresee being used by nonprofits in the future?

ACTIVITY

This chapter notes the salary levels of nonprofit CEOs. As a class exercise, try to find similar salary information for CEOs in the private sector. Are the compensation packages for private sector CEOs public information? If they are, find the salary amounts and determine what percentage of the company's total expenses is the CEO's compensation package? How does this compare to top CEO compensation packages in the nonprofit sector?

Websites

American Institute of Philanthropy's "Hall of Shame." http://www.charitywatch.org/articles/CharityWatchHallofShame.html

Videos for Discussion

Dan Pallotta: The way we think about charity is dead wrong. TED Talks. Published on Mar 11, 2013. http://www.youtube.com/watch?v=bfAz i6D5FpM

Description: Activist and fundraiser Dan Pallotta calls out the double standard that drives our broken relationship to charities. Too many nonprofits, he says, are rewarded for how little they spend—not for what they get done. Instead of equating frugality with morality, he asks us to start rewarding charities for their big goals and big accomplishments (even if that comes with big expenses). In this bold talk, he says, "Let's change the way we think about changing the world."

Additional Reading

Chertavian, Gerald. 2013. Nonprofits Need to Compete for Top Talent. *Harvard Business Review*. Accessed at http://blogs.hbr.org/2013/03/nonprofits-need-to-compete-for/

Notes

1   National Vital Statistics Systems. Birth Data. Accessed December 18, 2013 at http://www.cdc.gov/nchs/births.htm
2   Gelatt, Julie. 2007. *Annual Immigration to the United States: The Real Numbers*. May No 16. Washington, DC: Migration Policy Institute.
3   Minority population surging in Texas: Nonwhites now more than 50% of state's population. *msnbc.com*, *Associated Press*. August 18, 2005. Accessed: December 18, 2013 at http://www.bloomberg.com/news/2012–12–12/census-bureau-says-minority-youth-to-be-majority-by-2019.html/
4   Bass, Frank. 2012. Census Bureau Says Minority Youth to Be Majority by 2019. *Bloomberg*. Accessed December 18, 2013 at http://www.bloomberg.com/news/2012–12–12/census-bureau-says-minority-youth-to-be-majority-by-2019.html/
5   Language Spoken at Home for the United States: 2000. Source: US Census Bureau, Census 2000 Special Tabulation 224; Ryan, Camille. 2013. Language Use in the United States: 2011. *American Community Survey Reports*. US Census Bureau.
6   Schwartz, Robert, James Weinberg, Dana Hagenbuch, and Allison Scott. 2013. *The Voice of Nonprofit Talent: Perceptions of Diversity in the Workplace*. A national study produced in partnership with Commongood Careers & Level Playing Field Institute. Accessed December 18, 2013 at http://www.commongoodcareers.org/diversity report.pdf
7   National Center for Health Statistics, *National Vital Statistics Reports*. Accessed December 18, 2013 at www.cdc.gov/nchs

8   Getting Current: Recent Demographic Trends in Metropolitan America. 2009. *The Brookings Institution*. Accessed December 18, 2013 at www.brookings.edu

9   Getting Current: Recent Demographic Trends in Metropolitan America (2009).

10 US Census Bureau. Accessed December 18, 2013 at http://factfinder2.census.gov/faces/tableservices/jsf/pages/productview.xhtml?pid=ACS_12_5YR_DP03

11 Panousi, Vasia, Ivan Vidangos, Shanti Ramnath, Jason DeBacker, and Bradley Heim. 2013. Inequality Rising and Permanent Over Past Two Decades. *Brookings Papers on Economic Activity*. Spring, 2013: 67–142.

12 Anheier, Helmut. 2005. *Nonprofit Organizations: Theory, Management, Policy*. Routledge Press.

13 Allard, Scott. 2009. *Out of Reach: Place, Poverty, and the New American Welfare State*. New Haven, CT: Yale University Press.

14 Allard (2009).

15 Kenyon, Daphne A. and Adam Langley. 2010. Payments in Lieu of Taxes: Balancing Municipal and Nonprofit Interests. Policy Focus Report of the *Lincoln Institute of Land Policy*, Cambridge, MA.

16 Rezendes, Michael. 2011. City sends 'tax' bills to major nonprofits, Aims to triple voluntary payments within 5 years. *Boston Globe*, April 24, 2011. Accessed December 19, 2013 at http://www.boston.com/news/local/massachusetts/articles/2011/04/24/boston_sends_tax_bills_to_major_nonprofits/

17 Brodsy, Alyson. 2002. Northwestern University's fight with Evanston is headed for court. *Indiana Daily Student*, September 4, 2002. Accessed December 19, 2013 at http://www.idsnews.com/news/story.aspx?id=23252

18 Cordon, Lucia. 2010. Survey reveals public trust higher for charities than other institutions, *Future Leaders in Philanthropy*, November 30, 2010 9:29 PM. Accessed February 8, 2014 at http://www.networkflip.com/survey-reveals-public-trust-higher-for-charities-than-other-institutions/

19 Cordon (2010).

20 Kaufman, Leslie. 2012. David Oliver Relin, Adventurous Journalist, Dies at 49, *The New York Times*. Accessed January 30, 2014 at http://www.nytimes.com/2012/12/03/business/media/david-oliver-relin-co-author-of-three-cups-of-tea-dies-at-49.html

21 American Institute of Philanthropy's "Hall of Shame." Accessed January 10, 2013 at http://www.charitywatch.org/articles/CharityWatchHallofShame.html

22 Grobman, Gary. 2011. *The Nonprofit Handbook: Everything You Need to Know to Start and Run Your Nonprofit Organization*, 6th edition. Charlottesville, VA: Whitehat Communications.

23 Smith, Aaron. 2013. Top charity CEOs pay exceeds $1 million, *CNN Money*. Accessed January 30, 2014 at http://money.cnn.com/2013/10/10/news/nonprofit-ceo-pay/

24 Briody, Blaire. 2012. Ten Insanely Overpaid Nonprofit Execs, *The Fiscal Times*, December 20, 2012. Accessed February 18, 2014 at http://www.thefiscaltimes.com/Articles/2012/12/20/10-Insanely-Overpaid-Nonprofit-Execs

25 Pallotta, Dan. 2012. Charity Case: *How the Nonprofit Community can Stand Up for Itself and Really Change the World*. San Francisco, CA: Jossey-Bass.

26 Charity Navigator. Ten Charities Overpaying Their For-Profit Fundraisers. Accessed January 30, 2014 at http://www.charitynavigator.org/index.cfm?bay=topten.detail&listid=28#.Uurc8j1dUzs

27 Marvel, Mary K. and Howard P. Marvel. 2007. Outsourcing Oversight: A Comparison of Monitoring for In-House and Contracted Services. *Public Administration Review,* 67(3): 521–530.

28 Buettner, Russ and William K. Rashbaum. 2013. Whistle-Blower's Letter Led to Charity's Firing of Chief Executive, *The New York Times.* Accessed January 30, 2014 at http://www.nytimes.com/2013/09/16/nyregion/an-anonymous-whistle-blower-exposed-a-scandal-at-a-jewish-charity.html

29 Exceptions include religious institutions and organizations with revenues below $25,000.

30 Lecy, Jesse and Eric Chisholm. 2013. The End is Nigh: Limits to the Growth of the Nonprofit Sector. Paper presented at the 2013 annual meeting of the *Association for Research on Nonprofit Organizations and Voluntary Action,* Hartford, CT.

31 Grobman (2001).

32 Singer, Mark I. and John A. Yankey. 1991. Organizational metamorphosis: A Study of Eighteen Nonprofit Mergers, Acquisitions, and Consolidations. *Nonprofit Management & Leadership,* 1(4): 357–369.

33 Rampell, Catherine. 2011. More College Graduates Take Public Service Jobs, *New York Times,* March 1, 2011. Accessed February 25, 2014 at http://www.nytimes.com/2011/03/02/business/02graduates.html?pagewanted=all

34 Low-Profit Limited Liability Company. Vermont Secretary of State: Corporations Division. Accessed February 5, 2014 at http://www.sec.state.vt.us/corps/dobiz/llc/llc_l3c.htm

35 Zouhali-Worrall, Malika. 2010. For L3C companies, profit isn't the point, *CNNMoney.com,* Februrary 9, 2010. Accessed November 3, 2013 at http://money.cnn.com/2010/02/08/smallbusiness/l3c_low_profit_companies/

36 Lane, Marc, Brandon Bodor, and Mavara Agha. January 2013. Preliminary Report. Governor's Task Force on Social Innovation, Entrepreneurship, and Enterprise. Illinois General Assembly, Illinois. Accessed December 20, 2013 at http://social enterprise-chicago.org/site/wp-content/uploads/2011/12/Task-Force-Report_1.16.13-to-General-Assembly.pdf

37 The Nonprofit Technology Network (N-TEN). The 2012 Nonprofit Social Networking Benchmarks Report. Accessed January 29, 2014 at http://www.nten.org/research/mobile-social-media

38 The Nonprofit Technology Network (N-TEN).

39 Salamon, Lester. 2003. *The Resilient Sector: The State of Nonprofit America.* Brookings Institution Press and the Aspen Institute.

40 http://files.eric.ed.gov/fulltext/ED526915.pdf. Accessed September 5, 2013.

41 http://www.nytimes.com/2011/03/02/business/02graduates.html?pagewanted=all. Accessed September 5, 2013.

GLOSSARY/INDEX

Note: Page numbers followed by t indicate tables; those followed by f indicate figures.